P9-CJH-374

362.8
Rac   Racism and mental
          health

**Glendale College
Library**

RACISM AND MENTAL HEALTH

RACISM
AND

Charles V. Willie
Bernard M. Kramer
Bertram S. Brown
EDITORS

University of Pittsburgh Press

MENTAL
HEALTH

Essays

DISCARD

GLENDALE COLLEGE LIBRARY

362.8
Rac

Library of Congress Catalog Card Number 72-78933
ISBN 0-8229-3252-0 (cloth)
ISBN 0-8229-5233-5 (paper)
Copyright © 1973, University of Pittsburgh Press
All rights reserved
Media Directions Inc., London
Manufactured in the United States of America

Acknowledgment for permission to reprint portions of published material is made to the following:

American Sociological Review, the *Chicago Defender, Eugenics Quarterly, Integrated Education, Journal of Medical Education, Journal of Teacher Education, Journal of the American Medical Association, National Association of Secondary-School Principals Bulletin, National Medical Association Journal, New Generation,* the *Pan-African Voice, Psychology Today, Quarterly Journal of Studies on Alcohol,* the Seabury Press, *Social Forces,* the *World Book Year Book* (1969)

In Dr. Jackson's chapter, the quotation from *Psychology Today* is reprinted from the January 1971 issue. Copyright © Communications/Research/ Machines, Inc.

Portions of Dr. Powell's chapter are adapted from Gloria J. Powell, *Black Monday's Children,* 1973. Courtesy of Appleton-Century-Crofts, Educational Division, Meredith Corporation.

6/76

Publication of this book
was made possible by a grant
from the Maurice Falk Medical Fund.

Contents

Foreword

Mental health and the law—what if anything do they have in common? Both are concerned with the aspirations and problems of the human condition, and both deal with human rights and human responsibilities.

(The age-old problem is to balance individual freedom and social responsibility. Racism is demeaning to individuals and the nadir of social irresponsibility. Racism condones oppression and tramples on fundamental rights.)

Thus I welcome the first exploration in depth of the complex relationships between racism and mental health. Discrimination based on race, creed, color, sex, and national origin interferes with opportunities for individual expression by some and blinds others to their normal obligations. There is no health in a society afflicted by racism and discrimination.

The authors of this volume tell us that racism is oftentimes deliberate and sometimes unintentional. Nevertheless, the consequences are the same. The call for institutional change to overcome racism is a central theme in this book.

There are many ways of bringing about changes in the institutions of a society. The enactment of laws by way of democratic procedures is one way of effecting the necessary changes. But this is only part of the process of achieving a just and healthy society. People must support the law if it is to be effective. Such support is forthcoming only when the people have participated directly or indirectly in the lawmaking process. Through their participation, they achieve a feeling of belonging. This feeling in itself is something of value.

This book calls our attention to an aspect of social action that is often overlooked. It indicates how the struggle to achieve one's human rights is strengthening as well as debilitating. The story of despair is written in the pages of history and on the faces of the oppressed. This is a well-known story that need never have been written, according to the Constitution of this nation. Yet, it was. Some of the oppressions of the past have been overcome today simply because some of the oppressed had sufficient faith in the Constitution to confront the anomalies in society and to insist that they conform with the basic principles upon which this nation was established.

In the process of confronting injustice, the oppressed members of society have often grown strong, even stronger sometimes than those who maltreat them. Consequently, the self-concept of the children in many oppressed families has become exceedingly high, as pointed out by some of the authors in this book. It is my guess that this is an important finding for mental health as well as for the Civil Rights Movement.

That we can achieve two goals with one action is an idea worthy of considering. In overcoming racism and its debilitating effects, we may, at the same time, be achieving a better and more healthy society. This book is a contribution toward achieving these goals.

THURGOOD MARSHALL
Justice, United States Supreme Court,
Washington, D.C.

Preface

Racism is tearing this country asunder. Charles Silberman, who wrote a series of articles on race for *Fortune* magazine in the early 1960s, called American Blacks "the key to our mutual future."[1] Racism, then, is not a phenomenon which visits oppression upon the disadvantaged only; it could result in death and destruction for all.

Increasing urbanization of this nation brings all sorts and kinds of people into each other's presence. Racism makes it impossible for people who need each other to turn toward one another. No nation can set its people against each other and remain strong and healthy. As pointed out by Silberman: "Man cannot deny the humanity of his fellowman without ultimately destroying his own."[2]

The defeat of racism will require a breakthrough in the conscience of America—a conscience clouded over by a dense mass of tendentious rationalizations and contradictions. Witness the fact that among the signers of the Declaration of Independence were owners of slaves. Abraham Lincoln insisted that reunion rather than liberation was the aim of the Civil War even though he issued a proclamation to emancipate slaves. Witness, too, the current cruel attack upon poor Blacks as well as Whites in the wealthiest nation ever known. America has had a long history of failing

1. Charles E. Silberman, *Crisis in Black and White* (New York: Random House, 1964), p. 15.
2. Ibid., p. 16.

to face up to the racism that has had a debilitating effect upon its growth and well-being.)

This book puts aside camouflage and circumlocution and deals with racism and mental health from a behavioral science perspective that is at once polemical and analytical—polemical because the tragic human consequences of racism no longer will permit an even-tempered discussion devoid of passion; analytical because that is the essence of behavioral science. Recognizing these perspectives, we invited chapter authors to deal with racism and mental health from the point of view of their subjective experience as well as their objective research. Perhaps the abrasion in some chapters will hasten the needed breakthrough in the conscience of America so that the facts of the more analytical chapters may be received, understood, and acted upon.

(Decades of research into racial prejudice seem to have had little effect upon the culture and customs of this nation. Thus, in the 1960s and 1970s civil war has returned to the United States. The number of those who have died is mounting. And now the nation must deal with racism directly or cease to remain a united country. The late Martin Luther King, Jr., a victim of racial violence, said in his last book that this may be mankind's last chance to make a choice between chaos and community.[3]

(Violent eruptions in this nation due to racial injustice can only lead to more violence. When one group is attacked by another, the attack tends to stimulate self-preserving anxiety and a spiraling of counterattacks and escalation. The impact on national mental health should be evident to all)

A twofold approach is needed to obtain a reduction in the current level of destruction: institutional reform and self-renewal. The chapters in this book focus on this dual approach as a way of moving the nation away from imminent

3. Martin Luther King, Jr., *Where Do We Go from Here: Chaos or Community?* (Boston: Beacon Press, 1967), p. 191.

destruction and toward the possibility of freedom and fulfillment for each individual.

This book looks into the subtle ways in which mental
health institutions and treatment practices have contributed
to the perpetuation of racism and antihuman customs and
conventions. It highlights the social context that controls the
mental health system and calls for institutional changes at
local and national levels. But racism is a pathology with
personal and social consequences and must therefore be
dealt with at the individual as well as the group level. This
book focuses on both dimensions.

The editors call attention to the fact that in the text *Black*
and *White* are begun with capital letters. We assume that
Black is customarily capitalized to indicate the status of
Black individuals as a people. Noting how fine and beautiful
peoplehood is for Blacks, the editors have recognized the
peoplehood status of Whites too and thus have capitalized
White.

CHARLES V. WILLIE
BERNARD M. KRAMER
BERTRAM S. BROWN

Acknowledgments

The editors are most grateful to the Maurice Falk Medical Fund for initiating this book through its Technical Advisory Board and for the grant to the Department of Sociology at Syracuse University in 1970 to conduct a series of conferences at the University on racism and mental health, from which the chapters in this book emerged. We particularly appreciate the constant attention given to this project by Philip Hallen, President of the Fund. His advice and counsel have facilitated the development of this book, which could become a basic contribution in the newly emerging field of racism and mental health. The fund is devoting a considerable portion of its resources to continued support of research in this area.

This project has been a fine illustration of cooperation between the public and private sectors in jointly attacking a major public health problem. The National Institute of Mental Health, through the office of its director and several professional staff, have provided research assistance to several authors of chapters in this book. Especially helpful were the scientific literature search provided by the Clearing House for Mental Health Information and the data analysis presented by the Office of Program Planning and Evaluation of the Biometry Branch of NIMH.

The two conferences on racism and mental health held in Syracuse, N.Y., in the fall and spring of 1970–71 were ably assisted by Mrs. Marti Rawlings, Administrative Assistant, and Mrs. Mary Walsh, Conference Secretary, who were staff members of the Department of Sociology at Syracuse University. Copy-editing with care and compassion was a major contribution made by Mrs. Jane Keddy of Wakefield, Mass.

To all who contributed to this volume, including our racially diversified and interdisciplinary group of outstanding authors, we give our thanks and appreciation for their original chapters. As stated by Philip Hallen, we hope their work will help in the search for "some method of determining and subsequently lessening the effect of bigotry and hatred on the psychological health of Black and White Americans."

PART I

Overview

CHAPTER 1

Racism and Mental Health as a Field of Thought and Action

by Bernard M. Kramer

In the United States the mental health movement has had White middle-class Americans as its historic core of concern. While exceptions and changing trends are discernible, it is nonetheless a fact that race and class have decisively determined the character of the mental health movement. This book focuses on racism and mental health with the hope that readers will see how race and mental health have interacted to yield the present state of affairs, for clear-sighted understanding will help point the way to effective action.

Events of the past decade have made clear to all thinking citizens that which has been imprinted in the very fiber of every Black and Third World person: racism pervasively influences all the institutions of our society. As a nation we are now in the midst of a vast reappraisal of racial doctrines through a complex sociopolitical process. The process is visible and invisible, articulate and inarticulate, decisive and indecisive. Its mode of action oscillates between confrontation and accommodation, thrust and withdrawal, attack and counterattack, offense and defense, words and deeds, talk and double-talk. Popular sentiment contains elements of frustration, rage, despair, determination, vitality, retreat, and thrust. Paradoxes abound. But through it all one sees the outlines of a large national engagement with the issue of racism. The outcome, of course, is in no way clear. Indeed, prospects are gloomy for Blacks and other minority groups — and, ironically, Whites as well.

3

GLENDALE COLLEGE LIBRARY

Yet insistent pressure from these groups and their allies will surely not permit our society to slink away from the issues or to paper them over with small compromises. Pressures will continue unabated to power the nation's racial reappraisal. And the reappraisal will continue to poke into every corner of our nation's institutions: religion, education, sports, business, industry, commerce, travel, recreation, government, philanthropy, health. So, too, will mental health be scrutinized to reveal how racism has insinuated itself into the very core of a field otherwise marked by concern for human dignity and respect for personal integrity. This scrutiny is, in fact, already under way. Witness the formation of Black caucuses in the mental health professions, the emergence of the Center for Minority Mental Health in the National Institute of Mental Health, (NIMH), the publication of a special section on racism by the American Psychiatric Association (*American Journal of Psychiatry* 1970), and the publication of the present volume.

Many mental health workers support the Civil Rights and Black Liberation Movements. Yet this support is mostly expressed outside the mental health arena. Mental health professionals react in one manner to racism in general and in another to racism in mental health. They tend to finesse the question of race. An unspoken rationale for this split appears to be that mental health is an impartial helping discipline. Special attention to racial issues is, therefore, seen as inimical to a core conception of the field itself. Only through outside activity, in that view, can antiracist sympathies be promulgated. By contrast, this volume encourages mental health workers to tackle racism within their own professions and disciplines. Its conviction is that such efforts will produce a deeper, more broadly conceived humanism in mental health work.

But one needs to examine specifics in order to grasp the extent to which mental health has ignored or underplayed racial aspects of the field. Take, for example, the treatment of race in textbooks of psychiatry. One widely used text (Freedman and Kaplan 1967) contains 194 individual contributions organized in fifty-three chapters yielding 1,631 printed pages. Not one chapter nor one individual contribution carries a title showing specific concern for the topic of race and/or racism. In a chapter titled "Mental Health and Social Factors" one might reasonably expect a substantial treatment of racism. One is disappointed, however, to find only the barest mention of race and no analysis whatsoever of the impact of racism on mental health. Nor would the reader's appetite be satisfied studying the sections "Anthropology and Psychiatry" and "Sociology and Psychiatry." Moreover, in a long index, no reference is found to the words race, racism, Black, Negro, colored, prejudice, stereotypes, discrimination, segregation. Only in a unit entitled "Treatment of the Impoverished" do we find reference to conditions in Harlem. Even then, the point is blurred by placing it under the title "Characteristics of the Poor" and by omitting direct reference to Blackness and racism.

In another standard work on psychiatry (Arieti 1959), not one of 100 chapters deals centrally with issues surrounding minority mental health. Except for a short treatment of racial and ethnic groups in one chapter, "Statistical Data about Mental Illness," the handbook leaves the reader with the impression that matters relating to race and minority groups are alien or irrelevant to American psychiatry.

A recent compendium on community mental health (Bindman and Spiegel 1969) contains fifty-five articles, none of which deals frontally with the question of Blacks and mental health. Nor, again, are entries found in the subject index.

More striking is the void concerning race in the highly influential work *Action for Mental Health* (Joint Commission on Mental Illness and Health 1961) published under the aegis of the Congress of the United States. These omissions and inadequacies depressingly reveal the extent to which concerns of minority groups are neglected in major standard mental health publications.

A charitable analysis would be that this merely reflects a prevailing doctrine that mental health treats all people impartially without regard to race. Less charitable but more accurate would be the interpretation that psychiatry and other mental health disciplines are no less immune to the pervasive influence of racism and prejudice than other intellectual and service institutions of this country.

When we leave the realm of publications and turn to other components of mental health we find ample acts of omission and commission to heighten the desire to focus attention on racism and mental health. In traditional mental hospitals, segregation and discrimination continue through overt and covert action in all parts of the country despite efforts by some elements of government. Stronger laws along with stronger enforcement would be required to change the mental hospital system into one that fully respects the dignity, integrity, and culture of minority groups and their individual members. The need is great for a current restatement and reanalysis of the basic facts and figures relating to the operation of racism in traditional mental hospitals—particularly the large-scale facilities. Such reanalysis should serve as a keystone for rational action to strengthen the movement for equitable redistribution of financial and human resources in this well-entrenched bastion of racism in mental health.

More polite, but equally evil and unjust, is the growing use of psychiatric units in general hospitals as havens for the practice of psychiatry by and for predominantly White and well-to-do individuals. While exceptions are well known, no one who is familiar with psychiatric units in general hospitals would controvert the lack of easy access for Blacks, Chicanos, Puerto Ricans, Indians, and poor people. This fact partially accounts for the use of large state mental hospitals in the discriminatory way referred to above. In short, "they" have to go "somewhere," and that "somewhere" turns out to be the vast warehouse that is the large state hospital. From these observations, one begins to make out the rudimentary outlines of a dual system for handling the mentally ill. In this case, the dual elements are discernible as custodial care for the unfortunate and psychiatric treatment for the fortunate. One system controls and constrains; the other treats and heals. One is for outgroups; the other for ingroups.

Other components sharpen the outlines of the dual system. These are: (1) private mental hospitals, (2) private practice, (3) child guidance and mental health clinics, and (4) comprehensive community mental health centers.

Private mental hospitals are clearly beyond the reach of most Blacks and other minority groups at the bottom of the socioeconomic hierarchy in the United States. They came into being and continue to exist as institutions for the upper strata of our society. Likewise, a sober analysis of private practice in mental health would show, despite exceptions, an overwhelming focus on that sector of the population with ample resources. A study of mental health practice in Boston (Ryan 1969) showed how services in that city were sharply limited and geographically defined by racial and socioeconomic factors.

The child guidance clinics and the orthopsychiatric movement have been relatively more open to minority and low-income communities than has the private sector in mental health. Still, a frank accounting would reveal that the child guidance movement has also been largely oriented to and dominated by White, middle-class segments of the United States.

One sector of mental health practice with some chance of transcending this dominant trend is that of the federally aided community mental health centers. In its early days the community mental health center movement was prone to focus on the White middle class. The trend, however, is now being reversed. Resources are currently allocated for construction and staffing on the basis of a scheme giving highest priority to poverty areas. It remains to be seen whether the resources so allocated will be large enough to make a vital difference. It remains also to be seen whether programs will be suited to the way of life of Blacks and other minority groups.

Let us look now at manpower and its development. It is hard to disagree with the assertion that mental health workers over the years have been overwhelmingly White in numbers and spirit. Tiny numbers of Black mental health workers are found in subordinate positions or exiled places. There is, however, a movement afoot to increase the number of Blacks and other minorities in mental health positions. Likewise, there is substantial pressure to upgrade their role and influence. Mounting pressures of the Civil Rights, Black Power, and Black Liberation Movements coincide with increased awareness and granting of concessions in the mental health establishment. Time will tell how deep and broad will be the net results of interacting pressures and responses. Will more Blacks be trained and hired for less powerful positions? Will fewer numbers gain higher posts? Will a balanced program emerge for training and hiring minority members at all levels of competence and influence? It is safe to say that much will depend on the ability of mental health protagonists to grasp the connection between racism and mental health.

Another important, though less visible, area of concern is that of mental health research. Research dealing with institutional racism in mental health as well as psychic consequences of oppression has been sadly underrepresented in the national mental health research effort. Only quite recently has specific focus been brought to bear on this area of research. Up to now, allocation of research resources for this area has been subminimal and even the small amounts involved have turned out to be used largely by White researchers who have studied minority problems from a White point of departure. Moreover, the use of Black and other minority researchers has been minuscule not only in the area under discussion but in the general sphere of health research as well. This has tended to choke off development of minority manpower for research, thereby reducing the potential for future leadership in academic centers training new mental health workers and generating new ideas. As Pierce in chapter 13 of this book points out, the long-term interests of minority communities will be served by well-conceived and suitably implemented programs for nourishing their research-academic capacities, hitherto limited overwhelmingly to Whites.

One more example will perhaps suffice for our litany of racism in mental health practice, that of mental health education for the public. Conventional wisdom, with professional assent, has placed no small emphasis on the need to educate the public to use mental health services more effectively and to cope more effectively with the tensions of industrial life. But when one examines materials created with the help of public funds and intended for the edification of the public, one finds, sadly but expectably, material addressed to and picturing the familiar White middle class. No more cutting example could be adduced than the special Blondie cartoon series produced for the New York State Department of Mental Hygiene in the 1950s. In this series there is no hint whatsoever that Blacks exist or that they or their tormentors have or are mental health problems.

These examples of racism in mental health practice do not constitute a complete list. A task for our nascent field is indeed that of creating a full list with documentation and elaboration, for some will say that racism is not an urgent issue for mental health. But careful spelling out of facts and figures, both past and present, will help convince skeptics that racism is, in fact, the nation's prime mental health problem existing today.

Yet the reader might ask whether a book on racism and mental health is really needed. Some will say we need action, not books. Others will say that racism in mental health is so well known that no further study is called for. Some will say that mental health, of all fields, is least tainted by racism and that this spotlight is out of proportion to reality.

In contrast to these arguments we hold that action can be improved and made more effective by analysis and understanding. Moreover, the facts about racism in mental health are not at all widely known—either in the local communities or in the mental health community. Mental health practice is not untainted by racism, and the need to document and disseminate the relevant facts seems incontrovertible. But a clear conceptual framework has not yet been developed to subsume the many areas of investigation. Such a framework could give character and shape to a field of knowledge that would have developed long ago were it not for the impact of racism on the investigatory process itself. This chapter aims at speeding the emergence of racism and mental health as an organized field of thought and action with a conceptual framework that incorporates present knowledge and energizes the search for new knowledge.

How does a field come into being? How is it established as an authentic research domain? How do elements of thought and action come into public consciousness? The following appear to be critical conditions for the establishment and validation of a field:

1. A reasonable set of questions, problems, issues, and concepts
2. A critical mass of individuals interested in thought and action with respect to the above
3. A body of knowledge made public through books and articles
4. Machinery for compiling the results of research and practice
5. One or more periodicals in which results may be published efficiently and speedily

6. A conceptual framework embracing major issues and yielding meaningful questions for thought and action

7. Financial support to enable continued work

8. Educational programs to create a flow of competent and interested individuals

9. A constituency that helps nourish and support the field

Let us now review the status of racism and mental health in the light of the foregoing conditions:

1. There is a reasonable set of questions and issues which are spelled out throughout this volume.

2. There is a critical mass of individuals interested and working in the field. Among these are Prudhomme, Pinderhughes, Pierce, Comer, Thomas, Pouissant, Coles, Christmas, Butts, Pettigrew, Jones, Cobb, Grier, to name just a few.

3. There is a body of knowledge and experience exemplified by the lists of references at the end of the chapters in this volume.

4. To our knowledge there is no existing machinery for compiling the cumulative results of efforts in this field. Perhaps the new Center for Minority Mental Health at NIMH could be a force to create vehicles for compiling, reviewing, summarizing, and abstracting the results of research and experience in this field. Perhaps one or more universities could take the initiative toward this end. Perhaps a foundation or group of foundations could help make this possible. Or perhaps the Black caucus groups could be the leading force. In any case, the proper development of this field demands that such machinery come into being by one means or another.

5. There is no periodical now in existence for focused publication of work in racism and mental health. This, too, would appear to be vital for the field's development. Naturally, this does not imply that work on racism and mental health should be excluded from existing journals. Indeed, such a tendency should be resisted. Otherwise many mental

health practitioners and students would be restricted in their exposure to the issues. The purpose of such a journal would be to provide a sure outlet for technical and specialized work so necessary for substantive vitality. A *Journal of Racism and Mental Health* would encourage growth of scholarly works and sharing of practical experience.

6. Conceptual frameworks for mental health as such are abundant. One need only mention psychoanalysis, psychobiology, interpersonal relations, or symbolic interaction to reveal examples of conceptual frameworks widely used in mental health. Likewise, in race relations in general, conceptual frameworks are embodied in such words as nationalism, Marxism, self-determination, social conflict, pluralism, assimilation, separatism, American dilemma, group dynamics. But at the interface between racism and mental health the conceptual underpinnings appear discernible only in embryonic form. A conceptual framework stands as a goal to be achieved in this field.

7. Funds for the study of racism and mental health are so slim as to be hardly worth mentioning. Support from private foundations and from government funds would have to be forthcoming in substantial quantities to permit suitable growth. This volume should serve as a stimulus in this respect.

8. Financial support is perhaps less primary than education. There is at present no substantial educational machinery to assure the continual flow of new generations of professionals to master and forward the work of the field. Most academic departments in mental health pay little attention to the question of racism, and when they do it is frequently under the heading of "interesting" or "relevant" topics. Rarely is it accorded the status of a serious speciality for thought and action. Thus, for example, specialists in child psychiatry issuing from the nation's training centers may have a side interest in questions relating to race. Seldom, however, do

individuals come forward as specialists in the interaction between race and mental health. Indeed, many would argue that students must master the mental health disciplines as primary tools before pursuing an interest in racism. While many will follow this path, avenues should be opened to make concentrated study of racism and mental health legitimate and honorable for doctoral candidates and postdoctoral trainees. Clearly identified and well-supported educational vehicles will help assure the flow of scholars and specialists for the field's growth and development.

9. The matter of constituency is closely related to that of financial support. Decisions on financial grants from public and quasi-public sources often turn on the strength and influence of the constituencies that are backing the issue in question. The constituency for racism and mental health is, of course, a mixture of those interested in mental health of minorities and those who, from diverse standpoints, see racism as a major threat to the nation's mental health. Whether its supporters can be sufficiently unified to back this field is an open question, particularly in view of the primacy of survival questions for minority groups concerned.

Returning to the problem of articulating a conceptual framework for this field, the following questions might serve as a prolegomenon to a theoretical structure for thought and action:

1. What are the definitions of racism, institutional racism, personal racism, individual prejudice, group prejudice? How are these to be distinguished from each other? How do they overlap?

2. What is the extent of institutional racism and individual prejudice? How do these vary with respect to regional, socioeconomic, and ethnic groupings? What are the trends over time, for better or worse? What is the level of support for or hostility to racial justice across the nation, and how does this

vary with time? How are relevant rates to be measured? Can objective assessments that would command the respect of concerned parties be devised?

3. What are the causes of institutional racism and individual prejudice? What is the role of historical, economic, political, social, psychological, cultural, and international factors in maintaining, heightening, or reducing racism and prejudice? How can mental health disciplines contribute to an understanding of why racist discrimination, segregation, hostility, and violence have had such a tenacious grip on the psyche of so many members of the dominant White majority in the United States? In a phrase from an earlier period, why do men hate? This is, in fact, an ancient and haunting question — but if there is any single matter that mental health disciplines ought to be studying, it is this piercing question concerning the wellsprings of racial hostility. It strikes overarchingly at our national future and demands the highest order of intelligence from mental health disciplines. Now, during this great national period of racial reappraisal, it will not do to fall back on easy formulations of meliorism and benignancy. Hard, tough-minded, intense analysis will be needed to shape programs and policies to conquer racism and prejudice. No help will be gained from overoptimism about the ability of mental health disciplines to plumb the psychic depths of hatred. Nor can we expect that those who repress others will seek therapeutic help. This was the delusion of intergroup relations research of the 1940s and 1950s. But neither will help be gained from brutish Hobbesian oversimplifications. This is the Achillean weakness of those moved by raw antirationalism. For, in fact, there is a substantial role for reason in human affairs and in race relations. Its task is to harness sound research to the vehicles of change.

If racism is our endemic mental illness, then it follows that a major task for mental health is to discern its causes and direct its cure. Certainly a scientific challenge for psychology, psychiatry, sociology, and anthropology is to discover the causes, consequences, and means of control of maladaptive behavior. It would seem reasonable to hope that the creative energies of these fields would yield useful answers when turned to the question of why men and women hate and reject their brothers and sisters upon whom they are mutually dependent for personal and social survival. Although this was a significant preoccupation among social and behavioral scientists during and immediately after World War II, research lagged under the stifling influence of McCarthyism. It is to be hoped that a resurrection of interest in the causes and consequences of racism for public and personal mental health will achieve results commensurate with the current sense of urgency for just and humane relations between Blacks and Whites. Although research is hardly ever an acceptable substitute for action, it can frequently help in decisive ways, particularly when it goes to roots of a subject. Well motivated research into the dynamics of racism would be a welcome development.

4. What are the consequences of institutional racism and personal prejudice? What impact do they have upon oppressed, subordinated minority groups and their conditions of life, including their emotional, intellectual, spiritual, and physical health? What impact do they have upon the very capacity for personal and collective survival? What, too, are the consequences for the dominant, privileged White majority? How does racism affect their capacity for the use of intelligence? their capacity for judging self and others in the light of undistorted reality? their ability to perceive accurately? their ability to come to peace with themselves and live without hate in an atmosphere of mutuality based on trust? their very capacity for personal and collective survival in an age of worldwide atomic anxiety and realignment of national and racial power? How does the constrictive force of racism affect the ability of man to devise new and reticular forms in

response to the complexities of the technoindustrial era? What, in brief, is the impact of racism on human psyches and mores?

5. What are the responses to racism? How have oppressed minority groups reacted to the varied forms of racism found in this country? And how do they respond now? What are the role and extent of denial, confrontation, survival, counterattack, identification with the aggressor, rebellion, militancy, pragmatic action, accommodation? What are the positive and negative implications of varied responses to racism for personal and collective mental health? What are the counterresponses of the dominant groups?

6. What has been the impact of racism on mental health as an institution? How has it shaped mental health practice in its public and private forms? How has it sculpted the mental movement's programs, ideology, and style? How has it influenced the questions asked for research and the answers taught for education? How has it determined who shall enter the field, who shall teach and who shall be taught, who shall lead and who shall follow?

7. Finally, what has been the response of mental health disciplines to racism at large and racism in the sphere of mental health? What responses are emerging and which of these are suitable for encouragement and further development? To what extent have the response mechanisms that follow been operative or latent: denial, withdrawal, confrontation, counterattack, constructive action, search for alternatives? If the intellectual challenge to mental health is to build a thoughtful framework for its analysis of racism, then its challenge for action is to build a suitable scheme for its response to racism.

These questions set the stage for a conceptual framework that will emerge as the field of racism and mental health matures. The chapters that follow are part of that maturation, and the reader should find therein clues for further scholarly thought and humane action.

Chapter 2 by Charles Prudhomme and David F. Musto is a delight! The historian's perspective helps curb enthusiasm and naïveté; in this case the authors add to their historical overview the hair-raising tale of a repetitive racist compulsion to deny Black men and women their rightful place in the development of modern psychiatry. Prudhomme's own career as a distinguished Black psychiatrist reveals him not only as a witness to the events but also as a victim of discrimination and a combatant for racial justice. It is, therefore, only with utmost optimism that one dares to hope that patterns of discrimination and segregation will be broken in the immediate period ahead. In any case, Prudhomme and Musto permit no one to think that the struggle is new.

A seminal work of inspiration is the next chapter by Charles A. Pinderhughes entitled, "Racism and Psychotherapy," to which he brings a wide-ranging experience in psychotherapy and psychobiology. He develops a definition and conception of racism which are at once encompassing and powerful. Articulating the symbolisms and meanings of Black and White, he argues that racism underlies many superordinations and subordinations found in our society— rich-poor, Black-White, teacher-student, man-woman, master-slave. He illustrates his theme with psychobiological material and case histories from his therapeutic practice with Blacks and Whites. A veritable feast!

John A. Ordway's chapter, "Some Emotional Consequences of Racism for Whites," is a gripping statement of how racism creeps into the psychic tissue of a White community worker. Excerpts from psychoanalytic sessions highlight otherwise hidden tensions and biases in well-intentioned humanitarian activities. The pain and conflict on both sides, as reported by Dr. Ordway, leave the reader with a mixed sense of compassion, anger, incredulity, and insight into the many influences of racism on White lives.

Jeanne Spurlock's chapter shows how deeply racism affects the inner lives of Black children. Entitled, "Some Consequences of Racism for Children," it relies on clinical material to reveal several levels at which racism works its psychic powers. It also yields valuable insight into mechanisms at work in children's counterresponses, including the theme of "Black is beautiful." Hers is one of several chapters in this volume illuminating the life of Black children in the contemporary culture of the United States.

In their chapter "Racism and Mental Health Services," Claudewell S. Thomas and James P. Comer assert: "White racism . . . has created a great deal of mental anguish, has complicated mental illness, and stands as a formidable obstacle to the development of all kinds of mental health services. It interferes with mental health services at every step of the way." This authoritative statement comes from men in positions to know—Thomas in his top role at the National Institute of Mental Health and Comer in his varied roles at Yale. They pose the issues deriving from present patterns of discrimination and propose an advocacy approach to comprehensive mental health services. "Advocacy," they say, "can be seen as a technique for broadening the number of well-informed people who are active participants in the social screen, which ultimately selects out serious from mild defects. Advocacy involves a dialogue between the needy and the technical source of . . . fulfillment of need." In their conception, "part of the function of the professionals is to exchange their insights and know-how about the health care/mental health care system with . . . community people, receiving in return the insights of the community along with numerous complaints about the system and specifications as to how people adapt and actually live." Their discussions will surely engender lively action in mental health circles.

Jacquelyne Johnson Jackson's chapter is on the topic "Black Women in a Racist Society." Inherent in the title are all the obvious pressures and counterpressures of Black liberation, women's liberation, racism, sexism, priorities and counterpriorities, coalitions and countercoalitions. Yet, despite all, the issues need reasoned attention to add strength to the passionate advocacies in the wind. In this chapter Jackson presents data to counteract some of the prevalent flights and fancies about the role of women in Black communities and movements. She challenges widely held views about Black matriarchy as well as other current doctrines. She discusses advantages and disadvantages of potential alliances by Black women with White women, Black men, and the several socioeconomic and cultural groups in our society. Throughout she argues energetically for an egalitarian spirit that would enhance the mental health of all.

In his chapter entitled "Racism and the Mental Health of White Americans: A Social Psychological View," Thomas F. Pettigrew draws on concepts from social psychology to tease out interactions between racism and mental health. He sharpens the distinction between institutional racism and individual prejudice and points up the difference between the driven and the conforming racist. Making use of data from his studies of Black mayoral candidacies, he ties motivational aspects of prejudice to concepts of positive and negative mental health. The result is an insightful treatment of strategies available for reordering race relations in the United States.

In the chapter entitled "Self-Concept in White and Black Children," Gloria Johnson Powell presents data from her empirical study of self-concepts among Black and White youths in Northern and Southern sections of the United States. Her data may be startling to some, but they mesh well with developments in the country at large: Black youngsters have better self-concepts, as measured by Powell's instruments, than do White children. Likewise, Black students in the South have more positive self-images than Black youngsters in the North. Community development may indeed have spreading effects upon personal growth and development.

In his chapter, "Racism, Mental Health, and the Schools," Reginald L. Jones goes straight to the core in his opening paragraph: "The Black push for reforms in the schools is a mental health strategy. It is the Black American's assertion of worth and dignity. It represents a demand that the schools take account of the culture and heritage of Black Americans; that it remove vestiges of discrimination in the employment of Black teachers, counselors, and administrators; and that it deal with racism in the school curriculum. It represents a frank confrontation with institutional forces which dehumanize Blacks." Jones discusses the impact of neoracialist labels on the self-perceptions of Black children and pleads for eliminating labels on mental health grounds. He proceeds to analyze mental health implication of teacher expectations, curricula, and textbooks. Although his paper is in the scholarly voice, Jones does not refrain from raising a warning: "It may well be, if the social disease of racism is to be eradicated, that many of our current institutions — including the school — will have to be radically altered if not dismantled altogether." A fair warning!

In the chapter labeled "Definitions and Distributions of Mental Disorders in a Racist Society," Morton Kramer, Beatrice M. Rosen, and Ernest M. Willis argue that mental health policies and programs have emerged in the face of great ignorance about the distribution of various conditions among varying groups. The tools of epidemiology and biostatistics are vitally useful for developing creative solutions to difficult problems. The field of racism and mental health must come to grips with its basic epidemiology. The reader will be well served by careful study of this epidemiological contribution.

Preston Wilcox's chapter is entitled "Positive Mental Health in the Black Community: The Black Liberation Movement." It is by far the most uncompromising chapter in this volume. It defines "the concept of positive mental health from the Black perspective." Wilcox offers a powerful list of indicators of Black mental health, as follows: "1. Conscious awareness that this society is hostile to one's existence. . . . 2. A constant state of dynamic tension. . . . 3. Ability to deal with superordinates. . . . 4. Lack of desire to oppress or to be oppressed. . . . 5. A need to be involved in shaping and/or controlling one's own destiny. . . . 6. Steady involvement in self-confrontation. . . . 7. Being steeped in an identity not of one's own culture—history and values. . . . 8. A basic knowledge of the society's destructive characteristics: racism, capitalism, classism, sexism, materialism, etc. 9. An ability to perceive the humanity of oppressed people. . . . 10. Desire to think, feel, and act in a single motion—not to fragment oneself into emotion, intelligence, and action." He explicates the thrust of the Black Liberation Movement and highlights current self-liberating activities within the Black community. He argues for consumer control and the creation of new social values and institutions. Wilcox gives us an intense statement of the liberation movement's effects on Black mental health.

The next two chapters deal with current pressures on and responses of the mental health establishment in the realm of racism. Each, however, tells the story from diverging vantage points. Chester M. Pierce draws on the record of the Psychiatric Black Caucus in its efforts during the 1960s to impel mental health into action on racism. In "The Formation of the Black Psychiatrists of America," Pierce leads us up to the Black Caucus of May 1969 at the Miami Beach meeting of the American Psychiatric Association and takes us through events flowing from that caucus. He lists ten demands put forward by the caucus and tells the outcome of each. His version of the establishment of the Center for Minority Mental Health creates in the reader a sense of immediacy based on Pierce's personal participation in all the important events. The flavor is conveyed in these words:

In the early 1960s, while others were toasting HEW, some were in thirst for something more, something like a powerful minority center at NIMH. A center is here, but its power is yet to come. Even so, many of my White colleagues are ready to quench thirst by a toast to the new Center. But Blacks have a terrible dryness. Hence, they look about and realize that in the final analysis the only way that thirst can be slaked is by a massive and unprecedented commitment of effort and resources by White America. This is the only way that in two generations from now no person in this country will have to pause a millisecond a day in concern about skin color. This is the only way that the managers of American life can be seen on this globe as legitimate.

In their chapter, "Key Issues in Developing a National Minority Mental Health Program at NIMH," Frank M. Ochberg and Bertram S. Brown focus on the newly established Center for Minority Mental Health within the National Institute of Mental Health. They identify and discuss the following issues debated within and without the NIMH: definition of minority, relationships among minority groups, pros and cons of a segregated center, standards of excellence, scope and focus of the center, style and emphasis, power relations of the center vis-à-vis NIMH, and recruitment of a center chief. Their fundamental issue, however, is this: Can the mental health apparatus of this nation succeed in creating effective, well-funded machinery to support a concerted attack upon racism in mental health during a period of mounting attacks upon both the mental health movement and the Black Liberation Movement? This chapter offers an inside view of the forces at work to answer this question.

The value of this book is in no small measure attributable to the series of conferences on racism and mental health held at Syracuse University in 1970–71. Unanticipated was the extraordinary spirit that emerged in the flesh of the sessions. They were not melancholy exercises in pessimistic recrimination. Neither hopeless impasse nor childish Pollyannaism prevailed. Instead, there was a buoyant mix of hardheaded realism, mature and honest disagreements, and a sense of responsibility to accomplish the little that mortals can in their own fields of competence. Participants made special efforts to say in one way or another that they had experienced a positive emotional and intellectual impact in the course of the conference. Hopefully, the chapters that follow will convey that impact.

REFERENCES

Am. J. Psychiat. 1970. Special section on racism. 127(6): 787–814.

Arieti, Silvano. 1959. *American handbook of psychiatry.* New York: Basic Books.

Bindman, Arthur J., and Spiegel, Allen D. 1969. *Perspectives in community mental health.* Chicago: Aldine.

Freedman, Alfred M., and Harold I. Kaplan, 1967. *Comprehensive textbook of psychiatry.* Baltimore: Williams and Wilkins.

Joint Commission on Mental Illness and Health. 1961. *Action for mental health.* New York: Basic Books.

Pierce, Chester. 1973. The formation of the Black Psychiatrists of America. In *Racism and mental health,* ed. Charles V. Willie, Bernard M. Kramer, and Bertram S. Brown. Pittsburgh: University of Pittsburgh Press.

Ryan, William. 1969. *Distress in the city: essays on the design and administration of urban mental health services.* Cleveland, Ohio: Press of Case Western Reserve University.

CHAPTER 2

Historical Perspectives on Mental Health and Racism in the United States

by Charles Prudhomme
David F. Musto

The record of how mental health concepts and services have been formulated and delivered to Blacks and other minority groups reveals how deeply an institution such as the mental health profession is embedded in general society. Furthermore, it illustrates how scientific institutions may supply justification for what society wishes to do for reasons far removed from science. Relevant to this topic is the story of how Blacks began to obtain professional training in the area of psychiatry. Other elements binding together the history of Blacks as patients and professionals include the generally accepted theories and practices which were based on supposed distinctions between the personality structure of Blacks and Whites. When someday the interrelations of these factors are described in full, the history of racism in the American mental health professions will be appreciated in its many ramifications.

This chapter is not a comprehensive history but is intended to suggest avenues of research and interpretation which are needed today. Any attempt at present to describe the role of racism in the mental health professions is bound to be incomplete. Many of the basic records have yet to be made available, and much of the written history is too fragmentary or distorted in its descriptions to permit a full appraisal. However, it is possible now to suggest the general outlines of such a history and to bring together, in one place, information from several relevant areas. Hopefully, such an outline, by indicating opportunities for research, will encourage others to carry on this historical investigation. Certainly such research is essential if ever we are to appreciate fully how racism enters into social institutions ostensibly based upon objective principles of investigation. Although this chapter will be of special interest to the Blacks of America, it has a broader importance for anyone who wishes to learn and to understand how it happens that common and unverified cultural assumptions become part of what is presented as science.

This chapter will employ two kinds of evidence. The first, traditional historical documents, includes publications of various kinds which reveal statistics, theories, therapies, and descriptions of the mentally ill. Out of this immense literature some landmarks and a few reference points can be established. The second kind of evidence will be personal recollections which help close the gap between documents and the reality of life. In this account some of the experiences of one author *(CP)* in more than forty years of American psychiatry will be presented. Such recollections in the form of oral memoirs or autobiographies must be sought as energetically as the written records of the past, or one of our best opportunities to put documents into accurate context will be lost. For example, the desegregation in the 1950s of St. Elizabeths Hospital, the federal government's first and "model" mental institution, after almost a century of strictly separating patients by races and refusing to train and employ Black physicians and nurses, among other stigmata of racism, is a vivid personal narrative which cannot be captured in either government memoranda or formal letters expressing rejection.

In approaching the subject of opportunities available in the past to aspiring Black professionals, the life, work, and frustrations of Dr. Solomon Carter Fuller (1872–1953) provide classic illustration. An eminent neuropathologist, neurologist, psychiatrist, and teacher, Fuller was denied opportunities and yet achieved substantial professional recognition. Dr. Fuller embodies the spirit and determination necessary for a career as a Black mental health professional but also the angry frustration of being restricted by virulent racial discrimination. A brief account of his life and work is given toward the end of the chapter.

Unfortunately, the unpublished patient records of the nation's mental hospitals remain, for the most part, an unexamined research resource for the day-by-day treatment of the mentally ill.

Delivery of Mental Health Services

The establishment of mental hospitals in the late eighteenth and early nineteenth centuries in the United States was the occasion for some of the earliest decisions we find concerning the treatment of the mentally ill Black. At the Worcester State Hospital in Massachusetts, a landmark social institution established in 1833 by the state and sponsored by leading reformers, it was quickly decided that separate quarters would have to be provided for the races. A brick shop was remodeled to provide quarters for the Black mentally ill (Grob 1966, p. 50). Similar separation, believed to be required for the best treatment of the insane, was the rule in other asylums if they accepted Blacks at all. In the South there was generally little state provision for Blacks. If slaves, they were taken care of by their owners, perhaps at less expense than when being hospitalized at the owner's expense. The Eastern State Hospital at Williamsburg, Va., the first state mental hospital in what is now the United States, accepted free Blacks from its founding in 1774 (Dain 1971, pp. 19, 108–13). Following the Civil War, in 1869, a separate mental hospital exclusively for Blacks, Central State Hospital, was established in Virginia, ultimately located in Petersburg (Drewry 1916, pp. 731–71).

If no state hospital had room for an ill Black person, he was often confined to jail or an almshouse. In the history of the Central State Hospital in Virginia, for example, the hospital's success was measured by the jail's evacuation of Blacks awaiting treatment (Drewry 1916, p. 754). Although provision for Blacks in the South was meager and openly criticized by some Southern physicians, the North had conditions no better. In 1863 the American Freedman's Inquiry Commission discovered upon polling the superintendents of Union asylums that most institutions did not accept Blacks and those which did had miniscule numbers. Dr. Thomas S. Kirkbride of the Pennsylvania Hospital reported that most Blacks appropriate for admission to asylums in that state were actually in the poorhouses (Dain 1964, pp. 104–08). There does not seem to be any remarkable difference, prior to the Civil War, between the sections of the country with regard to the care of the mentally ill Black.

In the first half of the nineteenth century, environment and social conditions were seen as strong predisposing factors for the occurrence of mental illness (Dain 1964, pp. 108–13; Grob 1966, pp. 54–57). Moral treatment, pleasant surroundings and attendants, uplifting conversation, removal from the place of irritation, and good food were considered as "antidotes," so to speak, for the bad or stressful environment which was believed to cause the illness. Mental hospitals were planned by the most progressive reformers to be small, certainly caring for fewer than 250 patients, drawn from a relatively local area. The power of moral treatment, which is similar in many ways to milieu therapy of today, was accepted as immense. If a patient was treated in the first months of his illness, the chance for cure was perhaps 90 percent. If the illness had been ingrained for more than a year, the likelihood of cure was much less. Annual reports of the various asylums provided statistics which supported the belief in moral treatment and quick application of its healing powers to the mentally ill.

Along with the assumption that environment was a prime cause of mental illness, there was also the common opinion that the "uncivilized races" (for example, Indians and slaves) had much less or almost no mental illness. The forerunner of the *American Journal of Psychiatry* pointed out that the medical officer who oversaw the care of those Cherokees who were forced to move from their homes in Georgia and Alabama to the present state of Oklahoma "never saw or heard of a case of insanity among them" (Brigham 1845). Considering their treatment on the thousand-mile forced march – the "Trail of Tears" – which led to the deaths of 4,000 Cherokees from a total of about 20,000, this assurance of their remarkable sanity must have been encouraging to whoever was interested in their plight (Wilkins 1970, p. 315). Further evidence of the comparative insanity of the civilized included an old Cherokee chief's statement to a missionary that "he had never known a case of insanity among his people, such as he had seen at the Hospital at Philadelphia" (Brigham 1845). Similarly, as will be discussed below, it was believed that Blacks had little insanity.

Why this interest in mental illness rates? As hospitals in the United States and Europe began to compute statistics, it became apparent that the rate of insanity as measured by these methods was increasing in Western "civilized" nations and was at a much reduced level in the lower echelons of mankind, the "uncivilized" Blacks and Indians. What could medical science, psychiatry, offer in explanation of this alarming discovery? Although some reformers such as Dorothea Dix concluded that the character of civilized society was somehow defective and should be altered, the commonly accepted explanation for the apparent difference in rates of insanity was that the great stresses of civilization were unavoidable (Dain 1964, pp. 88–95). These stresses produced a lamentable tension in the nervous systems of the civilized. Other psychological theorists asserted that the constitution of the civilized was initially more sensitive, more liable to creativity and, unfortunately, to insanity. The lower races, the uncivilized, were less emotionally sensitive and were thereby protected from the strains of progress. Therefore, the American Indian, the Black slave, and various other apparently sluggard groups gave evidence of their retardation through an almost embarrassing lack of insanity, the presence of which thus became considered as a sign of progress.

Partly out of concern over the rising number of asylum residents, the U.S. government decided to enumerate the insane in the 1840 census. This produced a strange discovery: the South had almost no insane Blacks, but as one moved north the rate of insanity increased. This intelligence was communicated abroad and seized upon by the French geographer and statistician Jean Boudin. Taking the details of the census and assuming them to be correct,[1] he concluded that cold climates are destructive to the mental health of Blacks (Boudin 1857, pp. 143–44). The statistics on which he based his theory certainly pointed in that direction. In Louisiana, only 1 out of 4,310 Blacks was insane; in Virginia, 1 out of 1,309; in Pennsylvania, 1 in 257; in Massachusetts, 1 in 44; in Maine the figure was an impressive 1 out of every 14. Remarkable information, but not, as Boudin demonstrated, beyond the power of science to interpret.

Secretary of State John C. Calhoun of South Carolina similarly found the statistics intriguing. In fact, the secretary of state's office under Calhoun's predecessor had compiled and "corrected" the statistics, so one would naturally assume that Calhoun was familiar with the census. Soon after the figures had been published, he chided the British ambassador for wishing to abolish slavery since, as "science" had shown, the elimination of the protected condition of the Black would reduce him to a state of civilization in which he ran a 7

1. Interestingly, Boudin does not quote directly from the census, but from a book published in Mobile, Ala., in 1844 which had taken the census figures and used them as evidence of racial distinctions (Nott 1844).

percent chance of becoming an idiot or a maniac. Calhoun regretted that this was the case, but statistics proved it to be so, and these statistics were in harmony with the environmental causation of mental illness (Deutsch 1944). There was a specious reasonableness about how slavery's condition of dependency protected the Blacks from the worry of tomorrow and the trials of today. Since Blacks were thought to be fundamentally uncivilized, it was appropriate to fit the social condition to the bodily constitution, or "the punishment to the crime."

Northern abolitionists were upset by this census. It would seem the benefits which they sought for the slave were in fact hazards of almost inevitable consequence. A leading Massachusetts psychiatrist and medical statistician, Dr. Edward Jarvis, began a closer study of the census (see, for example, Jarvis 1842, 1852). He discovered that in New England, at least, the statistics had no relation to reality. For example, the city of Worcester had listed 133 colored idiots and insane. But this figure represented the total census (all White) of the Worcester Asylum. The census had also ascribed Black idiots and insane to some towns in the supposed mind-destroying climate of Maine when, in fact, there were no Black inhabitants in those towns whatsoever. The veracity of the sixth census of 1840 was undermined by Jarvis's research, but the federal government refused publicly to alter the figures or to admit error. Secretary of State Calhoun, when called upon by Congress to reexamine the census, brought back the Southern gentleman who had originally been in charge of the enumeration as an expert critic. Neither the reexamination by the former census taker nor further reflection by Mr. Calhoun revealed error. The census's revelation on the different rate of mental defect in the two races was to Calhoun "unimpeachable," and his conclusion was that the abolition of slavery would be to the African "a curse instead of a blessing" (Calhoun 1856, p. 461).

Interestingly, the proofs offered by Jarvis did not stop the use of the 1840 census as a support for racist policies. Through his work the scientific method was fulfilling its valuable role as a corrective to false and malicious pseudo-science, but the national climate was not conducive to accepting such correction, which ran counter to powerful emotional forces. Knowledgeable Northerners sneered at the apparent dishonesty of the 1840 census, while Southern slaveholders turned to such official government publications to rest their case on "unimpeachable" facts.

But ridiculing the patent distortion of fact to favor racial distinctions may have set somewhat uneasily in the minds of Massachusetts reformers when they then had to deal with an avalanche of aliens with strange customs and speech, and an "inherent" predisposition to insanity and pauperism, the Irish. New England progressives believed their conclusions rested on solid facts when they diagnosed what was wrong with the Irish (Jarvis 1855, introduction, pp. 59–60). The Irish were not accustomed to American ways and were suspicious of the established order in the Bay State. The Irish laborers, of whom there seemed to be no end, had a peculiar emotional makeup which made them especially susceptible to mental illness. Although the laborer required less to be happy than the "native" American, he seemed unable even to obtain that amount. Liquor was a severe problem. The Irish began to fill the asylums, and astonishingly, the hallowed moral treatment, which was so effective on the doughty New Englanders, did not cure the Irish, who were "different"; the poverty which engulfed them was, to Jarvis, who also studied this aspect of mental illness, the regrettable result of fundamental personal or constitutional deficiency. He believed the Irish paupers should be separated in asylums from the native paupers, for the two groups were so fundamentally alien.

Suggestions arose on how best to treat the Irish immigrant. Some eminent psychiatrists argued that segregation was required for their effective treatment. Isaac Ray, who was not only one of the founding fathers of the American Psychiatric Association (1844) but a great forensic psychiatrist of the century, in an article praising Jarvis's *Insanity and Idiocy in Massachusetts* (1855) saw a solution in the establishment of a separate asylum with a staff composed of Irish doctors and attendants. In this way, Ray suggested, the barriers in communication and confidence between the Irish and the New England psychiatrist would be overcome, and, after all, that was one of the fundamental bases for effective moral treatment (Ray 1856, pp. 95–96). Using a notion popular in the South, but there applied to free Blacks, the Massachusetts psychiatrist argued that the stresses of modern democracy brought out the constitutional weaknesses of the Irish and made the best of modern psychiatry ineffective in its ministrations. Such was the recommendation of some Northern medical psychologists for an apparently unassimilable social subgroup.

The dean of American mental hospital superintendents, Dr. Thomas S. Kirkbride of Philadelphia, argued for the segregation of the races as well as other categories of patients as the most efficient and acceptable form of asylum treatment. "The idea of mixing up all colors and classes," Dr. Kirkbride declared, "as is seen in one or two institutions of the United States, is not what is wanted in our hospitals for the insane" (Kirkbride 1855, p. 43). His views were followed with care in the establishment of the federal model institution, the Government Hospital for the Insane, or, as later known, St. Elizabeths. Founded with the indefatigable and enthusiatic support of Dorothea Lynde Dix, who is said to have personally chosen its first superintendent, Dr. Charles Nichols, St. Elizabeths opened its doors in 1855. From the start Dr. Nichols was in accord with the admonitions of his friend Dr. Kirkbride regarding construction, organization, and the separate care of the races. A building for the "colored insane" was constructed shortly after operations began, a signal event in the mind of Dr. Nichols. He located the cottage for Blacks in a somewhat scientific manner, since he had reasoned that "lodges for the colored insane should not be less than two hundred nor more than four hundred feet from the main edifice." Dr. Nichols's explanation for this calibrated *apartheid* was that "any distance within that range would exceed an objectionable proximity, but not the pale of an easy inspection" (Kirkbride 1855, p. 89).

This discussion of racial separation was raised in the august meetings of the Association of Medical Superintendents of American Institutions for the Insane (now the American Psychiatric Association) not simply because the federal hospital was the occasion for planning a model institution, but because the great Northern hospitals were under criticism by the superintendent of the Williamsburg, Va., asylum, Dr. John M. Galt II. Dr. Galt had declared some of the institutions to have the appearance of prisons and had also criticized by his practice the prevailing attitudes on the separation of the races. Both Drs. Kirkbride and Nichols were outraged at Galt for not only advocating, as Nichols phrased it, placing "Whites and Blacks all in together" but actually practicing this idea and then approving the result (Nichols 1855). In incidents such as this we get an insight into the complex attitudes toward Blacks which were found among psychiatrists in the North and the South only a few years before the Civil War erupted.

Dr. Nichols proudly reported to the secretary of the interior, under whom the hospital operated, that the new building "inaugurates, we believe, the first and only special provision for the suitable care of the African when afflicted with insanity which has yet been made in any part of the world" (St. Elizabeths Hospital 1856, p. 30). The desire to be the first led Dr. Nichols to the incorrect claim for the first such building. As noted above, the brick shed in Worcester had already been dedicated to this scientifically approved mode of medical treatment, and perhaps there were others. But whether St. Elizabeths was the first or not, Dr. Nichols evidently believed it should treat Blacks, since it was "particularly becoming to the Government of a country embracing a larger population of Blacks than can be found in any civilized state" (St. Elizabeths Hospital 1856). St. Elizabeths record of segregation was maintained until the 1950s.

Dr. William Alanson White, who became superintendent of St. Elizabeths in 1903, was one of the great American psychiatrists of the early twentieth century. After several controversial early years at St. Elizabeths, he took a firm command and made the hospital a center of research and care, fulfilling in many aspects the original plan that it be a model. There is evidence that near the close of his career he seriously pondered the problem of segregation and planned to appoint a Black physician for training in psychiatry, although his death on May 7, 1937, and the appointment of Dr. Winfred Overholser ended his early proposal to aid both Black patients and Black professionals.

Racial Theories of Mental Illness

Theories of mental illness among Blacks and Whites carried over into the realm of medicine a double standard similar to that in general society. Since the prevalence of mental illness among Blacks appeared to be low as compared with that among White Americans, the theoretical explanations of this discrepancy had some interesting convolutions. On first examination it would seem that a low rate of mental illness would be a very positive sign for any group, but, as noted above, in the nineteenth century such an occurrence was interpreted as a rather unsatisfactory state of affairs.

Generally, mental illness was explained as the effect of environmental and constitutional factors on the personality. An individual's constitution was the result of many generations of accumulated experience in society, a product of the inheritance of acquired characteristics. This past society might be civilized, as in the case of the representative New

Englander, or uncivilized, as in the case of the African slave. So there were two important variables, the present social environment and the constitutional makeup of the patient. In the first half of the nineteenth century the environment seemed to hold sway as the chief cause of mental illness; in the latter half of the century the bodily constitution seemed more important. However, both factors were always available for explanation.

When it appeared that the Black had less mental illness throughout the United States, this fact was explained as the natural result of his uncivilized nature. Like the American Indian, he was too simple to be insane. Insanity, Dr. Isaac Ray lamented, "was the price we pay for civilization" (Butler Hospital 1852, p. 19). Thus what at first might have seemed to be an advantage over White society turned out to be a sign of barbarism. If the theory which ascribed mental illness to education and independence was to be drawn to its logical conclusion, then slavery would have some advantage, since it circumvented this danger of freedom. Though the statistics of the 1840 census may have been adjusted by those with slave-holding sympathies, they were, all the same, adjusted in the direction which some psychiatrists would have declared to be reasonable. Even Dr. Jarvis, when he first examined the census figures, was able to interpret them in a way consistent with his psychiatric principles. Before discovering the errors of the census, he wrote that slavery, although "refusing many of the hopes and responsibilities which the free, self-thinking and self-acting enjoy and sustain," had the advantage to the slave of saving him "from some of the liabilities and dangers of self-destruction." The "false position" of the Northern freedman had a bad effect on his own character (Jarvis 1842, p. 119).

The supposed low insanity rate of the Black was often interpreted during the nineteenth century as a result of the comforts of slavery or the dull strength of the uncivilized. After emancipation, the reported number of mentally ill

Blacks began to climb. The arguments used by Southern psychiatrists about free Blacks before the Civil War were, after the war, reasserted, but apparently with less opposition from Northerners. For example, Dr. A. H. Witmer of St. Elizabeths looked back on slavery as a golden age, the exit from which caused the rate of insanity to rise dramatically. Witmer (1891) explained that

previous to their emancipation, the health and morals of the slaves were carefully preserved, and inebriety, excessive venery, and venereal diseases were closely guarded against; since their liberation, through overindulgence, exposure and ignorance of the laws of health, many have suffered from the effects of these fruitful causes of insanity. Untutored in a knowledge of the world, and without a sound philosophy or a religion deeper seated than the emotions to sustain them in adversity, many minds have failed under the constant strain of their advancing civilization.

Witmer expressed also a common view of heredity that acquired characteristics could be passed on to the next generation, but he believed that heredity had not yet played an important part in the rate of Black insanity. "It is too early," he explained to an international congress in Berlin, "in the history of their freedom for the denigrating effects of civilization to be manifest in the progeny of the recent slave" (Witmer 1891, p. 26). On balance, he argued for an approach toward mental illness which did not ascribe a multitude of distinctions between patients of various subgroups; but faced by the apparent rise of insanity rates among Blacks, he located causes which were widely accepted by his contemporaries. Rarely considered by writers on the subject were other factors which might account for an increased enumeration of the mentally ill such as changing patterns of health service delivery or a rising utilization of health services by groups such as Blacks.

In the late nineteenth century physicians were increasingly persuasive in attributing mental illness to organic factors. The *American Journal of Insanity* reported with interest a study by Dr. J. M. Buchanan (1886*a*) entitled "Insanity in the Colored Race." Dr. Buchanan, the superintendent of a Mississippi asylum, accepted a relationship between civilization and insanity, partly attributing to the effects of civilization an increase of insanity among Blacks from 1 out of 5,799 according to the 1860 census to 1 out of 1,096 by the 1880 census (Buchanan 1886*b*). The rate for Whites was about 1 out of 500. But other causes for this increase were listed as poor living conditions following emancipation, the increase of tuberculosis, and the general effect of bodily illness. Dr. Buchanan listed also specific organic factors as reasons why the Black would never reach the same degree of development as the White. This limitation was "owing, as some pathologists maintain, to the fact that the cranial sutures close much earlier in the Negro than in other races." Such an assertion might have comforted some who saw as one possible conclusion from an increase in Black insanity that the former slaves were becoming civilized.

Dr. Buchanan's observations on the social development of Blacks are of interest. As support for his cranial limitation theory he wrote that "in childhood Negroes are bright, intelligent and vivacious, and, as a rule learn as fast as whites of the same age, but on the approach of adult life a gradual change is manifested. The intellect seems to become clouded: they grow unambitious and indolent, and, losing interest in their books, their advancement grows slower and finally ceases altogether. . . . The growth of the brain is arrested by the premature closing of the cranial sutures and the lateral pressure of the frontal bones" (Buchanan 1886*b*, p. 69). A typical product of his times, this psychiatrist looked to farfetched theories of skull formation for an explanation of his observations, rather than considering the psychological consequences of growing to maturity in a hopeless social environment.

Even without being presented with the collection of skull

measurements, interpretations of facial features, and other scientificlike occupations of various investigators, one can see how the passage from a belief in the environmental causation of insanity to organic and inherited factors did not generally deflect the basic conclusion that Blacks were inferior. Before the Civil War a low rate of Black insanity established for psychological theorists the Black's lack of civilization. When the rate appeared to close in on that of the Whites, there turned out to be reasons why this was not a sign of "advancement." The turmoil of reconstruction and the subsequent disenfranchisement of the former slave was described as the tumult to which liberty is incident and to which the Black was unable to adjust because of constitutional inferiority. The common explanations for Black mental illness in the psychiatric literature were compounded of a mixture of political, social, organic, and hereditary causes which repeatedly led to similar conclusions of Black inferiority.

By about 1900 statistics on mental illness of various forms were widely available. One report might be mentioned in some detail. Dr. E. M. Green (1914), clinical director of the Georgia State Sanitarium, presented a comparative study of mental illness in two groups, White and Black, admitted during the years from 1909–1914 and totaling about 3,300 Whites and 2,100 Blacks. Dr. Green found alcoholic and drug psychoses, depression, neuroses, and mental retardation to be more common in Whites. In Blacks he found senility, general paralysis, mania, and dementia praecox (schizophrenia) to be more common. Both these sets of observations call for some comment. In the first decade of this century it was widely reported by newspapers and federal government spokesmen that cocaine was wreaking havoc among Southern Blacks, and, due to their excessive use of cocaine, male Blacks were a constant threat to womanhood.[2] Dr. Green

2. In the campaign to achieve a federal antinarcotic law, official government spokesmen dwelt on the supposed dangers from Southern Blacks, who were alleged to use cocaine in huge amounts. For example, Dr. Hamilton

points out, however, that of the 2,100 Black admissions only two had any involvement with cocaine, "although we all are familiar with the sensational statements made from time to time concerning the enormous increase in the use of cocaine by the Negro" (Green 1914, p. 702). The minimal use of cocaine was attributed by Green to poverty; if Blacks were prosperous, he opined, they might have more drug problems.

The reported excess of mania was explained by pointing to a "happy-go-lucky" attitude found among Blacks, along with a "peculiar mental attitude." This attitude was "not the result of a knowledge that his poverty, his social position, his unhealthy and cheerless surroundings cannot be bettered" and therefore are to be accepted with cheerful resignation, but rather due to "a simple nature which gives little thought to the future and desires only the gratification of the present" (Green 1914, p. 703).

The excess of schizophrenia was likewise subjected to an involved analysis. This disease seems to have been accepted as caused by traits which were considered by Dr. Green as characteristic of the White personality rather than of the Black, that is, the "shut-in personality . . . habits of introspection . . . sexual difficulties and sexual ruminations" (Green 1914, p. 707). Green's certainty that these factors could not be the cause of schizophrenia in the Negro reflects the introduction of modern dynamic factors as causes of mental illness. But as psychodynamics, the forces of the inner mental life, were introduced into psychiatry, the Black patient continued to be seen as a very distinct species who

Wright, U.S. opium commissioner in the State Department, declared before a House committee that "the crime of rape has largely been caused by the use of cocaine among Negroes in the South in the last 10 or 15 years" (U.S. Congress. House. Ways and Means Committee 1910, p. 23).

In the same movement, the Chinese living in America were pointed to as corrupters of White women, whom they enslaved by inducing them to smoke opium (U.S. Congress. Senate 1910, p. 45).

might well have reactions far different from those of the White patient.

Carl Jung also investigated the possible influence of race in mental processes. In 1912 he came to America where, with the permission of Dr. White, he analyzed the dreams and statements of fifteen Black patients at St. Elizabeths. He hoped to learn whether mythological motifs, which he later termed archetypes, were specific for each race or were common to all times and races. Jung believed that he was able "to demonstrate a whole series of motifs from Greek mythology in the dreams and fantasies of pure-bred Negroes suffering from mental disorders" (Jung 1971, p. 443).

By the 1930s, psychoanalysts in Washington, D.C., and Chicago were curious to learn whether it would be possible to analyze a Black patient successfully. Several made an attempt but without much success, and the procedure became a questionable undertaking. This uncertainty still persists among some analysts today. The late Gregory Zilboorg told one author (CP) that it seemed unwise to free a Black libido in an environment in which its free and uninhibited expression was restricted. In other words, he questioned whether a Black man could be truly free in our society. He further observed that the seeming success of women psychoanalysts such as Frieda Fromm-Reichmann, Viola Bernard, and Edith Weigert in the analysis of Blacks was probably due to the fact that these women were attempting to prove that they could succeed where male analysts had failed. But, whatever the interpretation, the possibility of successful analysis was ultimately established.

Some Personal Recollections of Charles Prudhomme[3]

At about the time of Jung visit, one of the earliest organ-

---

3. In order to relate more directly some of Dr. Prudhomme's recollections, this section is told in the first person.

izers of psychiatric training for Black medical students joined
St. Elizabeths staff. Dr. Ben Karpman (1886–1962), who introduced dynamic psychiatry into the medical curriculum at
Howard University in the mid-1920s, was an energetic and
well-liked teacher. He worked constantly to promote his subject and to stimulate in students a desire to study psychiatry.
Many showed interest but found very few places to do post-
graduate study. Early in his teaching at Howard University,
Karpman was able to persuade William A. White, Superintendent of St. Elizabeths Hospital, to give lectures to the
university students. The lectures were well attended and
well received. I attended several of these lectures while in
college and during my medical-school days. Ben Karpman
was a friendly man and active in many extracurricular activities in the Howard University community, especially the
Philosophy Club, established by the late Alaine Leroy
Locke. It was during these days that E. Franklin Frazier's
essay "The Pathology of Race Prejudice," first published in
The Forum (1927), was a frequent topic of discussion. Frazier
had adapted the mental mechanisms described in Bernard
Hart's *Psychology of Insanity* (1912) to the minds of Southern Whites in a very clever and convincing fashion. For his
efforts he was literally run out of Atlanta via a Lower Thir-
teen (the enclosed compartment located at either end of a
Pullman car).

Karpman required from senior medical students interviews
and case histories of Black patients at St. Elizabeths. All of
this was done in an "unofficial" arrangement but obviously
with the superintendent's approval. A series of studies prepared by senior medical students was arranged and edited by
Karpman and published by William A. White.

I met Dr. White in 1935 when a paper I had submitted as a
senior requirement was accepted by him for publication.[4] It

4. "The Problem of Suicide in the American Negro," *Psychoanalytic
Review*, 1938. This was the fourth in a series of studies under the general

was during this meeting that the subject of a Black's becoming an intern or resident at St. Elizabeths was addressed to Dr. White. He made no firm commitment, but told me about the civil service procedure and suggested that I apply. This I did as instructed, but my application was passed over for the year 1936–37. On a second visit, Dr. White urged me to reapply for the year 1937–38. I was then a resident in internal medicine at Freedmens Hospital which, like St. Elizabeths, was under the jurisdiction of the Department of the Interior. Seeing Dr. Phillip Graven[5] for psychoanalysis, I was in and out of St. Elizabeths as if I were an intern or resident. Such psychoanalytic experience had been arranged by Dr. Karpman for me and several others in the Howard University community including another young physician and two women social workers.

As mentioned above, Dr. White died in 1937 after a brief illness. Dr. Winfred Overholser of Boston was appointed by President Roosevelt as superintendent of St. Elizabeths. I approached the new superintendent and told him of my hope to become a resident at St. Elizabeths and how I had been encouraged by Dr. White. It was at this meeting with Dr. Overholser that I first heard that the laws under which St. Elizabeths operated specifically prevented any such possibility of an integrated medical staff. This meeting was not in an unfriendly vein but nevertheless quite disappointing. Dr. Overholser related his personal objections to such a state of affairs, but he was constrained by law and did not see how the former superintendent had expected to circumvent it. He spoke in asides of his own family background in New Eng-

---

title "Psychogenetic Studies in Race Pathology," arranged and edited by Dr. Karpman. Earlier publications in the *Review* included: Charles F. Gibson, "Concerning Color," 1931; R. A. Billings, "The Negro and His Church," 1934; and M. W. Allen, "Paul Lawrence Dunbar, a Study in Genius," 1938.

5. Dr. Phillip Graven was the first psychoanalyst in the Washington-Baltimore area.

land—of his ancestors' being sponsors of the underground railroad for runaway slaves—and he referred to Solomon Carter Fuller as being one of his favorite teachers while he was a student in Boston. These soul-wrenching soliloquies have continued to arouse sorrow and compassion in me for someone trying to explain away his blamelessness for such a state of affairs.

I felt defeated but resolved to fight back as best I could. I appealed to the NAACP, Secretary of the Interior Harold Ickes, Mrs. Eleanor Roosevelt, and my senator Harry S. Truman. All of my efforts, however, were to no avail, for segregation was the law of the land and remained so until the Supreme Court decision on school desegregation in 1954.

Shortly thereafter I secured an appointment, a Fellowship in Neurology and Psychiatry at the University of Chicago. Having finished my year of residency in internal medicine, I broke off my analysis and reported for duty on July 1, 1937. On arrival in Chicago, I walked into a rather nebulous and confused situation, as no real program for my training had been established or planned. I was warmly received in neurology by Drs. Percival Bailey and Paul Bucy, but as for training in psychiatry—well, they just wondered what to do with me. Finally, at the beginning of the medical school year, two Black senior medical students were assigned to me for their outpatient clerkship in psychiatry at the all-Black Provident Hospital. I felt that I was being used as a means of avoiding an assignment of the Black students to outpatient and inpatient services at the Billing's Hospital of the University of Chicago. These Black students and myself were assigned to the large "relief clinic" as it was dubbed at Provident. Another Howard University graduate, the late Dr. Walter Adams, my senior by a few years, was also assigned to these clinics. He was enthusiastic about psychoanalysis and was in analysis with Franz Alexander and later with Thomas Morton French, while working at the clinic.

Most of these patients were on relief or trying to get on the relief rolls. They were not really sick but just poor, destitute, and hungry, using the clinics as a means for survival during the Great Depression. I suppose it is reasonable to say that we clinic physicians were social psychiatrists.

I returned to Howard after this Fellowship and became a member of the two-man Division of Neurology and Psychiatry. I had not fully lost hope of breaking down the barrier at St. Elizabeths and again spoke with Senator Truman. Through his World War I army friendship with Dr. Charles M. Griffith, medical director of the Veterans Administration, I was offered an assignment as associate medical officer at Tuskegee Veterans Hospital. I accepted and reported for duty in January 1939. Dr. Griffith had formerly been the medical officer at Tuskegee when it was known as U.S. Government Hospital Number 91. He had been transferred as a result of the Veterans Bureau directive in 1923. He assured me that I would like it at Tuskegee and that there were some fine people working there. In 1943, after about four and a half years in Tuskegee, I returned to Washington and Howard.

One of my assignments at Howard was to teach psychiatry in the School of Nursing. The Nursing School was on notice that its accreditation was in jeopardy unless inhouse psychiatric case studies were provided for students. Having the support of Mrs. Roosevelt and Dr. Mary McCleod Bethune, among others, I went to Dr. Overholser with this problem. He "unofficially" acceded to our need for clinical teaching material. The solution was to transport each day the student nurses to and from St. Elizabeths. They were kept completely separate during work and mealtimes from the White student nurses from various schools on the East Coast that had "official" affiliate relations with St. Elizabeths.

Superintendent Overholser was also pressed to establish a cosmetology unit for Black female patients of St. Elizabeths since the one in existence would not accept any Black

patients. Again with Dr. Bethune's and Mrs. Roosevelt's vigorous support, Black students in the National Youth Administration, learning to become beauticians, were assigned with
their teachers to establish such a unit at St. Elizabeths.

In 1945 I participated in establishing a psychiatric service
as part of the University Student Health Services at Howard.
Somehow Frieda Fromm-Reichman heard about these
efforts, and after one of her lectures we held a long talk. She
invited me to her office at Chestnut Lodge, and after several
interviews she said she would like to work with me and also
to locate supervisors for Howard students of social work.
None of these arrangements, including my personal therapeutic alliance beginning in September 1945, was formally
related to either Chestnut Lodge or the Washington-Baltimore Psychoanalytic Institute. After a couple of
years, since I was in analysis and attending the institute's
lectures, I requested formalization of my work with Dr.
Fromm-Reichman and the institute. This was accomplished,
and I became a candidate in the then newly established
Washington Psychoanalytic Institute. I finished work with
Frieda Fromm-Reichman and, to my knowledge, all of the
prescribed requirements of the Psychoanalytic Institute in
June 1952. However, some questions were then raised on the
breadth of my training, and it was four more years before
everyone was satisfied that I had been properly trained.
While trying to satisfy the training requirements of the American Psychoanalytic Association, I had several interesting encounters with the leadership of the American Psychiatric
Association.

In 1948, the National Medical Association, having noted
the desegregation of the armed forces by President Truman's
executive order, asked the newly appointed head of the Veterans Administration, General Omar Bradley, for a conference in which plans could be made for a similar desegregation of the Veterans Administration. General Bradley cor-

dially met a group of concerned Black doctors and laymen and then requested his medical director, General Paul R. Hawley, to hold discussions in which both sides of this proposal would be aired. We met that spring in Washington for two days of lively exchange with those who opposed the integration of the Veterans Administration staff and patients. Dr. Winfred Overholser, who had recently become president of the American Psychiatric Association and was, as noted above, superintendent of St. Elizabeths, argued that such integration was not in the best interest of the patients, that psychiatric care could be best delivered in a segregated setting. We were initially disheartened by this opposition since Dr. Overholser spoke from a position of great eminence and authority. But at noon on the second day General Bradley came into our discussions and announced that he had had a telephone call from the White House. President Truman had decided to settle our question by ordering the preparation of an order desegregating all Veterans Administration hospitals. We were overjoyed by this action, and, as I look back upon many years in psychiatry, I believe that this presidential order was the first substantial breakthrough for Blacks in the mental health field (Truman 1948).

A few years later, in early 1952, I approached the American Psychiatric Association's leadership with a request which had been made of me by the Howard University team of lawyers who were preparing their arguments for the school desegregation case, *Brown* v. *Board of Education*. Their work, of course, resulted in the historic decision of May 17, 1954. I suggested that the APA file a brief *amicus curiae* supporting the contention that separate educational facilities are not equal. I was advised by the APA's "establishment" to withdraw from involvement in the case and remain aloof from such a political issue. One eminent leader described my proposal as simply one additional example of my continuing "acting out."

One final example of the resistance to integration on the grounds of "good politics" came from some prominent officers in the U.S. Public Health Service. During the early attempts to establish the National Institute of Mental Health, about 1945 and 1946, they suggested that I could make a significant contribution to the successful passage of the pending Mental Health Act and subsequent legislation for the burgeoning mental health field if I could persuade Representative Adam Clayton Powell not to attach an antidiscriminatory amendment to such bills. Such appeals are never couched in language which support racism, but rather as "reasonable compromises" which allegedly make progress possible.

Without touching upon further recollections, I will conclude by recommending that further research is needed into the history of the American mental health professions for the ultimate benefit of all concerned.

Professional Training — Dr. Solomon Carter Fuller

The life of Solomon Fuller (1872–1953) (figure 2.1) exemplifies some aspects of the training of Black professionals in past generations.[6] Born in Monrovia, Liberia, he received his undergraduate education at Livingston College, Salisbury, N.C. Disappointed in his application to Harvard Medical School, he was later accepted by Boston University, where he obtained his medical degree in 1897. After graduation Fuller became an intern and two years later the pathologist at the Westboro (Massachusetts) State Hospital. Fuller fell into pathology and later neuropathology by default, because of difficulties for Blacks at the time to enter private practice or to receive an appointment in clinical neurology

6. The following account is largely based on the research and publications of Dr. W. Montague Cobb, in particular his "Solomon Carter Fuller, 1872–1953 (Cobb 1954).

FIGURE 2.1. Dr. Solomon Fuller. This portrait, painted by Mrs. Naida Willette Page of Howard University, was commissioned by Dr. Charles Prudhomme and his wife and presented to the American Psychiatric Association.

FIGURE 2.2. The Psychology Conference Group, Clark University, Worcester, Mass., taken on the occasion of Freud's visit to America in September 1909. *First row, left to right:* Franz Boas, E. B. Titchener, William James, William Stern, Leo Burgerstein, G. Stanley Hall, Sigmund Freud, Carl G. Jung, Adolf Meyer, H. S. Jennings. *Second row:* C. E. Seashore, Joseph Jastrow, J. McK. Cattell, E. F. Buchner, E. Katzenellenbogen, Ernest Jones, A. A. Brill, Wm. H. Burnham, A. F. Chamberlain. *Third row:* Albert Schinz, J. A. Magni, B. T. Baldwin, F. Lyman Wells, G. M. Forbes, E. A. Kirkpatrick, Sandor Ferenczi, E. C. Sanford, J. P. Porter, Sakyo Kanda, Hikoso Kakise. *Fourth row:* G. E. Dawson, S. P. Hayes, E. B. Holt, C. S. Berry, G. M. Whipple, Frank Drew, J. W. A. Young, L. N. Wilson, K. J. Karlson, H. H. Goddard, H. I. Klopp. S. C. Fuller. Photo reproduced by permission of Clark University.

and psychiatry in the Massachusetts State Hospital system. Then, sensing a need to complete his American training by study at the great centers of European medicine, he went to Germany in 1904, visiting en route his Liberian home.

In Europe he studied psychiatry at the University of Munich under Emil Kraeplin and nueropathology with Alois Alzheimer. Fuller's family reports that he frequently recounted his initial examination by Alzheimer after which he was selected for advanced study while four or five white Americans were rejected at the same time as not being sufficiently experienced. Fuller first gained recognition and acceptance in neuropathology, but gradually he ventured into clinical neurology and psychiatry. At Boston University, Fuller finally rose to the rank of associate professor and on his retirement in 1933 was designated professor emeritus of neurology. Nevertheless, he felt neither that he had ever received his due academic recognition at Boston University nor that he was ever able to advance in the Massachusetts State Hospital system. Frequently he threatened to resign but simply could not afford to do so. He became, and remained for years, the editor of a scientific journal sponsored by the staff of Westboro State Hospital and was on the consulting staff of several hospitals in the Boston area. Increasingly he was sought as a lecturer and writer on neuropathology.

Karl Menninger recalls that while he was a student at Harvard Medical School, Solomon Carter Fuller was one of his teachers and has called attention to Fuller's presence in the famous group that gathered with Freud and Jung to commemorate the twentieth anniversary of Clark University in 1909 (figure 2.2). Winfred Overholser, commissioner of mental health in Massachusetts prior to succeeding White as superintendent of St. Elizabeths, asserted that Fuller "was my teacher and friend." Karl M. Bowman, president of the American Psychiatric Association from 1944 to 1946, also recalls Fuller clearly and particularly Fuller's rejection for a position at Johns Hopkins, although recommended by Adolph Meyer, because he was a "colored man."

Solomon Carter Fuller, an organically oriented psychiatrist, lectured along with other scientists at Clark University in 1909. His lecture entitled "Cerebral Histology, with Special Reference to Histopathology of the Psychoses" has not been located to date.

One of Fuller's signal accomplishments was to encourage the entry of Black people into the mental health professions. Recruitment was suddenly prompted when the Veterans Bureau directed that in sixty days the staff in the newly constructed U.S. Veterans Hospital at Tuskegee, Ala., should be changed from all White to all Black.[7] Fuller succeeded in recruiting and training four graduating Black students (three from Boston University and one from Harvard) into accepting the challenge of neuropsychiatry and becoming, in 1923, the nucleus of that service at the hospital in Tuskegee.

The sixty-day limit for Black recruitment was difficult to achieve, for there were few trained Black personnel available. In some categories, such as dieticians, none could be located anywhere. The drive to find the needed staff was vigorous, and it was at this point that Fuller was approached by Black leaders.

Of the 400,000 Black veterans of World War I, 300,000 lived in the South. They received some pretty shoddy treatment. Many with mental illness were labeled by the Veterans Administration as "behavior disorders" or "bad conduct cases" arising allegedly as sequelae to central nervous system syphilis. This diagnosis made them ineligible for veterans' benefits. The stigma and problem were resolved by the clinical and laboratory work of Fuller's students so that, after

7. Mr. Spurgeon O. Burke, who became the hospital's business manager at the beginning of the changeover, has generously assisted in the description of the events at Tuskeegee.

a time, mentally ill veterans began receiving their deserved benefits. But another injustice arose then because only Whites were allowed to be guardians and thereby be granted fiscal responsibility for these Black veterans. The entire Tuskegee story is a classic example of racism and its many exploitative aspects.

A recent visit with Fuller's two oldest sons in Hyannis, Mass., revealed further evidence of his concern for the welfare of the original four young men whom he had recruited and directed into the mental health field in the South. His two sons corroborated many of the previously unrecorded accounts of their father's life, work, and frustrations and also provided letters, papers, and pictures. Two recollections seem relevant to our major theme. Fuller was G. Stanley Hall's personal physician for years. They continued to be friends after most of Clark University's faculty departed en masse over President Hall's well-known irascibility. Fuller remained and always defended Hall for his broad knowledge and great intelligence. Although Hall's extensive publications are now viewed by many Blacks as having racist assumptions, there was seemingly no barrier to the mutual respect of these two men.

Fuller's sons described their father as a quiet, contemplative man, eclipsed in recognition by their mother, Meta Warrick, an extroverted and talented sculptress. She was commissioned to prepare and display her work in many places. In 1907 her exhibit of Negro life at the Jamestown Exposition was awarded a gold medal. Like their father, she too had studied in Europe. She was an acquaintance of Auguste Rodin, who advised and assisted her in securing commissions while abroad (Locke 1936, pp. 29 ff.).

Dr. Fuller's life, work, and frustrations certainly warrant a more thorough study. Records of all types, letters, photographs, memorabilia, and archives such as those at Westboro State Hospital, all need to be examined. One provocative item in the possession of the Fuller family is a geneological chart. This record is suggestive evidence that Solomon Carter Fuller is a descendant of a talented Virginia slave whom Benjamin Rush described in his abolitionist writings, a possibility that was raised by Betty Plummer in her master's thesis, "Benjamin Rush and the Negro" (Plummer 1969). It has already been determined that Fuller's immediate ancestors colonized in Liberia in the early 1800s from the same general area ot Viriginia as the slave in Rush's account. If this possibility could be established, a remarkable coincidence would exist in the lives of the Father of American Psychiatry and the First Black Psychiatrist.

Conclusion

At a time of accelerating protest, ethnic discontent, polarization, and fragmentation, we must ponder over these events with historical perspective. One strain in American history which has turned the proverbial "dream" into a nightmare for many is the virulence of racism which has been propagated from one generation to the next. Racism has been so much a part of our society that its assumptions take on the guise of "common sense" or "the way things are." The mental health professions are not somehow exempt from these pervasive influences. They take on the values and assumptions of society as well as operate within the customary restraints of contemporary social structure. This engagement with the rest of society should not be surprising, but it should not simply be accepted as inevitable or unalterable.

What record of the past we have sketched in these pages is meager in comparison with the extent and importance of the subject. Only a few highlights can be captured in the space available, but hopefully these episodes will encourage others to carry on and to document more adequately such subjects as the life of Dr. Fuller, patterns of service delivery and experience of treatment in the past, the ways in which rejection of an apparently alien group is transferred into the "impartial" language of science, and finally the patterns of incorporating into science distortions of its social environment. Such historical studies will represent a distinct service to science and to the mental health workers, for these analyses are necessary correctives to the kind of error that distracts the professions from their valid goals.

REFERENCES

Allen, M. W. 1938. Paul Lawrence Dunbar, a study in genius. *Psychoanal. Rev.*

Billings, R. A. 1934. The Negro and his church. *Psychoanal. Rev.*

Boudin, J. Ch. M. 1857. *Traité de géographie et de statistique médicales.* Vol. 2. Paris: Ballière.

Brigham, A. 1845. Exemption of Cherokee Indians and Africans from insanity. *Am. J. Insanity* 1:287–88.

Buchanan, J. M.
    1886*a*.   Insanity in the Colored race. *Am. J. Insanity* 2:278–80.
    1886*b*.   Insanity in the Colored race. *New York Med. J.* 44:67–70.

Butler Hospital for the Insane. 1852. *Annual report.* Providence, R.I.

Calhoun, J. C. 1856. Letter to J. W. Jones, Speaker of the House, February 8, 1945. *The works of John C. Calhoun,* ed. R. K. Crallé Vol. 5. New York: D. Appleton.

Cobb, Montague. 1954. Solomon Carter Fuller, 1872–1953. *J. Nat. Med. Ass.* 46:370–72.

Dain, N.
    1964.   *Concepts of insanity in the United States, 1789–1865.* New Brunswick, N.J.: Rutgers University Press.
    1971.   *Disordered minds: the first century of Eastern State Hospital in Williamsburg, Virginia, 1766–1866.* Williamsburg, Va.: Colonial Williamsburg Foundation.

Deutsch, A. 1944. The first U.S. census of the insane (1840) and its use as pro-slavery propaganda. *Bull. Hist. Med.* 15:469–82.

Drewry, W. F. 1916. Central State Hospital, Petersburg, Virginia. In *In-*

stitutional care of the insane in the United States and Canada, ed. H. Hurd. Vol. 3. 77:856–62.

Frazier, E. Franklin. 1927. The pathology of race prejudice. *Forum* 77:856–62.

Gibson, Charles F. 1931. Concerning color. *Psychoanal. Rev.* 18:413–25.

Green, E. M. 1914. Psychoses among Negroes — a comparative study. *J. Nerv. Ment. Dis.* 41:697–708.

Grob, G. N.

    1966.   *The state and the mentally ill: a history of Worcester State Hospital in Massachusetts, 1830–1920.* Chapel Hill, N.C.: University of North Carolina Press.

    1971.   *See* Jarvis (1855).

Jarvis, E.

    1842.   Statistics of insanity in the United States. *Boston. Med. Surg. J.* 27:116–21, 281–82.

    1852.   Insanity among the Colored population of the free states. *Am. J. Insanity* 8:268–82.

    1855.   *Insanity and idiocy in Massachusetts: report of the Commission on Lunacy*, reprinted (1971) with a critical introduction by G. Grob. Cambridge, Mass.: Harvard University Press.

Jung, Carl. 1971. *Psychological types*. In *Collected works*. Vol. 6.

Kirkbride, Thomas S. 1855. Proceedings for the Tenth Annual Meeting of the Association of Medical Superintendents of American Institutions for the Insane. *Am. J. Insanity* 12:43, 89.

Locke, Alaine. 1936. *Negro art, past and present*. Washington, D.C.

Nichols, C. H. 1855. Archives of the Institute of the Pennsylvania Hospital, Philadelphia.

Nott, J. 1844. *Two lectures on the natural history of the Caucasian and Negro races*. Mobile, Ala.

Plummer, Betty. 1969. *Benjamin Rush and the Negro*. Master's thesis, Howard University.

Prudhomme, Charles. 1938. The problem of suicide in the American Negro. *Psychoanal. Rev.*

Ray, I. 1856. Review of Jarvis, *Insanity and idiocy*. . . . *North American Rev.* 82:78–100, esp. pp. 95–96.

St. Elizabeths Hospital. 1856. Minutes of the meetings of the Board of Visitors of the Goverment Hospital for the Insane. July. Washington, D.C.: Archives of St. Elizabeths Hospital.

Truman, Harry S. 1948. Executive Order No. 9980. Regulations governing fair employment practices within the federal establishment. 26 July.

U.S. Congress. House. Ways and Means Committee. 1910. *Importation and use of opium, hearings*. 61st Cong., 2d sess., December 14.

U.S. Congress. Senate. 1910. *The opium problem.* 61st Cong., 2d sess., 21
    February. Doc. no. 377.
Wilkins, T. 1970. *Cherokee tragedy: the story of the Ridge family and the
    decimation of a people.* New York: Macmillan.
Witmer, A. H. 1891. Insanity in the Colored race in the United States.
    Alienist and Neurologist 12:19–30.

PART II

Clinical Context

CHAPTER 3

Racism and Psychotherapy

by *Charles A. Pinderhughes*

The origins of racism in humans are presented along with the history of racism in the United States. Description of psychotherapy of Black Americans before and after 1967 is given with case histories. The need for psychotherapy arises because of social and psychological repression. Biracial relationships in psychotherapy are considered as well as racism in therapists.

The chapter ends with a discussion of how the interlocked patterns of impressions from the body, the mind, and society may help us to understand universally encountered patterns in the dynamics of repression in all societies, along with twelve hypotheses based on these roots and the implications for societies that are based on competition or on sharing.

Racism as a Fixed Unequal and Hierarchical Relationship

The essence of racism lies in a relatively constant pattern of prejudice and discrimination between one party who is idealized and favored and another who is devalued and exploited in a common relationship. The relationships between Whites and Blacks, between Whites and Reds, between Whites and Yellows, and between Whites and Browns have been of this order. Relationships between men and women, between management and labor, between adults and children, between educators and students have also been of this order.

In a common relationship, equality of roles is rare. In order for peace and harmony to exist, the activity of each party in a relationship must be fitted together so they are not in conflict. When one is putting out, the other should be taking in. When one is talking, the other should be listening. This complementary peaceful and harmonious relationship is not an equal one. It involves an initiator and an accommodator—one who extends something of the self and one who adjusts to that.

In all human relationships these basic considerations are encountered, and forms of power or bribery are used to resolve them. Even reason and love are employed as instruments of power and mastery. In every culture, in every institution, in every family, in every relationship, power struggles define who will be the initiator and who will be the accommodator unless both individuals have been induced to employ some predetermined cultural guidelines for relationships.

Any and every aspect of one's personality may be available to participate in negotiations which define role relationships. Value orientation, cultural programming, and many other factors affecting personality development influence the quality of the roles sought and the intensity with which they are pursued. Our search for dependable conflict-free roles motivates the well-defined and rather stabilized patterns of role relationships in our institutions. Stabilized roles are seldom equal roles since, more often than not, one party is assigned the role of initiator and the other party assigned the role of the accommodator. This results in self-actualization for one party and self-surrender and subordination for the other.

Even the conflicts within a personality must be resolved in similar ways, with some components of each person being idealized and encouraged while others are devalued and repressed. It would appear that the only possibility for equality of roles exists when equally free parties negotiate in an ongoing way with equal power and resources.

In the long run, it may not be that what we want is equal roles. We may want only to be valued equally with other human beings, to be considered equally, to be appreciated equally, to be loved equally, and to have pain equally. As institutional and cultural pressures structure the behavior of people with one another, over a long time, these human components of the relationship become subordinated to the form, ritual, and structure.

A gradual erosion of the human aspects with resultant dehumanization takes place as an institution grows stronger and older. Persons in leadership roles have their sense of entitlement reinforced, and they function as racists toward the persons in hierarchical relationships below them. Upper ones feel more entitled and lower ones get neglected and exploited.

False belief systems aggrandizing the upper elites and denigrating the lower nonelites are promoted by influential persons in most human institutions. Elites are inclined toward narcissism and paranoia which glorify them while denigrating nonelites. Elites use their power to contrive reality and to limit the access of nonelites to resources, power, education, and privilege. For elites, self-aggrandizing beliefs and narcissism may be so strongly supported by contrived realities that their false belief in their superiority and entitlement may be inacessible to ordinary forms of psychotherapy. In psychotherapy, active confrontation processes may be as necessary for undermining and loosening these delusions as they are for altering racism and classism in institutions.

Nonelites are inclined toward paranoia which denigrates them while glorifying elites. Realities contrived in support of these false beliefs contribute to the oppression, depression, and disorganization which are so common among nonelites. The paranoid beliefs in racism or classism are shared by many people who have an intact capacity to relate socially to others and to trust and identify with other persons. Such group-related paranoias are nonpathological although they contain false belief systems based upon projection on non-elites of attributes which elites renounce in themselves. Contrived realities, initiated and maintained by both direct violence and processed violence, make the beliefs seem true.

By defining racism along such broad operational lines, we can see that the psychotherapy relationship may be a racist one whenever there is inequality of value, consideration, and appreciation between the therapist and the patient. We can also see that the shifting patterns of every dynamic interpersonal relationship may contain rare moments of equality for the participants but will be, for the most part, unequal and racist in nature.

When racism is defined this broadly, it can be viewed as a characteristic of human nature which may be employed for constructive or for destructive purposes. Roles of parents and children that are unequal and essentially racist may be employed to repress and exploit one party or to promote developments which equalize the parties and increase the freedom and mutuality in their interaction. Likewise, the unequal, essentially racist, roles of psychotherapists and patients may be employed to repress and exploit or to free and assist one or both parties.

Racism Within the Personality

Each personality may be regarded as a vehicle which contains aspects from all earlier developmental experience. There are immature aspects and mature aspects, aggressive aspects and passive aspects, controlling aspects and surrendering aspects, and masculine aspects and feminine aspects in every personality. Behavior is determined by those aspects which are dominant in the personality organization at the time. The following example may help to clarify this.

A twenty-six-year-old man sought psychotherapy for depression and anxiety two months after his roommate was killed in an automobile accident, four months after his male lover deserted him, and six months after he and his wife separated. He was preoccupied with the death of his roommate and with his feeling that he was a jinx to anyone near him. At times, in slips of speech, he referred to his roommate as "womb-mate." The sequence of disasters, accidents, and injuries and the feeling of being a jinx were traced back into early childhood. At six months of age, his identical twin had died of malnutrition. He was affected by the depression and mourning with which his caretaker grandmother had reacted, and in later life he fantasied that his own eating must have deprived and killed his sibling. His feeling of being a bad, no-good jinx was also tied to the fact that he had never known his father or mother, the latter having deserted by leaving the twins in the hospital after they were born.

At the wheel of this patient's personality was a child part of him that felt devalued, criticized, and perceived as a dangerous and contagious killer who took tragedy and death wherever he went. He lived dangerously and sought out companions and situations with which tragedies were likely to occur. He was unaware that he was living out his own child beliefs and fantasies which had been organized and embedded in his personality at an early age. As he became aware that the pattern of tragedies was tied to a script developed in early childhood and that this child part was in the driver's seat of his personality, he became aware that his life was dominated by and enslaved to this script.

In response to the therapist's insistence that children have no business driving automobiles or personalities, he began to work toward the goal of "getting the child's hands off the wheel and getting the most mature part of him into the driver's seat." Every decision on every issue, no matter how small, was examined to determine whether the decision had been made by an immature or mature part of himself. Over many months, his choice of companions and circumstances became more free of tragedies, accidents, and conflict. However, he missed the excitement and the sense of intense emotional involvement of his former life and began to bear the sense of loss and to mourn rather than to live out the repeated gaining and losing of objects to which he had been sensitized and programmed in his early life.

One might say that the patient had been enslaved to this program, that the child part of him had dominated and exploited his life in a very racist way. One might say, also, that an "evil," "undisciplined," "destructive," "black" part of the patient was the master of his personality and that the "good" "white" part had to be freed and put in charge. Every group encourages its members to enslave and rigidly control the bad, disruptive (black) aspects of their personalities in a kind of racist exploitation of some aspects of their personalities in order to make harmonious social life possible.

The patient in this example was White. He encountered in his community many influences which encouraged him to use more constructive patterns.

Black people in our racist society have had more opportunity than Whites to have early experiences of loss, pain, and deprivation which can imprint tragedy-seeking scripts in their personalities. Moreover, our racist society makes psychotherapy far less accessible to the Black person who needs it. Furthermore, our racist society has produced and perpetuated environmental circumstances for Blacks which do not encourage the use of constructive patterns and which provoke fear, degradation, uncertainty, and arousal and reinforcement of immature patterns. Many of these pathogenic circumstances are class related and found among the poor of any group. Racial factors merely doubly ensure membership among the nonelites, doubly ensure exposure to pathogenic circumstances, and doubly ensure exclusion from treatment.

The Unusually Pathogenic Nature of American Slavery

The nature of American slavery introduced pathogenic factors which were unique among slaves and their descendants.

No other American people have experienced a cultural press which prevented group formation by bonding them to outsiders, pressing them to trust outsiders and to distrust themselves, imposing a value system which undermined their self-esteem, and programming them to surrender, self-sacrifice, and defeat rather than toward mastery. This cultural press, introduced by American slavery and perpetuated by segregation, has increased the conflict, depression, distrust, and suffering among descendants of slaves. Conflict-resolving processes which require some relatively stable organization of people have rarely been effective in communities where these antigroup products of American racism abound, so that substantial preliminary group and community organization may be required. The ghettos of other groups abound with progroup pressures that are more likely to support and encourage any progress in psychotherapy. Black ghettos, on the other hand, abound with enormous antigroup pressures that are less likely to support and encourage any such progress.

The serious pathogenic circumstances in predominantly Black communities contribute to three major mental health problems: usually large numbers of people need psychiatric treatment, serious resistances to treatment are frequently encountered, and patients must return to the same pathogenic circumstances which spawned their pathology. The only broadly effective way to reduce the numbers needing treatment, to modify favorably the resistances brought to treatment, and to improve the circumstances to which Black patients return is to alter the pathogenic circumstances in their communities and the racism and classism which produced and maintained them. Under optimum conditions such changes come about slowly, for there is public resistance to the massive long-term social changes which are needed. It is unfortunate, therefore, that many years may pass before these three major mental health problems are solved in Black communities.

Psychotherapy of Black Americans Prior to 1967

The next part of this chapter deals with the treatment of individual Black patients in conventional one-to-one psychotherapy and delineates some of the common resistances encountered in the psychotherapy of Black patients between 1947 and 1967. The author of this chapter and Dr. Ruick Rolland, director of the Roxbury, Mass., Court Clinic, discussed the psychotherapy of Black patients at the Seventy-Second Annual Convention of the National Medical Association in St. Louis, Mo., August 1967. They had employed psychoanalytically oriented psychotherapy with numerous Black patients, and in their presentation they described the principles and tactics they employed in managing some of the resistances to this treatment. The principles and some of the tactics are transferable to other forms of psychotherapy. Two case illustrations are included from the records of twenty-five private patients and twenty-five public clinic and public hospital patients which were reviewed.

An additional section delineates the need for modifying the pathogenic nature of the social structure in Black communities. It deals more with the overall strategy of treating Blacks as a group of people in trouble and is referred to as the sociopsychological treatment of Black people by group formation.

Resistances to Psychotherapy in Black Patients

Racist sociocultural pressures in the United States have programmed most Whites to fit American institutions and most Blacks to be excluded. Under this cultural pressure some behavior patterns of Blacks in interactions with Whites have been important for survival and adaptation in the racist society but have served as obstacles to the office-type, therapist-controlled, more "racist" psychotherapy which prevailed prior to 1967. Subsequently, with development of community psychiatry, outreach methods, more trust-building, and better management of narcissistic and omnipotent feelings in psychotherapists, these resistances could be managed better and have been seen less often.

A partial list of obstacles to psychotherapy which were encountered frequently in Black patients between 1947 and 1967 includes:

a. Denial of problems or a vague commitment by which they relate to therapy as something done to them rather than with them

b. Transient paranoid feelings of persecution

c. Repeated signs of distrust

d. Silence or blocking

e. Claims of being passive victims of circumstances that interfere with therapy

f. Actions which precipitate crises in their lives

g. Lateness

h. Nonpayment of bills

i. Missed appointments

j. Quitting of therapy

While the above resistances may occur in persons of any racial, national, or ethnic background, they tended to occur with greater frequency in Black patients prior to 1967. Several of these resistances (c, d, e, g, h, i, j) sometimes represent indirect expressions of hostile aggression on the part of persons in whom more direct expression has been inhibited. Several (a, b, c, e) reflect a sense of victimization, pessimism, distrust, and fear which make denial of problems or passive surrender to them seem safer than an assertive attempt at problem-solving. When assertive action is taken, it may be undertaken in a manner which creates as many problems as are solved, since many Blacks feel that a price must be paid for any assertive activity. The pathogenic conditions imposed under slavery and segregation have promoted these patterns and ensured that child-rearing patterns would develop this feeling in large numbers of Black children. What was life-preserving and adaptive for Black people as slaves or servants has often proved maladaptive when some conventional psychotherapy styles have been employed with them. Black mothers, in order to rear children who would fit into slavery and segregation systems, had to exercise all the omnipotence of the ruling Whites to program and accommodate their children to the system. Their children accommodated in large numbers by showing indirect rather than direct aggression, by responding rather than initiating, by reading the thoughts of other persons while hiding their own, and by engaging in accommodating-subordinating ritualized behavior designed to make as few waves as possible in the system. Psychotherapy methods which encouraged discussion of thoughts, feelings, and problems in an open manner with a White person could not easily bypass a lifetime of conditioning in the opposite direction.

Let us look more closely at some of the resistances. One approach to a patient's denial of problems (resistance "a") involves delay in establishment of the treatment contract. Exploratory or evaluative interviews may be conducted indefinitely, without breaking off the relationship and without establishing a contract for therapy, until the patient and doctor together identify a problem needing treatment and find a mutually agreeable pattern of relating to one another. They may then work toward agreed-upon goals and methods of therapy. In hammering out what might be called a hard-nosed contract, direct and straight-from-the-shoulder confrontation occurs, providing the basis for reduced ambivalence, a sense of strength, trust, objectivity, and control. Throughout this process the therapist should maintain a positive regard and clearly manifest interest, or the patient may feel that the therapist's intent is to drive him away.

A paranoid posture with delusions of persecution (resistance "b") and intense rage may be adopted by some patients who have not lost capacity to test reality. They attack persons close to them to express the emotional distress of their disappointment and to express their wish to force compliance from a troublesome loved object.

In the midst of expressing such hate, the patient may be bluntly told that his feelings and behavior are a manifestation of love. Love for the therapist may also be interpreted. A sharp change in behavior often occurs. Crying with expression of relief at being understood may occur even in tough male patients. The events in the patient's life which have motivated the change in feeling and behavior are then examined in a conventional manner. All of this may occur in a single interview, or in a second scheduled soon thereafter, in order to nip in the bud the buildup of hostile destructive behavior which the patient unconsciously engineers by assuming the paranoid posture.

Quick identification of resistances and early vigorous interpretation of their meaning are important. Tactics which lift the resistance into bold relief are useful. Interpretations given with little supporting data may be formulated to discriminating tough-minded patients as guesses or speculations as to what may be limiting progress. Confrontation and encounter processes may be as useful in psychotherapy as in bringing about institutional change. Basically, they are useful in dealing with resistant structures whether they be in personalities or in societies.

Claims by some patients that they are passive victims of circumstances that interfere with therapy (resistance "e") may be dealt with by interpreting every act as a manifest decision. Statements such as "I couldn't come," "I was unable to be on time," "I can't talk," "I had to take a sleeping pill," and "I can't pay the bill" may be interpreted to the patient as meaning "You decided not to come," "You decided not to be on time," "You are deciding not to talk," "You decided to take a sleeping pill," and "You have decided not to pay the bill." These are simple statements of fact which interpret to the patient that he is not the helpless victim of fate that he claims to be. He has resources in terms of time, energy, and money and makes decisions on how to use them. To be sure, the patient's conclusions may seem reasonable, but implicit in his statements are an abdication of responsibility, of initiative, of decision-making, and of active mastery of reality. Such abdication of self-assertive roles has been developed and supported by the pathogenic conditions under which Black people have lived. Failure to encourage and stimulate use of the most mature ego functions available supports the patient's resistances and encourages a helpless attitude. A case illustration may make more clear some of the resistances and tactics described:

Case No. 1 (both patient and therapist Black)

A thirty-two-year-old, single, passive, quiet-spoken woman who "had difficulty paying for therapy" and who exemplified her obsessional rumination by "thinking about" but never carrying out constructive things she wanted to do — like learning to cook, to swim, and to visit relatives — was told that therapy appointments would be contingent upon her paying at the beginning of each hour and upon regular attendance at courses for cooking and swimming. At the conclusion of any course a new contract would have to be negotiated. At the next appointment she forgot her checkbook. The therapist refused to see her and rescheduled another appointment sooner than the next regularly scheduled one. She left in a rage. At the next appointment, she presented a check but neglected to sign it. The next two interviews are described below:

PATIENT [while making out check]: I'm having tremendous trouble remembering. I feel lost and not able to hold onto any information. I have no confidence and block on simple basic things so that I can't go on to complex ones. In everything I'm caught between giving and withholding. I don't know whether I'm being taken advantage of and I'm afraid of my anger. My friends say I play a dumb role and fail socially.

[The therapist suggested that her anger at him over the checks might have to do with her forgetting.]

PATIENT: I wanted to say, "Screw you." I'm a talker and a griper; I see everything wrong that other people do. I'm a good griper; I sound so erudite, it passes for thinking. You gripe me! But I get angry at myself when I hate others' guts.

THERAPIST: Why?

PATIENT: Last year I went on a rampage with another shrink to do myself in. He [the other psychiatrist] is a stupid asshole. He said I was shitting on myself when I was late to see him, even the time when I was late because of treatment by another doctor for my hemorrhoid. He took the finger out of the dike and I had to contend with the flood. You keep asking stupid questions! "Why! Why! Why!"

[She cried at this point and continued.]

PATIENT: I'm confused about giving—I give—I withhold—give—withhold—how can I get a decent job—if I don't, I won't be able to come here.

THERAPIST: That's your way to get rid of me.

PATIENT: I want to see some results, not years of talk, talk, talk, to stupid people. [in a rage at this point]. What would happen if everytime I got angry I expressed it? I'd scream and holler at others when I'm the one; I would look like more of an ass then when I'm quiet. I can't even do a stupid-assed child's puzzle.

[A contract had been set forth which threw some of her resistances into bold relief and made withholding more difficult. At the next appointment, she talked softly as she searched for the check she had misplaced in her bag as withholding was again in evidence.]

PATIENT: I don't want to speak loud—I want to mew. I want to do things and stop being so polite. [In a tortuous way she then described how other patients progressed with their psychiatrists but she did not. The therapist pointed out how roundabout she was in making her point.]

PATIENT: The other therapist let me get away with everything. If I'd worked with you, I would have staved off the feeling of loneliness and helplessness. He wasn't competent with me. I hate the way you sit there so smug and so superior. Why do you look at your appointment book now? Can't you do that later? You try to control everything.

THERAPIST: And to keep from feeling you're surrendering to someone, you refuse to produce; you just sit and put out nothing, or only mew a little out, speaking so softly you can't be heard. You've got an anal sphincter holding all your actions in check.

PATIENT: I hate myself for this—especially my typical posture of holding one hand with the other. I feel dead. I only feel alive when I go like this with each hand.

THERAPIST: When you claw with each hand, basically you want to kill!

PATIENT: I don't! I'm passive.

[As the therapist laughed at this and argued with her, she spoke louder and louder, at first vacillating between expression and suppression but finally speaking consistently strongly. She criticized three other therapists she had seen for being too nice, for not provoking her enough, and a fourth for provoking her too much without showing enough warmth along with his hostile manner.]

THERAPIST: No man could be satisfactory to you; you have to find things wrong with them, not trust them, and thereby relive what you felt about your own father—rage and disappointment that he let you down and left the family—now you say you wrecked your life last year because I was not with you and looking after you.

[The patient thoughtfully concluded the interview.]

PATIENT: I need vigorous interaction with someone strong enough to bring my feelings out and help me organize them. Otherwise I will destroy myself, the treatment, or you. I just don't know how to manage the feelings. They always had to be suppressed. That's what I mean by passive.

The anal content of these two interviews illustrates what the author considers to be of critical importance in the treatment of many Black descendants of slaves. The cultural press which has molded most Black American personalities has attempted to suppress aggression and rage and has not offered training in the management of aggression along acceptable self-assertive lines. Like rectums trained to compliance, they are to open up and produce or withhold on command.

Some difficulties in developing trust toward the therapist reflect problems Black American mothers have had in fitting care and nurture to infant needs in early development. It is the impression of the author that, in general, Black mothers have done a good job of providing care and nurture in the oral period. It has been in the anal period, when training in the control and management of internal impulses and mastery of the various body functions occur, that Black mothers have had difficulties which are reflected in the passive-aggressive resistances to therapy. The cultural press in which they have lived has insisted upon a passive and compliant child. Black mothers have used withdrawal of affection, disapproval, and punishment in abundance to achieve this. While the intensity of training to compliance has reduced in recent years, no significant training in acceptable, reward-gaining agressive behavior has taken its place. Massive attention to this area could pay great dividends in another generation. Rewarding socially acceptable sublimations and other patterns of managing agression indirectly would then be more prevalent.

Until recent years, management of emotions by withholding when with White people and by discharge when with other Blacks was the rule. Such periodic withholding and discharging is bound to be associated in the unconscious mind with management of the bowel and bladder. When they hold feelings in, they are seen as constipated, isolated, and unresponsive emotionally. When they let out freely, they are seen as uncontrolled or messy and disruptive.

At this point, the discussion of a second case may serve to refocus attention upon the psychotherapy of Black people with multiple problems:

Case No. 2 (Black patient and White therapist)

Repeated violent fights with women in authority brought thirteen-year-old Alice to the Court Clinic in 1964. She was placed on probation. While detained for study, she assaulted a matron at the Youth Service Board and personnel at the State Hospital to which she was sent. Study revealed that she and her mother were so angry with each other, and their fighting so continuous and violent, that immediate placement was indicated. This was not possible because no known facility would accept her. The Court Clinic accepted the case for temporary intervention in crises, and psychiatrists and social workers of the clinic joined personnel of the nine other social agencies already involved in stormy and irregular work with the family.

Initially Alice's mother was too upset and disorganized to give any history. During contacts over a few months she gradually developed a relationship which she used in emotional crises and ignored when she felt comfortable. She had led a nomadic childhood with a father who worked in a circus. When she was ten, her mother died, and at fifteen she married the impulsive and hostile father of Alice. She received many beatings and other sadistic behavior until 1962 when her husband was imprisoned for killing a man. Her life became settled in the absence of the husband, but two years later, in 1964, she developed a tumor which necessitated extensive surgery including a colostomy and ureterostomy. Extreme anxiety over attack and over loss of body integrity, of life, of femininity, and of all affection in the absence of significant supporting figures led to marked depression with associated disorganization. She made a violent attempt to control her daughter Alice and wrest from her the care, protection, and comfort she needed to maintain her sense of integrity. Alice experienced the loss of a mother figure and gained a panic-stricken, regressed, demanding, and attacking person who attempted to control her in a violent struggle. Alice became depressed as she was drawn into the intense and violent yet reassuring relationship with her mother. She related to surrogate mothers, wherever she found them, with the regressed, stormy fighting pattern which had come to be the only relationship she could find with her mother at home. In fact, they were like two frightened battling children seeking a parent strong enough and interested enough to hold and control them when they felt both furious and inconsolable. Simple directions were forcefully given about calming down, separating, using referees for fights, draining off anger by complaining to others, getting distance, avoiding fights, stopping those which started, and coming to the clinic in crises. They came daily, sometimes several times a day, always with crises, seldom keeping scheduled appointments.

As the fighting calmed down, long-term concerns were discussed, and the mother's depression was treated in interviews which proceeded along conventional lines. The mother and the daughter became able to use other agencies more effectively. The mother again assumed the mother role which she had abandoned when seriously ill. Alice's relationship flourished with a "Big Sister" in an agency. In the course of two years of treatment, the depression in both Alice and her mother lifted; their lives and home became organized, satisfying, and a source of pride. They longed to return to their family, to church, and to the less complex rural life in their hometown in the South, but remained in Boston in barely adequate adjustment.

Cases like this are common in most urban public agencies. Services are offered, but the patterns of resistance are slow to yield. It is important that therapists correctly interpret resistant behavior when it occurs. It does not mean that the patient rejects therapy. It means that particularly strong and tough-minded people who care deeply are wanted in an intense relationship.

The patients' provocative behavior is designed to induce their therapists to adopt patterns of response and a role relationship familiar to them in an early childhood era. The patients may be viewed as revolting against impersonal structure and pressing for an intense emotional interaction with powerful, emotional parental figures. The personal qualities and emotional attributes of the therapist assume importance. Treatment cannot be mechanical if a good effect is desired or if patients are to stay with the treatment.

Aspects of the therapist-patient relationship are reflected on a larger scale in the interaction of some Blacks with institutions. The Civil Rights Movement has been characterized by disruption of structure, breaking down the stereotyped, mechanical, dehumanized relationships which separate person from person. Some Blacks consider as White other Blacks who are absorbed with the academic, the intellectual, and the structural rather than with the human elements.

Sociopsychological Treatment by Group Formation

The violinist and composer, Clarence Cameron White, concerned with perpetuating the Negro idiom through the use of spirituals, based his work *Bandana Sketches* on four Negro spirituals: "Nobody Knows the Trouble I've Seen," "I'm Troubled in Mind," "No More Auction Block," and "Sometimes I Feel Like a Motherless Child" (Butcher 1957). It is possible that the vestiges of a slave culture and a sense of darkness and of trouble comprise the principle characteristics by which American Negroes are distinguished as a group. Their ancestry includes persons from many national origins, and every major religion has representation among them. They vary in complexion from white to black. Their ancestry varies in race from Caucasian to Indian to Negro or mixtures of these. Although the pattern of cultural pressures upon them was singularly of the United States, it contained influences from Europe, Africa, and the Americas. Bonds between American Blacks were systematically disrupted while they were bonded to American Whites, and for generations Blacks were trained to sacrifice themselves and to respect, honor, and obey . . . and love Whites.

The trouble American Blacks have is multiple. They have no principal national origin. To consider continental Africa as the homeland from which Blacks gain a sense of unity is as significant as considering continental Europe to be the unifying homeland of American Whites which brings Irish, English, French, German, Polish, Swedish, and Italian Whites into unity with one another. Blacks have no distinctive unifying religion, and they have been prevented from developing group feeling and an internal sense of authority, power, and organization, which are essential to the successful management of conflict among group members and to taking action in concert. In short, they have virtually no overall unifying ideology or group structure, although they are generally thought of as a group. Their only common elements are the vestiges of a slave culture and a sense of Blackness and of trouble. In urban ghettos where migration, separations, and inadequate organization have compounded the problems resulting from slavery and segregation, Blacks are far more at the mercy of conflict and trouble than are members of other groups who have more supporting family, social, economic, and political organization to assist them.

The models that are most available for Blacks to identify with are family and social groups which are disorganized, conflict ridden, and beset with troubles. Persons with such an identification tend to lead disorganized, conflict-ridden, trouble-filled lives like those with whom they identify. One effect of slavery and segregation is that larger numbers of such persons may be found among Black Americans than among other groups of people. No program that treats American Black individuals without altering the nature of the groups upon which they rely and with which they identify can be successful in treating Black people. An organized group will exert organizing effects upon families and individuals.

The Civil Rights Movement initially sought social change for American Blacks through integration and identification as first-class Americans. The intense resistance of Whites and the token changes which occurred convinced most American Blacks that so many American Whites rejected them that they must join other Blacks and help themselves. Each major attempt to improve the lot of American Blacks by integration on a large scale has failed, and each failure has been followed by a movement toward Black unification, group formation, and self-development (Isaacs 1963). One movement, led by Marcus Garvey, numbered three million persons among its supporters.

However, groups cannot form by merely deciding to do so and then setting up shop. They must go step by step through a long and complicated process. Without some unifying point of agreement, some flag around which persons can rally with feeling, group formation cannot take place. In early phases of group formation, identification of a common enemy provides the rallying flag that unites people by fantasied emotional bonds while they work out their many differences well enough to tolerate one another and form bonds based upon transference from earlier individual and group relationships (Day 1967; Standish and Semrad 1951). Integration in this country on a massive scale would probably be possible only if the country were under siege so that Blacks and Whites both had a common enemy.

Most Black people, with few bonds and with many

differences between them, constantly feel under siege. In an American society characterized by competing groups, only development of group formation, resources, and power can offer possibilites of significant mastery of their life circumstances. If White people could see this and encourage and support Black group development, then for Blacks some ethnic realization might be possible without intense conflict.

Unfortunately Whites cannot perceive that, when Whites united in power to foster White groups and oppose integration, they blocked development of democracy and encouraged Blacks to distrust Whites and to develop unity among themselves.

We should view the massive expression of hostility against Whites as simply a stage in a process of group formation by Blacks. This stage is being attenuated by the hostility and reactionary behavior with which Whites have responded. Whites, feeling threatened by Blacks, presented additional unified opposition, which helped the Blacks to reach more agreement as to the source of their trouble. Group formation then proceeded among Whites and among Blacks with each feeling victimized by the other as Whites marshalled power to maintain prejudice and discrimination against Blacks and Blacks marshaled power to resist and change the oppressive circumstances.

If clear limits are placed upon destructive components of group behavior of both Whites and Blacks, a strengthening of both groups will occur in the dynamic interaction between them. Both White Power and Black Power will be developed for constructive purposes. This will provide a giant step toward resolution of the troubles of Negroes. However, suppression of the destructive behavior of Blacks alone, accompanied by a permission for and rationalization of destructive behavior by Whites, will guarantee further unification of Blacks based on hatred, which could lead toward revolution by Blacks and genocide by Whites.

With less polarization along racial lines, coalition and

group formation along other axes would probably have occurred. There have been some trends toward coalition of powerless groups of Blacks, Reds, and Whites, but polarization and confrontation along racial lines have mitigated against development of other trends. Our present course perpetuates the undemocratic pattern of our past history. A confrontation of racially integrated have-nots and haves would have increased possibilities for basic changes in our behavior, institutions, and national character, which would be oriented toward a democratic society.

No strategy involving simple increase in the number of social agencies and professional therapists can be successful in treating the Black people who need psychotherapy. From practically every angle from which the treatment of Black people is viewed, it appears that, in addition to conventional medical therapies, innovative massive social therapy is needed. Without either rapid integration or development of Blacks into an effective group, their treatment and rehabilitation will continue to be an impossible task.

We can predict that if group formation among Blacks can be extensive and constructively oriented, lowered incidence of emotional disorder, fewer relapses following treatment, and altered resistance to therapy will occur. In fact, new honesty, forthrightness, and integrity have already begun to spread in Black communities and to affect constructively the values and behavior in White communities.

To the Blacks, Black has come to mean honest, direct, forthright, sincere, dependable, without guile or sham, close rather than distant, and emotional. The term *Soul* has come to symbolize much of this. If a therapist is to work with Blacks, his skin may be any color, but he should have Soul. There is recognition that verbal and intellectual approaches can be hypocritical, misleading, and fraudulent without any awareness of this on the part of the intellectual person. Nonverbal communications and relationships are more trusted. Blacks say that actions speak louder than words, and they can read the nonverbal messages well. They usually can detect whether sternness is or is not accompanied by respect and affection.

Treatment of Black people frequently provides a therapeutic experience for the therapist, who learns more about himself, becomes more of a Soul person, and becomes less rigorously devoted to impersonal methods.

Psychotherapy of Black Americans Subsequent to 1967

The confrontations developed by the Black Power Movement have initiated corrective effects upon racism in American social structures and upon the racism embedded in the psychology of Americans. New Black values, styles of behavior, and role models have emerged. Initiating has superseded accommodating. Passive compliance has been replaced by countermilitance.

Since 1967, group formation among Blacks has increased slowly, integration at the interface of Blacks and Whites has developed slowly, and some individuals have changed in psychology and behavior to a remarkable degree under the impact of new social pressures. Many more Blacks are aware of and accepting toward psychotherapy. More have access to it and more aggressively use it. Many young Blacks seek and use psychotherapy, and among these inquisitive, skeptical nonbelievers challenge and confront their psychotherapists with a new tough-mindedness which enables therapists to learn and improve as much as their patients do.

However, almost all the Blacks who have access to psychotherapy are in some metropolitan community and are members of some educationally or professionally elite group. The overwhelming majority of Americans of all colors simply do not have access to psychotherapy. The poor generally get none (Spurlock 1969), especially if they be Black. As long as professionals, universities, and other elites possessively retain custody of the knowledge and skills of psychotherapy, it will be dispensed along elitist lines. Psychotherapy can be divorced from the classism and racism which has pervaded it only when large numbers of nonprofessional psychotherapists are trained, accredited, and supervised in using more scientific methods under medical direction.

In order to have a balanced perspective, it is important to keep in mind that, in the racist society we have had in the United States, definitions, classifications, opportunities, privileges, and services have been developed along pro-White, anti-Black lines. The integration phase of the Civil Rights Movement was an expression of our most cherished national and religious beliefs in brotherhood, freedom, unity, and mutual consideration. Its theme of "Black and White together" was pro-White and pro-Black.

The militant White Power Movement of 1965 which gathered to neutralize and block integration efforts was divisive and polarizing in nature. It was commonly called the White Backlash. It undermined the integration movement until the movement became a futile and impotent exercise of conscience, and it derogated peaceful protests as disruptive, anti-American provocations to violence. By 1966, sixteen martyrs had been killed (Mendelsohn 1965), hundreds had been seriously injured, and thousands jailed and otherwise mistreated by Whites who violently reacted to the nonviolent integration movement.

The integration movement provided confrontations which revealed that most "true believers" in democracy were devout racists who believed in and wanted to maintain a pro-White, anti-Black world. The White Power Movement of 1965 made it quite clear that social structuring was determined by group strength and power. More and more Blacks became aware that they themselves were pro-White, anti-Black racists in their beliefs and behavior.

A study group of Black psychiatrists—Butts, Cannon, Comer, Davis, Elam, Pierce, Pinderhughes, Poussaint, Spurlock, Thompkins, Wilkinson, Young—and neurologist Calhoun has defined White racism as a paranoia in which dominant Whites and oppressed Blacks both believe in White superiority and Black inferiority in a *folie à deux*. Both Whites and Blacks have been duped by the contrived realities which keep producing human products who appear to verify the false beliefs. Both Whites and Blacks have been persuaded to retain their pro-White, anti-Black paranoia by the direct and processed violence encountered by any who oppose this paranoia.

Perception by Blacks of their own hypocrisy and paranoia, together with a growing sense of kinship among those in the Civil Rights Movement, led to new potentials for greater honesty, integrity, and idealism. These factors, associated with rising expectations and the emergence of new leadership, provided motivation and impetus to shift the main thrust of the Civil Rights Movement from integration to Black ethnic development.

In this context, the Black Power Movement was a movement of massive sociotherapy, group therapy, and individual therapy, attempting to develop more adaptive psychology, role relationships, and group structure for Blacks by:

a. Creating bonds between bondless Blacks and helping them toward the group formation needed to act in concert, to meet needs, to develop the internal cohesion and authority required for internal group discipline, and to develop and organize resources and power

b. Developing capacity for independent and autonomous function of Black individuals and Black groups

c. Taking the initiative and exercising options about what goes on within Black communities

d. Developing a more adaptive identity and culture in which self-esteem and a sense of worth may be justified

e. Generating the educational, economic, and political power needed to advance Black development

f. Judging personal worth of Black people by appropriate

criteria and realizing the value, limitations, and pitfalls of being a Soul person

g. Revealing to Whites limitations, pitfalls, and misuses of the intellect and reason so often worshiped in Western societies

h. Pressing for a more open society and for more democratic institutions

i. Pressing for justice and for special reparative programs to mitigate the crippling handicaps which directly resulted from the slavery and prejudice which were national policy.

j. Forcing Blacks with mixed identification and mixed interests to clarify their identity and define ·their allegiance either with Blacks or Whites (throughout the country, more middle-class Blacks established alliances with other Blacks)

k. Confronting Whites with their equality, with their weaknesses, with the strengths of others

l. Opposing "colonialism" of any kind

m. Generating responsive processes of interaction between Black communities and the power structure affecting them (Pinderhughes 1969; Barbour 1968; Carmichael and Hamilton 1967)

For many Blacks, the Black Power Movement meant learning and testing new roles; learning not to capitulate and surrender themselves; and experiencing a period of dictating, setting the structure, and running the show in the important areas of their lives. For most Blacks it involved a new relationship to their own emotions, especially to anger toward Whites which they could now permit, accept, and learn to master.

For many Blacks the goal of the movement is to develop sufficient power to make possible behavior that is in line with conscience and with national and religious ethics, since White power used without conscience and Black conscience without power result in continuation of an oppressive social order (Wright 1967). What most Whites perceive as an orderly American social system, most Blacks experience as un-responsive, unremitting, dehumanized, well-rationalized, quiet, courteous, institutionalized violence not unlike colo-nialism. Since influential and powerful persons and groups enjoy things as they are and are unwilling to change the society which they have opportunity to change, initiative for altering a destructive system and producing constructive change rests by default on the shoulders of the resourceless, powerless people who are better motivated, though often ill equipped for the task. The Black Power Movement repre-sented the next step on the part of Blacks in their quest to constructively change their society and themselves.

Since the movement had group formation as one goal, an essential element was the focus of verbal hostility upon a group perceived as a common enemy (which, in this case, has volunteered for the role). Many encouraged the development of sensitivity to the nature of that enemy and the use of force, if needed, to defend oneself from that enemy. For some Blacks, the movement included an intense interaction with Whites in which role relationships were modified by con-frontations and by interpretations which enabled some whites to understand the issues and to change. Counter-militancy reached its zenith in the riot interactions of 1967 between police and Black urban citizens.

Various forces within each Black community participated in dynamic interaction to determine the local forms the movement would take. A full spectrum, from inactive forms to the frankly revolutionary, existed in any sizable Black community. Black citizens who did not participate may have unwittingly surrendered control of their community to lead-ers who were inconsiderate or hostile — or even irresponsible. Creative conflict existed between the many forces in each black community. An abundance of new possibilities, new Black role models, and new pressures upon Blacks merged, along with crises, to loosen structure and make more change possible.

These processes have exerted profound effects upon many individuals. Confidence, self-esteem, assertiveness, and initiative have increased in many Blacks. Some have begun active struggles with self-defeating patterns in themselves. Unfortunately, these are so unconscious, so long-standing, and so deeply ingrained that few can change these self-destructive residues of racism without assistance. More often than not, psychotherapy is not available when it might help, and what is available is not trustworthy.

Despite the strong motivations of many Blacks to separate themselves from the White racist sources of sickness, few have the knowledge, skills, and tools to effect a cure in themselves. Those motivated to integrate and try to correct institutional racism often find themselves with inadequate knowledge, tools, and skills to effect the changes in social structure which are needed. Some cannot hold newly gained opportunities, and some find that appraisals by Whites are so based upon unconscious racist biases that Blacks are not respected in their new positions. Some are plagued by deeply ingrained self-defeating patterns which persistently follow them.

Increasing numbers of Black persons are seeking psychotherapy, and most of these show effects of the Black ethnic development movement and of frequent experiences in integrated settings. Many of the elements now encountered in the psychotherapy of Black patients were not present prior to 1967.

The psychotherapist is apt to see the advantaged Black who has experienced benefits from increased integration and from Black ethnic development. Unfortunately, such patients are an extremely small portion of our Black citizens, most of whom have great need for assistance, for social reforms, and for psychotherapy but are without access to any of these. Because there has been some change in the lot of Blacks at the narrow Black-White interface and for a few who have participated in well-organized ethnic development programs, there is a tendency to focus upon the Black-White interaction and ethnic development. This in itself contributes to the continuation of the racist oppression still experienced in most intense forms by 95 percent of our Black population.

A series of examples may serve to illustrate some expressions of racism which appear in psychotherapy. The expressions could not be listed completely for they are infinite in number. The following illustrations reflect some more common ones:

Case No. 3 (*A Black adult with a mild acute situational reaction but otherwise normal*)

PATIENT: A cat can't change his mental stripes overnight. Black was mighty unpopular before 1968. You can't reorient yourself in two years and undo the ingrained stamp of years of negative conditioning. I don't know how to deal with Whites and Blacks finding me attractive. Something in me feels the opposite. Something in me says, "Don't listen. It will turn your head. You might like being attractive, and your head might swell." Then too I always hated being thought of as one of those "good" Blacks. I've got a bad side too. Why can't that be me also? So I feel good but behave as if I don't. I don't dress up because then people will expect only that side of me. This way, anyone who counts, who really relates to me, will know my good qualities and my bad ones.

This statement was discussed in relation to several conflicts. First, he was reluctant to be assertive and masculine for fear that it would get out of hand ("head swell") or that he would have to renounce his feminine and passive wishes. Second, while functioning in a highly responsible way in his relationships and in his life, he wished to continue to do so on his own initiative. He felt that once he assumed the trappings of a responsible person like "neat adult coat-and-tie clothes," he would feel obligated and that expectations of others would be pressed upon him, that he would have to live up to the adult role he was assuming. At a still deeper level he was reluctant to give up the mildly rebellious, messy, willful, stubborn, but autonomous child role which was a source of pleasure and a sense of being in control. One senses struggles with values, with roles, and with images of himself which are tied to the struggle with the changing definition of Black. It used to mean the bad, messy, aggressive, willful child. Now, to Blacks, Black means the strong, resilient, mature, warm, forthright, attractive, desirable human adult. He is not willing to trade one for the other and seeks a way to remain himself, in touch with good and bad, with the adult and child parts of himself in a healthy integrative process.

It is notable that Black has at least three meanings to this man. Two years ago black meant unattractive, bad, poorly clothed, slurred speaking. However, it also could refer to a "good Black" who conformed and complied to White standards and hypocritically denied having a bad side. Finally, it means the strong, honest, attractive, emotional human adult.

Case No. 4 (a Black man with mild anxiety)

PATIENT: I've been pushing myself all alone, I mean all along. Taking people to the point when they are gingerly pussyfooting around used to be a habit with me. I used to resent people who were composed, cautiously articulate, and White . . . keeping the upper hand. Now I review my thoughts and feelings before expressing them and by the time I decide to express something, the opportunity is gone. I end up saying things which had not been on my mind when I first wanted to talk; however, I don't hide my hostility as I used to. I relate more honestly with my eyes, conveying my own maturity and understanding the maturity of the other person. I am more disciplined and can talk honestly for a couple of hours to someone I have not known well before. I'm not trying so hard to be Black. I was feeling I shouldn't do well in all areas, should have a jagged edge someplace. As

I've noticed that I'd do poorly alongside of doing well, I tried to correct it. It's not complete; these are the first stages of change. I'm not only trying to throw off old cultural restrictions; I'm trying to define where I want to be in things and how to get there. Being Black in this way has more meaning.

For this person White means unemotional, defensive, intellectual, and dominating, and, as he finds himself developing some of these characteristics, he is less critical of them. However, he is not satisfied by becoming White and strives toward a sense of maturity, honesty, and integrity which he perceives as a Black ideal. Also notable is the old meaning of Black, which meant having jagged edges and being alone—pushed and oppressed.

Case No. 5 (an adult Black woman with mild anxiety and depression)

PATIENT: Milton makes me feel comfortable and confident. I wonder if I'm trying to get out of my commitment to Raymond. You wonder if I'm replacing you with someone else. I went to a meeting—I notice you are tapping your leg, are you bored?

[The therapist replied that clearly one part of himself was giving a kind of attention to another part, that it was unconscious and could be explored, but that "we have an agreed-upon task of exploring your behavior that we do not wish to sabotage."]

PATIENT: At the meeting I was nervous. In fact even before the meeting. I was depressed the whole weekend and did some drinking. I felt inferior, felt quiet, don't like drinking—I don't like these alternations. What are you thinking?

THERAPIST: Why do you ask?

PATIENT: I want feedback.

THERAPIST: You want feedback, food, and talk of drinking—hunger and thirst?

[The patient cried.]

PATIENT: I'm tired of being this way, sick of being this way. [She chews gum vigorously.] It's like I can't control myself.

THERAPIST: You bring together drinking, eating, chewing, nervousness, and the meeting—what were your feelings?

PATIENT: I felt like the Black spokeswoman. It was just a bullshit meeting. I felt I could put in input.

THERAPIST: Input?

PATIENT: I talk of input-output a lot—work as a computer technician.

THERAPIST: Input-output, drinking and eating, and bullshit meeting; sounds like feeding and defecating.

PATIENT: I'm nervous to give input, to lead and have others follow.

THERAPIST: To be the feeding one.

PATIENT: I was nervous before coming in here, hoped I would not discover anything too shocking. There are a couple parts of my personality I don't want certain people to know about—I don't want to show a certain side. I act nice and sweet and giving when I first meet men; I know that's not me; I'm just trying to be accepted.

THERAPIST: What side do you not want them to see?

PATIENT: A Black side of me. I do think White is more acceptable. How do you get these Black things out of you? You can't run around the street saying, "Black is beautiful" and have that change your mind.

THERAPIST: There's a side of you that is not accepted—not giving?

PATIENT: It's giving in a different way, more aggressive, being messy. Who wants that shit?

[At the end of the interview the patient went to the bathroom and remained there for several minutes as was her custom after every interview.]

Once again we see that White means compliant, accommodating, sweet, and giving food and goodness. Black refers to the hidden, repressed, bad, aggressive, messy shit that also seeks expression. This patient experienced anxiety whenever she forcefully expressed herself to a peer or supervisor and associated forceful expression sometimes with an assertive masculine role, sometimes with an initiating controlling role, sometimes with an aggressive adult role, but always with a Black side (backside) of herself. She expressed the fear that she might "show her ass."

Whenever race comes up in psychotherapy it invariably symbolizes a part of the patient's or therapist's personality. Every patient has Black, White, Yellow, Brown, and Red parts of the personality and every human being psychologically is multiracial.

Every Black person has a "White mind" and a "Black mind" just as case no. 5 demonstrates, and every White person has a "White mind" and a "Black mind" (Pinderhughes 1966). The White mind constitutes the elements which are uniting and not disruptive to one's groups and are therefore socially acceptable. The Black mind constitutes those elements which are disruptive to one's groups and are therefore excluded from society. Racism prevails in every personality since the White mind is permitted free play in the personality and behavior whereas the Black mind is carefully censored and excluded from the mainstream of social experience. Disruptive sexual, aggressive, or other emotions, sudden loud noises, and exciting or annoying body parts or body products are associated with the Black mind and must be repressed.

This division occurs wherever human beings live in groups for, universally, group living imposes the same basic requirements upon individuals. Affectionate bonds and good "White" images are reserved for the group members while aggressive bonds and bad "Black" images are associated by projection with outsiders. In our racist society the "White part" of both Black and White persons is projected upon Whites, who are aggrandized, while the "Black part" of both

Black and White people is projected upon Blacks. Direct and processed violence is then employed to contrive and maintain a reality which supports the delusions about "good Whites" and "bad Blacks." One can see the importance of changing the conscious and unconscious value and meaning of the word *black* if the Black ethnic development movement is to be helpful. Some of the difficulty in accomplishing this relates to the deep-seated negative connotation of darkness arising from universal human experiences with night and day. In the dark, important objects are lost, and evil can approach unseen. For this reason light is valued over dark at primitive psychological levels in all societies.

We might bring to a conclusion the case illustrations by giving three examples of the White mind and Black mind in White patients:

Case No. 6 (a White adult female with hysteric and depressive symptoms)

PATIENT: Talking to Dad is like talking to a wall—his eyes have a glaze. You can't penetrate them, and he has nothing to give. He has more to give little children.

THERAPIST: What do you mean?

PATIENT: I remember him to be very dark, very browned from the sun, very warm, very physical, hugging and kissing me a lot. He always took me to the zoo. He could share in pleasure but not accept responsbility. He's so egotistical that he can only be interested in the response of others to him. He'd make a better grandfather than a father. My mother is just the opposite—colorless, emotionless, predictable, and dull.

Once again the White mind is the reliable, emotionless, controlled, nondisruptive one while the Black mind is masculine, unpredictable, undependable, physical, libidinal, pleasure oriented, associated with memories of animals.

Case No. 7 (a young White adult male patient with depression whose mother had died when he was age six)

PATIENT: I'd like to share my feelings with someone I can trust, but I can't find the one I can communicate with. I try, then I become silent and leave. I'm shy and uncomfortable with people. I'd rather be alone, in the dark. I wear this black. . . . I'm with a motorcycle crowd and plan to be a mechanic for motorcycle racers. I enjoy riding late at night, alone, fast, and not stopping. I'm convinced I'll die on a bike. I'm in contact with people who die or are injured. I've been injured myself. One friend committed suicide—he had just stolen my girl away—several of my family died. I am sad. Everything is black. I have a bleak [close to black] constricted life. Like being in a coffin. When I go by a cemetery, I want to cry. I hold back tears, like now.

In case no. 7 the Black mind is associated with feelings of loss, loneliness, devastation, and destruction, and with fantasies of violent death in which the patient is reunited with his lost mother. He retains control while flirting with death, with vivid fantasies of losing control and racing to his awaited reunion.

Case no. 8 (an adult White female with anxiety and hysteric symptoms who is struggling to terminate her therapy)

PATIENT: I'm keeping my coat on. You keep bugging me. I don't have much energy for you today. I wish I could throw up. [as if to say, "I'd like to get you out of me. You're inside me and bothering me"]. You are tight and not relaxed today either, and you have a hole in your stocking. You remind me of my husband. He's been difficult, a pain in the neck, a bastard—sloppy, disintegrated-looking. He drains me. [Her coat was still on; she opened it a bit and rubbed her eyes, mouth, nose, throat, ear.] And my daughter refused to go back to school after vacation. Once she gets involved, she never wants to give it up.

THERAPIST: She is sensitive to separation.

PATIENT: I always discipline my sentiments. I had plenty of guts and discipline. All right. So I'm in a black mood. I have no discipline now—you don't have to pound at it and make me feel guilty and embarrassed. I'm sick about the whole world, about you. I'm also scared to be free and go and live again. I make mistakes and need to set down rules and enforce them. Everything is going too far. It's a mess if I don't step into it now. I feel like screaming.

[The patient had shown rapid improvement in weekly interviews over a six-month period. Three months earlier she had less emotional control, exerted less control over her behavior, and used the word *black* much more often as she regularly came into the office and threw her coat on the floor. On one such occasion she wore an all-black sweater and all-black pants.]

PATIENT: Shit! [as coat was dropped] You're a bastard. I'm angry at you. I get upset and feel you hold me back. You know I get paranoid when you're a little late. And I'm ashamed at what comes out of me so spontaneously. I've always felt I was an outsider. I always kept isolated. Now I want to accept people and be accepted by people. When I was fourteen a Black family moved in behind us. No one welcomed them or gave them coffee as for the White neighbors. Now I feel like saying nobody gives me any! I was neurotic about dark skin—remember children talking about it. I remember a beautiful black cat I wanted to take home but I was reluctant to bring her home. I knew my mother would kill me. Once I offered to walk with a Black girl on the street, and she rejected the offer. She had some little Black children with her. I was in a rage but didn't show my anger. I get paranoid. You've done enough of your destruction; let's build now! I'm sick and standing there. You tore everything down now—help me build something!

For this patient Black means rejected, angry, discarded, worthless shit. It means something annoying inside which should be discharged by anus or by mouth and projected upon some deserving target. It means hiding sad feelings with rage. It means demonstrating loudly in an attempt to control and get proper treatment from an important person. It is the masculine, hostile, sloppy part which is inside her and to which she is wed. It is the undisciplined, sad, sick, scared, screaming child side of herself, which needs rules and controls. Although the therapist was Black in case nos. 3 through 8 and the content partially determined by the transference with a Black psychotherapist, black and white are commonly employed symbols where both patient and therapist are of the same race and complexion. Even more graphic examples of the White mind and the Black mind have occurred in the psychoanalyses of two other White patients, who perceived the Black analyst as White when they felt pleasure with him and as Black when they felt anger toward him. Both patients expressed amazement that the analyst could alter his racial characteristics so completely.

Psychological Repression and the Need for Psychotherapy

Just as the destructive social repression of racism often results in pathology requiring therapeutic processes, psychological repression often results in pathological derivatives which require psychotherapy. Psychoanalysts ascribe most psychiatric pathology to this cause.

The undoing of pathogenic psychological repressions can involve painful confrontations and interpretations analogous to those employed to undo social repressions. Modification of attitudes toward the repressed, increasing the strength of the repressed, and reentry of the repressed into the mainstream of social living, in modified or unchanged form, are steps common to the therapeutic processes employed in undoing both psychological and social repression. Many of the same factors which tend to perpetuate social repression tend also to perpetuate psychological repressions in the same victims.

In the United States, psychotherapy is coveted by the relatively privileged elites and is generally available only to them. Knowledge and skills in psychotherapy have been retained by circumscribed schools of professionals who strongly discriminate against those without access. There was a slow melting of the resistance of psychiatrists to accepting the psychotherapy of psychologists, social workers, and ministers, and now the line of resistances has moved to nonprofessionals, where the same slow integrative process is occurring.

All the dynamics and prejudice of interracial conflict may be observed in conflicts between members of different disciplines and even between differing schools of psychotherapy. Confrontation and encounter processes commonly occur in these interactions between persons who share group-related nonpathological paranoias which aggrandize their own group beliefs and denigrate others.

As polarization increases during encounter processes between members of different groups, projection and conflict increase, and additional delusions are born and lived out by all parties. One is the myth that an individual may be understood and successfully treated only by a member of his own group. Actually, anyone systematically using introjective processes and a scientific method can develop and validate understandings. Unfortunately, in times of intense polarization more patients and therapists have a reinforcement of projective processes in the presence of "outsiders."

The concepts in this chapter are consistent with the data from the sociopsychological research reported in Dr. Pettigrew's chapter. Jahoda's observation, referred to by Dr. Pettigrew, that the incidence of serious mental illness is lower in highly prejudiced people underlines the protection one gains from one's own aggression when it is focused on an external target. From this perspective, racism in America might be conceptualized as a public health program for Whites in which alternately red Indians, black Africans, yellow Orientals, black Irish, red Russians, and finally brown Asiatics have been dehumanized and used as health-promoting instruments by Whites. This is undoubtedly mediated in the psychophysiology of the body image and associated ego functions.

In the mind there is such an intimate association of the segregated images of Blacks with the segregated images of sexual and aggressive behavior that increased freedom for Blacks evokes in Whites all their fear of released sexual and aggressive impulses. Most Whites have had aggressive bonds associated with Blacks and perceive Blacks moving toward them as attacking rather than joining. Until recently, most Blacks had affiliative bonds associated with Whites and perceived their movement toward Whites as an act of love rather than hate. Only with the massive White Backlash of 1965 did the majority of Blacks try to give up aggressive bonds toward themselves and shift aggressive bonds toward Whites. At this point, for Whites the price for maintaining their aggressive bonds to Blacks became so high that they introduced more integrative behavior.

It is possible that the majority of influential American Whites believe it would be unhealthy to undo racial discrimination because pathogenic forces would be released among Whites by integration. This runs counter to the view that racial segregation is pathogenic and should be discontinued. Given these opposing views, what constitutes pathology and social therapy depends upon one's identification along group lines.

Many psychotherapists have value systems which encourage them to help patients to adjust to oppressive conditions rather than to seek change in the conditions. Prejudices against "action-oriented" patients may accompany this. This is one reason why psychotherapy has sometimes been labeled as an opiate or instrument of oppression.

Because so many blacks cannot afford or do not have access to private psychotherapy, a large percentage of them is exposed to the problems presented in psychotherapy in public clinic settings. Dehumanization, delays, a chain of contacts, less experienced therapists being used for teaching of medical students, and lack of continuity of therapy are common. The same psychotherapist often relates differently to his private and public patients. These patterns of racial and class discrimination may be largely unconscious, but teachers and supervisors often teach these attitudes by setting poor examples and by not treating clinic patients themselves.

The Biracial Psychotherapy Relationship

The biracial psychotherapy relationship may present special problems when the therapist employs a treatment method which relies heavily upon the empathy, the projections, or untested countertransference of the therapist. Under such circumstances the psychotherapist imputes to the patient all the qualities associated with the therapist's own feelings and thoughts. Of two therapists who feel convinced they have complete and valid understanding of a patient, one may be accurate while the other grossly misperceives the patient. From one moment to another, even the same therapist may have perceptions of the patient that are very accurate and highly inaccurate.

Psychotherapists should acknowledge that all of their thinking and evaluations of patients are based upon psychological mechanisms of projection and include paranoid content. Unfortunately most psychotherapists are quite unaware of this, and some are too narcissistic to acknowledge their own projection and paranoia when it has been demonstrated. Therapists vary greatly in the degree to which they rely upon introjection to test their own perceptions for reality by comparing their impressions to data repeatedly taken in from the patient.

In general, the greater the visible differences between the therapist and patient, the more the therapist relies upon untested projection without realizing it. Basically those who perceive themselves as members of the same group understand each other primarily by introjection and identification, while those who perceive themselves as members of different groups understand each other by projection.

Psychoanalytically oriented methods, meticulously used, should presume an ignorance and inaccuracy in the therapist which require ongoing spontaneous input from the patient for correction. Even with this method, therapists may be unaware of the false beliefs they are developing about the patient. Quite commonly inadequacies in therapists are projected upon patients. Whenever a therapist states that a patient is unsuitable for therapy, he expresses a paranoid idea even though many colleagues may agree with him. Invariably in such cases the therapist is unsuitable for treating the patient and is projecting his inadequacies upon the patient while renouncing inadequacy in himself.

In the final analysis, the psychological identity and self-image are the critical factors. In a large professional forum several years ago, two psychotherapists made case presentations which graphically illustrate this. The first psychotherapist was a Negro and highly trained, very organized and disciplined, and unusually perceptive in an intellectual way. This Negro psychotherapist presented a Caucasian patient who was unclean, soiled himself at school, required external structure to maintain order, and had so dependently attached himself to the therapist as to seek adoption. Discussion clearly revealed the predominately "White" identification of the Negro psychotherapist and the predominately "Black" identification of the Caucasian patient. From a psychological standpoint all persons have multiple identifications and are multiracial although, in any one moment, a single identification may be most evident.

The second psychotherapist was a Caucasian whose broad

GLENDALE COLLEGE LIBRARY

humanitarian interests, emotional style, and warm spontaneously open pattern of relating were quite evident. This
therapist presented the case of a self-contained Negro professional who never raised his voice, never expressed feelings,
never wore red, never ate chicken or watermelon, and was
more comfortable with Caucasians. Discussion of this case
brought out that the Caucasian therapist had a predominantly
"Black" psychological identity while the Negro patient had a
predominately "White" identity. All the data presented supported these conclusions.

Some persons repress and lose contact with the spontaneous, emotionally expressive side of themselves. Others
reinforce the emotionally expressive side of themselves but
permit the more highly disciplined and intellectual side to
be underdeveloped. Eldridge Cleaver had reference to this
when he observed that in the master-slave relationship the
White man lost his body and the black man lost his mind. He
observed that, as they struggle to become whole persons
again, the White man must get back his body and the Black
man his mind.

The most striking difference between the Black-White
relationship and relationships involving other cultural groups
is the completeness with which Black and White are viewed
as paired opposites. This was built into the social structure of
the master-slave relationship and has persisted in derivative
paired relationships of a master-servant nature. The
Black-White relationship is qualitatively similar to other
paired relationships involving minorities, but in this country
no other relationship between ethnic groups has been structured so completely and so rigidly into fixed complementary
pairs with one on top, the other on the bottom; one good, the
other bad; one having power and opportunity, the other not.
Personalities of Blacks and of Whites are structured along
these lines where segregation is strong and roles, behavior
patterns, living circumstances, education, resources, applications of law, and public services follow similarly discrepant

lines for the two groups. The Black-White pair thus serves remarkably well as a symbolic expression through which virtually all psychological paired opposites may be externalized and dealt with as if they exist in reality. The male-female, right-wrong, good-bad, and parent-child dichotomies and most conflicts of ambivalence find a close fit when projected upon the Black-White situation outside. Thus the Black-White external situation for most persons in this culture is intensely interlocked with their own internal conflicts, more so than with pairs of other cultural groups where the paired opposites are not so clearly polarized.

The view of reality of the therapist is more apt to differ from that of the patient in the intercultural situation. Each individual is apt to project and generalize reality for other groups from the specific realities in the family and social structure in which he has lived. Actions which may be logical and appropriate to the therapist may be impossible to accomplish in the context in which the client functions. The therapist then should, as usual, pay careful attention to responses following interpretations, suggestions, or advice. With greater frequency the feedback following therapist activity exerts a helpful corrective influence on the therapist's conceptualization of the patient. This is typical of the mental compartments in a bicultural situation. Each party may have to process messages twice before real communication takes place. The first reading is apt to be not quite on target; the second reading often achieves an interpretation closer to the perception of the other party. Sensitivity to feedback, ability to modify an initial appraisal, and ability to function beyond the limits of one's own subculture are important attributes in a therapist.

The inability of the therapist to take a second reading and correct one's course often does gross disservice to the client. Supervision provides a tool whereby some correction may take place. However, this tool is only as good as the person supervising. Repeated alterations in an erroneous or malad-

aptive direction too often take place. An inexperienced therapist with a healthy intuition may function more appropriately
without supervision than under a supervisor with an unconscious bias and rigidly compartmentalized thinking.

Racism in Psychotherapists

There has been too little awareness of the unconscious
racism which motivates large blocks of personnel in many
institutions. Many therapists have false beliefs that Blacks
are "nonverbal," that nonverbal persons are ill-suited for
psychotherapy, that Blacks do not trust Whites enough, or
that they have character disorders which are not likely to
change. These therapists perceive or elicit such data as support their delusions and define most Black patients as unsuitable for psychotherapy.

All too often the opposition to psychotherapy by a Black
patient is accepted at face value when the same opposition
by a White patient would be analyzed as resistance. Some
therapists unconsciously discriminate on a class basis. Most
psychotherapists tend to select patients with whom they
identify. We understand and relate to persons perceived as
members of our own group by introjection and identification
and to persons perceived as outsiders by projection and rejection.

One problem area for many patients lies in the unconscious needs of many psychotherapists to be in helping,
knowledgeable, or controlling roles. Unwittingly they wish
to be initiators and have patients accommodate to them or to
their style or approach. More Black patients than White perceive in this kind of relationship the basic ingredients of a
master-slave pattern.

Racism in psychotherapy may take subtle forms and may
even masquerade as consideration. I have supervised a
White therapist who was reluctant to treat a Black patient for
fear the patient would become too "White thinking" to again

adjust in her Black community. Underlying this rationalization was a fear that his neat composure would be
ruffled and that the patient would "get under his skin" arous-
ing "Black" angry feelings in the therapist. All persons, therapists and patients alike, have two mental contents: the accepted content and the renounced, ghettoized content. That
is, every social human being has both White thinking and
Black thinking with the White being open and free and in
front while the Black is more hidden, restricted, and behind.
Group members assume the former as characteristic of themselves and project the latter upon outsiders.

Most of the principles of psychotherapy can serve double
duty as principles for managing racism and other patterns of
social discrimination. The development of relatively conflict-free objects of affection and nonhuman targets of destructive aggression is often central in psychotherapy and in
managing racism.

The singular happenings experienced by each individual
result in highly individualized impressions and patterns in
the central nervous system of each person. No matter how
many similarities two individuals may find in each other,
eventually they will encounter differences which lead each
to perceive the other as an outsider. It is as if each person, as
a result of individualized experience and patterning, may
function as a separate race while sharing some characteristics
with others. Whether we lump people together in a single
family, group, class, or race or divide them into separate
families, groups, classes, or races is determined by whether
we focus upon similarities or differences. This in turn varies
with many factors including the relative strength of affiliative
(seeking, uniting) influences and divisive (aggressive, avoiding) influences of our personalities. In every personality
there are both integrationist and segregationist potentials
which may be reinforced in varying degrees by pressures
that are applied by the culture.

It is important for psychotherapists to relate to patients

with both uniting and separating patterns. Empathy, humanitarian attitude, and identification with the patient depend upon uniting, incorporative behavior. Collecting and taking in of information from the patient require incorporative, uniting behavior also. However, for objective understanding, the psychotherapist should realize that he and the patient are separate persons projecting upon and imputing certain characteristics to each other. The psychotherapist, then, should use some form of scientific methodology to develop and test each idea associated with the patient. Every thought a psychotherapist has about a patient is applicable to the psychotherapist but may or may not be applicable to the patient. Much too often psychotherapists assume their ideas and formulations are facts when they are merely psychological projections on the order of guesses, speculations, or partially validated hypotheses. Scientific methodology helps psychotherapists to manage better the racism that each psychotherapist has.

All interviewers have false beliefs of which they are unaware. Interviewers who formulate questions to bring out information are unaware that they try to validate false beliefs by eliciting information to support them. For this reason, interview methods which permit the patient to offer what is in his or her mind provide better data about the patient's concerns than methods which require the patient to respond to the interviewer's interests. During evaluative interviews, it is wise to get beyond the concerns of the patient after eliciting them and by directed questions to develop a comprehensive history of life experiences.

Summary of Relevant Principles

The organization of minds and societies may be altered away from closed, symptom-producing systems by reducing conflict, diminishing compartmentalization, and improving communications. Because of the linkages in the body image between mental representation of body activities, psychic activities, and social activities, the production of attitude change and more open organization of a society or a mind require attitude and behavior change toward body functions. Movements toward freer physical expression, sensitivity and encounter groups, miniskirts, nudism, sexual freedom, and increased illegal and official physical violence have accompanied social and psychological change and are probably a reflection of the linkages in the body image.

When societies become more closed, elaborate, and discriminating, then minds, bodies, and clothing become more differentiated, elaborate, and confining. If rigid, compartmentalized, dehumanized social structure is to be loosened and simplified, then minds, bodies, and clothing must loosen and become simpler also.

There are both benefits and problems associated with simple organization of behavior, and there are also both benefits and problems associated with complex differentiated organization. It would appear that differentiation of society and technology with simplicity in human values and human relationships might offer some middle ground. Some rotation of roles, feedback mechanisms, and constructive management of differentiation in society would be health promoting as well.

Finally, a cultural press which would encourage simple emotional and complex psychological development, which would encourage both Soul and intellectual development in persons of all groups, should promote healthier personalities and a healthier society.

We lack the wisdom to perceive whether this would be desirable or possible. What is quite clear is that only pain, fear, or profit can produce the eventual motivation for change since, on emotional matters associated with belief systems, humans do not respond to knowledge and reason.

The wish for constancy in relationships leads to a search for constant union with some. We just do not want to accept the facts of life. People do not unite constantly. They unite — separate — unite — separate. Only with belief systems can we have constant relationships; and, once we have them, we cherish them, cling to them, and defend them with the same physiological bonds we once had attached to our mothers. It matters no more that the beliefs are false than it mattered that mother wasn't perfect. We needed her, relied on her for relationships, for support, and for direction. We could not have lived without her. Destruction of her would have caused us to die. So it seems, also, with belief systems.

For many years the issue of race in psychoanalysis or in psychotherapy was seldom discussed in psychiatric forums or in psychiatric literature. A pioneering work by Kardiner and Ovesey (1962) reported the effects of racism on the personality and psychology of Black Americans who had been studied systematically by psychoanalytically oriented interview methods. Grier and Cobbs (1968) reported their analysis of the effects of racism on a very wide spectrum and large number of Black patients treated by psychotherapy. Both books made important contributions to the understanding and documentation of relationships between racism and psychotherapy and demonstrated clearly that psychotherapeutic interviews can offer one of the most productive methods of studying in depth the effects of racism upon individuals. Dr. Ordway's chapter in this volume is a pioneering effort which graphically depicts the effects of racism upon American Whites as revealed in psychoanalysis.

Notable among the studies of effects of race in psychoanalysis and psychotherapy are those of Bernard (1953, 1956) and Butts (1969), and the latter has also reported a study of the effects of racism upon the referral practices of private patients (Butts and Harrison, 1970).

Virtually every psychotherapist can cite anecdotal material concerning race and psychotherapy which broadens the dimensions of the subject. Two brief anecdotes may illustrate directions in which the sociopsychological dynamics of racism may influence which persons seek psychotherapy and which ones reject it. In the first, a Black female student was impregnated by a White student several years ago in a school which expelled students under these circumstances. The White student was expelled, but the Black one was permitted to remain, allegedly because the school was fearful of demonstrations by Black activist groups. The White student, separated from school and from fiancée and in conflict with his family, sought psychotherapy for depression. Feelings of being unfairly scapegoated and punished while his partner was permitted to continue in school were prominent.

In the second example, an emotionally disturbed Black man was fired when his lack of emotional control on his job led to repeated disruptions. His sympathetic White employer arranged for psychotherapy, which the man reluctantly and suspiciously accepted. In the first interview he acknowledged his loneliness associated with losses of family relationships and talked of the intense "crushes" he developed toward fellow workers. He was very sensitive to the slightest suggestion of rejection by those to whom he became attached and felt unable to control himself when his anger flared. He canceled his appointment for his second interview when an energetic White group decided to protest his dismissal as an act of racism. The man was the object of considerable attention, which gratified him and met long-unfulfilled needs, and he provided the protest group with a cause. The employer felt unable to divulge the confidential nature of details on which the dismissal was based. During one demonstration by the protest group, police were called, several people were jailed, several were hurt, and many thousands of dollars in fines were levied. No one could figure out how to close the information gap between the employer and the protest group or how to get the man back to the treatment he needed. It was notable that, while surrounded by staunchly loyal members of the protest group, the man felt he had a supportive "family" with him again, and he functioned without loss of emotional control. Psychotherapy offers a rich source of data for research on the interaction of individual psychodynamics and social phenomena.

Social sciences, psychological sciences, and medical sciences have developed along such separate lines that the phenomena defined in one science are seldom relatable to those in another because of basic differences in the terminology, concepts, and fields under study. In order to examine some of the relationships between somatic, psychic, and social fields, I have focused my attention for several years upon the parallel happenings, the analogous events, and the overlapping aspects of these three fields (Deutsch 1959, 1962; Brain 1951; Pinderhughes 1971a, 1971b).

There is one system in every individual where medical sciences, psychological sciences, and social sciences are intimately related. Every aspect of somatic experience, psychological experience, and social experience is represented within the central nervous system. The registering of impressions of body parts and body processes begins as soon as the central nervous system is sufficiently developed to accomplish this function.

Since some vegetative functions are ongoing throughout life, they provide continuing reinforcement of the earliest central nervous system impressions created by vegetative functions. I have offered the hypothesis that the dichotomy and antagonism in vegetative and other body processes program dichotomy and conflict into all thinking and behavior.

Impressions from the environment and from all social and psychological experience are superimposed upon and linked to impressions from the body in what we call the body image. The interlocked patterns of impressions (from the body, from the mind, and from society) which we find in the body image constitute the only point where everything is organically related that is going on somatically, psychically, and socially. This is the point where social, psychic, and somatic processes influence one another and where medical, psychological, and social sciences have common territory. In some instances phenomena arising in one field may have direct expression in the other as a result of the relationships in the body image.

In a series of studies of relationships between the body, mind, and society, I have concluded that the principles outlined in this section may help us to understand: (1) why racism, classism, and other forms of social discrimination are encountered universally in all societies; (2) why the forms, social structures, and dynamics of social discrimination everywhere are so similar; (3) why the dynamics of interaction between repressing forces and the repressed are the same whether the repression be in somatic, intrapsychic, interpersonal, or social fields.

Franz Fanon (1963) has brilliantly discussed these questions with a focus on the interaction of colonizing and colonized people. A great deal of his formulations are equally applicable to ghettoizing and ghettoized people. In several volumes which have come to make up a handbook for revolutionaries, he has described the psychology of these relationships, focusing upon the value orientations and power of the parties involved.

Juan Luis Vives in the sixteenth century discussed the same phenomena with many of the same conclusions, predicting the dynamics and conditions under which repressed people and repressed mental content rise (Zilboorg 1941, pp. 180–95).

Sigmund Freud attempted to study both the psychological and somatic dynamics associated with behavior and found all existing methods to be inadequate (1966). He postponed examination of the somatic factors and developed methods for studying psychological factors which were called psychoanalytic.

As of 1972 there are still no satisfactory methods for observing or describing somatic, psychological, and social phenomena within a unified framework. Consequently the principles summarized below as hypotheses are strange bed-fellows in that they are pulled together from different disciplines and frames of reference which are not suitable for comparison. Keep in mind the basic assumption that, since interactions between repressing forces and the repressed take place in somatic, psychic, and social fields, they may be analogous and following the same laws.

Hypothesis I

The physiological processes which mediate approach behavior also mediate acceptance behavior and the establishment of affiliative bonds (Maier and Schneirla 1964). The physiological processes which mediate avoidance behavior also mediate rejection behavior and the establishment of aggressive bonds. These dichotomous and opposing physiological patterns impose upon all thinking and behavior a drive to dichotomize, to perceive, and relate to two sides: one to seek and one to avoid. This drive to dichotomize underlies the ambivalence in early thinking and behavior processes which is universal.

Hypothesis II

Ambivalence is most prominent when relating occurs with a single object. Under such circumstances both affiliative and aggressive bonds are associated with the same person and the relationship lacks constancy.

Ambivalence can be resolved only by relating to two objects at one time, with affiliative bonds to one and aggressive bonds to the other. Establishment of constant relationships requires that psychophysiological processes mediating affiliation become attached to one object while processes mediating aggression are attached to another object at the same time (Hess 1964). Either affiliative or aggressive attachments may be developed to persons, to material things, to sensory stimuli, to body parts or processes, or to ideas. The physiology of the central nervous system makes possible attachments to any item of experience which has representation in the body image.

Hypothesis III

Invariably the object of the affiliative bond is aggrandized as the object of the aggressive bond is renounced. Universally, ambivalence is resolved by such paired paranoid processes (Pinderhughes 1970). The resolution of the oedipal conflict illustrates this. An affectionate bond and delusions of love become more constantly attached to one parent while an aggressive bond and delusions of hate become more constantly attached to the other parent in a process which reduces ambivalence and offers greater constancy in relationships.

Hypothesis IV

All constant relationships are basically paranoid. There is aggrandizement of objects of affiliative bonds and denigration of objects of aggressive bonds.

Hypothesis V

Groups are formed by developing paranoid affiliative bonds to group members and paranoid aggressive bonds toward common outside targets. The targets may be human or nonhuman. Common targets of aggressive bonds within the group also help the group to cement and purify itself while projecting (dumping) on the target. Human targets within the group are called scapegoats. They are sacrificed and attacked in order to protect group members from aggressive bonds toward one another.

Hypothesis VI

Wherever human beings live in groups, the group members must repress disruptive body parts, body processes, and behavior. Sexual arousal, hostile discharges, excretory behavior, and sudden loud noises are disruptive and are repressed in all societies. They are excluded from the group with "low" social value (although they may be highly valued in individual or private behavior). They are defined culturally as "low," "dark," "backward" (behind), and "wrong" behavior.

Since each group member must try to rid his social behavior of such impulses, there are needs for group members to find dumping grounds outside their group to project such ideas upon in order to purify their beliefs about themselves and their group members. Group members can then continue to love, aggrandize, and favor group members and to hate, denigrate, or neglect outsiders.

Hypothesis VII

Life experience determines what is assigned high value and affiliative bond and what is assigned low value and aggressive bond. Universal experience of human beings with night and day (Hartshorne 1934), with gravity, and with children and adults lead people all over the earth to value white over black and high over low. In each culture, characteristic objects for affiliation and targets for aggression are defined and reinforced by bribery or institutionalized and processed aggression. The patterns of prejudice and discrimination which characterize the culture are thus "learned."

Hypothesis VIII

Because of common bonds to "affiliative" physiology, the more highly valued component in each paired relationship is associated with the more valued component in other paired relationships. Thus, the "white," the "high," the "in," the "front," the "right," the "head," and the "top" are associated with one another in mental life. Also the "dark," the "low," the "out," the "behind," the "left," the "foot," and the "bottom" are similarly associated in human minds. In a society which segregates any people, the segregated will be associated in everyone's mind with hostile activity, sexual activity, feces, dirt, unpleasant odors, and other components of human life which must be segregated out of social living and kept in their place in order not to disrupt the group.

Hypothesis IX

Once a false belief system about a human target of aggressive bonds is developed, all relationships and all social structures are modified to express and validate the false beliefs. This contrived reality is produced and maintained by legitimized and institutionalized direct and processed violence.

The careful study of the historian Winthrop Jordan (1968) of the development of White English and American attitudes toward Blacks between 1550 and 1812 graphically portrays the projection and paranoid beliefs which developed in Whites from their earliest encounters with Blacks. The Puritans were unsuccessfully struggling with aggression, sexuality, and loss of discipline in their society much as we are struggling with the same problems in our society today. In the sixteenth century, the exploration and colonization which led to White-Black interactions themselves were an expression of trends toward more freedom and aggressive behavior not unlike the way our exploration of space expresses comparable trends in the present. Jordan's data reveal that, with the White-Black encounters, all the evils and immorality with which the English unsuccessfully struggled in their own society were imputed to the Blacks, and all the virtues and ideals of the Puritans were imputed to the Whites.

Realities were contrived to express and validate these false beliefs. Having attached to the image of Blacks all the base impulses in themselves which needed to be mastered, Whites had only to master the Blacks and debase them in order to express and verify their delusions and purify their image of themselves.

Shakespeare's Othello provides a remarkable social commentary upon this process. Othello starts out with as much dignity and nobility as any White person. The crafty White

Iago systematically undermines and destroys the dignity, the manhood, the confidence, the initiative, the self-esteem, the capacity for love and trust, and eventually the life of the Black Othello.

Only by believing that Blacks were less than human could a "free democracy" be developed with the most coersive institution of slavery on record (Elkins 1959). All political, economic, and educational institutions, all philosophies, role relationships, and psychologies, all aspects of American culture were modified to express and validate the delusions. The human products of these rigid divergent conditioning processes seemed to verify the delusions.

Every attempt to alter the contrived realities revives the delusions and activates intense behavior to maintain them. As long as the contrived realities in our institutions continue racial segregation, de facto or otherwise, the slave culture caste will be perpetuated in the descendants of slaves. As long as any group of people remain relatively isolated, the same cultural press tends to be passed on from generation to generation. Only with changes in the institution of segregation can the racist process and the pathology it spawns be undermined. Group development and ethnic development are important constructive processes which should be supported in parallel with integration in all institutions (Butts 1969; Comer 1967).

Hypothesis X

Paranoids are not aware of their paranoia. To them their beliefs are true. All their group members share their beliefs and cannot perceive their falseness. Only outsiders are aware of the falseness, and outsiders cannot be believed, but only rejected, denounced, or neglected. Outsiders, excluded from understanding and reason, must employ confrontation processes, in continuing conflict-filled relationship until again the outsiders are repressed or until conflict-reducing changes are introduced (Pinderhughes 1968).

Black people made many confrontations between 1954 and 1972 and doubtless will continue to make them. Delusions about Blacks have been altering. No longer are Blacks considered passive, and no longer are they easily neglected. The development of Black pride has been associated with increase in White rage, White respect, and White fear.

With each advantage gained by Blacks, every minority group on the hierarchical ladder above Blacks is quick to receive more fully these advantages, while Blacks get token changes. Some of the token changes are relatable to the crippling effects of pervasive American racism which has systematically prevented Blacks from gaining requisite preparation for meaningful participation in many institutions. Institutions which could not accommodate ten Blacks before 1968 have thrown open doors for scores and wonder why no Blacks step forward (Grier 1966). Institutions must find ways to develop the interest, knowledge, and skills which propel students from elementary school onto the tracks which lead to the institutions.

Unfortunately, Blacks will continue to be perceived as outsiders by most adults of this generation. Most adults also relate to their adolescent children as outsiders.

Hypothesis XI

When an object of affiliative bonds presents behavior which was previously renounced and projected upon outsiders, we have an opportunity to become less deluded about that behavior and more accepting of it. Some major confrontations of the late 1960s and early 1970s came from White youth whose minds were opened to the point where they could no longer identify with the double standards and false belief systems of their parents. The White parents identified with their children, but many White children no longer identified with their parents. As adolescents they modified social structure regarding sex and marriage, hair styles and clothing, and they "blew their parents' minds." To the parents, all which was so evil and black and far away was right at home in a previously loved person.

In these confrontations by loved ones, we find ourselves no longer certain and sure of our behavior, of our position, or of our beliefs. We have to acknowledge the bad as well as the good, the black as well as the white, in our group, in our family, in ourselves. Each of us is white and black too. As our paranoia is reduced, our ambivalence increases. So do our options and opportunities for change, since change from rigid structure can occur only with social, interpersonal, or physiological crises.

Repression will increase and so will the confrontations, and the process continues in a dynamic interaction. Possibly, if we learn enough or become frightened enough, we shall initiate the massive public health, mass media, and educational programs required to make it popular and rewarding to form affiliative bonds with and be concerned about outsiders as well as group members. A competitive society does not encourage such trends. It may be that, en route to the resolution of racial and other social discrimination, we shall have a massive national identity crisis of whether to attack and put down or share with and serve—the other guy.

Hypothesis XII

Human beings are normally paranoid. When socially healthy they can trust one another and form relationships in which their paranoid processes and content are shared by group members. When social capacities are impaired, they have idiosyncratic paranoid content and may be labeled sick (Freud 1948, pp. 444–66). At times they uncomfortably fluctuate between opposing beliefs in ambivalent states. At other times they achieve a more comfortable constancy in relationships by accepting one belief for themselves and projecting its opposite upon others (Knight 1940). Reasoning processes are generally employed in the service of paranoid processes to provide rationalizations and justifications, to deal with confrontations, and to contrive and maintain realities which support cherished delusions.

The data on human beings from all sources overwhelmingly support the conclusion that man is more paranoid than wise. This paranoia is not accessible to reason, and attempts to alter it lead to confrontations and often to violence. The paranoia is especially oppressive and deadly when it has been frozen into culture and when it has molded institutions.

When enough influential men in important institutions reform and humanize the structures over which they have power, then dissent, revolt, and revolution cease, and leaders are embraced with appreciation and affectionate bonds. However, there must be a sizable number of such leaders, enough to constitute a movement among influential men.

In essence, to eliminate racism, it would be necessary to develop a rededication to democratic and humanitarian values, a shift from the ethics of competition to those of sharing, and a new order of priorities in major institutions. That might be requesting more change than most influential Americans could accept. Social reforms of this kind were produced in Norway by a coalition of dedicated influential men working together for many years. Now that country is one of the few places on earth where low-, middle-, and upper-income people have equal access to the best hospitals and to the best in psychotherapy.

Factors like these determine, to a considerable degree, needs for psychotherapy, the nature of it, and who receives it. Factors like these determine the philosophies, the rationales, and the ethics with which psychotherapy is practiced and must be considered relevant in any discussion of racism and psychotherapy.

REFERENCES

Barbour. F. 1968. *The Black power revolt*. Boston: Porter Sargent (Extending Horizons Books).

Bernard, Viola W.

    1953. Psychoanalysis and members of minority groups. *J. Amer. Psychoanal. Ass.* 1:256–67.

    1956. Some psychodynamic aspects of desegregation. *Amer. J. Orthopsychiat.* 26:459–66.

Brain, W. 1951. *Mind, perception and science*. Springfield, Ill.: Charles C. Thomas.

Butcher. M. J. 1957. *The Negro in American culture*. New York: Knopf.

Butts, H. F. 1969. White racism: its origins, institutions, and the implications for professional practice in mental health. *Int. J. Psychiat.* 8:914–44.

Butts, H., and Harrison, P. 1970. White psychiatrists' racism in referral practice to Black psychiatrists. *J. Nat. Med. Ass.* 62:278–82.

Butts, H., and Schachter, J. 1968. Transference and countertransference in interracial analyses. *J. Amer. Psychoanal. Assoc.* 16:792–808.

Carmichael, S., and Hamilton, C. 1967. *Black power*. New York: Random.

Comer, J. 1967. Some parallels between individual and Afro-American community development. Paper read at the convention of the National Medical Association, St. Louis, Mo., August 11.

Day, M. 1967. The natural history of training groups. *Int. J. Group. Psychother.* 17:436.

Deutsch, F.

    1959. *On the mysterious leap from the mind to the body*. New York: International Universities Press.

    1962. *Body, mind and the sensory gateways*. New York: Basic Books.

Elkins, S. M. 1959. *Slavery*. Chicago: University of Chicago Press.

Fanon, F. 1963. *The wretched of the earth*. New York: Grove Press.

Freud, S.

    1948. On the mechanism of paranoia. In *Collected papers*. Vol. 3. London: Hogarth Press.

    1966 (1895). *Project for a scientific psychology*. Standard Edition 1:283–397. London: Hogarth Press.

Grier, W. H. 1966. Some special effects of Negroeness on the oedipal conflict. *J. Nat. Med. Ass.* 58.

Grier, W., and Cobbs, P. 1968. *Black rage*. New York: Basic Books.

Hartshorne, C. 1934. *The philosophy and psychology of sensation*. Chicago: University of Chicago Press.

Hess, W. R. 1964. *The biology of mind*. Chicago: University of Chicago Press.

Isaacs, Harold R. 1963. *The new world of Negro Americans.* New York: John Day.

Jordan. W. 1988. *White over Black.* Baltimore, Md.: Penguin.

Kardiner, A., and Ovesey, L. 1962. *The mark of oppression: explorations in the personality of the American Negro.* New York: World.

Knight, R. P. 1940. Introjection, projection, and identification. *Psychoanal. Quart.* 9:334.

Maier, N. R. F., and Schneirla, T. C. 1964. *Principles of animal psychology.* New York: Dover.

Mendelsohn, J. 1965. *The martyrs.* New York: Harper.

Pinderhughes, C. A.

　　1966.　Pathogenic social structure: a prime target for preventive psychiatric intervention. *J. Nat. Med. Ass.* 58:424–29.

　　1968.　The psychodynamics of dissent: with special emphasis upon racial activists. In *Science and psychoanalysis,* ed. J. Masserman. Vol. 12. New York: Grune & Stratton.

　　1969.　Understanding Black power: processes and proposals. *Amer. J. Psychiat.* 125:1552–57.

　　1970.　The universal resolution of ambivalence by paranoia with an example in black and white. *Amer. J. Psychother.* 24:597–610.

　　1971*a*.　Psychological and physiological origins of racism and other social discrimination. *J. Nat. Med. Ass.* 63:25–29.

　　1971*b*.　Somatic, psychic, and social sequelae of loss. *J. Amer. Psychoanal. Assoc.* 19:670–96.

Spurlock, J. 1969. Should the poor get none? *J. Amer. Acad. Child Phychiat.* Vol. 8, January.

Standish, C. T., and Semrad, E. V. 1951. Group psychotherapy with psychotics. *J. Psychiat. Soc. Work.* 20:143.

Wright, N. 1967. *Black power and urban unrest.* New York: Hawthorne.

Zilboorg, G. 1941. *A history of medical psychology.* New York: Norton.

CHAPTER 4

Some Emotional Consequences of Racism for Whites

by John A. Ordway

Emotional consequences of racism for Whites can be studied when and where they occur. Because in psychoanalysis the patient is encouraged to let his thoughts roam freely to whatever subjects enter his consciousness, the analysis of a White professional's reactions to his community work in a Black ghetto gives a direct view of what has happened when one White man has been confronted with his prejudices and participation in racist institutions.

Small portions of this analysis are presented and then followed by a discussion of some other isolated examples of racist psychology in other Whites and some implications for their mental health. Finally the thesis is briefly presented and discussed that racism is only one specific manifestation of general antihumanism.

The forty-one-year-old White community worker whose analysis will be discussed originally sought treatment because of a depression that began on his return from military service in Korea. After "toughing out" the discomfort of his depression for a number of years, he sought and entered psychoanalysis in the winter of 1966, not only to obtain relief from feelings of guilt and suicidal ruminations but also to "loosen up" a constricted, puritanical life-style.

During the early months of therapy he dutifully examined the sadistically strict Victorian background from which he was trying to free himself. He properly deduced that the physical and verbal whippings that he received from his ostensibly genteel parents had created his own habit of whipping and downgrading himself. He concluded, "If they felt that way about me, I guess I felt they must be right — that I was really no good." But when he tried intellectually to convince himself that he desired higher esteem and better treatment, he failed to improve his self-image until one day he rather suddenly realized the implications: "Now it's really in my guts. If a busy analyst will sit with me through two years and four hundred hours of treatment, I must be worth *something*." In succeeding hours he then made his therapist's assurances of his worth part of himself, felt "like a person instead of a schmuck for the first time," and began to give up the various ways in which he had been fond of torturing, defeating, and constricting ("jailing") himself.

As he felt freer of the pain of depression, more worthwhile, and less preoccupied with the past, he talked more about his work in the community and applied his newly found insights to work situations in the Black ghetto, where he had been a street worker for several years.

Previous to his current job, he had spent his life and career with a mixture of Whites and Negroes but has been with what he calls "new Blacks" in his work over only the past three years. During this period he has been helping put together several all-Black indigenous self-help programs — sometimes with the help of a few Whites, most of the time not, and always under the critical eye of some White city officials who had originally reacted to the 1967 rebellion in Cincinnati with a positive attempt to get at the "root causes of urban unrest." Later, however, these White city officials withdrew to a coldly suspicious law-and-order position about self-determining all-Black projects and, along the city grapevine, intermittently passed veiled threats to this White worker.

Some data relevant to prejudice and racism from the worker's ongoing psychoanalysis will help define his feelings.

Recently the worker has been wrestling with the problem of how much more deeply to involve himself in work that has left him chronically fatigued and/or ill because he feels too keenly the tragedy of Black-White hostilities between friends in both groups and because both Black and White militants constantly play on his loyalties, sympathies, guilt, and anxieties as he moves back and forth between Black and White communities. Further energies are consumed as he moves restlessly toward and away from an emotional and intellectual equilibrium and integrates further insights about his work. In the White community, on the one hand, he learns through the city hall grapevine that the police feel he has "become Black, gone over to the enemy, and is no longer trustworthy." On the other hand, in the ghetto, he feels that he "tells it like it is" to Black acquaintances but that his words are still greeted with suspicion. Seemingly good gifts, like job "opportunities," that he offers to Blacks are ignored or turned down flatly for reasons whose validity he can only dimly sense. He then has grindingly to work through the fact that the job he thinks he has offered in friendship is regarded as, and may be, only a part of the White racist establishment. He has therefore perhaps offered a racist trap instead of a gift. Thus a Black may angrily refuse what has looked to the startled White like a golden opportunity for his Negro friend. This offer then may further be interpreted as the Caucasian worker's participation in White racism. He has admitted, "Sometimes I get a little confused and tired of all this."

Our worker's fatigue is reflected in his recent rambling associations that contrast with the sharpness of his thinking two years ago when he had analyzed his own ghetto-spawned symptoms in a clearer crisper fashion. We see a mild, masochistic professional identity crisis emerging as he continues:

"It seems to me that this rapping is never gonna end. After three years of writing at least some successful applications for federal grants and bringing private monies and resources into the ghetto, this constant criticism, actual and implicit, goes on and on and on. I get mad as hell at 'them,' and as a matter of fact I seem to be mad every time I go over to the Black community. There seems to be no casual liking, agreeableness, affection, trust, charity, or anything positive in some of 'those people,' and I don't know if there ever will be. There is really no pleasure whatsoever in dealing with some of 'these' Black workers. 'They' seem more insistent on showing anger or finding loopholes or weaknesses in what I say or do than in working with me."

As the psychoanalyst, I replied, "Didn't you say that three years ago you and the regional NIMH office purposely picked out the most militant and angriest group with which to work?"

"Yes, I did," said the patient. "Consciously I did it out of a sense of challenge and some kind of a crazy wish to explore territory that I thought I understood before, but really didn't. But now it seems to me that I did it out of masochism. I'm fed up with the whole damned business. I'm really not. But then again I am. Everytime that I get on stable ground or what seems like stable ground with these people, they cut it out from under me and leave me wondering just what the truth is and where I am. I feel impotent and nagged and kind of beaten up."

"Didn't you say that the Black-White interface was marked by a struggle to see who is the master and the slave? Isn't everything you describe inevitable?"

"Yes, I suppose it is. They don't know that they're beating on me sometimes. Other times they do know they're beating on me. Sometimes they enjoy it and know what is going on. Other times I'm not sure that they really know how difficult it is for me to stay motivated to help when their main reaction is negative, critical, and hostile. And in fact they still seem to see me so much as a White master whom they unconsciously expect too much of or want to kill and destroy that I don't really know if we'll ever be able to work together. They say they're not racist, but I dunno."

There was a pause.

"You know, I hadn't thought of it before, but I think that I'm acting like a suffering slave. I don't really have to take all of this as an attack on me personally. It's an attack on me as a White. . . . Perhaps I can listen to all this anger but not react quite so much — 'quite so much' — that was an interesting kind of statement. I shouldn't react at all as a slave; but be myself, momentarily identify with the suffering slave and then go on to be me, a professional — empathic but objective. I don't have to live out slavery in order to understand it. Perhaps some of the people in my project were right when they said to go back to my White friends for a while and get them together. Perhaps what they meant also was for me to get myself together psychologically."

There was another silence.

"There's an awful lot of 'theys' and 'theirs' in what I've said. I haven't mentioned an individual all hour. Damned if I haven't lumped these complete individuals into one Black mass — or Black monster or monstrous master. Huh."

He next reflected further on his personal tendency to lump together and pigeonhole. Then he worried about his own identity and category as a professional whose training seemed of so little use in his current work.

In the next hour the patient recalled murderous impulses of two years ago that had helped him understand racism and his anger toward Blacks. At that time while he was closely involved with a number of militants in the Black ghettos, the patient noticed that although he was daily involved with a number of Negroes, he dreamed only about White people. At first he did not understand this situation. Then in a few weeks he reported a brand new symptom:

"I've had a peculiar kind of a headache: a dull nauseating feeling in the back of my head or rather at the base of my head and on top of my neck. It's a little bit to the left. It's funny to talk about a nauseating feeling in the head or the neck, but it's true. It's not in the center but to the left of center and like a knot."

Because this headache persisted on and off for eight to ten

hours of analysis, the worker talked about it frequently but got nowhere with understanding it until one day he came in after a particularly frustrating series of talks with his Black acquaintances.

"Goddamn it, I'd like to hang everyone of those Black sons of bitches by their necks. You can't get anything done. They say they'll show up and they don't show up, and you wait. You bring some people together, give them what they want, and then they do nothing that they've planned. They waste my time, they waste their time, and they're destroying themselves and they're also destroying me. I'd like to string 'em all up!"

And then there was a startled silence.

"Wow! That's it! 'String them up' is represented by the hangman's-knot position of my nauseating headache. But why nausea?"

No answer came for the moment. Instead, he went on like that in the several following hours to work through tremendous repressed anger at Blacks for their visiting c.p.t. ("Colored peoples' time") on him by being late or not showing up at all. Intellectually he understood, but, used to punctuality, emotionally he was really furious.

Finally he worked it out that the feeling of nausea and his headache were a wish to vomit up this anger and, with the vomiting, to get rid of his wish to lynch blacks. As soon as he had a more complete grasp of this type of anger, the "nauseating" headache gradually disappeared, and he felt more relaxed. As soon as he understood this desire to lynch, he began to think back on the absence of Blacks from his dreams and very shortly realized that this absence meant that he wanted to kill them all off. This was the casual racist genocide which his Black friends stated Whites wanted to visit on Negroes. Unconsciously the patient was only too willing to carry this out in his dreams—without much anxiety or guilt. He exclaimed, "I'd be glad to get rid of the whole mess."

About this time a new symptom appeared. It was the feeling of confusion after being rapped consecutively by three or four Blacks who presented "facts" that ostensibly sounded correct but were so extreme that he could not accept them as the truth or as part of his own White family's racist activities. Under these circumstances during the second hour of a "soul session," he would develop a confused feeling in his head. He struggled with this in analysis until he experienced the same kind of feeling at the moment just before defecation into the toilet. He described these moments as times of suspended activity in which there was great hope, excitement, pleasure, and approaching relief that he could get rid of the whole foul-smelling black mass and feel clean again. This feeling interfered with well-integrated and logical thought processes but unconsciously expressed a primitive and deep fury. At the same time another part of him felt like a good boy about to defecate in the potty just as he should.

He analyzed and understood this confused feeling in his head after some weeks. But this was not the last of his bowel symptoms. A month or two later when he expressed his anger finally with directness at a paranoid community worker, he became very guilty over his lack of understanding, and tried extra hard to be a good boy the next time "out" in the community. He bore down "hard" on this problem and, in bearing down harder in his work, also bore down harder with his rectum and anus and extruded a thrombosed hemorrhoid. As he analyzed what had happened, he discovered that he not only was trying to be a good boy "doing his duty" and emptying his bowels of whatever was there (like Blacks) that needed to be shed, but guiltily was trying to be extra good in even providing guilt-relieving, expiatory feces composed of his own blood, to make up for his crimes against the Blacks, whom he wished to shed. But it was some time before he realized the full sequence of his fantasies: a wish to gobble up his ghetto acquaintances, digest them, and then finally eliminate them via his gastrointestinal tract—with, of course, the just-described penitence at the end of the process.

Diverting from the course of the analysis for a moment,

one might speculate about how many of this man's reactions and symptoms were products of the ways in which he had latently and habitually *always* reacted generally to *all* people and how many were specifically reserved for Blacks. Difficult life circumstances can stimulate latent or unconscious reactions or habits to emerge in new and extreme forms or be channeled into new symptoms. It may have been that close association with aggressive Negroes constituted the difficult and upsetting life circumstances that stimulated previously dormant or little-noticed sadistic attitudes and wishes to emerge in symptomatic form. It was clear enough that he had genocidal wishes in his dreams in that he actively did away with all the Blacks in his life at least at night. This seemed to coincide with the genocide that Blacks indicate they fear from the White race. His curious conversion headache clearly represented a lynching situation. Since he had almost no associations in analysis to lynchings other than those of Negroes, it could be again stated that he wished to throttle his Black acquaintances. But it was not entirely clear that this wish was special for them because he may for years have wished to carry out these acts against Caucasians and other humans whenever they upset him. Expressions like "go hang" had long been in his vocabulary—always delivered with a smile, of course. Migraine headaches had characterized his preanalytic life and had been stimulated by situations in which he felt "let down" by women. He had had "cloudy" states of mind in "lily white" situations. So it was difficult to see exactly how many of his reactions were stimulated by prejudice and racism and how many by his meanness or antihumanism. It was only clear that he did have savage feelings against Blacks who frustrated him, that the symptoms mentioned above appeared for the first time in his life during his work with "new Blacks," and that attitudes revealed in analysis were by definition clearly racist.

On returning from these speculations to the course of the analysis, one finds the patient reviewing from earlier parts of his therapy his great surprise at the scholarship, general knowledge, high intelligence, and breadth of reading that the Black power leaders exhibited. He had been astonished at their dialectical ability and the insistent but charming and forceful use of logic as he was "rapped."

"They didn't turn out to be the pleasant, smiling, agreeable Negroes whom I had very easily accepted previously. Without realizing it, I think I had imputed a good bit of shallowness to my Negro friends in the 1940s and 50s. But I guess it wasn't that they were shallow but that they were repressing a lot of anger that they felt it wasn't safe to express toward Whites and just giving us and me a kind of pleasant song and dance that covered real feelings underneath."

The analysand continued, saying that he had no idea that there were so many Black universities and Black students at universities like Howard and Tuskegee. Also he had been astonished to find that in the South all Black students in most areas were forced to take courses in Black history and in a sense forced to be Black and part of a Black and not White system. A Black identity had been thus encouraged in the "separate but equal" school systems.

Pressed by my questioning, he had admitted early in analysis that he had thought of Blacks going through about the eighth or ninth grade and then doing very unskilled labor for the rest of their lives unless they happened to be exceptions. He then realized in a flood of emotion that he really had prejudged Blacks to be undereducated, less intelligent, cloudy minded though friendly, lacking in scholarship and general knowledge—although of course there had always been those "exceptions" with whom he had gone to college, been in service, and attended casework school and casework placement.

"I always assessed them correctly because they were in class with me, and their intelligence was obvious and their attainments great. But I think I kind of turned them White in my mind, thus made them friends, and was able to date the girls and stand up as a best man for one of my Negro friends who was marrying a White girl. The idea of Blackness as a separate culture in its own right simply had never occurred to me."

In the same hour when he described a pleasant Negro girl he dated once, "having made her properly White, unconsciously," he also described his inability to empathize with the White men he saw cruising along Reading Road in the Avondale district of Cincinnati to pick up Black prostitutes. He had understood Malcolm X's account of White businessmen rushing into Harlem for a "quick one" before going to work, in an attempt to get a little love and affection and "Soul" when they couldn't get it from their own wives. But somehow the sight of White men actually doing this in front of his eyes he initially could not accept. Bit by bit he began to work it out that when he had read Malcolm X, he had thought of the Harlem prostitute as having first been made White by contact with the White man. But he was not able to apply the same process to the Avondale prostitutes because he had begun unalterably to see Blacks as Blacks, not to be "Whitized." When he was unable to change her into a White, the Black woman became something alien and threatening and dangerous.

At first he could not understand why she had become so dangerous; but, as Black militants filled him in on the way their Black great-great-grandmothers had been misused sexually by their White masters, he came to see that he feared the same revenge from the women that he feared from the Black men who were also emerging from a kind of slavery. He had fantasies of instruments inside the black women put there to tear away his penis and testicles, just as during his first days in the ghettos he also fantasied knives and guns in the hands of Black men waiting for him.

"I never asked myself where all the mulatto women came from, but unconsciously I must have known that Negro women had been 'used' by their White masters. It never occurred to me consciously."

The analysand never "meant" in any way to gobble up and digest for his own purposes his Black friends and then flush them down the toilet. But he did so in the fantasies underlying and giving rise to his gastrointestinal symptoms, and he "unmindfully" attempted actual damage to his Negro acquaintances by offering destructive job "opportunities." Consciously his fears of Blacks and/or the very idea of genocide seemed ridiculously unreal to him, but his dreams unquestionably revealed his wishes to annihilate. Also his own assumption of a slave role covered the opposite unconscious wish to enslave. In other words, his personal offensive against Negroes was carried out at a largely unconscious level by this ostensibly kind and unprejudiced professional.

As with this patient, the real meanings of many racist techniques or methods never do occur consciously to Whites, but they nevertheless constantly carry out modern "slave-breaking" activities in thought, word, or deed. For example, a common racist technique is to reduce Blacks to less than human status in thought or word. A distinguished Negro physician says, "The Black has never really been regarded as a human, but as a thing." His words recall the dehumanizing, thingizing words of a highly placed decision maker, a White executive, on tennis courts located in a Negro neighborhood. Some Black youngsters, on the other side of the fence, of course, asked for some tennis balls to play with in the street. This momentary distraction led to a missed shot by his opponent. Across the net came a laughing, "What's the matter, got some soot in your eye?" On another occasion this ostensibly warm and charming man remarked, "The mud balls are really out tonight!"

"Well," a White may protest, "name-calling happens everywhere. Everyone dehumanizes or insults or gets slandered or insulted. Why such a big deal? Who's hurt by a few names?"

"It's the heavy repetitiveness of what you do," answers a Black professor. "You repeat again and again that you consider us subhuman. It's every day, every day, every day—not just occasional but constant slander for us, it's a black trip through a white landscape, and everything in that landscape reminds us that you consider us second rate."

"Second-rating," devaluing, or depreciation are used in a myriad of ways against Negroes. Only a few examples are given here—chosen, however, from some of the most secure and intelligent elements of the White population.

In a university setting a Black professional "raps" his white colleagues hard, attacking institutional racism with considerable logic and persuasiveness. His words sound clear and reasonable. But a faculty member takes care of the whole argument.

"You know how Jim is," he said. "Jim's not very smart and tries to make up for it by attacking other members of the faculty. I really think he is paranoid and ought to 'go.' " And "go" he did.

In order to hide the mechanism of depreciation and make it hard to combat, the White may additionally cover the depreciatory attitude with the opposite attitude of over-appreciation, oversolicitude, or overcompensation as in the following episode reported by Lillian Rubin (1968) after a group of White women had been jailed in the same quarters with Black women following an antiwar demonstration in Oakland: The Blacks had been smuggling goods to the White inmates after their arrest. When the White women's privileges were restored, they repaid their benefactors ten times the amount in cigarettes, chewing gum, etc. As the Black women scurried around gathering their reward as though they were "on the make," they flashed that differential smile of thanks that acknowledges White "superiority." They made the peace sign, and someone commented that the next time she would be helping in the demonstrations.

The White women perhaps did not understand that by returning "the maximum" tenfold to their benefactors, they implied that this was the usual White-Black situation, namely, that the first-rate White always has ten times as much to give as the second-rate Black.

This incident reminds one of a self-respecting Black man trying, and without "whipping a game," sincerely to borrow a ten spot from a White social worker at a meeting. In a ludicrous exchange, the White kept insisting that the immediately offered money was to be a gift and not a loan. The Negro worker kept wearily trying to explain that he wanted to repay it and just needed a temporary short-term loan. The Caucasian grandly refused, put the money in the other's pocket, and moved to another group of people, thus ending the exchange. Within a short time the Black went to work for the Office of Economic Opportunity and tried to repay the loan. Still unconsciously insisting on the Negro's inferiority, the White refused to accept repayment, making some kind of statement about his being in better circumstances than his Black acquaintance. A whole year passed after this episode before it finally dawned on the White that his debtor was making only a few thousand dollars less at the OEO than he himself made from city hall and that his Negro acquaintance was fully able to carry out a borrowing-repayment contract. He had repressed for a year the understanding that he had second-rated his Black colleague.

Repression of the recognition that they are using racist techniques not only blinds Caucasians to the knowledge that such mechanisms exist even in themselves but also permits prejudicial attitudes to exist and be utilized daily without the racist's being confronted with his methods. Even in the calmest office situation far from an Oakland jail, very stable, sensitive, intelligent Whites, whose professional duties specifically include the analysis of their own and others' hidden attitudes, blind themselves to the presence of racism in even their most intensely studied relationships. Several years ago, for example, a group of experienced White psychoanalysts meeting in a New York City workshop on relations between patients and analysts solemnly agreed that, during their experience analyzing Black people, racism and prejudice had never been issues between them and their Negro patients.

Such experiences run counter to the impressions of sociologist C. Eric Lincoln and Lorentho Wooden (1968), who say:

It is as inconceivable to me that a White person who has lived in this Western world would be without racial prejudice as it is for a Black person who has lived in this Western world not to have to deal with deep feelings of inferiority because of it — we're talking about a culture (America) in which racism is absolutely pervasive, where it finds its expression in every single one of our basic institutions, and it conditions the lives of all of us in very specific kinds of ways. From the time that an American White or Black is old enough to recognize color differences he begins to be shaped and conditioned by the recognition and in terms of the way in which those people who are significant in his life react toward color: his parents, his teachers, his Sunday school teacher, his minister. . . .

and, we might add, his psychoanalyst.

If, therefore, race, color, racism, and prejudice all are realistic parts of a Negro's daily life, any White psychoanalyst who is unaware of and fails to deal with these issues must be blinding himself by the amount he fails to deal with them. Furthermore, it seems that a White analyst would be deceiving himself to believe that his relations with his Black patients are not touched by racism or prejudice.

At the workshop in New York one White psychoanalyst seemed to have partial vision. He reported the first dream in therapy that Paul, a Black teen-ager patient, had revealed. The patient had been sullen and silent for the first three sessions, had begun to talk a little in the fourth, and then in the fifth hour reported the following dream: "Two cars bumped into each other. One was black, one white. They were towed away to the garage. Only one could be repaired. I don't remember the color. It drove out of the garage and went away."

Later in the hour Paul laughed as he said that he thought

maybe the black car had driven away. At the analytic meeting itself the analyst recounted that, from the boy's subsequent interpretation of the dream, he understood that the patient had a feeling that a destructive clash between patient and doctor was inevitable and that the patient only hoped that he could survive his trip to the hospital (garage). He understood that the patient's fury at Whites had led him in the dream wishfully to "bump off" his White therapist. But the psychoanalyst laughed heartily at the "unrealistic" thought that Paul had anything to fear from *him*. Only after the meeting, over an introspective drink, did he see that his hearty laugh was in large part sadistic joy over Paul's discomfort and his ability to "make a nigger patient squirm." His self-vision had partly improved.

Of course, one can discern in the exchanges reported above, in addition to depreciation and self-blinding or repression, the mechanics of denial used to support the present Black-White status quo and to continue the serious difficulties of the black trip through a white landscape. Such denial of the serious difficulties of the black trip through a white landscape is evidently rather widespread if we give credence to the report below from the National Advisory Commission on Civil Disorders (Rossi 1968, pp. 69–215):

A survey was made in 15 American cities of the racial attitudes of police, teachers, social workers, political workers, merchants, and employers. Interviews were concerned mainly with the images respondents held of the Negroes in their cities in general, and as clients, customers, students, and potential employees. Findings showed that although respondents were aware that their cities faced severe problems of housing, education, poverty, crime, and employment, their views can be characterized as *optimistic denials of the full seriousness of the position of the urban Negroes* in their cities. More than half felt that Negroes were being treated on a par with whites. They were willing to concede that important sources of civil disorders lay in basic conditions of slum life but they gave a much more important role to militants and "agitation" than the commission was able to find. There were considerable differences among the six occupational groups. Police, merchants, and employers generally took positions on most issues which strongly denied that there was inequality for Negroes in their city, which tended to blame riots on agitators, and which held unfavorable images of the Negro population. In contrast, educators, social workers, and political workers took opposite stands, recognizing inequality and accepting an environmental rather than instigational theory of riot causation. For example, only 21 percent of the police thought that Negroes were treated generally more poorly than other groups in the city in contrast to 71 percent of the educators.

During the racially stormy days of 1968, in another example of self-blinding, a very upper-class White industrialist in Cincinnati put himself in "a bag" during an attempt to form an urban coalition. He had called a meeting of all groups and all races and seated them in a large circle. The Blacks attending the meeting were seated to his right and very close. On his left and at a distance were many White business, political, and labor leaders. In the course of the meeting raised hands signified wishes on the part of the attendants to speak. Fascinatingly, the White leader utterly failed to see a forest of Black hands going up over the first fifteen or twenty minutes, despite his announced intention to bring together all groups. A White professor watched the process. "I don't believe it," he said and thus succinctly stated the process of denial that was struggling to remain alive in his own mind.

Unlike the serene patrician merchant secure in his remoteness from "the poor," some sadistic, guilty Whites fear retaliation by Blacks. To defend against this fear, they identify with the aggressor and defensively elevate Blacks to the status of gods of vengeance, ally with them, talk like them, and hope thus to avoid the final disaster in which all Whites are crushed by Black revenge. This is an energy-sapping, uncomfortable series of psychological events and therefore one of the least desirable for racist Whites.

Damning with faint praise is a less stressful occupation of skillful and sophisticated Whites accustomed to subtle infighting with White or Black.

"They're all right when they're willing to work," states a White medical specialist from northern Minnesota. "I used to play football with one of them. He was a real smart man, but never quite 'made it.' I still see him, as a matter of fact. He does odd jobs and cleans up a filling station down at the corner. Every time I drive by, he waves.

" 'Hi, Dr. Bill,' he hollers.

" 'Hey, boy, how ya doin?' I yell back."

Evidently the Black man is not on a first-name basis with "Dr. Bill," and the good doctor feels perfectly free to reduce a sixty-year-old man to the status of "boy." Although the two of them have gone to school together and played football side by side and may even have originally been of equal intelligence, a socioeconomic gap has widened between the two of them, a gap which Dr. Bill takes for granted as part of his "superior" position.

The mental mechanisms described in the foregoing paragraphs yield a mixed harvest to the White racist. Techniques of depreciation, self-blinding, denial of reality, paranoia, and identification with the aggressor not only reduce an American's view of a whole segment of his countrymen but also may produce similar attitudes toward *all* his fellow humans because the techniques he uses with "inferior" Blacks he will tend to use not only with many whom he considers "inferior" but also with many whom, instead of understanding, he would like to dismiss as inferior. He thus easily and unconsciously robs himself of many rich friendships and associations. The paranoid racist constantly lives with fear, and the man who identifies with an aggressor is in constant suspense as to whether the aggressor will turn on him. In other words, whatever the brave "front," racists like these live in a fantasy world of dangerous attack and counterattack, of thrust and parry, of sadism and vengeance. And these fantasies consume mental and emotional energies that no person can afford to expend.

On the other hand, although a racist's unconscious mental mechanisms may sap his strength, he may not realize this and may consciously feel comfortable and happy. After all, a man who feels superior because of an unconscious delusion that he *is* superior is in a comfortable position emotionally because he is not aware of the extra work being carried out in his unconscious to keep alive that delusion of superiority. When a man feels that he can "make a nigger squirm" any time he lies, he directs his hostile energy into that channel and is then left free to direct his love toward Whites and may even be known as the "nicest man in the world" to his wife, family, friends, clubmates, labor union, or political party members.

In the racist's heart and mind, the "nigger" (and, for that matter, the "kike, Polack, Canuck, greaser," or whoever) is the victim, and the racist is the victor. The latter then, delusionally to be sure, feels stronger, more efficient, more skillful, and superior to the step-'n'fetch-it who is ridiculed. Prejudices and racism, in other words, are apparently so profitable for many White people that they are pleased and in no conscious way disturbed by these attitudes. In fact, they may crow in delight at stories of lynching and torture.

After all, such crows of delight at human suffering have long been heard. Racism is only one specific system in which people attack each other. There are other systems by which the human race expresses its general antihumanism. In order to give some perspective to these specific considerations of racism, it may be well briefly to discuss the general antihumanistic or inhumane matrix in which racism is set. Such a discussion may partially explain the ease with which Caucasian prejudice operates in the United States.

For purposes of the discussion, therefore, antihumanism might be defined as a generic term for all the ways in which human beings damage each other psychologically or physically within their own racial group or outside it. Racism may then be included as simply one species of such antihumanism. Antihumanism ranges from the physically fatal shot to the subtle psychological put-down, from torture slaying to the sadistic serfdom in which many Americans are held. Antihumanism has a long and bloody history and unfortunately is not a recent and easily uprooted spectrum of sadism. Wars, genocide, enslavement, persecution, and racism are rampant today and will abound tomorrow unless the human race makes the remarkable decision to preserve itself not only by its creativeness but also by giving up its self-destructiveness.

In the face of the glory still accorded by large groups of our population to disastrously illogical antihuman activities like war, it cannot be assumed that the less spectacularly cruel acts of prejudice and institutional racism, which receive their own glory in song and story, will disturb or hold the attention of a nation long enough to get it truly to rehumanize its attitudes to a "minor" part of itself. In any consideration of the emotional consequences of racism for Whites, therefore, one must reflect that, since antihumanism is deeply rooted and has an honored history, we cannot assume that one species of antihumanism in Whites will necessarily disturb them emotionally.

Some Whites may habitually carry out inhumane acts with pleasure, without much change in emotion, or with some degree of displeasure. Group attitudes and reactions may reinforce such prejudicial participation in a racist society. On the other hand, of course, individuals vary widely. Although a large group's sanctions may encourage or permit sadistic acts against members of another group, one individual may not be able to make use of these sanctions because he is emotionally unable to tolerate, for example, such inhumane horrors as the physical and psychological circumstances in which many Blacks are forced to live.

Other individuals, however, may be experts in antihumanism who make use of dehumanizing group sanctions to keep White "nine-to-five slaves" in just good enough physical and mental health to serve as cogs in an industrial, academic, or medical machine. Two health-center secretaries report:

"We're just 'its.' They use us like machines, and when our machinery stops, their interest in us stops." A telephone operator reports: "We're robots in a line with a supervisor breathing down our necks. We don't dare to move, go to the bathroom, do anything except the mechanics of the job." Physicians have been dismissing people as "cases" for centuries. A new-breed mental health executive adds: "Cases produce data, statistics; and statictics produce more money. Get 'em in and get 'em out. Complete cases. Complete cases look good on applications for federal money." A corporate executive calls his personnel director: "Joe, I want a body at that desk tomorrow," and also, "Get a unit behind that lathe."

These individual instances of dehumanization can then be systematized by keeping groups of people locked into jobs far below their human potential, sometimes from generation to generation, not only at low health and income levels but also at such low levels of education that their constricted horizons do not allow them to venture beyond the daily grind. For example, in a maritime state, caseworkers persistently report that entrepreneurs manage whole "stables" of poverty-stricken "worm diggers," who supply the middle-class fisherman with his bait. Many "diggers" are reported to make less than $1,000 a year at this important craft, an income which keeps them alive and existing and able to carry out their work—and little more. These almost-serfs are of course from old American White stock, long rooted in their seacoast towns. The more prosperous individuals who manage the diggers and who collect and market the worms are possibly unaware that these low incomes and the consequent bad health and education perpetuate a kind of slavery because people thus handicapped are simply not strong enough to reach out for their full rights as free men under the Constitution of the United States. They are even shamed out of asking for appropriate welfare assistance by more prosperous members of their local community who sit in positions of some power.

In Maine a newspaper report, referring to a study of the pulp and paper industry, quotes the initiator of the study: "Wage rates among woodcutters . . . are really little above subsistence level in many cases" (Bangor 1971). The woodcutters are allowed to subsist.

In another subtle system of bondage, the busy housewife's personality is blanded out in committees, chauffeuring, and household imitations of a perpetual-motion machine that make it difficult for her to think creatively, freely, and objectively about the world in which she is hustled along from one action to another. Busyness and "flat-out" involvement in a system, of course, also keep a person from having time to question or alter the very system which has mastered him. And at the head of each little pyramid of power sits the master or mistress: a social arbiter, a boss, a professor, a chairman, police chief, or whoever. And he says: "My job is to make the system work. The people are unimportant."

Such systematic use of humans as parts of a machine or system may tend successfully to perpetuate the machine or system, but is hardly calculated to produce a full-blooded, self-respecting, unique human being. Furthermore, it trains him in turn to look at other people in limited terms of their industrial or professional functions rather than in terms of their human uniqueness inside or outside the office.

Such a system traps even those who run it from executive positions. Office get-togethers, for example, are often constructed along the lines of a hierarchical gathering, with the boss still the all-important figure because he is the all-important figure in the business system. Even though the gathering is ostensibly social, the system is really mastering the socialization of the individual humans who watch the boss's every move and react in terms of what he and therefore some given system demand. Says one executive: "I may be a vice-president, but when I go to his parties, I take my cues from him, and I expect my juniors to do the same from me. That's the way it goes."

If a human exercises humane creative talents, he may be

destroyed or become a reject if the exercise of these talents is regarded as destructive to some system: "You're a good mechanic, Mac. Your jobs are perfect. But we don't want that. We want the job to be done well enough to get the cars in, do a little to 'em, and get them out. We want a big turnover and big profit. We have to let you go."

It is unimportant that Mac later turns up at a mental health clinic, unemployed and depressed. The system takes care of its rejects in charity hospitals and clinics. They there become cases, computerized data, and subject to rapid turnover in order to obtain the maximum federal dollar. The system continues to flourish. Meanwhile a self-respecting human being with talents, high standards, and a wish to serve and please his fellows is diminished. This reject takes his place beside niggers, kikes, Polacks, and greasers. And meanwhile the WASP community worker, coming from a middle-class but "genteel" background with some "connections" and correct social graces, has full access to the highest quality of medical treatment, is being helped to recover from any temporary ill effects of his racist tendencies, will realize a great deal of his potential, and in good health will go on to serve the very institutions that have created the conflicts between his racism and his humanism.

REFERENCES

Bangor, Me. 1971. *Bangor Daily News,* May 16, 1971.
Lincoln, C. Eric, and Wooden, Lorentho. 1968. *A conversation about Black America,* a compatible stereo-mono 33 rpm microgroove record. Copyright by Seabury Press, New York. The conversation is between Professor C. Eric Lincoln, the Reverend Lorentho Wooden, and their wives.
Rossi, Peter H.; Berk, Richard A.; Boesel, David P.; Eidson, Bettye K.; Groves, W. Eugene. 1968. *Between White and Black: the faces of American institutions in the ghetto.* Supplemental Studies for the Na-

tional Advisory Commission on Civil Disorders. Washington, D.C.: U.S. Government Printing Office.

Rubin, Lillian. 1968. The racist liberals: an episode in a county jail. *Trans-Action* 5(9):39–44. Summary from National Clearinghouse for Mental Health Information, National Institute of Mental Health.

CHAPTER 5

Some Consequences of Racism for Children

by Jeanne Spurlock

Psychiatric and psychonanlytic work with children shows that racism affects both Black and White children.) Case histories are presented. Adaptive strengths are discussed and also ways which children find to cope with discrimination. Implications of "Black is beautiful" are explored as well as the effects of racism on parents and the price that is paid by the nation for racism.

For several reasons, not the least important of which is that I am Black, I have long been interested in the topic of this chapter. Professional work, as a child psychiatrist and psychoanalyst, with children and adolescents — both Black and White — in both the North and South, as well as less formal contacts with youth who have been active participants in the Civil Rights Movement, has provided multiple opportunities to observe the many ways that racism affects our children. These experiences have prompted the conclusion that the consequences for all children, although primarily for Black children, are negative for the most part.

The situation in which seven-year-old LaVerne B. developed is distinctly illustrative. The Black child, the eldest in a sibship of five, was referred for a psychiatric evaluation because of learning and behavioral problems. The family was intact with both parents living in the household, an overcrowded unit in a public-housing dwelling in a Northern ghetto. Each parent, a high school graduate, had migrated north during adolescence. Both cited numerous discriminatory experiences in their past and current life situations. These experiences were much more burdensome to the mother in this family and were intensified around the situation of her first pregnancy. She recounted the distressing experiences, when she sought prenatal care, of being turned away at one clinic and of enduring the racial slurs "whispered" by some professionals at another clinic, which did provide her with the necessary physical care. So, early in her pregnancy this mother experienced considerable psychological discomfort, focused on her pregnant status but precipitated by society's response to her Blackness. Added to this discomfort in the then current situation was the reactivation of the experience of deprivation this mother had experienced in her own infancy and childhood. Her own mother, who had been the primary support of her family, had returned to work as a domestic within a fortnight of the birth of all of her seven children.

LaVerne's early life was studded with instances in which she underwent deprivation of mothering, experiences which illustrate the passing on of the burden of deprivation from one generation to the next. Mrs. B. had an intense need to be a good mother to LaVerne, but it was equally apparent that she felt driven to have some of her own unmet needs gratified. Frequently such gratification was obtained through the child, at the price of LaVerne's development. For example, the infantile stage was prolonged; Mrs. B. cited a number of situations indicating her reluctance to help LaVerne advance through the separation-individuation phase. On occasion the urgency of the family's reality needs required the mother to supplement the father's income by day work as a domestic. This provoked Mrs. B. to elevate LaVerne to a mother-surrogate role. At times of similar stress, as with an unplanned pregnancy, the mother would turn inappropriately to LaVerne. LaVerne was clearly a deprived child, deeply loved but deprived of adequate mothering because racism had shattered the basis for a fully stable, reliable, nuturing family climate. The nature of her parents' environment *had not* permitted them either the resources or the opportunity to guarantee optimal neutralization and integration of the child's raw affects, the expression of which made for many painful experiences. Significantly LaVerne, like her mother, displayed pronounced depressive features which were clearly related to seeing herself as a devalued person, as did her mother and her mother's mother.

Psychoanalytic and psychiatric literature is studded with references to support the thesis related to the effects of the dominant culture on the mothering experience. Erickson (1968) writes: "A person's and a peoples' identity begins in the rituals of infancy when mothers make it clear with many preliterate means that to be born is good and that a child is deserving of warmth." Although disturbances that are unrelated to ethnic background occur in the mother-child relationship at an early period in the child's development, a mother's own cultural experiences are pertinent influencing factors. Davis (1968) calls attention to the fact that there is a decrease in a mother's capacity to provide emotional security for her child if she is hampered by an inability to obtain the necessary physical, economic, and emotional support for herself in the mothering role. She notes: "The chances for successful negotiations of infantile stages of personal development are significantly decreased for the child of any family at the lowest end of the socio-economic scale, but there will be a larger proportion of dark-skinned children emerging from infancy with specific vulnerabilities to later damaging experience since their families occupy a disproportionately large segment of the population at that end of the scale."

There are numerous references to the residual influence of slavery on the psychological development of the Black American. Pinderhughes (1966) writes that "severe alterations in the personalities, family and group structure, and culture of black people were made forcibly by whites in the slave and segregation systems." Hunter and Babcock (1967) reported findings, based on long-term psychoanalytic studies of intrapsychic phenomena in some Black patients, suggesting that the culture of the dominant White population continues to graphically influence the intrapsychic structure of Blacks. In accounting for the "breakdown" of the Black family, Herzog (1970) suggests poverty as an important factor and points to the experiences of deprivation and discrimination which effect every facet of life of the majority of Black Americans.

The psychodynamics of narcissistic personality disorders, as discussed by Kohut (1968), have many parallels to the burdened psychological development of Black children. Kohut writes: "Under optimal circumstances the child experiences gradual disappointment in the idealized object—or, expressed differently: the child's evaluation of the idealized object becomes increasingly realistic—which leads to a withdrawal of the narcissistic idealizing cathexes from the object imago and to their gradual (or more massive but phase-appropriate) internalization." Should the child experience a traumatic disappointment in the relationship with the idealized object, especially with respect to the regulation of self-esteem, personality development is impaired. For example, the child as he grows into adolescence and adulthood may continue "to be dependent on certain objects in what seems to be an intense form of object hunger." In such instances the child's superego does not acquire the essential elevated state necessary to raise self-esteem to healthy, comfortable levels. For the majority of Black children, the required idealized (parental) object is a depreciated one—made so by a racist society. As Pinderhughes (1966) has so vividly illustrated: "America has structured the white group toward a pattern of characteristics viewed as superior, and the black group toward a pattern of characteristics viewed as inferior."

Contrary to the findings reported by many social scientists, most often by those who are White, there is ample evidence of the adaptive strengths of the Black ghetto dweller. Such strengths are reflected in a report of a home visit made by a psychotherapist working in a predominately Black mental health clinic in the South. The report reads:

The description, as written in the clinic record, of the mother was that she was ineffective, limited, tired, and overburdened. She was said to have provided little emotional warmth for her seven children, five of whom were under five years of age – the youngest, a set of twins who were nine months of age. The child for whom there was particular concern at this time was the four-year-old boy, a child with virtually no speech, hyperactive, destructive, and often uncontrollable. There was more than a suggestion on the part of the staff that had previous contact with the mother that a large part of the problem had to do with her inadequacy.

To adequately evaluate the problem, I felt it advisable to make a home visit. The family lives in a Black Community on the outskirts of the city. As I drove, on a beautiful spring day, toward the family's home, I was struck by the beauty of the countryside – the soft, rolling hills, the blossoms of shrubbery and flowers. I noticed the well-kept, modest homes, each with enough surrounding grounds to accommodate flowers and one or two flowering shrubs. As I made the necessary turn to reach the family's home, I noticed a decided change in the scenery; the change became more striking the farther I drove away from the main road. The air was still soft, the hills still rolling, the temperature still pleasantly warm, but the change was unmistakable. It was as if flowers and shrubbery struggled to stay alive. The houses were shabby. By anyone's standards, the home of the O. family was a shack; the furnishings, charitably described, were worn. Yet, the warmth, the apparent organization, and the strength that emanated from Mrs. O. could not be missed. She presented herself much differently in the setting of her home than she apparently had in the clinic setting, staffed by both Blacks and Whites, which she had apparently viewed as an alien and somewhat hostile environment. Her ability to handle frustration was striking. Her interactions with her children clearly evidenced that she, in spite of the burdens of her present life situation and deprivations of the past, was able to mobilize energy for warm mothering. She displayed an ability to anticipate the needs of her children and appropriately responded, exhibiting much warmth. Limit-setting was accomplished in a nonpunitive manner, and the older children (with the exception of the identified patient, who later was clearly diagnosed as mentally retarded) were quickly responsive.

I could not help but wonder what kind of life would be possible

for her, how much more she could give if she had a few of the
supports that would be available to her if only she were not black in
America.

Specific patterns of behavior are frequently developed
through the Black child's effort to find ways to cope with the
conflicts triggered by his experiences with discrimination. Of
course, the nature of the patterns that are developed depend
upon several interrelated factors, including such things as the
socioeconomic status of the family, local cultural norms, and
the stability and nature of the family relations. Often these
behavior patterns are viewed as pathological and maladaptive by the majority group. Such defenses so employed
may be properly viewed as adaptive in some environments,
independent of the question of whether or not they prevent
psychological scarring. Indeed, there is no question that the
successful utilization of some of these defensive patterns has
permitted survival. Perhaps the behavior pattern that has
provoked the most attention is that of aggression. Too
frequently, the description of this pattern, be it by the press
or the novelist, has been presented in a dramatized form.

Clark (1955a) advises that "the meaning of hostile, aggressive, and social behavior among Negroes should be considered in the light of the following question: Are Negroes as a
group subject to a more general condition of social isolation,
rejection, and frustration than other groups in America?" He
further suggests that "to the extent that Negroes as a group
are still bombarded with negative social pressures, to this
extent a relatively large minority of them will be driven to
express their humiliation and defiance in self-destructive and
antisocial behavior. The importance of race as a factor is that
this is the basis upon which Negroes are oppressed." The
concerns of a middle-class Black mother and father, who
sought help for their sixteen-year-old son, John, illustrate this
pattern. They spoke of their son's active participation in antisocial activities, his growing pattern of renunciation of all

authority figures. Significantly, this behavior was of rather recent origin, had not been observed prior to his attending a newly integrated school. The parents were concerned that John was no longer interested in extracurricular activities which had interfered, or so the mother felt, with his "studies." Additional information (gleaned from interviews with John) pointed to a long history of this lad's experiences of frustration and rejection, many of which could be clearly traced to racial discrimination. The recent experiences had served to reopen old wounds as well as to inflict fresh ones. It was apparent that John's behavior was, to a great extent, a reaction against a racist environment to which he was daily exposed; the triggering of regression had yielded deneutralization and primitivization of behavior. Like so many Black youths, John had come to feel that the social values that had significance for "accepted" people held no meaning for him, one who had been repeatedly rebutted and isolated by society.

With the approach of adolescence many Black children, especially those at the lowest rung of the socioeconomic ladder, come to feel even more alienated from society and become entangled in a life of antisocial behavior. It would seem that this antiauthoritative rejection of society, combined with antisocial aggressive activity, serves to maintain a newly insulated, vulnerable self-esteem. Malcolm X and Claude Brown have provided us with vivid and shocking illustrations of this in their respective autobiographies.

Other survival techniques make for considerable constriction, stunting the development of many a Black child. We see this all too frequently in the area of learning and academic achievement. The majority of Black children who are psychologically evaluated because of poor academic performance display depressive features; they reflect, in so many ways, that they have given up. A striking specific characteristic often observed is the limitation of their range of fantasy. "Why bother even to fantasize," they seem to say. "I can't experience gratification there either!" Erickson (1950) has written about "a colored boy who, like our boys, listens every night to Red Rider. Then he sits up in bed, imagining that he is Red Rider. But the moment comes when he sees himself galloping after some masked offenders and suddenly notices that in his fancy Red Rider is a colored man. He stops his fantasy." The estrangement provoked by such experiences can quickly trigger a sense of inferiority, which becomes reinforced in many instances as the Black child's experiences with the wider society are broadened and serves as a barrier against academic learning. Other Black children cope with the burdens of racism by excessive use of denial and/or the continuous expenditure of energy, seeking ways and means to remain invisible. The energy utilized in these extensive defense maneuvers leaves little available for the ideational elaborations and experiments necessary for creative academic learning. However, the coping maneuvers of other children may well make for extraordinary achievement. My observations of many Black children who have this latter experience support the conclusions of Clark (1955a) and others that this achievement is often reflective of compensatory behavior related to racism. This is not to negate the fact that the teacher's attitudes and expectations are pronounced influencing factors, as shown in the Rosenthal and Jacobson study (1968).

Until the very recent past, the concept of blackness has held an unfavorable connotation for most Americans — Black and White. Blackness has long been associated with sinfulness and evil in contrast to the purity and goodness of white. It has been suggested that Black children no longer experience their Blackness as negative, but they see Black as beautiful. We frequently see Black faces on the television screen, in magazine and newspaper advertising. Now parents can purchase for their young children coloring books which are geared to Black identity; Black dolls are flooding the market. But it is questionable if these changes have erased, for the majority of Black children, the stigma of Blackness based as it is on early, intense, diffuse, and almost preverbal influences. Some Black children with whom the author has had contact, in professional and social situations, clearly indicate Black awareness in their drawings and proclaim "Black is beautiful," yet they reveal negative feelings about Black identity.

But would it not be in the nature of a miracle if these youngsters felt differently since there continue to exist the multitude of situations that daily illustrate that racism is alive and actively operating — influencing the early infantile developmental experience and then intermittently reinforced throughout childhood? How often does the White press give coverage to the activities of blacks, unless the story relates to some sports event or a crime committed? How many history books still in use in the public school systems are devoid of facts related to the contributions of Black America and/or perpetuate myths of inferiority of Blacks? Black youngsters are aware that seventeen years after the Supreme Court decision outlawing segregated education the majority of communities throughout the nation have not complied with the law. They are aware that open-housing ordinances are most often a farce. Certainly, they are constantly made aware, as are their parents, that Blackness is unacceptable to the nation as a whole. Coles (1964) in *Children of Crisis* has presented a vivid illustration of this when he writes of six-year-old Ruby who had been enrolled in a previously segregated school and who responded to her abusive experiences with anorexia and a repetitive question: "Is it only my skin?" I continue to hear similar questions from Black children.

A few years ago I initiated a study (Spurlock 1969) to determine the changes in identification in young Black children as related to the development of Black consciousness. Children between the ages of four and nine, in whom there was no demonstrative evidence of psychopathology, were contacted and asked (1) to identify which of two dolls — one

Black and one White — they saw as the prettier, and why, and (2) to draw and color a picture of a person and himself. The findings of the study were highly suggestive that the mouthing of the beauty of Blackness by many Black children is a reaction formation. A striking finding is that this characteristic appears most frequently among those children from lower socioeconomic groups; that is, they react by saying that Black is beautiful, but they do not really feel it as being so. It is speculated that these youngsters are more consistently exposed to more forcibly racist and rejecting experiences than are other children. These are the children who attend overcrowded schools and who may frequently hear from their teachers (Black and White) comments implying that "they can't learn," "don't want to learn," and/or "all 'ADC' [Aid to Dependent Children] children are just alike."

Seven-year-old Donald P. was identified as a severe behavior problem in the overcrowded second-grade classroom in an inner-city school of a large Northern city. The fourth child in a sibship of five, Donald lived with his mother and siblings in a high-rise public housing complex. The father, who is said to have been erratic in his work record, disappeared intermittently and was last in the home three years previously. The family had been on relief continuously since the father's last desertion. Mrs. P. impressed the interviewer as being extremely depressed, manifesting no indications of a reservoir of energy. The developmental history of the child revealed two strikingly significant features: absence of significant elements of object constancy during Donald's very early years and an intense use of the child for the mother's pregenital need gratifications. As in the case of the aforementioned B. family, Mrs. P.'s relationship with Donald reflected her own traumatic experiences of her early development and the passing on of the burden from one generation to the next. But here we see an additional factor in relation to the profound difficulties experienced by the father. Mr. B., as described by the mother and a paternal great-aunt, fit the description depicted by Davis (1968) of some other Black American fathers. Davis writes:

A man whose confidence in his ability to fulfill the paternal role is low because of inadequate skills, unstable employment and marginal earnings may view the new baby primarily as an additional burden and a threat to an already shaky self-concept. A father, so threatened, is less able to evidence the pride and joy he feels in his child, and less capable of responding reassuringly when the mother's anxieties erupt. If, as sometimes happens in the Negro families at the lower end of the socioeconomic spectrum, pregnancy or birth of a child becomes, by virtue of the above mentioned circumstances, the precipitating factor for desertion by the father, the mother's own security is even further disturbed.

During the course of the interviews, Mrs. P. recalled that her husband had lost his job at about the same time she became aware of her pregnancy with her youngest child and had let out an angry outburst when she apprised him of the pregnancy.

A report from Donald's teacher reflected a tendency toward stereotyping. For example, she noted that his behavior was "typical of the children from the housing project": he seemed to have no interest in learning and was continuously "clowning." In the initial interview, Donald displayed an air of haughtiness. During the course of the interview (and subsequent contacts) this presenting attitude was sharply abated. It was determined that Donald was a very curious, knowledgeable, and sensitive child but had underlying depressive features. When asked to describe himself, he loudly proclaimed, "I'm Black and I'm proud." However, the depressive features and accompanying expressions of self-disparagement surfaced. These were acutely apparent when referring to his father (i.e., "He never kept his promises to me") and his school situation (i.e., "She [referring to his teacher] act like us kids who live in the project are dumb").

It was quickly apparent that Donald's expressions of pride and his air of haughtiness were defensive and utilized to disguise his feelings of depreciation.

This same expression of a feeling of pride holds a different significance for other Black children. Certainly, the theme "Black is beautiful" has other than intrapsychic determinants and has provided many youngsters with a positive feeling of unity, peer acceptance, and protection against the onslaught of a hostile world. I have come to know well a number of children for whom the theme has apparent developmental significance in that it has provided a necessary, though fantasied, ideal ego image.

As a psychotherapist for a representative number of White children, I have had occasion to observe that they and their peers, too, have been adversely affected by racism. In many instances these youngsters had parents who were clearly not active perpetrators of racist attitudes, but they were certainly exposed to the racist attitudes and symbols that are woven into the fabric of American society. These children have also become victimized, be it to a lesser degree than Black children, by institutionalized racism.

Several years ago I had occasion to talk with a White youth, Southern born and bred, who had become active in the Civil Rights Movement. The lad came from a poverty-stricken family and had limited formal education himself. He spoke of his earlier ideas about becoming somebody and of the way in which even the fantasied expressions of such wishes were thwarted. He recounted numerous experiences of hearing, "You got it better than those niggers," in response to his requests for something more for himself (a salary increase, etc.). This was most often voiced by people for whom he worked. As a late adolescent, he felt convinced that he had come to believe that he was superior to "niggers"; simultaneously, his ambitious drive to "become somebody" was diluted. How many poverty-stricken White children have had similar experiences? For how many has racism been used as a tool of manipulation to allow more room at the top for a chosen few? How many have experienced the crippling of self-esteem and the drive to realize their ambitions from the pervasive influence of the fantasy of "natural superiority" which has invaded them?

The arousal of guilt, frequently of paralyzing dimensions, is often a consequence of racism for the majority-group child. The reflections of fourteen-year-old Robert illustrate this crippling effect. Referral for a psychiatric evaluation had been advised by Robert's pediatrician, to whom the parents had expressed concern about the lad's tendency to isolate himself, especially his growing inclination to estrange himself from his father. The oldest of two children, he had been primarily cared for, in infancy and early childhood, by the Black live-in maid. He remembered her with fondness and recalled the many times when she had been the only one to offer him comfort when he awoke from a frightening dream or when he ran into the house with a skinned knee. He remembered her as being so soft and nice and black and how confused he felt when, in the first grade, he heard other kids talk about the "colored people," heard them referred to as "dirty, lazy niggers." He recalled speaking to his parents about this and his father's response: "Martha's different; she's taken good care of you and she's a good housekeeper." Reference was made to Martha's move back South. Then, he didn't miss her too much because he had begun to spend so much time with Little League practice. Recently, he had thought a great deal about Martha.

"Maybe," he suggested, "it has something to do with all the talk I hear from my father. He's always up tight about having trouble collecting rents from his Black tenants. He says they're all alike—no good. How can he say that when Martha was so good to us, and I know some swell Black kids at school? Dad has met you; he knows you're Black. Gee, I just realized that you remind me, in some ways, of Martha." In subsequent sessions it became increasingly more evident that the passive estrangement with his father was rooted in guilt-evoking conflicts.

Renunciation of authority is a common phenomenon in adolescence as the youth struggles with his dependency-independency conflict. For many White adolescents, their awareness of institutionalized racism and resultant cynicism tend to initiate or reinforce their disrespect for authority. This is certainly not a new finding, but one for which many of the majority group have a blind spot. One of the conclusions of the Mid-Century White House Conference on Children and Youth (Clark 1955b, pp. 168–71) was that "confusion, conflict, moral cynicism, and disrespect for authority may arise in majority group children as a consequence of being taught the moral, religious and democratic principles of the brotherhood of man and the importance of justice and fair play by the same person and institutions who, in their support of racial segregation and related practices, seem to be acting in a prejudiced and discriminatory manner."

Sixteen-year-old Susan, an honor student in a surburban high school, talked of her "awareness" stemming from her interest in history. She was at a loss to explain why she suddenly felt driven to delve into the history of slavery. At any rate, she did and began to learn much about American history that was not a part of her textbooks and/or was a distortion. At the same time, she was a participant in an exchange-student program and came to know Blacks other than the household help. As she became more exposed to the "real world," she became more aware of the great discrepancies in what she had been taught and "what's for real." Having always been a verbally aggressive and questioning child, she felt no hesitation in questioning instructors about the value of texts selected for use in her school. She raised the same question and related ones with her parents, from whom she got "double-talk" as a response. The budding cynicism spread like wildfire during her spring-vacation experience of working as a volunteer in a social agency, the clients of which were mostly inner-city Blacks.

Her parents had initially supported her in this venture. Her mother had always been active in several charitable organizations, and she knew her father had frequently made sizable financial contributions to liberal causes. So it seemed as if she was simply carrying on a family tradition. But the more she raised questions about what she saw as institutionalized racism and questioned her parents' support of the same, the less enchanted her parents became about her volunteer services. They expressed concern that she was being wrongly influenced by the kind of people who came to the center and strongly suggested that she abandon her plan to spend a month of her summer vacation working at the agency. Susan angrily exclaimed that she got the same kind of response from their minister, whom she had previously viewed as a "true liberal" who had genuine concern for all people. As Susan's cynicism grew with leaps and bounds, she became increasingly less effective in any undertaking. Susan has experienced a disastrous, intense deidealization of parental imagos and/or the good superego, leading to defensive patterns to protect her from archaic superego remnants. The precipitant is clearly racism.

In each direction we look, it becomes increasingly more apparent that racism affects all children, and most often the consequences are negative. A conclusion of the Committee on Children of Minority Groups of the Joint Commission on Mental Health of Children relates to the devastating effects of racism. The report states that "in terms of mental health, racism is a more pervasive and a far more serious threat than childhood schizophrenia, mental retardation, psychoneurosis, or any other emotional derangement. Its destructive effects severely cripple the growth and development of millions of our citizens, both young and old alike. Yearly, it directly and indirectly causes more fatalities, disabilities and economic loss than any other single factor" (Joint Commission on Mental Health 1969). As concluded in the following statement by the forum, Children Without Prejudice, of the 1970 White House Conference on Children:

Racial policies and attitudes pose a serious threat to our society whose viability depends on everyone's achieving a full measure of growth and development. Discrimination perpetuates poverty, crime, semi-literacy, poor education and poor physical and mental health. While financial costs of eradicating racism will obviously be immense, millions who would have been wasted human beings will become contributing members of society. They will become new consumers for all national products; commercial relationships with other nations will be improved, and welfare spending will be cut. The investment appears to be unusually sound.

REFERENCES

Clark, K. B.

    1955*a*.   The Negro child and race prejudice. In *Prejudice and your child*. Boston: Beacon.

    1955*b*.   The effects of segregation and the consequences of desegregation: a social science statement. Appendix 3. In *Prejudice and your child*. Boston: Beacon.

Coles, Robert. 1964. *Children of crisis*. Boston: Little, Brown.

Davis, E. B.1968. The American Negro: family membership to personal and social identity. *J. Nat. Med. Ass.* 60:92–99.

Erickson, E. H.

    1950.   *Childhood and society*. New York: Norton.

    1968.   Race and the wider identity. In *Identity, youth and crises*. New York: Norton.

Herzog, E. 1970. Is there a "breakdown" of the Negro family? In *The family life of Black people*, ed C. V. Willie. Columbus, Ohio: Merrill.

Hunter, D. M., and Babcock, C. G. 1967. Some aspects of the intrapsychic structure of certain American Negroes as viewed in the intercultural dynamic. In *The psychoanalytic study of society*. Vol. 4. New York: International Universities Press.

Joint Commission on Mental Health of Children. 1969, *Digest of crisis in child mental health: challenge for the 1970s*. New York: Harper and Row.

Kohut, H. 1968. The psychoanalytic treatment of narcissistic personality disorders: outline of the systematic approach. *Psychoanalytic Study of the Child* 23:86–113.

Pinderhughes, C. A. 1966. Pathogenic social structure: a prime target for preventive psychiatric intervention. *J. Nat. Med. Ass.* 58:424–35.

Rosenthal, R., and Jacobson, L. 1968. *Pygmalion in the classroom.* New York: Holt, Rinehart & Winston.

Spurlock, Jeanne. 1969. Problems of identification in young Black children — static or changing? *J. Nat. Med. Ass.* 61(6):504–07.

CHAPTER 6

Racism and
Mental Health Services

by Claudewell S. Thomas
James P. Comer

Working definitions of the concepts of mental health and racism are developed. Consideration is given to how the myth of individual responsibility for illness affects societal structures for services to individuals and the community and how it affects the self-image of the individual. The adaptive strengths of Black groups and the double jeopardy of the Black child as he grows up are pointed out. An assessment is made of the implications for therapy that arise from acceptance of societal and group responsibilities, and final consideration is given to the problems connected with mental health services–their incidence, prevalence, and utilization–with projection into the future for such patterns as consumer and special group advocacy for mental health services.

While the precise definition of mental health still eludes students of the problem and provokes passionate debate when an effort at definition is made, it is generally agreed that mental health encompasses an order of concerns considerably broader than those represented by categorical mental illnesses. We understand mental health to include both illness and health. Most importantly, mental health includes people's feelings of worth in the context of the total cultural and societal system as well as within the identifiable groups to which they belong. It is quite true that some people manage to adapt to society in a way that appears at first blush to be more universalistic than group bound. It is probable, however, that such individuals have come to grips with the issue of group identity and have made a universalistic resolution thereto. Such a resolution implies maturity and experience; and underneath it, if it is to be of any value, must be a positive identification with one's group.

Mental health, then, encompasses the issue of the availability of the "good life" within a given social, political, and economic context. The absence of opportunities to meet basic and culturally determined needs constitutes the gap between individual aspiration and the availability of satisfaction. This gap is the source of a great deal of mental anguish and sometimes precipitates or complicates mental illness. Obviously, such issues as employment opportunity, education, recognition, and some margin of safety for the individual and his family become quite critical. Sometimes the margin of safety is definable in economic terms; sometimes it is definable in social status terms.

For the purposes of our discussion, the state of being mentally healthy represents possession of the ability to cope or function within society in an adaptive way. In this discussion we will address ourselves only to the concept of a positive adaptation. By positive adaptation we mean the results of everyday endeavors to cope which produce in turn a heightened capacity to cope and an increased willingness to engage the society. It is implicit here that the underlying phenomenon which is critical to the above outcome is success in a number of instrumental endeavors.

Racism can be defined as the belief that race, or identifiable physical characteristics related thereto, is the primary determinant of human behavior and sets the limits for human accomplishment. Thus, the inherent superiority of certain races to other races is an important part of a racist belief system (Allport 1954, p. 2). Allport identifies prejudice as the result of overcategorization based upon misconception and closely related to the human potential for prejudgment. He indicates that "prejudgments become prejudices only if they are not reversible when exposed to new knowledge" (p. 2). Allport's definition of ethnic prejudice seems consonant with the sense in which we wish to explore racism in this paper: "Ethnic prejudice is an antipathy based upon a faulty, inflexible generalization. It may be felt or expressed, it may be directed towards a group as a whole or towards an individual because he is a member of that group. The net effect of prejudice thus defined is to place the object of prejudice at some disadvantage not merited by his own misconduct" (p. 2). It is clear from this series of definitions that racism or ethnic prejudice, while it is often expressed individually, is basically an intergroup phenomenon, the malignant manifestations of which accrue to individuals only in the context of their membership in groups.

We also understand racism to be a projective mechanism often rooted in unconscious or preconscious processes. However, racism is also a conscious adaptive mechanism by which members of a dominant group exploit members of a vulnerable group in order to meet their own perceived social, psychological, and economic needs. While it is probably not possible for anyone to be free of the racism based on unconscious needs, it is quite clear that the condoned and promoted adaptive use of racist attitudes is an alterable phenomenon.

In the context of this discussion, our primary concern will be with White racism directed institutionally and individually against Black Americans. We are fully cognizant that racism exists in relation to Indians and Spanish-speaking Americans and toward sundry ethnic groups. We are also aware that racism is not only a matter of White against Black; Adolf Hitler's genocidal endeavor against the Jews, the recent Nigerian-Biafran conflict, the recurrent conflict between Mohammedans and Hindus, and the caste conflicts of India and Japan are convincing examples to the contrary. Nonetheless, it is through the particular window of White racism and its effect on Black Americans that the authors have come to much of their insight. In addition, as the most numerous minority group in the U.S.A., Blacks have been the recipients of the most widespread form of American White racism.

For those of us who are concerned with mental health and mental illness in a statistical public-health sense, a logical emphasis is the concern with group membership and institutional racism over and above concern with individual psychological capacity and individual racism. This is so because it is the basic assumption of individual responsibility for attainment or lack of attainment that must be challenged, not on the basis of exceptional individuals, but on the basis of the predisposing sociological factors extant within society that maximize or minimize the degree to which the individual may make use of his inherent and learned characteristics.

There are direct linkages between the quality and level of mental health in individuals and groups and the opportunities and limits that exist within the society. Such areas as education, employment, and housing opportunity are more directly related to the presence or absence of a desirable quality of mental health than they are to the presence or absence of healthy organ systems within individuals. Social conditions then become a major concern of mental health workers. Racism's effects outside the professional mental health area must also be of major concern to the mental health worker.

Because of racism, a disproportionate number of Blacks cannot enjoy the desirable quality of mental health to which they are entitled. Indeed, White racism—because it is the block between individual aspiration and opportunity— has created a great deal of mental anguish, has complicated mental illness, and stands as a formidable obstacle to the development of all kinds of mental health services. It interferes with the delivery of mental health services at every step of the way, from identification of the problem to the development of problem-solving strategies and the delivery of services. In this discussion we will address ourselves to but a few of these difficulties.

Jack Ewalt, in a review of the approaches to the study of the psychological content of positive mental health suggested by major investigators, came up with the following six (Jahoda 1968, p. 4):

1. Attitudes of the individual toward himself
2. Degree to which the person realizes his potentialities through action
3. Unification of function in the individual's personality
4. The individual's degree of independence of social influences
5. How the individual sees the world around him
6. Ability to take life as it comes and master it

A look at any of the six approaches reveals that the individual's capacity to cope with both himself and the environment is involved in each. However, items nos. 2, 4, and 6 reveal the age-old paradigm of individual responsibility for all behavior and capacity for action independent of the influence of environment. Here again, in terms of statistical reality, it is more than likely that the input from one's environment will produce an adaptive response. The exceptional individual who appears to transcend his environment indeed is the happy possessor of an adaptive response which is deemed worthwhile in terms of behavioral manifestations by the major society, and very often little attention is paid to the internal costs of that adaptation until such time as they show up in behavioral dysfunction.

The myth of individual responsibility for illness constitutes a basic paradigm which is operative in many of the systems that serve ill people. The standard of individual responsibility at times seems to be successfully challenged in the field of general health but appears to be relatively unchallenged as far as mental illness is concerned. This probably relates to society's inability to make up its mind as to whether mental illness is indeed illness or whether mental illness is a form of social deviancy. There are other "crimes" of circumstance that are laid at the doors of individuals; and these also are in an area where societal ambiguity, if not negative sanction, is manifest. Individual responsibility for poverty, individual responsibility for Blackness, or other major minority statuses constitute cases in point. And it is this basic issue, the issue of societal responsibility for individual maladaptation, that determines the structure of existing services. While lip service is paid to the power of social deterministic factors, the underlying assumption is somehow in line with the tradition of social Darwinism, that is, the worthwhile individual will somehow transcend his circumstances.

The model of individual responsibility for misfortune is slowly giving way in the area of general health to a broader acceptance of the need to structure services so that there is some sharing of risks between the healthy and the unhealthy. Even here, it is apparently giving way only for those who are seen by the society as gainfully employed. In the area of mental anguish, mental illness, and mental health, the realities of group responsibility for individual dysfunction are at least as evident as in the case of general health. However, the notion of societal responsibility has been met historically by putting the bulk of mental health services in the public sector. Such services have been structured in such a way as to insure that those who participate in public-sector treatment will receive negative sanctions from society. The comprehensive community mental health center, with its bold new approach, has been a giant step away from the negative overtones of public treatment, but it too has not gone as far as is desirable and necessary.

But even the private patient does not escape. So pervasive has the negative sanction connected to mental illness been that it has even managed to affect the individual private patient within the sacrosanctity of his private therapist's office.

The problem is greatest for the minority group member. The most powerful tool in the armamentarium of mental health therapeusis is the communicative use of another human being for the purposes of resolving conflict. This becomes less than an optimal tool when used in relation to Black or minority people by members of the dominant White group who subscribe to the basic philosophy of assigning individual responsibility for misfortune. When this placement of responsibility is made, it offers the possibility that the individual will understand himself and be able to achieve limited conflict resolution only at the cost of accepting values and standards that tend to deny the reality of minority group membership.

Consider a background-polarizing value that exemplifies the racist attitude within the society, to wit, Black is bad, White is good. Within this basic paradigm a Black individual can find no resolution for his inner conflict because any acceptance that he can find for himself must come at the price of rejecting his Blackness. Any effort in the direction of helping a Black individual must encompass some effort at changing the basic racist background paradigm. Otherwise the individual will have to attempt to deny a basic part of his own identity.

Much has been said to the effect that the basic inequity in opportunity and achievement between Blacks and Whites arises from different familial structures (Moynihan 1965). And the proper solution is seen as the strengthening of the Black family, which is identified as primarily matriarchal with an absent or inconsistently present male. At this point in history it is clear that the measurement of family strength by the criterion of instrumental adaptability in the face of normal external demands is probably an improper criterion for studying Black families. Clearly the yardstick that must be used, is the criterion of being able to survive under shifting, treacherous, and highly vulnerable circumstances. With such a frame of reference, the Black family, far from being maladaptive and disordered, becomes highly adaptive and strong.

From the beginning of slavery in America, racism has affected the mental health of Blacks. Prior to the past half century, however, little was required to acquire good instrumental coping skills beyond a limited developmental experience. Earning a living could occur by the sweat of the brow and the bend of the back. Even oppressed parents living under marginal and difficult circumstances could earn a living for their families and provide them with relatively good developmental experiences and good, if not progressive, coping skills. This is no longer the case. Gaining a living is far more difficult in this age of advanced technology, or, as some have called it, the age of the postindustrial society. A medium to high level of academic and social skill is required if one is to be able to earn even a reasonable living in today's job market.

The makers of social policy have the responsibility for preparing all people for this age of technology. Racist social policy over the past fifty years has produced a disproportionate number of Blacks without the skills appropriate to the age. This policy in turn has limited coping capacity and all the related psychological functions for a disproportionate number of all minorities. The varieties of mechanisms used by Blacks to offset the impact of racism must be of interest to mental health service personnel concerned with the needs of minority people. Likewise, the mechanisms used by Mexican Americans, Indians, and other large non-White groups must be studied and understood. The place of strong and extended family ties must be measured against the emphasis on the conjugal family in terms of the differential requirements of minority and majority group membership.

Farley and Harmelin (1971), in a recent article, systematically examine familial stability issues between Blacks and Whites and note:

The evidence suggests family instability is associated with some- what lower levels of the life chance variables examined. At the same time it appears that in nearly all cases the differentials are modest. Often the effect of the instability factor is much less important than other factors examined in the work cited and by itself the family stability variable does not go far in accounting for differences be- tween the races. One implication of this is that programs designed to strengthen Black family structure in the hope of thereby improv- ing the socio-economic status of Blacks may be less effective than alternate strategies. At any rate, the potential gains from different approaches must be carefully appraised if scarce resources are to be used to maximum advantage.

It is possible to see in such a set of conclusions that there are massive adaptive strengths in the Black family that are missed in the usual overview of the situation.

The very process of focusing on an intermediate variable such as family stability is in the service of the paradigm of individual (here extended to family and group) responsibility for maladaptation. In going one step beyond, into the different criteria that are required for establishing family sta- bility in the face of different external threats, one comes up against the alternative paradigm: that of the societal respon- sibility for individual, family, and group defect. The mytholo- gy that the yardstick can be the same prevents coming to grips with the issue of the overwhelming determinancy of the social process. Again, considered even in terms of the simple yardstick of coping adaptability, the Black child is in double jeopardy while he is growing up.

The first level of jeopardy involves procuring the basic sense of trust (versus mistrust, in Ericksonian terms) which is related to the nurtural figure, the mother, and the degree of security and love which she brings with her into that nurtural situation. Clearly, the prospect of having a basic loving and trusting orientation available for the nurtural Black mother cannot be good in a society in which in the last years of the nineteenth century the number of Blacks lynched in the South is estimated conservatively at three thousand; where in the 1920s race riots accounted for the deaths of hundreds more; where there is an ever present fear that it can happen again (Yette 1971, p. 9). Her chances undoubtedly are below the chances of having such a fundamental substrate available in a White mother. This is independent of the individual vicissitudes to which all individuals are subject. It represents an overriding statistical sociological determinism.

At this very basic maturational level, the interaction between father and mother is certainly important in the provision of some sense of security to the mother. Here again, the Black child is apt to be at a disadvantage. Now assuming that the mother has made a compensatory adaptation so that the major brunt of her inner distress is not communicated to the child; the child grows up between birth and three-and-one-half at no disadvantage compared with a White child who is growing up in a less threatening social system. The child gradually becomes aware of the father's limited instrumental role. With that awareness comes the awareness of his family and its position vis-à-vis the broader society. The societal stereotype (e.g., Black= no good, Black = evil, Black = inferior) is introduced into the child's assessment of self, father, and family. While all the social dynamics are not comprehensible at this tender age, certainly there is the availability for comparison of other patterns that display more instrumental activity of father and family. The story is told by the work of the parents, their relationship to authority figures, and their ability to influence the environment beyond the home. The child observes, listens, and learns.

A burden which the young Black child cannot escape is to see apparent superior White achievement without having knowledge of superior White opportunity. The child often decides that the problem is either with himself, with his family, with his race, or conceivably with all three. Feelings of inadequacy are often associated with these identities, and this association may result in an attempt at differentiation of self away from Black persons. Since there is no acceptance to this particular response within the broader society, this flight from Blackness is doomed in advance, and so the child must accept the societal definition of self and family and the psychological implications of that societal definition. Thus the second step in the double-jeopardy process is achieved. It is unnecessary to belabor the point any further. Clearly, developmentally, epigenetically, the path is skewed, and the slide is greased toward identity confusion.

Therapeutic endeavor in the light of the dominant culture repeats the developmental invitation to abandon one's group identity in an attempt to find exception to the basic racist societal paradigm. Part of the power of the Black-is-beautiful philosophy today is that it carries within itself the repudiation of and possibly even the guilt related to the Black man's having entertained seriously the belief that Blackness was no good. Clearly, in and of itself, it is not a sufficient expiation of that attitude, which is still widely internalized. But it exists on the same societal paradigmatic level as "White is right, Black stay back" and has within it the challenge to the basic societal assumption that determines the available psychological choices for Black individuals. There is thus enormous energy connected to it. However, the useful application of that energy depends once again upon acceptance by the surrounding culture and not only on the efforts at rebirth of the Black man.

The only successful way of dealing with a Black person in a psychotherapeutic mode is to fail to accept and even to raise the challenge to the basic societal assumption and not to offer solace to an individual at the potential price of leaving the group behind. The therapist clearly does not have to engage in the reorganization of his society. Indeed, it is important at some point in the treatment of all patients to help them realistically assess themselves and their responsibilities. But first the interactional set must reflect the acceptance of the reality that the society can be wrong and can be responsible; that makes the difference in the degree of communicative intimacy and trust that can be attained.

We are not suggesting that there is no mental illness in the traditional sense in the Black community. We are not suggesting that Blacks avoid treatment for mental illness. In fact, we expect a high incidence and prevalence of psychoses and personality disorders among groups who live under difficult social circumstances. It is more difficult to predict a pattern of neurotic disorders in an oppressed group, and existing epidemiological data have too many methodological errors to be useful here. We have attempted to underscore a point to which mental health workers have given too little attention—the critical impact of the society on individual development and mental health. We are suggesting that this awareness is necessary both to design and to provide services for minority group peoples.

We have talked about the psychotherapeutic relationship as an example of an area in which the basic racist paradigm can operate to the detriment of Black individuals. The organization of services also reflects the basic paradigm. It has been pointed out in relation to Spanish Americans that, when the therapeutic help is offered in English, it reaches an entirely different group from the Spanish Americans who speak Spanish only and have different subcultural values (Phillipus 1971; Torre 1970).

The problem of reaching American Indians in terms of mental health services is one that is struggled with consistently by various agencies on many levels. Here, too, there is a growing awareness that the key must be the development of a cadre of individuals who can relate to illness and health within the Indian culture in terms of an understanding of that culture and an acceptance of its norms, many of which appear contradictory to the norms of the surrounding White culture. This means, of course, that there may be as many intermediate kinds of helping groups as there are separate and distinct Indian tribes.

The important activity of identifying the incidence, prevalence, and service utilization of mental health services by minority groups is hampered by our failure to study the adaptational impact of society on groups and individuals. Given the reality of societal limits to coping, and the cultural alternatives and compensatory mechanisms utilized by subgroups, we do not know the meaning of figures on mental illness incidence, prevalence, and service utilization. Utilization figures may or may not reflect the efficacy of available mental health services. Relative increase in mental health resource utilization by Blacks may mean little expect that the societal alternatives for Blacks are fewer than those available for other groups. The efficacy of the therapeutic help offered is an entirely different and separate matter. Thus we can learn little from utilization data in relation to minority groups beyond that resources are either used or not used. If they are not used, we are certain that they are seen as inappropriate. If they are used, we have no guarantee that they are seen as appropriate. While it is not useful to present utilization data here, it is important to refine our data-collection techniques and develop ways to understand better their meaning and implications.

A Future Pattern of Mental Health Services

Recently the notion of consumer and special group advocacy has attained a position of prominence within the mental health field. The notion of advocacy, while containing some useful elements, is at the same time a confusing and sometimes misleading concept. It contains ideological elements which may bespeak a moral commitment to the cause of another human being. Underlying this position may or may not be an identification with the problems of the person whose cause is being championed. While there is nothing wrong with this notion of advocacy, it is quite insufficient to deal with the system needs that seem to pervade modern organized corporate society. The following is suggested as an instrumental interpretation of the term which may be useful in developing a comprehensive mental health services system that is more broadly representative of some of the needs of people who diverge greatly from generally accepted standards of health care and for whom the health resources are least available. In this sense advocacy can be seen as a technique for broadening the number of well-informed people who are active participants in the social screen which ultimately separates the serious from the mild defects.

We suggest an advocacy approach which involves a dialogue between the consumer and the technical source responsible for providing mental health services. This dialogue is mediated through the so-called advocate. Advocacy without this assumption takes on the overtones of *noblesse oblige* and is unacceptable as a viable approach to people in this day and age. The person who wishes to advocate the cause of another person cannot do so in the abstract, but must be in close communication with that person and must operate as an assistant to that person until such time as the individual is able to express his own needs. With children the process of advocacy is a necessary and protracted one because of the limited intellectual capacity and social skill that are appropriate to this period of life. Advocacy for disadvantaged adults becomes a different matter. Here it must be antitipated that the role of advocate will be given up at such time as the person whose cause is advocated is sufficiently trained and cognizant to express his own needs.

How can such a system work? A certain body of people trained technically and conversant with the technological side of health care (i.e., professionals), in this case mental health care, is in communication with community people (broadly defined in terms of subcultural identity). Part of the function of the professionals is to exchange with those community people their insights and know-how about the system for health and mental health care. In return, the mental health professionals receive the insights of the community, along with numerous complaints about the system and specifications as to how people adapt and actually live. The possibility exists here for the identification of those areas in which the health care system does not fit and does not meet people's perceived needs.

Clearly, basic assumptions about societal rightness and appropriateness of technical know-how must be abandoned if such a system is to be employed. Armed with the information about the lack of fit between the system and perceived need, the mental health advocate can then proceed to deal with hiw own institution or profession to make known the specific needs of the clientele. This is one level of potential operation of advocacy.

On another level, the original client or client group, armed with the specific knowledge of the more conversant person, can be more effective in making his own needs known. This process in turn leads to the development of a group of people who are more than somewhat knowledgeable about the technical-care system and who preserve much of their indigenous quality that comes from community living. As the number of such people increases to a point where a certain percentage of that community's social screen is occupied by such people, the quality of care demanded will be necessarily higher. If at the other end of the advocacy equation the process is equally successful when the advocate is dealing with his own institution and profession, then the adequacy of appropriate care proffered will also increase.

We have defined a broad educational task increasing the receptivity of professionals within the system, on the one hand, and increasing the articulateness and cognizance of the community person on the other. This sense of the notion of advocacy contains within it the healthy prospect of challenging basic societal assumptions about individual responsibility and the rightness of a system for dealing with human needs purely on the basis of the existence of individual responsibility. This broad model implies that the services should be located within identifiable subcultural complexes. It implies the responsiveness on the part of the system to progressive increases in sophistication in the populace's recognition of need. Such responsiveness is primarily the province of government rather than the province of the private sector although there is no necessary exclusion. This may imply that governmental agencies and governmentally funded resources must lead in the development of such a model.

One of the implications of this model is that a mental health worker from the same subculture as that of a given client has the best chance—all other things being equal—of establishing the communicative intimacy and trust required for treatment. Obviously, all other things are not always equal, and groups who have lived under difficult circumstances produce fewer therapists. Nonetheless, an important part of the thrust of dealing with the mental health problems of Black Americans must be the training of many more Black professionals. It is quite clear that the broadening of the number of cognizant community people—cognizant in terms of some of the aspects of the technical side of health care, cognizant in terms of increased capacity to express needs—also becomes a critical parameter in the thrust toward greater mental health for Black Americans. The basic determinant of Black and minority mental health is within the context that change must be made in the structure of institutions to the degree in which institutions accept cultural pluralism, minority status, and the thrust of self-definition. We see the necessity of moving the mental health care system closer to a position in which, in the spirit of advocacy, it can challenge the appropriateness of institutional structure and the definition of needs.

DeVos and Wagatsuma (1967, p. 18) state in their introduction to *Japan's Invisible Race: Caste, Culture and Personality:*

In the United States the plight of the American Negro persists. Despite ameliorative changes that are taking place, the segregating barrier of caste status has not been completely lowered. The social and psychological stigmas of 100 years of repression after slavery are still visible and will remain so for some time to come. The persistent effects of caste, social and economic exploitation and the continuing prejudice in American society are reflected in the statistics of illiteracy, unemployability, family dislocation, illegitimacy, disease, drug addiction, mental illness, as well as delinquency and crime. Such statistics not only reflect present social conditions, but are also the inheritance of the past crime of enslavement. The *"karma"* of this crime is transmitted from one generation to the next. On the descendants of the oppressors it bestows a brutalizing burden of unfaced guilt yet to be expiated, but the true horror is more keenly felt by the descendants of the victims. In many cases the debilitation of the human spirit is passed on from mother to child and will take the concerted effort of the total American society to break this chain of causation.

We agree!!

REFERENCES

Allport, Gordon, 1954. *The nature of prejudice.* Reading, Mass.: Addison-Wesley.

DeVos, G., and Wagatsuma, H. 1967. *Japan's invisible race: caste, culture, and personality.* Berkeley, Calif.: University of California Press.

Farley, R., and Harmelin, A. 1971. *Am. Soc. Rev.* 36:8.

Jahoda, M. 1968. *The current concepts of positive mental health.* New York: Basic Books.

Moynihan, D. P. 1965. Employment income and the ordeal of the Negro family. *Daedalus* 94:7.

Phillipus, M. S. 1971. Successful and unsuccessful approaches to mental health services for an urban Hispano-American population. *Am. J. Public Health* 61:12.

Torre, E. F. 1970. The irrelevancy of traditional mental health services for urban Mexican Americans. *Stanford M.D.* 9:12.

Yette, Samuel F. 1971. *The issue of Black survival in America.* New York: Putnam.

PART III

Social Context

CHAPTER 7

Black Women in
a Racist Society

by Jacquelyne Johnson Jackson

The first function of this chapter is to reflect on the Black matriarchal and emasculatory theories, with the conclusion that they serve as masks for the effects of White racism and that they imply the subjugation of the Black woman as a sine qua non for Black racial progress. Its second function is to destroy the myths of the presumed superiority of Black women, in comparison with Black men especially, by an analysis of demographic data relative to education, occupation, employment, income, and family stability, and to suggest the importance of the Black sex ratio in any evaluations of Black family life. A third and related function is to stress the imperative of simultaneous priorities for both racial and sexual liberation for Black women now.

Black Matriarchy and Emasculation: Reflections

The overriding emphasis of my round-table presentation at the 1968 annual meeting of the American Sociological Association (Boston) was based upon the immediate need to reexamine theoretical assumptions and political implications surrounding "the Black matriarchy," so as to reduce existing

Especially would I like to acknowledge the varying assistance received from the Public Documents Room, Perkins Library, Duke University; Charles Willie; Ronald Koenig; Robert Staples; Nampeo McKenney; Carl Eisdorfer; Erdman Palmore; Henry Norwood; and others unnamed who have made gaps between the assumptions and reality. I stressed a critical need to investigate with great care the motivations of those persisting in perpetuating myths that effectively place blame for Black social pathologies *within* the subcultural group, rather than *outside,* where it more properly belongs.

The relatively cool reception that my ideas received was not surprising. The White social scientists gathered around that table basically reasserted their beliefs about Black female dominance over Black society. Yet they were alarmed by the then recent riots in which the dominant participants were male and about Black numerical increases in certain cities (most specifically, Washington, D.C.). In the latter instance, I gingerly reminded them that the White House could always be removed to the rolling grasses of Mount Vernon.

My later reflections on that round table were primarily concerned with (a) the guilt expiation so readily available to White social scientists when they employ a matriarchal theory in causal analyses of many of the *effects* of racism, and (b) the striking similarity between much that they expressed and what some Black men in particular *(but not all)* express. Both points, I think, are worth noting.

For example, White social and behavioral scientists dissecting Black families usually employ a social-disorganizational approach, heavily buttressed by a "Mother-God" psychoanalytic paradigm, as apparent in greater or less degree in *The Mark of Oppression* (Kardiner and Ovesey 1951) and *Black Suicide* (Hendin 1969). (To be fair, these specific works explicitly blame racism as a crucial phenomenon in creating and maintaining disruptive or dysfunctional

suggestions about the content of this essay or provided technical assistance. I have used some of those suggestions and discarded others—either through lack of time to implement them or because they were at variance with my conceptualizations. *Above all,* special appreciation must be extended to my daughter, Viola Elizabeth Jackson, for her, at times, cooperative—at other times, noncooperative—assistance in entertaining herself so that I could complete this chapter.

familial and sexual relationships among Blacks, with especial emphasis upon lower-class Blacks. In this respect, they transcend most of the current literature by Whites on Blacks by their continued and emphatic hammering away about the centrality of racism.) Needless to say, most of these White scientists have been overwhelmingly male.

Absent Black fathers and husbands are usually treated much more sympathetically than are Black mothers and wives. Some limited illustrations may be in order. Kardiner and Ovesey (1951, p. 341) call attention to certain characteristics that they feel to be typical of Negro novels, namely, that most novels about Blacks by Blacks predominantly had females as the chief characters, with male fates being determined by them, with few masterful male figures, and with extremely limited dialogue among two people. This is an extremely interesting comment since most Black novelists have been male. Nevertheless, there is a need for a systematic examination, which was not attempted within this paper, of the extent to which White writers, including social and behavioral scientists, have expressed their sympathy in differential ways toward the Black sexes.

In *The Mark of Oppression* Kardiner and Ovesey (1951, pp. 381–82) tend to be more sympathetic toward males than toward females in that they apparently accept the "correctness" of a patriarchally oriented society and are most concerned about effecting economic changes necessary for the establishment of Black patriarchal families:

We wish particularly to stress the effect that lack of subsistence has upon the family. The position of the father in our patriarchally oriented society suffers. He is the great provider and source of all bounties within the family. When he fails in his provident function, his psychological position falls. . . . He cannot be idealized. If the mother can work and does so, the father takes his place as one of the siblings. One cannot retain paternal authority if one ceases to be the source of basic life satisfactions during the normally dependent period of the child.

If the mother now has to work, she cannot be the mother she ought to be. By her mere absence from the home for the greater part of the day, she imposes restrictions and frustrations on the child. She takes the psychological position of the father, in which cases she automatically elevates the female role as provider and derogates the established role of the male. Her idealization is, however, mixed with a great deal of ambivalence; she inspires fear as well. . . . The result of all this is that the affectivity potential of the child is undermined. The child has no one to trust and idealize.

The sex-segregated roles are clearly evident. The mother is subordinate to the father. The "bad mother" does not stay home with her child. Nowhere do these authors question the restrictions and frustrations and consequent psychological damage which may be inflicted upon some wives and mothers forced to submit to patriarchal authority (as if they, then, were one of the children). They also fail to consider those cases where "mothering" may benefit when the mothers are not confined to the home.

Even more clear-cut is the statement by Kardiner and Ovesey (1951, p. 71) that "the basic reason for the instability of the lower-class marriage lies in the fact that it is generally entered on for economic purposes by the female." Thus, the basic blame is placed upon the female. The male is let off the hook. If the statement were to read that "the basic reason for the instability of the lower-class marriage lies in the fact that the male fails to provide economic support," then the authors would be more inclined to shift the blame to the society. If, as the authors have noted, these females were products of families and subcultures where the males could not be depended upon for sole economic support, where they may have witnessed working females (including those who worked to assist their spouses in providing for the families), and where they may have been enculturated to avoid relying solely upon male support, one must then assume that they are extremely naïve females, which is probably not the case among many Black females.

Other instances include a tendency for Kardiner and Ovesey to assume that employment opportunities for Black females have been better than those for Black males: "The
Negro female's chances for employment are better and more
constant than those of the Negro male" (1951, p. 54). As I
shall demonstrate later, close examination of this myth does
not provide the expected substantiation. One finds no sympathy expressed toward the deplorable conditions under which
many Black women have worked nor any suggestions for
improving the conditions for those who are both workers and
mothers so that they may be more effective in both roles,
other than, again, that of mothers remaining home and being
economically dependent upon their husbands. They are basically sympathetic toward those Black males who are prevented from assuming their *proper* malehood roles of subju-
gating women and children.

Hendin, who counted Kardiner and Ovesey among his
intellectual mentors, tends to avoid sex preferences for sympathetic purposes. In his study of suicidal Blacks, he de-
bunks the myth about the greater vulnerability of Black
males to racism (Hendin 1969, p. 44):

The impression that the Black female suffers less than the male
because racial institutions strike so directly at the male's image of
himself as a worker and provider is not borne out by the case
histories. The most disastrous impact of racial institutions seems to
be felt so early in life and so overwhelmingly that the plight of the
female seems as bad as that of the male.

He does, however, tend to place greater emphasis upon maternal, rather than both maternal and paternal rejection of
children, as suggested by the following quotation: "Equally
important, the mother who has herself been neglected as a
child finds it hard to react differently to her own children, no
matter how bitter she is toward her own mother for comparable treatment," (Hendin 1969, p. 140). The omission of
any reference towards possible bitterness directed at the fa-

ther is glaring. In this sense, Hendin and other writers tend to be more sympathetic toward males than females by the rare attention, if any, focused specifically upon paternal and maternal rejection, or by the far greater consideration given to maternal rejection, without having previously established that one can be regarded as being significantly more detrimental than the other. In other words, there is a great tendency to assume that maternal rejection, *ipso facto*, is more devastating than is paternal rejection.

Although the very welcome *Tally's Corner: A Study of Negro Streetcorner Men* (Liebow 1967) provides insufficient evidence to deduce precisely the Black sex group, if any, to which Liebow would be more sympathetic, his treatment of absent Black fathers and husbands appears more sympathetic, more gentle, than that more often found in works concentrating principally upon the Black females. Perhaps this possible difference may be due to the fact that he, unlike most White writers on Blacks, actually knew his subjects through interaction with them in their sociocultural environment, on their territory. They emerge as human beings with feelings, rather than as statistical categories steeped in the misery of their own mud. This latter description is more aptly reserved for the Black females described in *The Negro Family, A Case for National Action* (Moynihan 1965).

While recent studies (e.g., Gurin and Epps [1966]) suggest that the low income mother's influence on a child's decision to go to college is probably minimal — if existent at all among most Blacks — and that of the teacher is probably far more significant, as may be that of siblings and peer group members, Cramer et al. (1966, pp. 143–44) tend to attach undue importance to the mother's influence, as may be deduced from the following quotation from their work:

It might be said that decisions must involve both parties, but with a fair degree of independence allowed the child in order for optimum educational planning to occur. What is even more striking, however, is the markedly reduced level of educational goals for children experiencing either the extremes of parental autocracy or parental abdication of authority. This seems especially true when mothers are involved. When the mother uses either an authoritarian or a complete laissez-faire approach to decisions concerning what the child should do, the chances are especially bleak that the child will expect to go to college and very high proportions, especially of Negroes, may even drop out. When we remember that Negroes are more likely than whites to report their parents as autocratic (especially their mothers), we see another possible contributor to the overall racial gap observed in educational plans. Negroes are again overrepresented in a situation that is associated with low college ambitions regardless of race.

Such a statement tends to attach far too much importance to the decisive influence of the low-income mother with respect to her interpersonal relationships with children and far too little importance to the sociocultural environment in which such mothers and children find themselves; that is, it is not clearly demonstrated that such great significance should be attached to the role of these mothers in influencing advanced education for their children.

In *The Eighth Generation: Cultures and Personalities of New Orleans Negroes,* Black matriarchs are depicted as particularly hostile toward males, as evidenced in the following quotation from that work (Rohrer and Edmonson 1960, pp. 161–62):

The matriarchs make no bones about their preference for little girls, and while they often manifest real affection for their boy children, they are clearly convinced that all little boys must inexorably and deplorably become men, with all the pathologies of that sex. The matriarchal mother usually projects the blame for this result on the bad boys that lead her own little angel astray, and not infrequently attempts to counteract such influences with harsh if erratic punishments, but these frequently mask her own unconscious expectations of her son, and may do a great deal toward shaping in the image of men she knows and approves or fears and represses.

The psychoanalytic paradigm which the authors utilize in

characterizing the matriarchs tends to imply blame upon them for failure to permit their "boy children" to develop. In this respect the study can be regarded as an unsympathetic treatment. In addition, the authors fail to explore more fully the complex dynamics of the situations in which the matriarchs (by their definition) may operate or to distinguish fully between those who would be regarded as matriarchs merely by virtue of being household heads and those who (even if not legally considered household heads) may, indeed, exercise patterns of unhealthy psychological relationships with their offspring, as well as other alternative matriarchal patterns.

Gans (1970, p. 585) tends to be much more sympathetic toward Black males than toward females in that he depicts the latter as being emasculating, while he utilizes social and economic factors in the larger society quite explicitly in explaining the "instability" of Black males. While he depicts the marginal and insecure position of the males, there appears to be no explicit recognition of even the possibility of a marginal and insecure position for Black females. In fact, one general implication may well be that Black females do not occupy such a position, which is probably quite removed from reality. While he expresses concern about the influence of a predominantly female household upon male children, there is no concomitant concern about that influence upon female children. The following quotation from his work tends to substantiate the greater sympathetic stance assumed toward the males:

The reason for [the matrifocal] pattern among Negroes can be found in the fact that in the present and past, they have lived under conditions in which the male's position in the society has been marginal and insecure. Under slavery, for example, the formation of a normal family was discouraged, although the female slave was allowed to raise her own children. Since the days of slavery, the Negro's economic position has been such as to maintain much of this pattern. The man who has difficulty in finding a steady job and is laid off frequently finds it difficult to perform the functions of a male breadwinner and household head. Moreover, when the woman is able to find steady employment or can subsist on welfare payments, she tends to treat the man with disdain and often with open hostility, especially if he complicates her life by making her pregnant. Under these conditions, there is no incentive for the man to remain in the family, and in times of stress he deserts. Moreover, when the male children grow up in a predominantly female household — in which the man is a powerless and scorned figure — their upbringing encourages ambivalence as to male functions and masculinity.

Such literature as this rarely, if ever, considers the undue hardships placed upon those Black women who find themselves having to play both mother and father roles to their children; nor does it consider the possible relationships where the men, finding it difficult to assume the role of household head, may castigate their females by displacing the blame for their own inadequacies upon them instead of upon White society. It is as if many Black women have been the alter egos, for it could be hypothesized that those Black men, inordinately fearing Whites, have transferred that hostility upon Black women.

As a final illustration, let us contrast two statements in *Black Rage* (Grier and Cobbs 1968, pp. 79, 80), with the second statement appearing on the page following the first one:

Mothers have wanted fair girls for their sons and fair husbands for their daughters. Until very recent times, beauty among Negro girls has been synonymous with fair skin and a minimum of Negroid features. . . . *The issue has been of less importance to men,* since male beauty is of less significance in this country. (Italics added)

She . . . is probably fairer than her husband, and in fact most Negro couples are likely to show this color difference. The man pursues the woman, the beauty; and the frequency with which *Negro men choose women fairer than they attest at least in part of the connection in the mind of the black man between fair skin and beauty.* (Italics added)

In the first statement there is an inference that mothers (females) have been skin-color conscious, preferring the fairer shades. Men have been much less concerned, and, presumably, much less guilty in their rejection of darker skin hues. Yet the second statement does indicate quite correctly that many Black men select spouses lighter than they and that they, too, are often concerned (or at least in the past have been concerned) about the color of the mates selected by their children. For example, I have heard any number of Black men relating their preferences for lighter mates. One male friend married to a woman several hues lighter than he informed me that, when he was a college student at a Black institution, his major professor often advised him and his friends to avoid marrying anyone darker than they. The above contrast in *Black Rage* can be interpreted as being more sympathetic toward the males in this instance by the explicit denial that males attach as much importance to skin color as may have been true of the females.

The historical burdens of Black women have been many. They have, in fact, included a charge for furthering the progress of the entire race: "Above all let the Negro know that the elevation of his race can come only, and will come surely, through the elevation of its women." (Kletzing and Crogman 1969, p. 191. We have been praised for furthering that progress and we have been blamed for impeding that progress, as evidenced especially by the Black matriarchal and emasculatory theories. These are unique charges. No other women of any subordinate or any dominant group have ever been so charged. Even now, some persons apparently feel that Black females bear a peculiar responsibility for racial liberation. Much of the basis for this statement comes from listening to speeches and other pronouncements at various formal and informal sessions where the specific topic of the role of Black women in racist and feminist movements was of concern. One formal statement bearing upon the issue may be found in Hare and Hare (1970, pp. 65–68).

Concerns about Black female liberation may be far less frequent. In that respect, it might be well to articulate further the point mentioned earlier about a striking similarity between expressions of the Whites gathered around that round table in Boston in 1968 and some Black men. Careful monitoring of both serious and idle conversations with some Black men since 1968 has led me to conclude that some of them (I do not know the precise proportion) seek to emulate powerful White men. Largely interested in liberation for themselves, they are far less sympathetic toward Black females, for Black female subordination is one of their chief goals. Some even seek to emulate those White men who have or who have had sexual access to both Black and White women. They now seek similar access while simultaneously attempting to restrict Black women to a racial endogamy.

Some Black coeds on predominantly White Northern campuses have privately described specific instances fitting this pattern. They have experienced minimum social activity in that some Black male students, when possible, prefer to date White coeds, thereby reducing the dating pool available to the Black coeds. On some occasions, however, when the Black coeds have participated in interracial dating, a few Black male students have castigated and threatened them. Such highly insecure Black males exaggerate their masculinity—particularly their authority and their right to authority over Black women. Their sexist attitudes reveal their internalization of existing norms and their general failure to emphasize the human dignity of each individual, male or female. Sadly, it was so long ago and now, as indicated by Mrs. Anna J. Cooper as quoted in Flexner (1959, p. 128): "While our [Black] men seem thoroughly abreast of the times on every other subject, when they strike the woman question they drop back to the 16th century logic." This "sixteenth century logic" is characteristic of many of the supporters of the theories under discussion, but the fault does not lie with the sociologist who may be considered "the theoretical father of the Black matriarchy." The late E. Franklin Frazier's matriarchal theory has been overextended by others, as has his theory of Black family disorganization, for example, in the unfair criticism to which it was subjected in *Culture and Poverty* (Valentine 1968).

It is important to examine Frazier's own writings if one wishes to determine his conceptualization of the "Matriarchate." G. F. Edwards (1968, pp. 325–31) has Frazier's bibliography. The most useful source is probably *The Negro Family in the United States* (Frazier 1966). If I am right, Frazier has merely described "The Matriarchate" as *one* of the prevailing Black family types, not the sole type. While its prevalence could not be measured precisely, his supporting statistical data did not indicate that the matriarchal was even *the* extant dominant type.

Frazier's matriarchate is roughly the equivalent of female-headed households. It roots were partially established in slavery. Following emancipation, women who were "schooled in self-reliance and self-sufficiency during slavery" and who were without "the assistance of a husband or the father of their children" exercised their self-reliance and proceeded to support themselves and their children. Often naïve about institutionalized marriage and divorce, their chief perception of marriage was largely "as a means of co-operation in the task of making a living" (Frazier 1966, pp. 102–03).

Not all of the roots of the matriarchate were confined to Blacks following emancipation. Some irregular unions between White men and Colored women continued, although they gradually diminished with "growing sentiment against it on the part of both blacks and whites" (Frazier 1966, pp. 102–06). These women were often left with the responsibility of providing for their mulatto children, but they, too, met the challenge as best they could.

The matriarchal families were "largely organized on the basis of the personal and sympathetic relations existing between the members of the various family groups," with mothers generally exhibiting strong filial attachments, even though they may have, on occasion, detrimentally affected their children through overindulgence, such as the establishment of adverse dietary patterns through food gratification. In any case, many mothers gained prestigious elevation as grandmothers (Frazier 1966, pp. 107–13).

Around 1910, Black family stability tended to decline as the "Great Black Migration" ballooned. But some Black men had long since insisted upon female subordination (Frazier 1966, p. 127):

A worker among the freedmen during the Civil War observed that many men were exceedingly jealous of their newly acquired authority in family relations and insisted upon a recognition of their superiority over women. It was not unnatural.... But it required something more concrete than the mere formal recognition of the man's superior position to give substance to his authority in the family and to create in him a permanent interest in marriage.

Many families concretized that permanent interest through "subordination of the woman in the economic organization of the family." Other favorably developing factors included the male-dominated Black church's emphasis upon male ascendancy and the male purchasing of wives and children from their slave masters, for "in some present-day Negro families of the *patriarchal* type, it appears that the male ancestor's original interest and ascendancy in the family were due in part at least to the fact that he purchased his wife and children" (Frazier 1966, pp. 127–28; italics added). In stressing the inverse relationship between patriarchal authority and female economic subordination, Frazier also noted instances of the carry-over of male authority among Blacks from slavery in that the male's permanent familial interests rested chiefly upon his property rights to his wife and children, whom he had bought from their master and placed under his authority. The institutionalized family was first established by these free Negroes, who numbered almost one-half million before the Civil War (Frazier 1966, pp. 140–41). The subsequent continuing female subordination contributed to "The Downfall of the Matriarchate."

The matriarchate's prestige was not to rise "In the City of Rebirth," although this family type inherited from slavery continued to exist on a relatively large scale. Urbanization induced family desertion and "outlawed motherhood" as well, for Blacks themselves were developing negative attitudes toward illegitimate children. Blacks of the dominant family types in the city frowned upon illegitimacy. These included the upper class, the Brown middle class, and the patriarchal Black proletariat, all distinguishable from the matriarchal Black proletariat. The small group of families comprising the upper class were readily distinguishable from the masses by their higher moral standards and their superior culture. The Brown middle class, a new class developing during the rapid urbanization around World War I, could be differentiated from the upper class through their newness, their salaried positions by and large (often with both spouses employed), and their tendency toward egalitarian, rather than patriarchal, family authority.

Actually, Frazier's typology of "The Black Proletariat" contained three subtypes, categorized by the sex of the family head and the employment status of the wife: (a) matriarchal proletariat; (b) working husband and working wife, where the latter was not completely subordinate to the former; and (c) working husband and nonworking wife, where, on occasion, harsh or brutal male authority prevailed (Frazier 1966, pp. 296, 324, 344).

Improved economic status was not perfectly correlated with family stability, for avenues of escape from paternal dependence did exist. In addition, although the more resourceful would escape it, increasing disorganization awaited those urbanizing Black families evolving "within the isolated world of the Negro folk," unless a socially supportive environment (including adequate housing) was constructed around them to promote organization (Frazier 1966, pp. 365, 367). Frazier's concerns were grave and perhaps no more grave anywhere than those about the matriarchal family in the city. It appears to me that his emphasis upon that family type contained his concern about effective environments to thwart the portending disasters. It should be clear by now, however, that Frazier never characterized the matriarchal family as the dominant family type among Blacks following emancipation. That characterization has come largely from outside the Black race.

One of the most rewarding of the recent emerging critiques of the Black matriarchy is that written by Staples (1970). Although he could not have known it, he expressed eloquently certain of my long-standing thoughts. After labeling the Black matriarchy as a hoax masking "historical and semantic inaccuracies" and noting African patriarchies and absences of any "true" matriarchy, he quickly cites variables, "made in America," contributing toward greater Black female independence from the male. Defending that great mass of Black women defenseless against onslaught on their bodies by Whites and the vile slandering by those insisting that the Black woman and the White male were the only ones free in the South, Staples demythologizes Black male economic dependence upon the female, maternal lowering of their sons' educational achievements, and the "inevitable" maternal hatred by the son. Ignoring those research studies which reveal no sex role preferences by Black mothers, "the practitioners of White social science have not been content with pitting husband against wife but also wish to turn sons against mothers, brothers against sisters" (Staples 1970, p. 13).

He also joins in disparaging the validity of any Black solution dependent upon a reigning patriarchy, for he understands (1970, p. 8)

how the typical black female would react when told that the problem of black liberation lies on her shoulders, that by renouncing her control over the black male, their other common problems such as inadequate education, chronic unemployment and other pathologies will dissipate into a dim memory.

" 'T aint true, 't aint true, and it ain't." A beautiful Black man, may his tribe increase!

Black women have not been idle in this recent surge of literature, with the best single available work being *The Black Woman, An Anthology*. It forces attention upon our arising consciousness that "if we women are to get basic, then surely the first job is to find out what liberation for ourselves means, what work it entails, what benefits it will yield." (Cade 1970, p. 7).

Two of the best articles from this anthology can enlighten any discussion of the emasculation theory. Beale's "Double Jeopardy: To Be Black and Female" disposes quickly of the customary fabled myths and laments the failure of Black people to understand the victimizing brainwashing processes operating against them. Then, proceeding to the heart of the matter, she comments (Beale 1970, p. 92):

Since the advent of Black power, the Black man has exerted a more prominent leadership role in our struggle for justice in this country. He sees the system for what it really is for the most part, but where he rejects its values and mores on many issues, when it comes to women, he seems to take his guidelines from the pages of the *Ladies' Home Journal*. Certain Black men are maintaining that they have been castrated by society but that Black women somehow escaped this persecution and even contributed to this emasculation.

After deploring economic and sexual exploitation of Black women and stressing a societal need for highly developed academicians and technicians, she clearly comes out on the side of righteousness: "Black women likewise have been abused by the system and we must begin talking about the elimination of all kinds of oppression," inasmuch as "Black women sitting at home reading bedtime stories to their children are just not going to make it" (Beale 1970, p. 94). What remains to be said is, "Tell it like it is, Sister."

In "Is the Black Male Castrated?" a successful and rational castration of the matriarchal and emasculatory theories emerges. In the words of Bond and Peery (1970, pp. 114–16):

The emasculation theory, as interpreted by Blacks, is two-pronged, one version being primarily followed by women, the other commanding the allegiance of both men and women. Version number one alleges that Black men have failed throughout our history to shield their women and families from the scourge of American racism and have failed to produce a foolproof strategy for liberating black people. It is therefore concluded that black men are weak, despicable "niggers" who must be brushed aside and overcome by women in the big push toward freedom. Version number two also arrives at the point that Black men are weak via the route that Black women have castrated them by, among other things, playing their economic ace in the hole. . . . Also linked to this thesis is the woefully misbegotten notion that Black women complied with their rapists and used their bodies to rise on the socio-economic ladder, leaving Black men behind. What this all adds up to is that Black men and women are placing ultimate blame for their subjugation on each other, a propensity which fairly reeks of self-hatred.

They contend that Black men have not been stripped of their virility, for, if this castration were "a *fait accompli* of long standing, why the frantic need on the part of Whites to replay the ritual of castration over and over again in a hundred different ways?" (Bond and Peery 1970, p. 116). Good question. Whites try over and over again and are, no doubt, successful in some cases, but they continue to find, perhaps much to their dismay, that some Black men cannot be robbed of their virility. It is as in the days of slavery: some Black men, and some Black women as well, refused to be bought and sold.

Bond and Peery are quite aware of the illusory power of Black women and their *double* victimization, through being both Black and female. They also see through the clever devices that Whites have employed, consciously or unconsciously, to damage Black ingroup relations, and they warn about the dangerous consequences if Blacks accept an emasculatory theory, for one must then accept all the "out-

GLENDALE COLLEGE LIBRARY

rageous misrepresentations of the Black personality." Finally, they recognize, as does Staples and as do all of us knowledgeable about our history, that Black men have been, and continue to be, the dominant sex in Black protest leadership (Bond and Peery 1970, p. 118). Such a recognition does not negate the notable roles of some very prominent Black women.

It is obvious that Bond and Peery do not accept the outrages that have been inflicted upon Blacks. Neither do I. Neither will any beautiful Black men accept these emasculating theories. Black *men* do not need to hide behind the skirts of White society in furthering female subordination, for Black *men* truly in quest of freedom quest freedom for all mankind and womankind. Even if higher education has sissified some Black men, as some have claimed (Grier and Cobbs 1968, esp. pp. 147–52), it is not the case, as some otherwise reasonable Black men are wont to believe, that feminist liberationists are lesbians bent on rejecting and destroying men. Such outrageous indictments mask their male chauvinism.

The simple truth is probably that most Black women are fed up with the disrespect (sing it, Aretha Franklin!) heaped upon us by this racist and sexist society. We know that the Black matriarchal theory demands careful reexamination and perhaps restriction to those for whom Frazier apparently intended it: female-headed families bereft of husbands and fathers. *The vast majority of Black families are not matriarchal.* In fact, the vast majority contain a married couple—a husband and a wife. Husbands are more powerful than wives in some, wives are more powerful than husbands in others, and, in still others, husbands and wives approximate egalitarian relationships. In all, that is their personal business.

Temporary—if not permanent—dropping of the Black emasculatory theory is necessary until such time as no more pressing issues remain to be considered. Whatever male oppression that Black women may have been guilty of cannot begin to equal the oppression imposed by White racism.

Heretofore, Black women have been powerless to control their own lives, let alone the lives of others. Black men clamoring about Black female emasculation must cease their whimpering; they must, instead, put on the armor of battle and confront the real enemy—White racists and their institutions—and stop dodging behind Black women. In so doing, they must also be concerned about Black women, whose lot, as we shall now see, has been most victimized.

Black Women and Demographic Comparisons

A focus upon the specific social status variables of education, occupation, employment, income, and family stability has an added value of directing attention toward major issues currently surrounding Black women. *The overriding hypothesis is that, since family- stability is positively correlated with education, occupation, employment, and income, Black family stability should increase with qualitative and quantitative expansions of the educational, employment, and income levels of Black women.* Hence, expanding Black opportunities during most of the past decade should have been free of sex preferences, although certain of those efforts appeared unduly to have favored males. As will be pointed out shortly, however, the expanding educational opportunities in higher education especially for Black males seem to have been highly ephemeral in that the consistent increase in the percentage of Black males, twenty-five to thirty-four years of age, completing four or more years of college that was evident from 1960 through 1969 has failed to continue into the seventies.

Innumerable examples of sex discrimination favoring Black males, as opposed to Black females, during the bulk of the 1960s have come to my attention. Such actual knowledge and the reports of others were based upon experiences with academic, governmental, and industrial recruiters. Although systematic documentation may be useful in highlighting these reports, since permission was not obtained to cite spec- ific instances obtained from informants, I have not included any here. However, more recently, several instances of less concentration upon Black males in some institutions of high- er education have been reported. For example, it has been suggested that certain institutions may have increased re- cruitment of Black females out of a feeling that Black women would be less threatening to the system and certainly less likely to engage in violent behavior, including the carrying of guns. Careful research about the various ramifications of the Black campus protests upon largely White campuses is cer- tainly needed, including information about dropouts, partic- ularly among the Black students, by sex, matriculating during the period from 1965 to 1968.

TABLE 7.1. Age and geographical distribution of
the Black population by sex, 1970

Characteristic	Females (N^a = 11,885,595)	Males (N^a = 10,786,795)
Percentage base	100.0%	100.0%
Age		
Under 5 years	10.4%	11.3%
5–14 years	23.4	25.9
15–24 years	18.5	19.0
25–34 years	12.3	11.4
35–44 years	11.0	10.1
45–54 years	9.6	9.1
55–64 years	7.3	6.9
65 + years	7.5	6.3
Geographical distribution		
Northeast	19.5%	18.8%
North central	20.1	20.2
South	53.2	53.2
West	7.2	7.8

SOURCE: U.S. Bureau of Census 1971.
a. N = total number of females or males.

In 1970, there were approximately 11,885,595 Black females in the United States, comprising 52.4 percent of the total Black population, 11.4 percent of the total female population, and 5.8 percent of the total population of the country. Table 7.1 shows the age and geographical distribution of the 1970 Black male and female population. As can be seen, about 52 percent of the females and 56 percent of the males were less than twenty-five years of age. The modal age range for both sexes was between five and fourteen years. Although no significant difference characterized the sexes by the proportions under twenty-five years of age, in actual numbers there were more females (6,214,605) than males (6,063,140) or only 97.6 males per every 100 females. Between twenty-five and sixty-four years, we find 4,783,387 females and 4,045,541 males, or 84.6 males per every 100 females, with such numerical differences impacting marriage and family stability among Blacks. For example, the excessive number of females may increase the probability of female-headed households, while the paucity of males reduces the possible husband-wife families. Among those sixty-five or more years in age, there were 887,603 females and 678,294 males, or 76.4 males per every 100 females. Hence aged Black females, as compared with younger ones, are most likely to be without spouses and least likely to obtain spouses, since, *inter alia*, men tend to seek younger mates.

The median age of the Black population is declining, as is that of Whites which is at a slower rate. The median ages of the Black population increased consistently from at least 1890 until 1950. In 1890 the median ages were 18.5 years for the males and 18.3 years for the females. As can be seen, the males were slightly older, as they continued to be through the 1940 census: the 1900 median ages in years were 20.3 (male) and 19.5 (female); in 1910 they were 21.7 (male) and 20.7 (female); in 1920 they were 23.1 (male) and 21.9 (female); in 1930, they were 23.9 (male) and 23.1 (female); in 1940 they were 25.3 (male) and 24.9 (female); and in 1950, they were 25.9 (male) and 26.1 (female). In 1950, the pattern reversed, and the females were slightly older, as can be seen. By 1960, while the median age dropped for both sexes (22.7 years for the males, and 24.3 years for the females), the females continued to be slightly older.

Also the Black population continued to be younger than the White. The 1960 median Black age was 23.5 years; the White, 30.3 years. The 1969 median Black age of about 21 years was eight years younger than that of the White 29 years. Thus, although both racial groups were becoming younger, the gap between Blacks and Whites had actually widened from seven years in 1960 to eight years in 1969. By sex and race, the median 1969 ages were 22.4 years for Black females, 19.8 years for Black males, 30.3 years for White females, and 28.2 years for White males. On the average, the females were older than the males, with Black females being 2.6 years older and White females being 2.1 years older than their respective male counterparts. One immediately apparent implication is that of the possible dysfunctionality of a norm specifying older male marital mates.

Concomitant with the increasing youthfulness of the Black population is a phenomenon bearing our especial attention: the proportion of those sixty-five or more years of age is also increasing. This aged Black population, 6.9 percent of the 1970 Black population (7.5 percent among the females, 6.3 percent among the males), was up about 1 percent from its proportion in the 1960 population. In 1950, 5.7 percent of all Black females were between the ages of fifty-five and sixty-four, and an additional 5.7 percent were sixty-five or more years of age. In 1960, the proportions in each age group among these Black females had risen to 6.7 percent and 6.3 percent respectively. Among the males, 6.3 percent were between fifty-five and sixty-four years of age in 1950, and 6.9 percent were in this category in 1960 while 5.7 percent were sixty-five or more years of age in 1950, with an increase to 6.0 percent in 1960.

This trend may necessitate the reordering of social priorities by age among Blacks. That is, in addition to the continued need for program expansions providing educational, employment, and other opportunities for Black youth, program expansions (such as comprehensive preretirement and retirement services, and ensured adequate housing, health, and income resources) for those in their middle and later years are mandatory. The changing statuses and roles of aged Blacks must be continuously directed toward those enhancing family stability and satisfactory adaptation to old age. Particularly affected are those who may find themselves in quadruple jeopardy because they are *old and Black and female and poor.*

More and more Black women are coming to understand that a longer life triples that jeopardy by their being at least Black, female, and old. The National Caucus on the Black Aged (organized November 1970 under the chairmanship of Hobart A. Jackson) is immediately concerned with the jeopardizing conditions of Black aged, but it also recognizes clearly that the major thrust has to come from a significant improvement in the lives of the young so that when they, too, are old, they will no longer be jeopardized. This is especially important for Black females. It might also be noted that Black women have been among the pioneers in establishing facilities for the aged, as evidenced by the opening of the Alpha Home for Aged Colored Women in Indiana in 1886, the founding of the New Bedford Home for the Aged by Elizabeth Carter-Brooks, and Susan McKinney Steward's service as a board member of the Brooklyn Home for Aged Colored People.

As is also evident in table 7.1, most Blacks were still in the South in 1970, while the remainder were fairly evenly divided between the northeastern and the north central regions (about 20 percent each). The fewest (about 7 percent) were in the West. The geographical disproportionment by sex prevailing in 1970 was not new, as it was clearly evident in earlier censuses. The proportions of males in the western and north central regions in 1970 were significantly larger than those of the females. Black males were, in fact, *numerically* greater in nineteen states. Black females were particularly more numerous within the South. The possible significance of this disproportion may be profitably examined by looking at Black family stability.

Family stability. In general, demographic data provide relatively little information on family stability per se. Indices usually employed to impute family stability include: (a) the proportion of female-headed households, (b) illegitimacy rates, (c) percentage of minor children residing with both parents, and (d) separation and divorce rates, even though the latter rates (as some writers clearly recognize) are measures of *marital* stability, whereas the former also really reflect marital rates as well. Also, the usual encroachment of the social disorganizational approach upon an explication of the various rates deflates the stable and disproportionately inflates the relatively fewer instable ones.

To refer again to the matriarchal theory, many erroneously assume that slavery is a sufficient explanation for contemporary Black marital and familial patterns, despite Frazier's valid pronouncement that "the progressive stabilization of Negro family life continued throughout the nineteenth century and during the first decade of the twentieth" (G. F. Edwards 1968, p. 10). Notwithstanding certain factors rooted in slavery, social factors that continue to emerge since then (including urbanization) have probably had the greatest impact upon the existing Black marital and familial patterns.

Data in table 7.2, on Black and White marital statuses, tend to bear out Frazier's observation. Unfortunately, however, separation data were not reported in the 1900 census. In any case, while not directly comparable, the data show increasing proportions of married and widowed black females over the sixty-year span with the accompanying decreased proportion of those returned as single. Moreover, the data suggest in-

TABLE 7.2. Black and White marital statuses
by sex, 1900, 1940, and 1960

Marital Status and Year	Black Females	Black Males	White Females	White Males
Percentage base	100.0%	100.0%	100.0%	100.0%
1900, 15 + years of age[a]				
Single	39.8%	39.2%	40.1%	39.7%
Married	55.5	54.0	55.4	54.9
Widowed	4.3	5.8	4.0	4.5
Divorced	0.2	0.4	0.3	0.4
Unknown	0.2	0.6	0.2	0.6
1940, 15 + years of age[b]				
Single	23.9%	33.5%	26.0%	33.2%
Married	58.5	60.0	61.2	61.3
Married, spouse absent	14.3	12.1	4.3	4.4
Widowed	15.8	5.5	11.1	4.2
Divorced	1.7	1.0	1.7	1.3
1960, 14 + years of age[b]				
Single	22.3%	30.5%	18.7%	24.5%
Married	60.1	62.1	66.5	69.9
Separated	8.3	5.6	1.3	1.0
Widowed	14.0	4.9	12.0	3.5
Divorced	3.6	2.4	2.7	2.1

SOURCES: U.S. Census Office 1902; U.S. Bureau of Census 1943*b* and 1964.
a. Data for Whites in 1900 are for native Whites of native parentage only.
b. Data for Blacks in 1940 and 1960 are for all non-Whites.

creasing shifts in marital statuses since slavery (i.e., greater movement within and outside of the category of married, with spouse), which are insufficiently explained by those patterns found within slavery. Consequently, the matriarchal theory is far less potent today in analyzing marital disorganization than are economic theories, as demonstrated by the relationships Moynihan (1965) showed between rates of Black male unemployment and female-headed households.

Precise comparisons of Black and White marital statuses are prohibited inasmuch as the 1900 data shown for Whites were for natives of native parentage only, and the 1940 and 1960 Black data were, in fact, non-White data. However, the 1900 data reveal great similarity by marital status among both racial groups. By 1940 significant differences were apparent among those married with spouse absent and those widowed. As shown, approximately 14 percent of the Black females and 12 percent of the Black males fell into the former category, as compared with about 4 percent each for the White females and males. In both racial groupings, widowhood rates were higher among Blacks than Whites and higher among females than males. Similar trends, with some rate changes, were evident in 1960 as well. If those "married, spouse absent" in 1940 are equated with those "separated" in 1960, the proportions in all four groups declined over time, as did those widowed, with the exception of White females, in which group the rate rose from 11.1 percent to 12.0 percent between 1940 and 1960.

Also in 1900 White females were those most likely to be single whereas Black males were least likely to be single. In that same year, Black females were most likely to be married and Black males most likely to be divorced. By 1960, although 60.1 percent of the Black females were married, the Black females were those least likely to be reported in the "married" category, whereas the highest proportion of married persons was found among White males. The highest rates of separation, widowhood, and divorce were among Black women. Divorce and widowhood rates were also higher among White women than among Black males.

Most racial comparisons of marital and familial stability fail to consider differential factors affecting those comparisons. Given the strength of the racially endogamous marital norms and the tendency for those few exogamous ones involving Blacks to contain Black male, *rather than female* partners, one extremely important difference often overlooked is that of the racial sex ratios. *Black females have always had less access to mates than have White females.*

In 1850 the Black sex ratio was 99.1 (i.e., 99.1 males for every 100 females), whereas the White ratio of 105.2 (i.e., 105.2 males for every 100 females) contained an excessive number of males. By 1900 the Black ratio was 98.6; the White, 104.9. By 1950 the respective rates were 94.3 and 99.1. In 1970 the continually declining Black ratio was 90.8. This rate appears to have had some inverse relationship upon marital stability in that, as it decreases, separation and divorce rates have tended to increase among Black females. At the very least, the 1970 ratio suggests the need that Black females have for more Black males, for more other males, or, failing that, perhaps for legitimation of polygyny or the sanctioning of other marriage and family patterns.

Until 1950 the census revealed a continued excess of males among Whites, but in that year a reversal occurred, and the sex ratio was 99.1 (precisely the same as it was among Blacks in 1850, one hundred years earlier). Since that time, it has continued to decline and was about 95.3 in 1970. If the female excess among Whites continues and is accompanied by significant changes in their sex and marital norms (as is already evident), one unanticipated consequence may well be more realistic interpretations by social scientists of similar — and earlier — norms among Blacks. That realism may be hastened by the development of a significant cadre of Black and White female social and behavioral scientists. In fact, that hope underlies this entire chapter.

Having called attention to the disparate racial sex ratios, it is now time to return to the geographical disproportion of the sexes among Black people in 1970. The significance of that disproportion is our main concern. Table 7.3 gives the Black sex ratios and the percentage of Black female-headed households within each state and the District of Columbia in 1970. Hawaii, with the highest sex ratio (192.6) was among the states containing the lowest percentage of female-headed

TABLE 7.3. Black sex ratios and the percentage of female-headed Black families and their rank orders in the United States, 1970

State	Sex Ratio	Rank[a]	% Female Heads	Rank[b]
Hawaii	192.6	1.0	7.1%	49.0
Montana	169.2	2.0	24.2	36.0
North Dakota	160.3	3.0	2.9	51.0
Idaho	158.5	4.0	9.0	46.5
South Dakota	157.0	5.0	6.2	50.0
Utah	151.6	6.0	21.6	42.0
Alaska	147.3	7.0	7.8	48.0
Vermont	139.3	8.0	13.0	44.0
Maine	136.9	9.0	9.0	46.5
New Hampshire	130.4	10.0	9.9	45.0
Wyoming	114.2	11.0	13.2	43.0
Washington	113.0	12.0	23.1	40.0
Colorado	105.2	13.0	22.1	41.0
Rhode Island	102.5	14.0	31.7	3.0
Minnesota	102.4	15.0	28.5	15.5
Arizona	102.2	16.0	25.5	31.0
New Mexico	101.1	17.0	24.3	34.5
Nevada	100.8	18.0	23.6	39.0
Oregon	100.5	19.0	26.1	26.0
Kansas	97.9	20.0	27.2	23.0
Iowa	95.9	21.0	28.9	10.0
California	95.2	22.0	28.1	17.5
Virginia	94.7	23.0	23.7	38.0
Wisconsin	94.0	24.0	30.8	6.0
Michigan	93.6	25.5	25.7	29.5
Nebraska	93.6	25.5	30.5	7.0
Kentucky	93.0	27.0	27.9	19.0
Maryland	92.8	28.0	27.0	25.0
Indiana	92.7	29.5	24.7	33.0
Delaware	92.7	29.5	28.1	17.5
Texas	92.4	31.0	24.0	37.0
North Carolina	92.1	32.0	25.8	28.0
Florida	91.7	33.0	28.5	15.5
South Carolina	91.4	34.0	26.0	27.0
Ohio	90.6	35.0	27.1	24.0
Mississippi	90.1	36.0	25.7	29.5
Louisiana	90.0	37.0	27.6	20.0

TABLE 7.3—*Continued*

State	Sex Ratio	Rank*a*	% Female Heads	Rank*b*
Arkansas	89.8	38.0	24.3	34.5
Connecticut	89.7	39.0	30.4	8.5
New Jersey	89.5	40.0	30.4	8.5
Illinois	89.4	41.0	28.8	11.5
Oklahoma	89.3	42.0	31.1	5.0
Missouri	89.1	43.0	28.8	11.5
Massachusetts	88.6	45.0	34.3	1.0
Georgia	88.6	45.0	28.6	14.0
District of Columbia	88.6	45.0	28.7	13.0
Tennessee	88.3	47.5	27.9	22.0
Pennsylvania	88.3	47.5	31.3	4.0
Alabama	88.0	49.0	27.4	21.0
West Virginia	87.6	50.0	24.8	32.0
New York	85.9	51.0	32.1	2.0

SOURCE: U.S. Bureau of Census 1970.
a. Rank ordering is from high to low, with the state (Hawaii) having the greatest number of males per 100 females ranked 1.0 and the state (New York) having the fewest number ranked 51.0
b. Rank ordering is from high to low, with the state (Massachusetts) having the largest percentage of female-headed families among Black families ranked 1.0 and the state (North Dakota) having the lowest such percentage ranked 51.0.

Black households (7.1 percent). Only two states, North Dakota (where only 2.9 percent of such heads were females) and South Dakota (where only 6.2 percent of those heads were females) exceeded Hawaii in the proportion of Black male-headed households. Both of those states were highly ranked by the variable of sex ratio: North Dakota was third with 160.3; South Dakota was fifth with 157.0.

On the other hand, New York, where the sex ratio of 85.9 was the lowest, ranked second highest in terms of the percentage of female-headed households among its Black population (32.1 percent). Massachusetts, with the highest proportion of female-headed households among all the geographical areas (34.3 percent), had a sex ratio (88.6) identical with those of Georgia and the District of Columbia (ranked fourteenth and thirteenth respectively in terms of highest proportion of the female heads) and was exceeded only by Tennessee, Pennsylvania, Alabama, West Virginia, and New York in terms of lower sex ratios.

Using the Pearsonian r, we find that there is a significant inverse relationship between these sex ratios and the percentages of female-headed families ($r = -0.68$, $df = 49$, $p > 0.001$). That is, the percentage of female-headed families tends to decrease as the sex ratio increases, or the greater the availability of males, the smaller the number of female heads. In general, the highest sex ratios tend to be located within areas sparsely populated by Blacks (such as Hawaii) and outside the largest megalopolises of the country (such as North and South Dakota). A trend of higher median incomes for Blacks within those areas, a greater proportion of Black military families, a greater prevalence of the most resourceful Black migrants, as well as any number of other factors' may all contribute toward this inverse relationship. To be sure, it is not a perfect relationship, therefore not *proving* that an increased proportion of Black female household heads is *caused* by a decreasing availability of Black males. Relationships, of course, are not automatically equatable with cause. But the significant relationship suggested above does warrant causal investigation. It may be that geographical location is an important variable affecting Black marital and family patterns. If so, reasonable redistribution of that population through enticing lures (such as maximizing employment and income levels for the sex that a state wishes to attract) may not be a farfetched proposal for social policy.

The most important point, perhaps, about Black family stability is the need for reorientation of social conceptions of family stability, since, in reality, the usual conceptions are quite misleading as applied to Blacks. For example, a Black female-headed family maintaining itself over time is not unstable. It is stable. To put it another way, the presence or absence of a male head is an insufficient criterion for family stability. Black family stability, then, should not be measured by such inappropriate criteria but, rather, by the extent to which the members meet their functional obligations. In this respect, Black females, in particular, are jeopardized, because they, as compared with Black males and White females and males, are those who most often occupy the lowest rungs on the educational, occupational, employment, and income ladders, as indicated below.

Education. Oft-cited myths about Black women and education purport that they are better educated than Black men, having received their education at the expense of Black men and being less threatening to the dominant power structure. These myths contain some fact, as myths do, but they also contain some fables.

Prior to emancipation, a greater proportion of *Free Colored* males than females received formal education. The first Black recipients of college and professional degrees were males. No Black female received a Ph.D. until 1921, forty-five years after Yale University had awarded a Ph.D. to a Black male, a first in American education. The proportionate excess of Black males in lower education was also an early pattern. For example, in 1880, 38.1 percent of all colored males, five through seventeen years of age, were enrolled in school, as were 37.5 percent of their female counterparts. Illiteracy rates in 1880 were higher for the females than for the males, although for those between the ages of ten and fourteen, the male rates were higher. A greater percentage of Black females were reported as illiterate (i.e., "unable to write") in each census from 1870 through 1910. Thereafter the pattern reversed.

Although highly refined educational data on Blacks were not available in the 1920 and 1930 censuses, females averaged a greater median level of education. But the males were still overrepresented on doctoral and professional levels. In

1940, although females still maintained the lead in gross education, 1.3 percent of all non-white males twenty plus years of age had completed four or more years of higher education, whereas only 1.2 percent of non-White females had achieved a similar level. A total of 0.3 percent of those males, as compared with 0.1 percent of the females, had received further education beyond college.

Table 7.4 contains selected educational data for Blacks by sex. For the years from 1940 through 1970. It shows that in 1960 females had surpassed the males in the percentage falling into the gross category of four or more years of college. That finding may be an oversimplification, however,

TABLE 7.4.   Selected educational data on Blacks
by sex, 1940 through 1970

| | Percentage of | |
Characteristic	Black Females	Black Males
25 + years of age with no school years completed		
1940	8.9%	11.4%
1960	4.2	6.4
1967	2.6	5.1
25 + years of age with less than five years of schooling completed		
1940	37.5%	46.8%
1960	19.8	28.3
1967	13.9	21.6
1969	13.5	18.0
1970	12.1	18.6
25 + years of age completing four years of high school only		
1940	4.9%	3.5%
1960	14.3	11.3
1967	21.3	18.8
1969	23.0	21.4
1970	24.4	22.2

TABLE 7.4—*Continued*

Characteristic	Percentage of	
	Black Females	Black Males
25 + years of age completing four or more years of college		
1940	1.2%	1.3%
1960	3.3	2.8
1967	4.4	3.4
1969	4.5	4.8
1970	4.4	4.5

	Median for	
	Black Females	Black Males
School years completed, 25 + years of age		
1940	6.1	5.3
1960	8.4	7.7
1967	9.6	8.7
1969	9.8	9.4
1970	10.2	9.6

SOURCES: Bressler and McKinney 1968; U.S. Bureau of Census 1970*c* and 1970*d*.

since it obscures sex differences in professional education especially. The gross reversal can be explained by a number of factors. In addition to segregation and discrimination, such factors ought to be noted as Black male participation in World War II and the Korean War and the impacts of legal desegregation in higher education. The impact on legal desegregation of the 1935 *Pearson* v. *Murray* and 1938 *Gaines* v. *Canada* legal decisions may be of particular importance. They led to the circumvention of "equal education" in a number of Southern states. About 1940 the emergence of "overnight" creations of programs for advanced degrees, mostly master's, in education in largely state-supported Black institutions had the practical benefit of increasing graduate education among Black women. The process was further speeded by the increasing requirements for obtaining bachelor's degrees for public-school teaching positions and periodic certificate renewals through more education.

More specifically, almost all the master's degree programs developed in these Black state-supported colleges were for elementary education, where the vast majority of the employed and employable Blacks were females. Far fewer programs were developed in secondary education and in administration and supervision, but, when they were, the latter programs did attract a larger proportion of males. After 1940, especially, when Black female principals have been disproportionately replaced by Black male principals, courses in administration and supervision (serving mainly principals) have become increasingly populated by males. In recent years, accreditation requirements for principals of secondary schools to earn master's degrees have also involved a larger number of males on that level. However, the overwhelming majority of these programs were, as aforestated, largely developed for Black female public-school teachers. Very few of these institutions developed master's degree programs in specific subject content outside of education. When they did, however, the degrees were most likely available in areas more likely to attract females than males, such as that of English.

A few of these institutions developed professional programs, principally in law (as at North Carolina Central University, Southern University and A. and M. College, and Florida A. and M. University), in pharmacy (Florida A. and M. University), and in library science (North Carolina Central University). The last program, about thirty years old and not yet accredited, has always enrolled a female majority, whereas the legal and pharmaceutical programs have catered primarily to males, or, as in the case of some, have closed.

Therefore, the greater female percentage for those completing four or more years of college in 1960 was due primarily to changing public-school teaching qualifications during the past several decades, which meant at the very least that normal school certification no longer met the new standards and that additional education was required for those without the qualifications. Thus, since Black females were largely affected by these changes, inasmuch as they constituted the majority of Black public-school teachers, the proportion completing at least four years of college among them rose, as did the proportion obtaining master's degrees, again largely in education and in direct response to changing occupational requirements. Inasmuch as far fewer Black males were affected by these changing occupational requirements, a similar trend did not occur. Nevertheless, it is significant to note that, without the major shift in occupational requirements affecting them, the proportion of males completing four or more years of college was only 0.5 percent less than that of the females.

As can also be seen in table 7.4, in 1967 the proportion of females completing four or more years of college among Blacks was higher than that among the males. The increase among the males from 1967 to 1969, however, was greater than that among the females, and a larger proportion of males had completed four or more years of college in 1969 than had the females. By 1970 both groups had experienced a slight *decrease*.

In general, table 7.4 suggests that the increasing convergence of the median number of school years completed by Black females and males from 1967 to 1969 did not continue through 1970. By 1969 the gap of 0.9 year, apparent in 1967, had narrowed to 0.4 year, but by 1970 — one year later — it had increased to 0.6 year. Such census data may well point toward the highly ephemeral educational changes previously noted.

More recent census data, shown in table 7.5, reveal clearly that the proportion of Black females twenty-five to thirty-four years of age, completing four or more years of college actually declined between 1966 and 1969, while those propor-

TABLE 7.5.   Selected educational attainment data by
race and sex, 1960 through 1970

| | Percentage of | | | |
Characteristic and Year	Black Females	Black Males	White Females	White Males
Persons 25–29 years old completing high school or beyond				
1960*a*	41.0%	36.0%	65.0%	63.0%
1966	47.0	49.0	74.0	73.0
1967	55.0	52.0	75.0	74.0
1968	54.0	58.0	75.0	76.0
1969	52.0	60.0	77.0	78.0
1970	57.8	54.3	77.8	79.3
Persons 25–34 years old completing four or more years of college				
1960	4.6%	3.9%	7.8%	15.7%
1966	6.1	5.2	10.4	18.9
1969	5.6	7.6	12.3	20.2
1970	6.4	5.8	12.4	20.9

SOURCE: U.S. Bureau of Census 1970*a* and 1970*e*, pp. 51–52.
a. 1960 high school data for Blacks include all non-Whites.

tions among Black males and Whites rose. In 1969 cumulative factors tending to favor higher education for Black males
produced a situation relatively unique in recent years: the
proportion of Black males in the specified age groups completing four or more years of college (7.6 percent) was *greater* than that for Black females (5.6 percent). Thus by 1969, of
the four groups shown, only the Black females had lost
ground. In fact, between 1966 and 1969 the gaps between
Black females and the other groups widened. In 1966, although a larger proportion of Black females than males had
obtained a college education, only 1.1 percent difference
separated them; in 1969, with Black males then ahead of the
Black females, the separating distance was 2.0 percent. But
clearly the Whites continued to outdistance the Blacks. In

1966 we see that 4.3 percent more of the White than the Black females were in the aforementioned educational category, but by 1969 the gap had widened to a separating distance of 6.7 percent. The biggest gap was that between Black females and White males. With the latter consistently in the lead, it increased from 11.1 percent in 1960, to 12.8 percent in 1966, and to 14.6 percent in 1969.

Thus not only were Black females least likely to complete a college education, as judged by our 1969 data, but they were also being victimized by the widening educational gap between themselves and Black males and Whites. However, by 1970 we find that the proportion of Black females in the group from twenty-five to thirty-four years old had *risen* slightly since 1969 (from 5.6 percent to 6.4 percent) while the proportion among Black males had *decreased* (from 7.6 percent to 5.8 percent). The increases characteristic of Whites in the earlier years continued.

The 1969 and 1970 data for Blacks are peculiarly striking and explanations for these patterns should be sought quickly so as to prevent significant reductions in the higher education of both the Black female and male population. It is highly likely that certain years around the mid-1960s were more propitious for Black males, but that campus protests and other activities in the demise of the Civil Rights Movement produced a backlash which affected Black males in higher education more drastically than it affected Black females, whereas a more favorable attitude toward civil rights tended to affect the females more drastically than it did the males. If so, it could well be hypothesized that the major societal institutions in the United States tend to favor Black males during periods of "goodwill" toward Blacks, but, as those moods recede, then Black males are less favored and Black females are either more favored or at least less affected. Also it should be emphasized quite strongly that such data as those presented in table 7.5 do not permit the resolution of the issue concerning the supposed unnatural superiority of

Black females in education. They neither confirm nor deny any superiority of Black females in education. They neither confirm nor deny any superiority for either of the two groups.

The percentage of Black females twenty-five to twenty-nine years of age who had completed or gone beyond high school, as also shown in table 7.5, decreased as well from 1967 to 1969 and then resurged in 1970 whereas, following the pattern noted earlier for college education, the Black males continued to increase through 1969 and then noticeably declined from 1969 to 1970, falling from 60.0 percent to 54.3 percent in this category. Again, the proportions among the White females continued to rise throughout the decade, with the greatest increase from 1967 to 1970 occurring among White males.

These alarming data about the widening gaps between Whites and Blacks as they relate to higher education are of particular significance if one considers the possible impact upon the participation of the Black labor force. Insofar as Black females especially are concerned (since they constitute the primary interest within this chapter), such data should force immediate causal analyses and rectification of what can be regarded only as a highly undesirable situation. While a number of factors, most certainly racism, are responsible for this trend, the issue of Black female school dropouts due to pregnancies deserves special emphasis. It does not deserve such emphasis — let it be clear — because of numerical importance per se, but because of the general lack of sufficient policies and programs permitting such females to continue their education. In other words, since this group may contain a significant proportion likely to become household heads, it deserves significant consideration.

Probably the Black subgroup most in need of improved education and employment is that of expectant and unmarried mothers. In the past many were forced to become school dropouts by overzealous principals, including Southern Black principals. The fact that few of the scant efforts to

improve their socioeconomic statuses and prestige have been
originated by Blacks themselves is an insult. This highly
visible need is one of the ironies of the "world of
make-believe." Given reliable statistics indicating a need for
increased earning powers among them and given a sense of
commitment, Black school principals especially should have
been foremost among those bucking the inapplicable norms
of White society to these women, as, indeed, White society
itself bucked its own norms for its unmarried mothers.

Irrespective of primiparous age, when the need exists,
adequate and relevant education for these women must be
ensured so that they may quadruple the standard of living for
themselves, their children, and their children's children,
with or without a man in the house. In view of the rising
rates for households headed by females, the need is acute.
Present efforts in this direction, although sparse and characterized by varying degrees of success, should be applauded.
Some efforts, of course, are not free from controversy about
their ideological stances.

The existing programs are various, including those developed by both the public and private sectors with various
local, state, and regional areas, such as those of The Salvation
Army Homes for Unwed Mothers or the Florence Crittendon
Homes (as in Charlotte, N.C.). (Some of these programs may
now be in the process of closing due to decreased utilization
because of increased use of birth control techniques and
abortions, the growing tendency for unmarried Whites to
carry their children and give birth in other settings, etc.)
Unmarried mothers meeting the eligibility requirements
have, in some areas, been encouraged to participate in various work-study and cooperative education programs. The
Manpower Development and Training Act of 1962 has been
of some assistance through its institutional vocational training courses and its on-the-job training (OJT) programs. A
number of the women enrolled under the institutional vocational training program have been disadvantaged Blacks,

such as female heads of welfare families. Many serious problems which these women may have encountered, such as the
failure to obtain employment after satisfactory completion of
such programs, can usually be attributed to factors external to
the women themselves. Other programs include the Neighborhood Youth Corps, New Careers, Special Impact, and
Work Incentive Program, and the Concentrated Employment
Program.

Lest there be any undue exaggeration of the scope of the
problems of Black female school dropouts due to pregnancies, it should be strongly emphasized that the actual
number of students so affected is very small, certainly far less
than 5 percent. It is not the size of the problem which is of
concern but the fact that, no matter how small that problem
may be, each such individual should have the right to continue her education. Provisions should be incorporated into all
public school systems for that purpose. Illegitimacy data are
highly inaccurate for all the usual reasons. In addition,
such data never reveal the race of the father. Nevertheless,
some indication of the size of this problem may be found by
inspecting the 1967 data in *Vital Statistics of the United
States*, 1967 (U.S. Department of HEW 1969). Although the
non-White illegitimate rates among teen-agers have been
declining, the rate for those under fifteen years of age in 1967
was 891.6 per 1,000 births for that age group (up from the
1966 rate of 878.8). For those from fifteen to seventeen years
of age, the rate was 656.7 as compared with 635.2 in 1966;
and for those from eighteen to nineteen years of age, the
1967 rate was 416.5 and the 1966 rate, 400.4. In terms of
actual numbers involved, data based upon the thirty-five reporting states in 1967 indicate that a total of 4,052 mothers
under fifteen years of age were included, as were 63,840
between the ages of fifteen and nineteen years. We could
then estimate that about 100,000 non-White females under
twenty years of age would represent the maximum range of
our population of concern. If so, to reiterate, we are referring

only to a very small proportion of Black female teen-agers, *inasmuch as the overwhelming majority of them do not become school dropouts due to pregnancy. Such a label is probably applicable to far less, again, than 5 percent of that population.*

The second factor mentioned above — that of the probability of greater concern about higher education for Black males than for Black females — is, of course, potentially controversial. There are at least two aspects surrounding this issue. A more obvious one can be said to be the critical need for increased higher education among both sexes. If so, the chauvinistic motives of those disagreeing with that conception need continued exposure. One current disaster may be the probable preference for Black males, as opposed to females, which is apparently evident in many college and university admissions and scholarship policies. I have made this assertion primarily from examining a number of requests for assistance in recruitment from largely White institutions made to me and innumerable friends and acquaintances. Most often, definite male preferences have been explicitly stated or can be inferred (particularly so for graduate and professional schools, including, interestingly enough, candidates for school of social work). My experiences do not extend much beyond the liberal arts and sciences, social work, law, and medicine (and in the last instance does not include nurses, pharmacists, and technologists). Most of the top-level administrators of these institutions and of the specific degree-granting programs are male. Most tend to justify their male preferences on the grounds that Black males are more in need of higher education (particularly beyond college) than are the females. Quite recently, however, some institutions appear to be interested in "killing two birds with one stone" by filling their racial and sex quotas with a minimum number of Black females. Such a strategy, if successful, is less likely to affect spaces for White males. One policy in such instances of racial and sex quotas should be that an individual *cannot* be counted in more than one category (e.g., one may be counted either as female or as Black).

A second aspect is far less clear. It may be, perhaps, that the developing saturation points in the need for most public school teaching positions, coupled with the increasing influx of males into these traditionally female slots, may have been reached. It may also be, as shall again be noted later, that school desegregation has reduced a need for Black teachers in the Southern public schools especially. If so, it could well be the case that some Black females who, in earlier years, would have readily sought higher education with the assurance of a teaching position upon graduation are now less likely to embark upon such a course and less likely to be motivated by others to follow that course. Thus changes in the proportion seeking to complete at least four years of college may be evident, as shown in table 7.5. In fact, some of those females who would earlier have been channeled into four-year colleges to prepare for teaching are probably now being channeled into the various two-year business colleges sprouting up around the country, including the South. If this is so, then there is clear support for the *utilitarian theory of Black female education.*

Scanzoni, in indicating that Black females accrued certain socioeconomic gains from having greater access than did Black males, to the opportunity structure, especially between 1865 and 1914, has held that even now "black females complete more years in school than do black males and are more represented than they in high status occupations" (Scanzoni 1971, p. 6). As I have already shown, recent data do not bear out this assumption if one examines more closely specific educational levels and age groups, for we found that, in 1969, a larger proportion of Black males from twenty-five to thirty-four years of age than Black females were more likely to have obtained formal education at or beyond the high school level. As will be shown in greater detail later, the overrepresentation of Black females in the high-status occupations as suggested by Scanzoni is much too pat. Modification of that statement is definitely in order, inasmuch as a majority of the lower-status positions with the "high-status" positions are held by Black females (e.g., elementary public school teachers, librarians, nurses, and social workers), while a majority of the higher-status positions within the "high-status" positions are held by the males (e.g., physicians, dentists, lawyers, judges, and college presidents). Scanzoni seems to lose sight of the far more refined generalizations about education among Blacks, as do Bressler and McKenney (1968, p. 17) when they simply note, without sufficient further qualification, that "the Negro woman has generally surpassed the Negro man in attaining a higher level of education."

Now, let us return to the utilitarian theory of Black female education (i.e., education as a means to an occupation to produce income needed for living): the educational motivation of Black women has been largely work oriented (Noble 1956). If this is so, as all available evidence suggests, then *Black women have probably not been better educated than Black men*. If "better educated" is defined as greater and wider access to employment, then Black women have clearly not been better educated across the board. Those receiving a college education have been far more restricted than have the males, and the greater educational restriction has obvious consequences for occupational restriction.

Both Scanzoni's and Bressler and McKenney's observations about the greater educational level of the Black female become quite trivial upon examination of the precise differences to which they refer. It may be recalled (table 7.4) that the median years of schooling completed by Black females twenty-five plus years of age in 1940 was 6.1, only 0.8 year more than that of the males. In 1960 the difference was 0.7 year; in 1967 the difference was 0.9 year. In each case, *the difference is less than one year of schooling*. In utilitarian terms, what was the real difference between some sixth-grade education for the females and some fifth-grade education for the males in 1940 or between some ninth-grade education for the females and some eighth-grade education for the males in 1967? There is literally no difference. This is another instance when comparisons are less useful than are analyses about the extent of education and programs to improve that education for both Black females and Black males.

The greater victimization of Black women in higher education, due to their greater restriction to largely elementary education — and, hence, to elementary schoolteaching as an occupation — has already been mentioned. For those who may be unaware, it is also important to note that educated Black women (i.e., those completing at least college) have more likely been overrepresented in Black colleges and universities, *with the critical exception of professional programs* (as at Howard University and Meharry Medical College), and seriously underrepresented in the most prestigious American colleges and universities than have Black males. It is not without significance that two of the four Black fraternities were originated at White institutions (Kappa Alpha Psi at Indiana University and Alpha Phi Alpha at Cornell University), whereas all of the Black sororities were formed at Black institutions. Even more important historically is the greater conferring of undergraduate degrees by prestigious White institions upon Black males than upon females. If it is the case, as some of us would agree, that the best education available within the United States has been that available at the Harvards, the Browns, the Radcliffes, the Yales, and others in that genre, then it would follow that the subjugation of Black females to more inferior higher education (as that available, for example, in segregated state-supported institutions) has always exceeded that of Black males, since Black females have formed the bulk of the student population at these Black institutions. If it is the case, as some others of us would agree, that there have been differences in the education received from the most prestigious institutions and those which were Black (and especially, again, the state-supported institutions), it would then follow that the Black female's education has been different from that of the Black male. It is true, of course, that some few Black women have graduated from the most prestigious American institutions and that many Black males have graduated from the Black state-supported institutions.

Black parents, mothers and fathers, to the best of their abilities and circumstances, have usually motivated their children, girls and boys, to seek an adequate education. To be sure, they have often failed, with such failure probably more attributable to external than to familial factors. But these high parental aspirations are often measured merely by the children's educational accomplishments, as if they were synonymous. Such measurement may provide mistaken support for the myth of parental (most often, read mother) preference for more education for their daughters than their sons.

Additionally, many parents may operate within the realm of the possible. Their reported educational preferences for females may represent a realistic perception of available labor force openings. Studies about these educational preferences by sex rarely report concomitant data on desired and expected incomes and occupations for male and female children. A probable finding of such a study would be that even when the parental educational preference favors the female, the income and occupational preferences favor the male. These studies also fail to correlate the parental perception of the child's educability with the sexual preferences.

Typically, Black females have been judged as more academically successful in elementary and secondary schools that Black males. Admittedly, this may be an artifact of the school environment. Although there is no definitive proof, it could also be that those Black females in those specific instances may have been intellectually superior to those Black males with whom they were in competition. It has been suggested elsewhere that, at the very highest levels of education, those women admitted to various programs tended to be scholastically superior as a group to the men within those programs, largely because admitting procedures included a wider latitude of scholastic competence for the males (Bernard 1964).

A realistic historical assessment of Black preferences for more education for females, where preferences may have existed, should be functionally related to the greater educational requirements for obtaining an occupation as a public school teacher, with almost the only other visible occupation for Black females then being that of domestic employment, whereas most educational requirements for occupations open to the males (generally at higher income levels) were not so stringent. Hence, what has usually been translated as a greater preference for educating a daughter than a son may really have been translated as merely trying to keep the daughters away from "Mr. Charlie's house" as a domestic servant and as a more vulnerable sexual object.

While most Black families have stressed as much education as possible for their children, familial variations, to be sure, have existed. Presently, however, there appears to be no evidence supporting any systematic preference of Black mothers to educate their daughters at the expense of their sons or their sons at the expense of their daughters. The same generalization applies to Black fathers as well. What may be more important are the various associations between higher education among Blacks and such variables as those of social class, family size, and ordinal position of the siblings. In general, the higher the social class level, the greater the likelihood of higher education for Black offspring, with the greatest likelihood emerging for those offspring of parents who themselves had received higher education and who hold high-status and high-income jobs as compared with the remaining Black population. Chances are considerably better for only children and those with only one sibling than they are for offspring from larger families. Among larger families especially, middle children tend to be less likely to receive higher education than are the first and the last born. Parental influence is especially strong for those outside the poverty level, whereas teacher influence appears to be more dominant in affecting higher educational aspirations for Black students from severely deprived poverty families. The lower the social-class level, the greater is the influence of siblings and peer groups as well, as shown by Gurin (1966), which also contains references to recent studies providing reviews and analyses of relationships between educational aspirations and achievements and other variables affecting Black youth.

Some years ago, in his *Negro College Graduate* (1938), Johnson analyzed changing patterns of origins of Black college students. "College students of a generation ago came, more often, from homes of meager education and income, but with aspirations definitely fixed above their status." But "in the succeeding generation there were more high school and college graduate parents; education was no longer a highly exceptional achievement." Moreover, "while the majority of college matriculants still come from lowly homes, which must make serious sacrifices to support their education, there are increasing numbers of graduates, who, in the security of good incomes and familiarity of learning, look upon college as simply a normal phase of the development of children" (Johnson 1938, pp. 90–91). It is probably true that this latter pattern has continued to persist.

At any rate, some Black poverty-level offspring do reach college. Gurin and Epps, in their investigation of such students, have raised some critical issues about the "importance of family structure and early socialization for motivational development." Associations influencing college attendance which they stressed should be noted (Gurin and Epps 1966, p. 35):

Regardless of intactness of the home . . . the lower the family income, the greater is the importance of nonfamily figures (particularly the high school teacher) as influencers in the decision to go to college; furthermore, considering only family members themselves, the lower the family income the less likelihood there is that the father or both parents will play an important role in the college decision process while the influence of the siblings increases the lower the family income. We find no differences in the proportions of the income groups mentioning the mother alone as an influence in the decision to attend college.

Thus it appears that very low-income mothers, including those who are family heads, are relatively uninvolved in significantly influencing college attendance for their offspring and are, therefore, relatively inactive in exercising sex preferences for such education.

In summary, then, it appears that Black parents tend not to exercise preferences among the sexes in providing higher education for their offspring but that, among the higher-status parents, differences may lie especially within the preferred educational curricula and occupational choices they consider to be most appropriate for their offspring by sex. Females tend to be channeled more nearly into the conventional female occupations (e.g., teaching or social work), while males are more often urged into nontraditional (i.e., for Blacks) educational and occupational tracks. The latter generalization is probably also applicable for daughters of highly educated fathers in high-status occupational positions (Gurin 1966).

Pacified, educated Black women? Most have been locked into White-controlled public school systems. Thus very few have been economically self-sufficient or, in lieu of that freedom, economically dependent upon other Blacks (rather than Whites), as is usually the case for Black attorneys, dentists, ministers, and physicians. Hence educated, employed Black women have been less free than men in openly defying the Establishment.

Recent research findings suggest that Black women, as compared with Black men, may be less prone to violence (Campbell and Schuman 1968, pp. 1–67), although it may well be that they are not less prone or that they may have been socialized differently from the males (with violence being more accepted or expected from the latter). It has also been reported that the females tend to find more meaning in civil rights demonstrations (Butler and Carr 1968). Comparatively fewer social conformists may be among the female ranks as well (Iscoe, Williams, and Harvey 1964). One study has specifically suggested that mothers of those children arrested for rioting in one metropolitan city may have unconsciously encouraged that behavior by leaving those children unattended at that critical time (Komisaruk and Pearson 1968). As previously noted, Black men have always been more prominently placed in protest struggles, but Black women have certainly contributed to fights against racism in a variety of ways.

There is another sense in which Black females offer fewer threats to the Establishment. Generally the acceptance of sexism has not mandated fair employment practices for Black females. More recently, the employment of Black males subjected to inequitable career-ladder progressions has invoked direct confrontations upon racism. These direct confrontations can still be avoided, unfortunately, merely by hiring a Black female, but increasing attacks upon both racism and sexism can reduce this subterfuge. Black males, then, on their own behalf have a vested interest in attacking these twin-headed phenomena.

A parenthetic commentary (N = 1) prior to concluding this section on Black women and education: to be young (in my younger days), Black, female, and a Ph.D. has represented an impossible combination for some persons whom one encounters. A few, Black and White, simply regard you as a freak equipped with stolen goods. Some apologize for you. Others deny you (e.g., introduce simultaneously two Black Ph.D.s, one male, one female, and the male will usually be acknowledged as "Dr.," the female as "Miss" or, in the South, "Miz"; or verify to a long-distance telephone operator that you are in fact the call recipient and note the exasperation in that operator's voice as she requests again and again that you place the "Dr." on the line).

Blacks and Whites tend to prefer higher educational achievement among males than females (a process of societal conditioning), so one can readily encounter sex discrimination in all-Black institutions, as well as in non-Black institutions. The underrepresentation of Black females holding higher professorial and administrative positions, even when educational training and experience are held constant, in Black institutions extends to the fields of public school education and social work administration. Those responsible for school desegregation apparently tend to prefer male staffers at the outset. Impressionistic judgments suggest that they may be right for all the wrong reasons. I would be among the first to concede that desegregation may proceed with less conflict and friction under such conditions. If so, causes are surely contained within norms surrounding expected male authority.

I, myself, have experienced several Southern situations where my educational attainment surpassed that of White female employees. Usually the racial undertones were onerous. In one specific local community mental health center, several educated Black females were categorically rejected for positions as nurses and social workers by the director (a psychiatrist of foreign birth), despite their *overqualifications*. They were superior to the White females then employed. The inexperienced and racially prejudiced director catered to those White female prejudices. These females believed that it was too difficult for them to view any Black female in any working relationship exclusive of domestic service. The director assumed that the Blacks ought to understand that and wait until the attitudes of the Whites had changed. In the meantime, he apparently considered himself to be free of any racial prejudice inasmuch as he was of foreign birth. However, he was highly supportive of the White females and of a single lowly educated Black woman staffer (who was observed performing cleaning chores for White female staffers not required by her job description), but he highly rejected any educated Black female. That was 1969–1970, in a clinic existing in part to (would you believe?) serve mental health needs of low-income Blacks. Incredible, but the late Malcolm X was quite correct: a *nigger* by any other title is a *nigger*.

Overall, this section about education portends a need for increased education among Black females, currently most likely to receive the least education, as compared with Black males and Whites; for more relevant education for all segments of the Black female population, with especial emphasis upon those most likely to become family heads; and for much greater participation of Black women in liberationist movements. Clearly, Black women have been grossly shortchanged in education.

Occupations, employment, and income. This section emphasizes the myth of greater Black female accessibility to employment. Educational inequities have affected the Black woman's occupational, employment, and income levels, for most have had the greatest access to the worst jobs at the lowest wages. Occupational and employment data in table 7.6 show clearly that males have been dominant in the Black labor force, despite their long-standing numerical minority in the total Black population. Even in 1880 males comprised about two-thirds of all colored teachers.

In 1910 employed Black females comprised only 38.8 percent of the total Black labor force; the remaining 61.2 percent of that force included the Black males. In other words, more males than females were employed. In that year, Black males, comprising 56.5 percent of all Black professionals, held the margin in professional services.

In 1920 much the same situations prevailed except that the total number of employed Black females had actually decreased over the decade, whereas the male employment

TABLE 7.6. Selected occupational and employment data on Blacks by sex, 1880-1960

Year and Characteristic	Black Females	Black Males	Black Females	Black Males
1880				
Negro teachers	5,314	10,520		
Percentage of Negro teachers			33.6%	66.4%
1910				
Negroes employed, all occupations	2,013,981	3,178,554		
Percentage of				
Total Negro population employed, by sex			54.7%	87.4%
All Negroes employed			38.8	61.2
Total Negro population			50.3	49.7
Total Negro employment, by sex				
In agriculture			52.2	56.1
In manufacturing, mechanical industries			3.4	18.5
In domestic and personal service			42.4	8.4
In professional service			1.5	1.2
All Negroes in professional service			43.5	56.5
1920				
Negroes employed, all occupations	1,571,289	3,252,862		
Percentage of				
Total Negro population employed, by sex			38.9%	81.1%
All Negroes employed			32.6	67.4
Total Negro population			50.2	49.8
Total Negro employment, by sex				
In agriculture			38.9	46.8
In manufacturing, mechanical industries			6.7	24.5
In domestic and personal service			50.3	8.4

1920—*Continued*

In professional services	2.5	1.3
All Negroes in professional service	47.9	52.1
1930		
Negroes employed, all occupations	1,840,642	3,662,893
Percentage of		
Total Negro population employed, by sex	38.9%	80.2%
All Negroes employed	33.4	66.6
Total Negro population	50.9	49.1
Total Negro employment, by sex		
In agriculture	26.9	40.7
In manufacturing, mechanical industries	5.5	25.2
In domestic and personal service	62.6	11.6
In professional service	3.4	2.0
All Negroes in professional service	46.4	53.6
1940		
Negroes employed, all occupations[a]	1,542,273	2,936,795
Percentage of		
Total Negro population employed, by sex	23.4%	46.8%
All Negroes employed	32.2	65.6
Total Negro employment, by sex		
In agriculture	15.9	40.9
As craftsmen, foremen, operatives, kindred workers	6.4	17.0
As domestic service workers	59.5	2.9
In protective service, other service work	10.4	12.3
As professional and semiprofessional workers	4.3	1.8
All Negroes in professional and semiprofessional work	55.3	44.7

TABLE 7.6—*Continued*

Year and Characteristic	Black Females	Black Males	Black Females	Black Males
1950				
Non-Whites employed, all occupations	1,882,000	3,528,000		
Percentage of				
Total Negro employment by sex			8.7%	22.7%
In agriculture			15.5	29.1
As craftsmen, foremen, operatives, kindred workers			5.9	5.6
As clerical and sales workers			40.9	1.1
As private household workers			18.9	13.5
As service workers			5.6	2.3
As professional and technical workers				
1960				
Non-Whites employed, all occupations	2,565,000	3,887,000		
Percentage of				
Total Negro employment, by sex			3.3%	10.9%
In agriculture			13.7	34.2
As craftsmen, foremen, operatives			10.4	6.6
As clerical and sales workers			33.9	0.7
As private household workers			21.0	13.7
As service workers			7.6	4.0
As professional and technical workers			4.2	0.9
All Negroes in teaching, except college				

SOURCES: United States Censuses of Population, 1880–960.
a. Except for public emergency work

showed a slight increase. Black males had thereby increased their proportion of all gainfully employed Blacks to 67.4 percent; females were only 32.6 percent of that labor force. One out of every two employed Black females was in domestic and personal services, occupations usually rejected by the males. Although proportionately more females were classified as professionals than the males, the majority of Black professionals were *male*.

By 1930 employed Black males comprised two-thirds of all employed Blacks. About four-fifths of all males in the Black population were then employed, as were about only one-third of the females. About three out of every five females, rates higher than those in earlier decades, were in domestic and personal services. The majority of all Black professionals remained male. Altogether, there were 63,027 Black female and 72,898 Black male professionals in 1930. In short, about eight out of every ten of these females were teachers; one of every ten, a nurse. Almost none were physicians, dentists, lawyers, judges, chemists, veterinarians, architects, authors, clergywomen, etc. The male professional latitude was significantly wider. Males far outnumbered females in all professional occupations, save those traditionally reserved for females — teachers, nurses, librarians, and social workers.

By 1940 the severe economic restrictions imposed upon Blacks by the economic depression of the 1930s were clearly visible. Only about 80 percent as many males and 84 percent as many females were employed as had been employed a decade before. About 66 percent of the males fourteen or more years of age were gainfully employed, as were about 32 percent of the females. Still more males than females were working. Unemployment rates were higher among the females than among the males. About 60 percent of the females were domestics. More females than males were classified as professionals *and* semiprofessionals.

In 1940 the greater male professional heterogeneity persisted. About eight out of every ten Black females were yet teachers, and one was a nurse. Perhaps that *depression* was much more critical than any Black matriarchy in affecting Black male education and employment. Certainly, Black women were not the cause of that depression, which really "socked it" to the Black males. Nor have Black women ever been responsible for any significant hiring of Black males, before then, since then, or now. What is most important is that the actual number of Black employed professionals among the males *decreased* from 1930 to 1940.

In 1960 Black females were still more numerous only within the traditional professions of teaching (excepting college, music, and art), social work, nursing, and librarianship, but the trend toward slightly greater inroads by males was evident. Black females had continued to make some inroads into the traditional male fields, such as medicine and law. However, it is significant to note that, from 1920 to 1960, the proportion of females among Black college presidents, professors, and instructors actually declined.

Comparisons of Black occupational distributions by sex can be utilized effectively in dispelling any myth about greater opportunities for black females, for, as has been partially demonstrated, the only employment opportunities available to these females, with extremely rare exception, were of two kinds: (a) those traditionally reserved for females, such as teaching, and (b) those almost solely reserved for Black females in the South, such as domestic employment. Hence, it could not have been the case that Black females, by virtue of their employment, kept Black males from gaining employment. For the most part, the two sexes have not been in competition for the same jobs, and, when they have been, as in the case of school principals and other administrative positions, Black males have in most cases received the greater preference.

It is a phenomenon that originated after the turn of this century for Black females to have greater access to public schools than Black males have. This "safe haven" for Black female professionals, however, is being destroyed by a combination of such factors as male influx, salary upgrading, and educational desegregation. The resulting competition may be welcomed, provided it produces greater Black female professional diversity and strengthens quality education for Black children. It is well, however, to be circumspect about certain current rationalizations about maintaining Black teaching positions largely "for the sake of the children." More critical analyses and resolutions of the entwined educational and employment issues must be the order of the day.

TABLE 7.7.   Selected occupational data for employed persons by race and sex, 1969

| | Non-White | | White | |
| | Females | Males | Females | Males |
Occupation	N = 3,601[a]	N = 4,768[a]	N = 25,377[a]	N = 44.075[a]
Percentage base	100%	100%	100%	100%
Professional, technical, and managerial	12%	11%	19%	29%
Clerical and sales	22	9	44	13
Craftsmen and foremen	1	14	1	21
Operatives	18	28	15	19
Service workers, except household	25	13	15	6
Private household workers	20	—[b]	3	—[b]
Nonfarm laborers	1	18	—[b]	6
Farmers and farm workers	2	7	2	6

SOURCE: U.S. Bureau of Census 1970*a*, p. 42.
a. N = total number of females or males employed. Number is in thousands.
b. Represents or rounds to zero.

Table 7.7 permits an inspection of the 1969 occupational distribution of non-White and White males and females. Almost one-half of the females classified as non-White still occupied the very lowest status positions, justifying the conclusion that, of the four groups presented, they occupy the worst occupational positions in the United States. Almost two-thirds of all employed White females held professional and kindred positions (19 percent) or clerical and sales jobs (44 percent), and almost one-third of all White males held the highest positions. While the percentage of non-White females in professional, technical, and managerial positions exceeded non-White males by *only* 1 percent in 1969, males were 54.8 percent of that category (524,480 males and 432,120 females, an excess of 92,360 males). Thus, it now appears as if the females may be losing ground. Refinement of these data would probably also yield the typical pattern of females in the lowest-status positions within the high-prestige occupations.

Bowers's commentary on the relative paucity of Black women in medicine also illustrates his linking of the Black physician shortage and the matriarchal theory. He asks this: "Should not the medical schools be more active in identifying and preparing Negroes for the study of medicine—including Negro women?" (Bowers 1968). A legitimate concern. Very much so. But a few paragraphs earlier, he characterized Negro society:

Although Negroes constitute over 10 percent of our population, they represent only 2 percent of our physicians. The Negro society in the United States is matriarchal, as are the societies in West Africa from which the American Negro originated. Slavery was the crucial factor in establishing the dominant role of the woman in the American Negro society. Developments . . . since the beginning of World War II . . . have strengthened the position of the Negro woman to a greater degree than the Negro man.

He continues by concurring with reports that "in the Negro society today, the man is the focus of bias rather than the woman . . . [and] the Negro family prefers to invest funds for college or university in a daughter while a white family prefers to invest in a son." It has already been shown that the stereotypes depicted in the above quotations misrepresent

reality. But, even if Bowers's attitudinal data can be momentarily assumed to be correct, how does his theoretical stance
about Black female dominance explain the indisputable fact
that well over 95 percent of all Black physicians in this
country have not been female when it is simultaneously
recognized that most of those physicians have been trained
in only two institutions, both predominantly Black?

Would a controlling Black matriarchy, I ask, operate in that
fashion? This and related questions hit at the core of the
matriarchal and emasculatory theories, for they seek to determine who has been controlling whom and what! Thus far,
most of the social scientific literature is sufficiently vague on
that point, the Bowers tries desperately to mask the issue by
his adjacent statements about the underrepresentation of
Black physicians in the population at large and the imputa-
tion of the existence of a matriarchal Negro society, as if the
latter were the cause of the former. A rewriting of Bowers's
statements follows: "Although Negroes constitute over 10
percent of our population, they represent only 2 percent of
our physicians. The United States society has been racist,
and the American Negro, male and female, has been victimized by that system created by Whites. The issues of matriarchy are irrelevant in accounting for the failure of this
country to produce Black physicians, both male and female."
End of statement. It may also be noted, in passing, that
Bowers provides another illustration, perhaps even a better
one than those cited, of greater sympathy toward Black males
than toward Black females.

Non-White unemployment rates by sex for 1954 through
1966 do show some rate fluctuations. When non-White males
and females fourteen to nineteen years of age are compared,
one sees that the females had the highest unemployment
rates in each of those years. For example, in 1954 their rate
was 18.4 as compared with the male rate of 12.5; in 1960 the
female rate was 22.7 with a male rate of 22.0; and in 1966 the
female rate was 31.1 as compared with a male rate of 21.2. By

1966 the female unemployment rate was 6.6, while that for
the males was only 4.9.

It is recognized that these rates fail to reveal the true
unemployment rates for either sex, but it may be conjectured
that, if the true rates were available, they would probably
remain consistently higher for females at this point in time.
Earlier data, such as those of 1940, also indicate a higher
female unemployment rate. Thus, such data tend to confirm
the observation that Black males have, in fact, had greater
access to employment, notwithstanding the fact that, in certain years, the adult male unemployment rate may have exceeded that of the female. It is useful to restate the fact that,
except for public school teaching and certain limited service
jobs in particular, Black men and women have not been in
competition for the same jobs. This by no means negates the
specific instances of Black females obtaining employment
when their spouses (in search of different jobs) have failed,
but, even here, studies have not refined their data so as to
permit comparisons of the working potentials of these mates.

Even when Black women have worked twenty-five hours
per day, eight days per week, and fifty-three weeks per year,
their income has been consistently lower than that of Black
males, and, for that matter, Whites. Table 7.8, containing
1969 median income data for recipients twenty-five plus
years of age by education, race, and sex, shows that White
males have the highest earnings, followed by Black males,
White females, and, finally, Black females. If those with the
highest average earnings, White males, are used as the measuring standard, a comparison of the median earnings of the
remaining groups with that standard is very useful in illustra-
ting the rough impacts of racism and sexism upon income.
Black males earn 60.2 percent as much as White males, with
White females earning 31.8 percent as much as White males,
and Black females 26.3 percent. By education, for those with
an elementary education, Blacks earn 72.5 percent of our
standard, if they are male, but, if female, only 26.9 percent,

TABLE 7.8.   Median income for recipients twenty-five plus years
of age by education, race, and sex, 1969

	Median Income				
Educational level	Black Female	White Female	Black Male	White Male	% BF/ WM[a]
Total income	$2,078	$2,513	$4,748	$ 7,890	26.3%
Elementary education	$1,221	$1,448	$3,291	$ 4,539	26.9%
Less than eighth grade	1,195	1,303	2,973	3,613	33.1
Eighth grade	1,320	1,688	4,293	5,460	24.2
High School	$2,711	$2,943	$5,729	$ 8,171	33.2%
1–3 years	2,268	2,355	5,222	7,309	31.0
4 years	3,257	3,234	6,144	8,631	37.7
College	$5,395	$4,372	$7,667	$11,117	48.5%
1–3 years	4,247	3,427	7,051	9,575	44.4
4 years or more	6,747	5,707	8,567	12,437	54.2

SOURCE: U.S. Bureau of Census 1970*b*.
a. % BF/WM =the Black female median income expressed as percentage
of White male median income, with this index computed from raw data.

while White females earn 31.9 percent as much as White
males. For those with a high school education, Black males
decrease to 70.1 percent while Black females rise to 33.2
percent and White females, to 36.0 percent. For those with a
college education, the statistics are 69.0 percent for Black
males, 48.5 percent for Black females, and 39.3 percent for
White females. Thus, as may be evident, Black females are
affected far more than Black males.

In fact, in 1969 Black females earned 43.8 percent as much
as did Black males. By education those with an elementary
education earned only 37.1 percent as much as their male
counterparts, increasing to 47.3 percent as much for those
with high school education and to 70.4 percent for those with
college education. Among Black females and males, the income gap lessens as their level of education increases,
whereas among Black and White males the income gaps

remain relatively constant at each educational level, decreasing only from 72.5 percent at the elementary to 69.4 percent at the college level.

Table 7.8 also shows that, when education is held constant, in 1969 Black females with more than three years of high school education outranked comparable White females in median income. This may be attributed to a number of factors, other than higher salaries for the Black females. Perhaps the White females tend to be employed part-time more often than these Blacks. Also, in the South especially, the median educational level of Black female public school teachers is higher than the Whites, as is their length of tenure. Finally, more Black mothers are likely to be engaged in full-time employment, even when their children are under six years of age, than are their White counterparts.

Table 7.9 contains data on the median income of families

TABLE 7.9.   Median income of families and unrelated individuals by race, 1969

Income Recipient Category	Median Income		% B/W[a]
	Black	White	
Total, family and unrelated individuals	$6,059	$ 9,794	61.9%
Total, family	$7,273	$10,211	71.2%
Male head, total	7,329	10,241	71.6
Male head, wife in labor force	9,134	11,886	76.8
Male head, wife not in labor force	5,612	9,111	61.6
Male head, other marital status	6,223	8,818	70.6
Female head	3,341	5,500	60.8
Total, unrelated individual	$2,106	$ 3,078	68.4%
Male	3,058	4,468	68.5
Female	1,612	2,500	64.5

SOURCE: U.S. Bureau of Census 1970*b*.

a. % B/W = the ratio of Black to White income (e.g., Black family and unrelated individuals earned 61.9% as much as did their White counterparts).

and unrelated individuals by race in 1969. Blacks earned less than Whites; females earned less than males of both races. Black families and unrelated individuals earned 61.9 percent as much as the Whites. Black male-headed families with their wives in the labor force earned 76.8 percent as much as similar White families, but, without their wives in the labor force they only earned 61.6 percent as much as did similar White families. That gives some indication of the significance of a Black working wife. When both the Black husband and wife were working, their combined median income of $9,134 was only $23.00 more than that of the $9,111 earned by a White male head whose wife was not working. The Black female head earned only 60.8 percent as much as the White female head, 53.7 percent as much as the Black male head not living with a spouse, and only 37.9 percent as much as the equivalent White male head. These income gaps between Black females and the remaining groups have significant implications for these females — particularly in gaining access to opportunities designed to have some impact upon their own upgrading of skills and knowledge — and their families, including educational aspirations of their children. Black working wives provided more monetary benefits for their families, too, than did White working wives, which may be one of the underlying factors in the relative reluctance exhibited by employers in providing day-care centers for children. However, the current increase in working White wives who may become significant contributors to their "family pot" can be an added benefit for Black employed females with children.

Bressler and McKenney have already convincingly demonstrated that Black women's income level is below that of Black men. "Holding class of worker, occupation, and education constant, the income level never reaches parity" (Bressler and McKenney 1968, p. 33). That point is well taken, and table 7.8 substantiates their findings about education and income. Nevertheless, what is missing here and elsewhere are definitive statements demonstrating the income differentials between Black women and White men, when education, occupation, etc., are all held constant. The traditional literature tends to compare the low incomes of Black women only with those of White women and Black men, as if any other comparisons are unnecessary. An implication may be that the income level of White men should not be the standard on which to base the ideal income level for Black women, but that is a false contention. Future studies should stress the income differences between the group under investigation and those enjoying the highest returns for their labors and thoughts.

The issue of working Black women has often centered upon power. That is, matriarchal power has been ascribed to the working Black woman merely because she may be employed. Staples (1971) has already criticized the invalid assumption—which generally underlies the matriarchial theory—that the Black wife has an inordinate influence upon family tasks and decisions. In addition to the evidence that Hyman and Reed provided in their secondary analysis of three surveys of family dominance, where they reported "that the actual white pattern [of female influence] is almost identical to that for Black families" (Staples 1971), Middleton and Putney's study of forty Southern couples of both racial groups, with an equal number of male spouses employed as college professors and skilled workers, also points toward certain misconceptions about the Black matriarchy. They failed to find any significant family dominance (on a continuum from matriarchy to patriarchy) between the Black and White families; nor did they find any between those families engaged in different occupations. Specifically, they indicated (Middleton and Putney 1970, p. 20):

Thus we find no evidence that whites and Negroes, professors and skilled workers, differ as to which spouse dominates in the making of daily decisions. Contrary to the literature, our data suggest that all these groups are predominantly equalitarian. In view of this, it would be interesting to conduct further investigations with lower-class whites and Negroes to see whether they deviated from the predominant equalitarian pattern.

They also suggested the need for further research to determine the differences, if any, which may exist among the racial and occupational groups when the focus is upon the specific decision-making areas. One major finding that they reported is pertinent to our discussion of Black working wives as well. "Families in which the wife works are significantly *more* patriarchal in decisions than those in which the wife does not work in direct contradiction to findings of previous studies" (Middleton and Putney 1970, p. 21). Such a finding clearly bears further examination among Black working couples — particularly those among the lower classes, inasmuch as they were excluded from the Middleton and Putney sample.

In an intriguing account "Where the Black Matriarchy Theorists Went Wrong," Delores Mack, a Black psychologist, has demonstrated quite convincingly that "blacks and whites do not differ on their perceptions and uses of power in a marriage relationship." Her findings were based upon novel experimental conditions well worth replication, for she used questionnaires, direct observations, and couple bargaining. From her sample of eighty married couples representing Black and White middle and working classes (and carefully matched), she has stressed her most significant finding, namely, that class differences are far more important than race. She has also warned us (Mack 1971, p. 87):

This absence of racial differences [in husband-wife power] is startling when one considers the emphasis placed upon them in the literature. What my findings suggest is that researchers have not carefully evaluated the logic of their assumptions of their hypotheses. They have looked at the white community and seen that education, occupation and income are important sources of power.

They note that in the black community black women have more control over these resources than black men, that frequently black women schoolteachers are married to janitors or, if they're lucky, to blue-collar workers. From this they have concluded that black women are more powerful than black men. They have ignored the possibility that the sources of power in the black community may be different from those in the white community.

The possible differences she specifically referred to were those of sex, which she posited as "a potent form of power in any marriage, but particularly in black marriages."

All of the above demographic commentary simply lends further credence to the observation by Logan (1954, p. 336) that, of all groups, the equal rights of Colored women have been those most violated. By education, occupation, employment, and income and by any of the usual measures of marital and family stability,[1] Black women are enmeshed in the worst position in this racist society, necessitating the need for Black female liberation *now*.

Black Female Liberation

Really relatively little remains to be said since my position is already clearly stated. Flexner (1959), too has described greater educational deprivation of the Black girl (as compared with her brothers) in earlier years and, later, her severely limited educational and occupational aspirations. Of greater importance, she has written of the great debts Blacks

---

1. It is probably worth restressing the fact, as Bressler and McKenney have noted, that "the majority of the Negro families are of the traditional type with a husband and wife present. Of the 4.5 million Negro families, approximately three out of every four had a husband and wife present; one-fourth were headed by a woman" (Bressler and McKenney 1968, p. 10). For related articles on occupation, employment, and marital and family stability especially, see Willie (1970). For a viewpoint on Black college-educated women differing from that expressed here, see Fichter (1967*a*, esp. chap. 5, pp. 77–102). See also Bock (1969).

and Whites owe to women such as Harriet Tubman, Sojourner Truth, Frances Ellen Watkins Harper, Mary Ann Shadd Cary, Charlotte Forten, Anna Mae Douglass, Sarah Remond, Charlotte E. Ray, Caroline V. Still, Hallie Q. Brown, Fannie Barrier Williams, Ida B. Wells, Josephine St. Pierre Ruffin, and Mary Church Terrell.

Much earlier, that distinguished scholar and gentleman Benjamin Brawley (1937) had praised the strong character of Black women: "In the history of the United States no more heroic work has been done than that performed by the Negro woman." Those not familiar with those great women mentioned above, and with such women as Margaret Murray Washington, Lucy Smith Thurman, Mary B. Talbert, Eva B. Dykes, Sadie T. Mossell Alexander, Georgiana R. Simpson, Otelia Cromwell, Ruth Whitehead Whaley, Violette N. Anderson, Elizabeth C. Wright, Cornelia Bowen, Nannie H. Burroughs, Arenia C. Mallory, Virginia E. Randolph, Ruth Anna Fisher, Maggie L. Walker, Fanny Jackson Coppin, Maria L. Baldwin, Lucy Laney, Charlotte Hawkins Brown, Maudelle Brown Bousfield, and that Dean of Negro Women, the incredible Mary McLeod Bethune, should read his *Negro Builders and Heroes* (Brawley 1937, chaps. 37–39; see also Donnett 1964, 1966).

Black women have been great organizers and have most often used their organizations to work toward improved conditions for others. That is, their organizations have tended to be altruistically motivated. They have also heavily contributed their services as members of the most active Black protest movements since slaves first jumped off those ships and went home to their masters to be free. Black women have kept alive the faith and hope that the world can and will be a better place.

In recent years, there have been two perhaps related trends. One is the significant shift in the literature about Black women. That shift from praise to blame may be understandable since most early writings about Black women were by Blacks, whereas most between 1940 and the late 1960s were by Whites. To be certain, Black female participants in the Abolitionist Movement, particularly when that participation was joined with women's suffrage, were not always welcomed, but the disparagement characteristic of the later literature was conspicuously absent.

The second trend is the significant decrease in effective public participation of Black women in civil rights or protest movements (as they become more institutionalized—hence more patterned upon White society) and in various professions (most notably, medicine and law). That trend has also accompanied increased attempts to subordinate Black females, to make them more "equal" with White females.

Both trends, currently reversing, demand Black female action to ensure an irreversible reversal. A most serious need is for increased, meaningful Black female participation within Black liberationist and feministic movements right now. A second is an insistence that Black men in decision-making positions (such as directors of Black studies programs, personnel officers in the government and major industries, and admissions and recruitment officers in academia) must share that power with Black women. They must stop behaving as if they were, at long last, "masters of the plantation." Black women must also insist that Black and White children be taught about the Truths, the Tubmans, the Terrells, and the Bethunes, instead of largely about the Kings, the Malcolm Xs, and the Washingtons. Black women must demand equal opportunities for their Black daughters. Black women must insist that White female liberation cannot mean Black women in their homes, taking care of business as usual, for Black women must stop working as domestics for White folks. The elaboration of "domestics" to "glorified homekeepers" leaves a thorn, a thorn. This last reason is one of the most critical reasons why Black women cannot leave women's liberation to White women!

Finally, Black women must write their own history, and

they must make a critique of that history which is written about them by others, because, as long as the social and behavioral sciences, at least, are largely in the hands of males, reality will be less plausible. What Black women need – and must produce – is a series of highly sophisticated and highly relevant studies, for there is none currently about them. The paucity of the literature on Black women noted by Flexner (1959) yet prevails. Some indication of the type of literature currently available may be gleaned from the bibliography at the end of this chapter. Unfortunately, it is not an exhaustive one. Its very incompleteness attests to the need for an exhaustive, annotative bibliography on Black women, so as to provide Black female scholars with assistance in locating work about themselves, criticizing that work, and developing new works.

One critical area needing study may well be that of the greater victimization to which Black women may be subjected. Insight might be found from investigating psychological distresses affecting them. Among the sampled subjects obtaining medical examinations in the 1960–62 National Health Survey, Black females reported more symptoms of psychological distress than did the Black males. The self-reported percentages for nervous breakdowns included 10.4 percent ($N = 6,208$) among the females eighteen to seventy-nine years of age and 2.8 percent among the males ($N = 5,177$). Comparable percentages for specific symptoms follow: (a) feelings of an impending nervous breakdown (16.1 percent female, 8.2 percent male); nervousness (55.2 percent female, 31.3 percent male); inertia (29.5 percent female, 17.1 percent male); insomina (40.0 percent female, 20.4 percent male); hand-trembling (12.3 percent female, 7.1 percent male); nightmares (14.3 percent female, 13.0 percent male); perspiring hands (16.0 percent female, 16.8 percent male); fainting (20.5 percent female, 13.8 percent male); headaches (31.0 percent female, 11.9 percent male); dizziness (15.7 percent female, 9.2 percent male); and heart palpitations (6.4

percent female, 4.8 percent male). The mean numbers of positive symptom responses were 2.65 female, 1.55 male, while the median numbers were 2.31 and 1.04 respectively. The higher magnitude among females is generally consistent with the usually reported higher rates of mental illnesses among them. Their lower suicide rates may be a function of greater familial constraints upon them. Black women may tend to be somewhat less healthy than Black males, but mortality rates are higher among the latter. Some would stress the greater distress that Black women experience daily; others, that of the males. Here, I suspect data are much too inconclusive to permit a reasonable choice; there may be no difference. Nevertheless, whatever the causal nexus, such data as that presented above about reported psychological distress does suggest anew that Black women may be aptly characterized as that group whose rights have been most violated.

Summary

Black women, the most disadvantaged group in the United States, as evidenced by their unenviable occupational, educational, employment, income, and male-availability levels, have been "messed over" by distorters of reality. The worst distorters include the overextenders of the Black matriarchal and emasculatory theories and those Black males especially who seek female subordination as proof of their masculinity (an unnecessary emulation of the White man). This distortion successfully continues the oppression of Black women and, indirectly, Black men, thereby masking the real racist and sexist culprits (with the latter being joined by some Black men as well). The concept of the Black matriarch needs considerable restriction, limiting it to those for whom Frazier intended it — Black female family heads bereft of husbands and fathers for their children. Matriarchies, in

fact, constitute a minority of all Black families. The emasculation theory, possible only in a sexist society, must become
inoperable as this society learns to respect the human dignity
of all.

Black women have traditionally occupied positions of
lower status than is true of Black men, assertions to the contrary notwithstanding. Black women can never afford to be
fooled by those Black men who seek to trick them into believing that the first responsibility of Black women is the
freeing of Black men. Black men have never been their cap-
tives. Few seek to be their liberators. Black women must
increase their participation in racial and feminist liberation
movements, and they can find no better role models than
Sojourner Truth and Mary Church Terrell. Their direct participation in women's liberation is very critical, so that there
will be no question of the Black woman's being left out in
the kitchen or the nursery. The "heat" should be placed
upon those White women who persist in believing that Black
women do not wish to become liberated!

Expansion of professional roles among Black women is one
of the critical needs of the time, for Black women must
become their own historians, sociologists, psychologists, and
psychiatrists, ably assisted by those beautiful men who both
"know and understand." An eminent need for historical and
contemporary studies of Black women exists, for no adequate
work is presently available. Black women must sing their
own praises today, so they will not get left out in the shuffle,
as is evidenced by the recent decline in educational attainment among younger Black females. This trend must be reversed.

No matter how critical conditions may now be, "O Mary,
Don't You Weep, Don't You Mourn," but get out there and
help drown Pharaoh's chauvinistic armies, and search on for
the phoenix spied by those great Black women seeking relief
from racism and sexism, such as Sojourner Truth, Mary

Church Terrell, and Mary McLeod Bethune. Concerted, constructive activism can repay that debt. That is my message to all Black women.

Epilogue

Toward men, and toward God, she maintained a respectful attitude, lightened by the belief that in a crisis she could deal adequately with either of them. (Nathan 1935)

Although *all* the opinions will never be in, publicity about the paper that foreran this chapter has cast me in the role of a polemicist. Perhaps the most significant impressions that I can share with any reader are two.

The first is that agreement or disagreement with my major conclusions concerning the relative position of Black women is far more affected by socioeconomic status than by race. Among those Black men and women especially who have shared with me their evaluations of what I have said about Black women in a racist society (in personal conversations or correspondence), those who occupy the higher socioeconomic positions among Blacks have generally given me their blessing, whereas those Black males of lower socioeconomic status (as measured by education, occupation, and income) or first-generation representatives of "Black bourgeoisie" within their families have been extremely concerned about my *failure* to recognize the *necessity* for Black women to "take a back seat" to Black men.

One of the most interesting pieces of correspondence I received came from a Black male inmate in a Northern correctional institution, and his comments are especially worth recording not only for their own intrinsic value but because they represent a view which should also be heard:

. . . I found [your comments] to contain much truth.

When I was younger, I use to wonder to myself, why many Black Families were headed by the woman, and not the man; but of course after many years, and my getting involved into the many circumstances surrounding "we Blacks," I became quite aware of why Black women headed the Family. I found that the Black men have been seriously emasculated by the whites, through dehumanized methods of mental and physical slavery. Stripped mentally of our unique capability of leadership, placed in such a dehumanized state of mind, that we were stripped of all senses of responsibility toward ourselves and toward our women, children, and Families. Being denied jobs, etc., forced our Black women into our pants along with her dress, to take on the responsibilities of providing for the children, the men and trying to maintain family ties. From the Black women's strength and determination to survive the unhumane treatment, we were able to survive, but with little or no efforts on our part. To keep the Black men in their past and present state of mind, the whites invested the matriarchal theory to keep the Black men and Black women mentally divided and perhaps in some cases it's keeping them physically divided as well. (Hence interracial marriages and dates). Today the Black men have accepted their Afros, with attaching, etc., symbols of power, and they have even tried to pull back their pants. But still they have not fully accepted their responsibilities as men toward themselves, women, children, and families. This is one of the biggest problems confronting the Black struggle today for liberation. I found that where there is no responsibleness for self, there can be no respect for self or others. Perhaps a prefabricated image of responsibleness and respect for self and others, but not the real thing that would substantially contribute to the Blacks' struggle.

In viewing the irresponsibleness of the majority of Black men, eyes also must be focused on the Black women. Some of my sisters believe that they are truly suppose to be the provider and head of the family, but then again, this falls right back to the dehumanized slavery, which was inflicted upon we Blacks. Accordingly, the Black men have the responsibility next are endeavored as men to be strong enough to replace the Black women, back in their proper perspectives. And of course she to must be willing to accept her perspective as a measurement of awareness and respect to her newly awaken Black man. However where the Black men's irresponsibility continues to prevail, Black women will continue to be cautious and maintain their alleged role as the provider and head of the family for fear of being left in the Ghetto Projects with a House full of children, and no responsible or respectable man to attend to their needs.

Dr. Jacquelyne J. Jackson, I didn't mean to take up to much of your time. I merely wanted to let you know that it's plain to see that the Black woman's strength and determination still prevails toward survival of the Black Race.

1 June 1971

The second impression is simply that those Black women currently most likely to be supportive of Black female liberationist movements are those who, educationally and occupationally, are the most unconventional, perhaps because they function principally within "a man's world." Their educational and occupational reference groups are significantly different from those found among the typical public school teachers, nurses, social workers, and librarians. They do not deny their womanliness, but they also know, along with Friedrich Schiller, that "equality is the sacred law of humanity."

BIBLIOGRAPHY

Black Women Authors

Brooks (1949)   Guy (1966)   Hansberry (1959)
Negro woman (1966)   Vroman (1963)   Walker (1966)
Wheatley (1773)   Wright (1969)

Black Women: Educational, Occupational, and Political or Civic Participation

Bates (1962)   Barton (1948)   Bluestone (1968)
Carter (1965)   Carter (1968)   Chappelle (1970)
Chisholm (1970)   Cooper (1892)   Daniel (1931)
Engs (1969)   Fichter (1967b)   Field (1948)
Gurin (1966)   Hare and Hare (1970)   Haughey (1969)
Haynes (1969)   Hobson (1896)   LaRue (1970)
Miller (1969)   Mossel (1894)   Nat. Manpower (1957, 1959)
Noble (1964)   Quarles (1940)   Reed (1970)
Russell (1962)   Shockley (1967)   Strong (1967)
Swift (1969)   Williams (1893, 1900)

Black Women: Demography

Cowhig (1967)	Demographic Aspects (1970)	Farley (1966)
Goldstein (1963)	Grabill (1958)	Nicol (1964)

Black Women: Marriage and Family

There are so many publications in this field that the reader can best encounter them by looking through the references that follow.

REFERENCES

Anders, Sarah F. 1969. New dimensions in ethnicity and childrearing attitudes. *Am. J. Mental Deficiency* 73:505–08.

Anders, Sarah F., and Dayan, Maurice. 1967. Variables related to child-rearing attitudes among attendants in an institutional setting. *Am. J. Mental Deficiency* 71:848–51 (1966–1967).

Anderson, Robert E. 1968. Where's Dad: parental deprivation and delinquency. *Arch. Gen. Psychiat.* 18:641–49.

Barton, Rebecca. 1948. *Witnesses for freedom: Negro Americans in autobiotobiography.* New York: Harper.

Bates, Daisy. 1962. *The long shadow of Little Rock.* New York: McKay.

Baughman, Earl, and Dahlstrom, W. Grant. 1968. *Negro and White children, a psychological study in the rural South.* New York: Academic.

Beale, Frances. 1970. Double jeopardy: to be Black and female. In *The Black woman, an anthology,* ed. Toni Cade, pp. 90–100. New York: New American Library.

Bell, Robert R. 1965. Lower class Negro mothers' aspirations for their children. *Social Forces.* 43:493–500.

Bernard, Jessie.
    1964. *Academic women.* University Park, Pa.: Pennsylvania State University Press.
    1966. *Marriage and family among Negroes.* Englewood Cliffs, N.J.: Prentice-Hall.

Biller, Henry B. 1968. A note on the father absence and masculine development in lower-class Negro and White boys. *Child Development* 39:1004–06.

Billingsley, Andrew.
    1968. *Black families in White America.* Englewood Cliffs, N.J.: Prentice-Hall.

1969. Family functioning in the low-income Black community. *Social Casework* 50:563–72.

Billingsley, Andrew, and Billingsley, Amy T. 1966. Illegitimacy and patterns of Negro family life. In *The unwed mother*, ed. Robert W. Roberts, pp. 131–57. New York: Harper.

Blood, Robert O., and Wolfe, Donald M. 1963. *Husbands and wives: the dynamics of married living*. New York: Free Press.

Bluestone, Barry. 1968. The poor who have jobs. *Dissent* 15:410–19.

Bock, E. Wilbur. 1969. Farmer's daughter effect: The case of the Negro female professionals. *Phylon* 30:17–26.

Bond, Jean Carey, and Peery, Pat. 1970. Is the black male castrated? In *The Black woman, an anthology*, ed. Toni Cade, pp. 113–18. New York: New American Library.

Bowers, John Z. 1968. Special problems of women medical students. *J. Med. Educ.* 43:532–37.

Brawley, Benjamin. 1937. *Negro builders and heroes*, chaps. 37–39. Chapel Hill, N.C.: University of North Carolina Press.

Bressler, Tobia, and McKenney, Nampeo. 1968. *Negro women in the United States*. Paper presented at the annual meeting of the Population Association of America, Boston, Mass.

Brooks, Gwendolyn. 1949. *Annie Allen*. New York: Harper.

Burma, John H. 1963. Interethnic marriage in Los Angeles, 1948–1959. *Social Forces* 42:156–65.

Busse, Thomas V. 1969. Child-rearing antecedents of flexible thinking. *Developmental Psychol.* 1:585–91.

Butler, Alan C., and Carr, Lester. 1968. Purpose in life through social action. *J. Soc. Psych.* 74:243–50.

Cade, Toni, ed. 1970. *The Black woman, an anthology*. New York: New American Library.

Campbell, Angus, and Schuman, Howard. 1968. Racial attitudes in fifteen American cities. In *Supplemental studies for the National Advisory Committee on Civil Disorders*, pp. 1–67. Washington, D.C.: U.S. Government Printing Office.

Carter, Barbara. 1965. Integrating the Negro teacher out of a job. *Reporter* 33:31–33.

Carter, Genevieve W. 1968. The employment potential of AFDC mothers. *Welfare in Review* 6:1–11.

Chappelle, Yvonne R. 1970. The Black woman on the Negro college campus. *Black Scholar* 1:36–39.

Chisholm, Shirley. 1970. Racism and anti-feminism. *Black Scholar* 1:40–51.

Clarizio, Harvey F. 1968. Maternal attitude change associated with involvement in Project Head Start. *J. Negro Educ.* 37:106–13.

Clark, Kenneth, and Parsons, Talcott. 1966. *The Negro America*. Boston, Mass.: Beacon.

Cooper, Anna J. 1892. *A voice from the South by a Black woman of the South*. Xenia, Ohio: Aldine Printing House.

Cowhig, James D. 1967. The Negro population of the United States. *Welfare in Review* 7:14–16.

Cramer, Richard, et al. 1966. *Social factors in educational achievement and aspirations among Negro adolescents*. Survey study, cooperative research Project No. 1168. Vol. 2. Chapel Hill, N.C.: University of North Carolina.

Dandes, Herbert M., and Dow, Dorothea. 1969. Relation of intelligence to family size and density. *Child Development* 40:641–45.

Dannett, Sylvia G. L.
    1964.   *Profiles of Negro womanhood, 1619–1900*. Vol. 1. Yonkers, N.Y.: Educational Heritage, Inc.
    1966.   *Profiles of Negro womanhood, 20th century*. Vol. 2. Yonkers, N.Y.: Educational Heritage, Inc.

Daniel, Sadie Iola. 1931. *Women builders*. Washington, D.C.: Associated Publishers, Inc.

Davies, Vernon. 1966. Fertility versus welfare: the Negro American dilemma. *Phylon* 27:226–32.

Demographic aspects of the Black community. 1970. *Milbank Memorial Fund Quarterly* 48:11–361.

Dreger, Ralph M., and Miller, Kent S. 1968. Comparative psychological studies of Negroes and Whites in the United States. *Psychol. Bull. Monograph* 70:1–58. Supplement.

Duncan, Beverly, and Duncan, Otis D. 1969. Family stability and occupational success. *Social Problems* 16:273–85.

Edwards, G. Franklin. 1963. Marriage and family life among Negroes. *J. Negro Educ.* 32:451–65.

Edwards, G. Franklin, ed. 1968. *E. Franklin Frazier on race relations*. Chicago: University of Chicago Press. See pp. 325–31 for a listing of Frazier's bibliography.

Edwards, Harry. 1968. Black Muslin and Negro Christian family relationships. *J. Marriage and Family* 30:604–11.

Engs, Robert F., and Williams, John B. 1969. Integration by evasion. *Nation* 209:537–40.

Epps, Edgar G.; Katz, Irwin; and Axelson, Leland. 1964. Relation of mother's employment to intellectual performance of Negro college student. *Soc. Prob.* 11:414–18.

Epstein, Ralph, and Komorita, S. S. 1966. Prejudice among Negro children as related to parental ethnocentrism and punitiveness. *J. Personality Soc. Psychol.* 4:643–47.

Erickson, Erik H. 1968. *Identity: youth and crisis,* pp. 295–320. New York: Norton.

Farley, Reynolds. 1966. Recent changes in Negro fertility. *Demography* 3:188–203.

Fichter, Joseph H.
>1967*a*. *Graduates of predominately Negro colleges, class of 1964.* Washington, D.C.: U.S. Government Printing Office.
>1967*b*. Career expectations of Negro women graduates. *Monthly Labor Rev.* 90:36–42.

Field, Emma L. 1948. The woman's club movement in the United States. Master's thesis, Howard University.

Fischer, Ann; Beasley, Joseph D.; and Harter, Carl L. 1968. The occurrence of the extended family at the origin of the family of procreation: a developmental approach to Negro family structure. *J. Marriage and Family* 30:290–300.

Fischer, Joel. 1969. Negroes and Whites and rates of mental illness: reconsideration of a myth. *Psychiatry* 32:411–27.

Flexner, Eleanor. 1959. *Century of struggle, the woman's rights movement in the United States.* Cambridge, Mass.: Belknap Press of Harvard University Press.

Frazier, E. Franklin.
>1939. *The Negro family in the United States.* Chicago: University of Chicago Press.
>1966. *The Negro family in the United States.* Rev. and abridged. Chicago: University of Chicago Press.
>1968. *See* Edwards, G. F. (1968) for Frazier bibliography.

Friedman, Niel. 1966. James Baldwin and psychotherapy. *Psychother. Theor. Res. Pract.* 3:177–83.

Frumkin, Robert M. 1954. Attitudes of Negro college students toward intrafamily leadership and control. *Marriage and Family Living* 16:252–53.

Gans, Herbert J. 1970. The subcultures of the working class, lower class, and middle class. In *The logic of social hierarchies,* ed. E. O. Lauman et al., pp. 575–88. Chicago: Markham Publishing Co.

Geisman, Ludwig L., and Gerhart, Ursula C. 1968. Social class, ethnicity, and family functioning: explaining some issues raised by the Moynihan report. *J. Marriage and Family* 30:480–87.

Goldstein, Marcus S. 1963. Longevity and health status of the Negro American. *J. Negro Educ.* 32:337–48.

Grabill, Wilson H.; Kiser, Clyde V.; and Whelpton, Pascal K. 1958. *The fertility of American women.* New York: Wiley.

Grier, William H., and Cobbs, Price. 1968. *Black rage.* New York: Basic Books.

Gurin, Patricia. 1966. Social class constraints on the occupational aspirations of students attending some predominantly Negro Colleges. *J. Negro Educ.* 35:336–50.

Gurin, Patricia, and Epps, Edgar. 1966. Some characteristics of students from poverty backgrounds attending predominantly Negro colleges in the deep South. *Social Forces* 45:27–40.

Guy, Rosa. 1966. *Bird at my window.* Philadelphia: Lippincott.

Hansberry, Lorraine. 1959. *A raisin in the sun.* New York: Random.

Hare, Nathan, and Hare, Julia. 1970. Black women, 1970. *Trans-action* 8:65–68.

Haughey, John C. 1969. Black sisters become soul sisters. *America* 121:67.

Haynes, Alfred M. 1969. Distribution of Black physicians in the United States, 1969. *J. Am. Med. Ass.* 210:93–95.

Heer, David M. 1966. Negro-White marriage in the United States. *J. Marriage and Family* 28:262–73.

Henderson, George. 1967. Role models for lower class Negro boys. *Personnel Guidance J.* 46:6–10.

Hendin, Herbert. 1969. *Black suicide.* New York: Basic Books.

Henton, C. L. 1961. The effect of socio-economic and emotional factors on the onset of menarche among Negro and White girls. *J. Genet. Psychol.* 98:255–64.

Herzog, Elizabeth.
  1966.   Is there a "breakdown" of the Negro family? *Social Work* 11:3–10.
  1967   *About the poor: some facts and some fictions.* U.S. Health, Education and Welfare Children's Bureau publication no. 451. Washington, D.C.: U.S. Government Printing Office.

Herzog, Elizabeth, and Bernstein, Rose. 1965. Why so few Negro adoptions? *Children* 12:14–18.

Himes, Joseph, and Hamelett, Margaret L. 1962. The assessment of adjustment of aged Negro women in a Southern city. *Phylon* 23:139–47.

Hobson, Mrs. E. C., and Hopkins, Mrs. C. E. 1896. *Report concerning the Colored women of the South.* Baltimore, Md.: Slater Fund.

Hyman, Herbert H. and Reed, John S. 1969. "Black matriarchy" reconsidered: evidence from secondary analysis of sample surveys. *Public Opinion Quart.* 33:346–54.

Iscoe, Ira; Williams, Martha; and Harvey, Jerry. 1964. Age, intelligence, and sex as variables in the conformity behavior of Negro and White children. *Child Development* 35:451–60.

Jackson, Jacquelyne J.
  1970.   Aged Negroes and their cultural departures from stereotypes and rural-urban differences. *Gerontologist* 10:140–45.

1971. Sex and social class variations in Black aged parent-adult child relationships. *Aging and Human Development* 2:96–107.

Johnson, Charles S. 1938. *The Negro college graduate*. Chapel Hill, N.C.: University of North Carolina Press.

Kaplan, Henry K., and Matkom, Anthony J. 1967. Peer status and intellectual functioning of Negro school children. *Psychol. in Schools* 4:181–84.

Kardiner, Abraham, and Ovesey, Lionel. 1951. *The mark of oppression*. New York: Norton.

King, Karl. 1967. A comparison of the Negro and White family power structure in low income families. *Child and Family* 6:65–74.

Kletzing, H. F., and Crogman, W. H. 1969. *Progress of a race, or the remarkable advancement of the Afro-American*. New York: Negro Universities Press. Originally published 1897 in Atlanta by J. L. Nichols and Company.

Komisaruk, Richard, and Pearson, Carol E. 1968. Children of the Detroit riots: a study of their participation and their mental health. *J. Urban Law* 45:599–626.

Kunstadter, Peter. 1963. A survey of the consanquinal or matrifocal family. *Am. Anthropol.* 65:56–66.

LaBarre, Maurine. 1968. Strengths of the self-supporting poor. *Social Casework* 49:450–66.

Lansing, John B.; Clifton, Charles Wade; and Morgan, James N. 1969. *New homes and poor people: a study of chains of moves*. Ann Arbor, Mich.: Institute of Social Research.

LaRue, Glenda J. M. 1970. Black liberation and women's lib. *Trans-action* 8:59–64.

Lawder, Elizabeth A. 1966. Quasi-adoption. *Children* 13:11–12.

Lefcowitz, Myron, J. 1968. *Differences between Negro and White women in marital stability and family structure: a multiple regression analysis*. Madison, Wis.: Institute for Research on Poverty.

Lessing, Elise E.; Zagorin, Susan W.; and Nelson, Dorothy. 1970. WISC subtest and IQ score correlates of father absence. *J. Genet. Psychol.* 117:181–95.

Liebow, Elliot. 1967. *Tally's corner: a study of Negro streetcorner men*. Boston, Mass.: Little, Brown.

Logan, Rayford. 1954. *The Negro in American life and thought, the nadir, 1877–1901*. New York: Dial.

Mack, Delores E. 1971. Where the Black matriarchy theorists went wrong. *Psychol. Today* 4:24 ff.

Maxwell, Joseph W. 1968. Rural Negro father participation in family activities. *Rural Sociol.* 33:80–93.

Middleton, Russell, and Putney, Snell. 1970. Dominance in decisions in the family, race and class differences. In *The family life of Black people*, ed. Charles V. Willie, pp. 16–22. Columbus, Ohio: Charles E. Merrill.

Miller, E. Eugene. 1969. The woman participant in Washington's riots. *Federal Probation* 33:30–34.

Mossell, N. F. 1894. *The work of the Afro-American woman.* Philadelphia: Geo. S. Ferguson Co.

Moynihan, Daniel P. 1965. *The Negro family, a case for national action.* Washington, D.C.: U.S. Government Printing Office.

Nathan, Robert. 1935. *The road of ages.* New York: Knopf.

National Manpower Council.

1957.   *Womanpower: a statement with chapters by the council staff.* New York: Columbia University Press.

1959.   *Work in the lives of married women.* Proceedings of the Conference on Women, Oct 20–25, 1957. New York: Columbia University Press.

The Negro woman in American literature. 1966. *Freedomways* 6:8–25.

Nelson, John C. 1968. Section C: interests of disadvantaged and advantaged Negro and White first graders. *J. Negro Educ.* 37:168–73.

Nichols, Robert C. 1964. Parental attitudes of mothers of intelligent adolescents and creativity of their children. *Child Development* 35:1041–49.

Nicol, Helen, and Drake, Merci L. 1964. *Negro women workers in 1960.* Publication of the Women's Bureau, Department of Labor. Washington, D.C.: U.S. Government Printing Office.

Noble, Jeanne L.

1956.   *The Negro woman's college education.* New York: Bureau of Publications, Teachers College, Columbia University.

1964.   The American Negro woman. In *The American Negro reference book,* ed. John P. Davis, chap. 13, pp. 552–47. Englewood Cliffs, N.J.: Prentice-Hall.

North, George E., and Buchanan, O. Lee. 1968. Maternal attitudes in a poverty area. *J. Negro Educ.* 37:418–25.

Parker, Seymour, and Kleiner, Robert J. 1966. Characteristics of Negro mothers in single-headed households. *J. Marriage and Family* 28:507–13.

Payton, E.; Crump, E. P.; and Horton, C. P. 1960. Growth and development VII: dietary habits of 571 pregnant Southern women. *J. Am. Dietet. Ass.* 37:129–36.

Pope, Hallowell. 1967. Unwed mothers and their sex partners. *J. Marriage and Family* 29:555–67.

Quarles, Benjamin. 1940. Frederick Douglass and the women's rights movement. *J. Negro Hist.* 25:35.

Rainwater, Lee. 1970. *Behind ghetto walls.* Chicago:Aldine.

Reed, Julia. 1970. Marriage and fertility in Black female teachers. *Black Scholar* 1:22–28.

Reiner, Beatrice S.1968. The real world of the teenage Negro mother. *Child Welfare* 47:391–96.

Reiss, I. L. 1964. Premarital sexual permissiveness among Negroes and Whites. *Am. Sociol. Rev.* 29:688–98.

Rohrer, John H., and Edmonson, Munro S., eds. 1960. *The eighth generation: cultures and personalities of New Orleans Negroes.* New York: Harper.

Russell, R. D. 1962. Experiences of Negro high school girls with domestic placement agencies. *J. Negro Educ.* 31:172–76.

Scanzoni, John H. 1971. *The Black family in modern society.* Boston, Mass.: Allyn & Bacon.

Schenck, Mary-Lou. 1969. A Southern Negro girl in a White Northern family: a case study. *Social Work* 14:77–83.

Schulz, David A.
  1968.   Variations in the father role in complete families of the Negro lower class. *Soc. Sci. Quart.* 49:651–59.
  1969.   *Coming up Black: patterns of Negro socialization.* Englewood Cliffs, N.J.: Prentice-Hall.

Schwartz, Michael. 1965. Northern United States Negro matriarchy: status versus authority. *Phylon* 26:18–24.

Shockley, Ann A. 1967. Negro librarians in predominantly Negro colleges. *College and Res. Libraries* 28: 423–26.

Smith, Mary, 1968. Birth control and the Negro woman. *Ebony* 23:29–32.

Solomon, Daniel; Parelius, Robert J.; and Busse, Thomas V. 1969. Dimensions of achievement-related behavior among lower-class Negro parents. *Genet. Psychol. Monographs* 79:163–90.

Staples, Robert.
  1970.   The myth of the Black matriarchy. *Black Scholar* 1:8–16.
  1971.   Towards a sociology of the Black family: a theoretical and methodological assessment. *J. Marriage and Family* 33:19–38.

Strodtbeck, Fred L. 1964. The poverty-dependency syndrome of the ADC female-based Negro family. *Am. J. Orthopsychiat.* 34:216–17.

Strong, Augusta. 1967. Negro women in freedom's battles. *Freedomways* 7:302–15.

Swift, David W. 1969. Interracial effectiveness of sub-professional aides. *Phylon* 30:394–97.

Teicher, Joseph D. 1968. Some observations on identity problems in children of Negro-White marriages. *J. Nerv. Ment. Dis.* 146:249–65.

Tulkin, Steven R. 1968. Race, class, family and school achievement. *J. Personality Soc. Psychol.* 9:31–37.

U.S. Census Office.
  1883.   *Statistics of the population of the United States at the tenth census.* Vol. 1. Washington, D.C.: U.S. Government Printing Office.

1902.   *Census reports.* Vol. 2, pt. 2: Population. Washington, D.C.:
         U.S. Government Printing Office.
U.S. Department of Commerce. Bureau of the Census.
1913.   *Population, general report and analysis.* Vol. 1. Washington,
         D.C.: U.S. Government Printing Office.
1922.   *Population, general report and analytical tables.* Vol. 2. Wash-
         ington, D.C.: U.S. Government Printing Office.
1931.   *Fifteenth census of the United States: 1930.* Vol. 1. Washing-
         ton, D.C.: U.S. Government Printing Office.
1933.   *Population, general reports on occupations.* Vol. 5. Washing-
         ton, D.C.: U.S. Government Printing Office.
1943*a*. *Population, the labor force, occupation, industry, employment
         and income.* Vol. 3, pt. 1: United States summary. Washington,
         D.C.: U.S. Government Printing Office.
1943*b*. *Sixteenth census of the United States: 1940.* Vol. 2: Character-
         istics of the population; pt. 1: United States summary, Ala-
         bama–District of Columbia. Washington, D.C.: U.S. Govern-
         ment Printing Office.
1943*c*. *Sixteenth census of the United States: 1940.* Vol. 4: Population,
         characteristics by age, marital status, relationship, education,
         and citizenship; pt. 1: U.S. summary. Washington, D.C.: U.S.
         Government Printing Office.
1953.   *Seventeenth census of the United States: 1950.* Population,
         characteristics by age, marital status, relationship, education,
         and citizenship, pt. 1: United States summary. Washington,
         D.C.: U.S. Government Printing Office.
1964.   *U.S. census of population: 1960.* Vol. 1: Characteristics of the
         population, pt. 1: United States Summary. Washington, D.C.:
         U.S. Government Printing Office.
1970*a*. *The social and economic status of Negroes in the United
         States,* 1969. BLS Report no. 375, Current Population Reports,
         Series P-23, no. 29. Washington, D.C.: U.S. Government Print-
         ing Office.
1970*b*. *Current population reports.* Series P-60, no. 75: Income in
         1969 of families and persons in the United States. Washington,
         D.C.: U.S. Government Printing Office.
1970*c*. *Current population reports.* Series P-20, no. 194: Educational
         attainment, March 1969. Washington, D.C.: U.S. Government
         Printing office.
1970*d*. *Current population reports.* Series P-20, no. 207: Educational
         attainment, March 1970. Washington, D.C.: U.S. Government
         Printing Office.
1970*e*. *Statistical abstract of the United States: 1970.* Washington,
         D.C.: U.S. Government Printing Office.

1971.   1970 *Census of Population.* PC(V2)-1: United States, advance report, general population characteristics. Washington, D.C.: U.S. Department of Commerce.

U.S. Department of Health, Education, and Welfare.

1969.   *Vital statistics of the United States, 1967.* Vol. 1: Natality. Washington, D.C.: U.S. Government Printing Office.

1970.   *Vital and health statistics.* National Center for Health Statistics, Series 11, no. 37: Selected symptoms of psychological distress, United States. Washington, D.C.: U.S. Government Printing Office.

Valentine, Charles A. 1968. *Culture and poverty, critique and counterproposals.* Chicago: University of Chicago Press.

Vincent, Clark. 1961. *Unmarried mothers.* Glencoe, Ill.; Free Press.

Vroman, Mary Elizabeth. 1963. *Esther.* New York: Bantam.

Walker, Margaret. 1966. *Jubilee.* Boston, Mass.: Houghton Mifflin.

Watkins, Elizabeth L. 1968. Low-income Negro mothers—their decision to seek pre-natal care. *Am. J. Pub. Health* 58:655–776.

Wheatley, Phillis. 1773. *Poems on various subjects, religious and moral.* London. Reprinted 1966, edited, with an introduction, by Julian D. Mason, Jr. Chapel Hill: University of North Carolina Press. Apparently this represents the first published work by an Afro-American in the United States.

Whitehead, John S. 1969. *Ida's family: adaptations to poverty in a suburban ghetto.* Yellow Springs, Ohio: Antioch College.

Williams, Fanny Barrier.

1893.   *The present status and intellectual progress of Colored women.* Address delivered at the Congress of Representative Women, World's Congress Auxiliary of the World's Columbian Exposition, Chicago, May 1898. Other data lead us to believe that the correct date for this is 1893.

1900.   *A new Negro for a new century.* Chicago: American Printing House.

Willie, Charles V., ed. 1970. *The family life of Black People.* Columbus, Ohio: Charles E. Merrill.

Wright, Sarah E. 1969. *The child's gonna live.* New York: Delacorte.

CHAPTER 8

Racism and the Mental Health of White Americans: A Social Psychological View

by Thomas F. Pettigrew

Working definitions are given of such concepts as prejudice, ethnocentrism, direct and indirect discrimination, and individual and institutional racism. Social and personality contexts of prejudice are explored, particularly with respect to personalities rooted in authoritarianism and conformity, showing their relation to mental health. Four generalizations are offered concerning racism and the mental health of White Americans, and necessary remedial action in reducing institutional racism is emphasized.

Jack Hess is a big, friendly steelworker who grew up in a small town in Iowa and came to Gary, Ind., after completing high school and his armed service in Korea.[1] He proved to be a cooperative respondent for a survey interview that was being administered to a representative sample of the city's Whites. The survey focused upon Richard Hatcher, who made political history in 1967 by becoming Gary's first Black mayor. Hess was bluntly direct when he forcefully stated that he had not voted for Hatcher for mayor, nor was he planning to vote for him in the future.

"Tell me," followed up the interviewer, "is there *anything* Richard Hatcher could do as mayor to cause you seriously to consider voting for him in 1971 for mayor?"

Hess thought a moment. Then he explained his position.

---

1. "Jack Hess" is, of course, a pseudonym.

"Well, to tell you the truth I don't like the present mayor because he's Colored, and I didn't like the previous mayor, Katz, for he's a Jew. I'd just rather have one of my own kind in there running things. But there is this stinking city dump just two blocks down the street that all of us here on the block have been screaming about for years. And if this new mayor would just close down this damn dump, I swear I'd vote for him even if he is Colored."

Relevant Definitions

This frank survey response illustrates for us the basic distinctions we need in order to understand racism from a social psychological perspective. Hess evinces outgroup *prejudice* and a generalized *ethnocentrism* when he rejects Gary's former mayor as a Jew and its present mayor as a Black. He apparently would prefer to have "one of my own kind in there running things" — almost solely on group criteria rather than individual qualifications. Note that prejudice and ethnocentrism are broader terms than racism and do not include just Black Americans. More formally, we can define *prejudice as an affective, categorical mode of mental functioning involving rigid prejudgment and misjudgment of human groups.*[2] Ethnocentrism is a similar concept involving an individual's thinking about and relation to human groups. As employed by Adorno et al. (1950), *ethnocentrism is an organized system of items, or ideology, characterized by rigid ingroup and outgroup distinctions, stereotyped and hostile attitudes of outgroups generally, stereotyped and submissive attitudes of ingroups generally, and a hierarchial, authoritarian view of group interactions.* Ethnocentrism, then, is a broader term than prejudice. It emphasizes the bigot's tendency to draw sharp dichotomies between ingroups and out-

---

2. For a thorough discussion of the concept of prejudice, see Allport (1954).

groups and to be prejudiced against a wide variety of out-groups.

Discrimination is the action component of intergroup prejudice. While stereotyped beliefs and prejudiced attitudes are cognitive, discrimination requires an active conative means of expressing the outgroup hostility and rejection. Hess is a solid supporter of the Democratic Party in both national and local elections; yet when Hatcher ran in November of 1968 as the Democratic nominee, he cast his ballot for the almost unknown Republican nominee for purely racial reasons. Such a vote on these grounds is obviously discriminatory. More formally, we may define *discriminatory behavior as the acting out of intergroup prejudice against an outgroup on largely ascribed and particularistic grounds of group membership rather than on achieved and universalistic grounds of ability. To constitute direct discrimination, such acting out must limit the opportunities and choices open to the victimized group.* Important as this phenomenon is in American race relations, *indirect discrimination* is even more common for it refers to *restrictions in one realm,* such as politics, *created by direct discrimination in another realm,* such as education. For example, if Mayor Hatcher had been *directly* discriminated against and prevented from attending and graduating from the Law School of the University of Indiana—his alma mater—then this would have had the *indirect* effect of causing him to be unqualified to run for mayor.

Myrdal (1944) pointed out a generation ago in his *American Dilemma* that racial discrimination in the United States has formed a vicious circle, with restrictions in housing, politics, employment, education, or any one realm complexly interwoven with restrictions in all others. Thus authorities in each realm can point to the "true" core of the problem as lying elsewhere. In reality, each realm's restrictions contribute to the web of direct and indirect discrimination that has encircled Black Americans for years. But Myrdal also pointed out an interesting property of vicious circles of causation: they can be broken at any point and evolve in time into self-correcting benign circles of affirmative racial change.

Since Myrdal wrote his classic volume, progress bears out his contention with one vital qualification. Racial change does not come evenly across all realms; rather, discrimination is alleviated in some areas faster than in others, with the retarded areas acting through indirect discrimination to slow progress in other areas. During the 1940s and 1950s, direct discrimination in employment proved to be the primary barrier to general improvement. More recently, direct discrimination in housing and in primary and secondary education have become especially crucial (Pettigrew 1971a). At any rate, remedial efforts in a given realm are most effectively fashioned against the direct discrimination involved rather than the indirect discrimination stemming from other realms (Fein 1966; Pettigrew 1971a). More effective yet, of course, are broad-scaled antidiscrimination efforts which attack systematically the whole process across realms.

Social psychology has focused considerable attention upon the relationship between prejudice and discrimination, for the ties between the two are more complex and problematic than generally thought. There is, of course, a positive relationship between the two, with discriminators generally more prejudiced than nondiscriminators. But the relationship is not at all perfect. Many relatively prejudiced Whites rarely engage in direct racial discrimination, and many relatively unprejudiced Whites engage in it virtually every day of their lives. These "error" cases are typically caused by immediate factors of the interracial situation and broader social factors of the culture and society. Much prejudice as well as discriminatory behavior represents conformity to what is situationally and societally expected of us (Pettigrew 1971a). Jack Hess's views, for instance, are highly consistent with those of his neighbors. Thus, the social milieu can importantly affect prejudice, discrimination, or both. Put

differently, we must always view these phenomena in their
social context—a critical point to which we shall return.

Within this perspective, then, *individual racism involves
both prejudicial beliefs and discriminatory behavior of individuals specifically directed against Black Americans.*[3] Its
anti-Black orientation is *fundamentally based on superior-
ity-inferiority assumptions of race* that trace straight back to
Count Arthur de Gobineau's *Essai sur l'inégalité des races
humaines,* published in the nineteenth century.[4] Indeed,
over the years, the arguments of de Gobineau have changed
surprisingly little in racist thought despite repeated efforts to
dress them up with pseudoscientific respectability (Pettigrew
1964, chaps. 3–6).

But two basic misconceptions have become widespread
since the concept of individual racism was popularized by
the National Advisory Commission on Civil Disorders Report
(1968)—better known as the Kerner Commission Report.
First, individual racism is often discussed as if it operated in
a psychological vacuum, apart from a person's other values
and beliefs. But Jack Hess, our steelworker from Gary, makes
it clear that such a view is naïve. He readily admits to individual racism but easily cites something more important to
him than racism—". . . if this new mayor would just close
down this damn dump, *I swear I'd vote for him even if he is
Colored.*" Or, paraphrased, "Even though I'm a racist, I care
more about closing the stinking dump than I do about the
race of the mayor." Clearly, then, individual racism is *not*
operating in a psychological vacuum. Rather, it is always
acting in concert or in conflict with other values and attitudes

3. "Racism" can, of course, apply to a range of outgroups who are perceived to be racially distinct from the ingroup. Thus, anti-Semites are more
likely to perceive Jews as a "race" than others, and, hence, their feelings
against Jews might thus be described as "racist." But we are using the term
in its narrow and current North American application to Black Americans.

4. For an excellent treatment of the early origins of racist thinking in the
United States, see Stanton (1960).

to form a crudely ordered hierarchy of what is most important to the individual. For Jack Hess, closing the dump and living in an improved neighborhood environment rank over racism. For some other respondents, racism ranks much higher in their hierarchies. This point is a basic contribution of social psychology to an appreciation of this social problem, and we shall return to it shortly when we attempt to sketch out a theory of racism and mental illness.

The second misconception abroad is that individual racism acts in a social and institutional vacuum. Just as an exclusive focus upon prejudice blinds us to the more immediately crucial issues of discrimination, an exclusive emphasis upon individual racism blinds us to the dominant issues of institutional racism. Consider again the social context of Jack Hess's blunt response in Gary. To interpret what he says meaningfully, one must know that political racism had prevented Blacks from ever becoming mayor of the city prior to the rise of Richard Hatcher. Had Gary boasted previous Black mayors, the rejection by Hess of Hatcher as mayor would take on deeper personal significance. But the institutionally racist milieu within which Hess lives means that his aversion may represent in part a sense of threat of the new and the strange. It is significant, too, in judging Gary's racial norms that its White community gave Governor George Wallace one of his largest voting percentages for president in 1968 of any community outside of the South.

We can define *institutional racism*, then, as *that complex of institutional arrangements that restrict the life choices of Black Americans in comparison to those of White Americans.* Such a definition can rightfully be challenged on the grounds that it is too all-encompassing, that it covers virtually all the nation's institutions and their operations. But is this the fault of the definition, or is it a reasonably accurate picture of American society? In this chapter the contention is that the latter is the case and that the broad definition therefore proves useful.

Three points need to be made about institutional racism. First, as we have seen in the case of Jack Hess, institutional racism avidly supports individual racism as if it were a fifty-two-week-a-year antibrotherhood reminder. An attack upon institutional racism specifically is more needed than all of the brotherhood sermons and dinners conceivable. Second, racist institutions need not be headed by racists nor designed with racist intentions to limit Black choice. Indeed, it makes little difference to Black Americans what the formal intentions are, for the restrictive consequences are the same.

Finally, institutional racism is extremely difficult to combat effectively. We have already determined that one reason for this is the complex system of racial discrimination that spans the various realms and institutions of American society. A second reason concerns the positive functions of institutional arrangements with racist effects. Many of these arrangements, perhaps even most of them, were originally designed and established to serve positive functions for the institution without thought of their racial implications. They have been maintained precisely because they do in fact accomplish these positive functions. Thus Harvard University in the 1930s set up a variety of meaningful criteria, including publication of scholarly works, to select their tenured faculty. The aim was praiseworthy—namely, to ensure a faculty of high quality. Yet the publishing requirement effectively acted to restrict the recruitment of Black professors, for most of them carried heavy teaching loads in predominantly Black colleges, which limited their time to write. Not surprisingly, then, Harvard University in the 1960s found itself with only a handful of Black faculty members. Yet the university is understandably loath to give up a selection procedure that has served its intended function well, though its unintended racist consequences are a matter of record. This example can be repeated almost endlessly in American society. The problem, then, is not simply to eliminate racist arrangements, difficult as that alone would be, but to replace these arrangements with others that serve the same positive functions equally well without the racist consequences.[5]

Racism and Mental Health in America

A principal mission of social psychology is to combine the individual and social levels of analysis in formulating meaningful models of social behavior. In recent years this focus has been applied more and more to the broad area of mental illness with increasing success (Freeman and Giovannoni 1969; Wechsler, Solomon, and Kramer 1970). Some of these contributions are reflected in the group therapy and the community mental health movements. Some of them have been applied, especially by Jahoda (1961), to the relationship between prejudice and mental illness.

Jahoda joins the numerous students of the field who have objected to the simple dichotomy of "sick" and "well." She points out that at the very least a middle category of "not healthy" is necessary to account for the empirical data that have been collected on the subject. Positive mental health, she argues convincingly, is not merely the absence of mental

5. The Harvard example is provided because it is close to the author's experience. It is also cited to illustrate how each of us can find prime examples of insitutional racism in our immediate lives. For those who question what they can personally do to combat racism, the answer is to work for structural change in the very institutions of which they are participants. Here the Harvard example is also useful. With very little alteration in the selection system, the university could set aside a certain proportion of faculty funds for Blacks which, unlike the usual faculty salary budget, would not be proportioned off in fixed amounts to each school and department. In other words, the competitive system would be inverted to where each unit of the university would have an incentive to find relevant and competent Black faculty. There are still other problems not met by this new structure. It is at best transitional. Nor can it be allowed to encourage talent raids on predominantly Black campuses (Poinsett 1970). The ultimate need, of course, is an enormous expansion in qualified Black Ph.D.'s, an expansion that has only begun at present (Pettigrew 1971b). Yet this suggested rearrangement serves to illustrate the type of transitional device needed in many realms.

illness. Many individuals do not meet the criteria of either mental health or mental illness; they can best be seen as simply "not healthy."

Survey data gathered and analyzed by Bradburn (1970) support and extend Jahoda's contentions. In this important new study he repeatedly interviewed over two thousand respondents in five contrasting areas ranging from middle-class suburbia to the inner city to learn how the common problems of life relate to "psychological well-being." The closed-end interviews first evaluated perceived happiness by asking the respondents to rate themselves "very happy," "pretty happy," or "not too happy." A third described themselves as "very happy" compared with from 5 percent to 15 percent as "not too happy." But more than 20 percent of the respondents residing in an economically depressed area rated themselves as "not too happy"; and older persons evaluated themselves as less happy than younger persons. However, no sex differences in rated happiness emerged.

Bradburn next obtained measures of psychological well-being by asking his respondents whether they had experienced within the past few weeks a variety of positive and negative feelings. The most striking finding of this research, perhaps, is the fact that these two components of well-being — one of positive affect, the other negative affect — are independent of one another. That is, knowledge of a person's positive affect does not permit prediction of his negative affect. Moreover, neither a positive nor a negative feeling state significantly relates to the self-reports of happiness. Yet the *difference* between the positive and negative components is highly associated with happiness and is called by Bradburn the Affect Balance Scale. In short, an individual experiences a sense of psychological well-being when he has an excess of positive over negative feelings and a sense of diminished well-being when negative feelings are in excess of positive feelings.

Once established as the crucial measure, the Affect Balance Scale was then related to a host of other variables. Women possessed slightly lower scores than men, though few age differences were noted. Blacks reported lower scores and less sense of well-being. This racial difference appears to be largely a result of differences between Black and White Americans in education and income. Those respondents with higher education and income experienced considerably greater positive affect than others and felt greater psychological well-being. This not-too-surprising result seems to be traceable in part to the typically increased amount of social participation for persons of higher socieconomic status. And much of the positive value of social participation was the increased likelihood of the participant's experiencing novel experiences, which increased his sense of well-being. Likewise, Bradburn found that male unemployment, marital tensions, and not being married all acted to heighten negative affect and, without compensating increases in positive affect, to lead to impaired well-being.

Bradburn's work connects directly with Jahoda's contentions when the Affect Balance Scale is related to more traditional conditions of anxiety and mental health. Both anxiety and mental illness are highly correlated with negative but not with positive affect. They could, therefore, be compensated for by extensive positive experiences to achieve a modicum of psychological well-being. At any rate, Jahoda's three categories of "sick," "well," and "not healthy" can be roughly translated into Bradburn's Affect Balance terms as follows: "sick" can refer to an unusual degree of negative affect uncompensated for by increased positive affect; "well" can refer to a surplus of positive over negative affect; and "not healthy" can refer to states of near parity between positive and negative affects or where negative affect slightly outweighs positive affect. Jahoda and Bradburn agree, then, that positive mental health, or "psychological well-being," constitutes a great deal more than the simple absence of mental illness.

Such a view is necessary to untangle what appears at first to be a basic contradiction in the findings of research on prejudice and mental illness. One set of studies has utilized mental patients and has failed to detect simple relationships between the intensity of their intergroup animosities and either the severity of their psychiatric disorders or the particular diagnoses (Ackerman and Jahoda 1950; Adorno et al. 1950; Jensen 1957). A closer look, however, at the underlying personality dynamics does reveal some differences between the highly prejudiced and the unprejudiced patients. The former "usually displayed very little awareness of their own feelings and psychological problems" (Adorno et al. 1950). They often suffered from vague anxiety or physical signs of anxiety and rage with somatic complaints. Significantly, two of the investigations note the conspicuous *absence* of depression among the highly bigoted (Ackerman and Jahoda 1950; Adorno et al. 1950). By comparison, the unprejudiced patients often suffered from serious inhibitions and neurotic depression with feelings of inadequacy. They were as a group "more familiar with themselves, more aware and accepting of emotional experiences and problems" (Adorno et al. 1950). Jahoda notes that these findings are in line with personality theories of prejudice: namely, the tendency of bigots to externalize their problems by projecting feelings of discomfort onto such definite objects as somatic symptoms.

Research data on psychiatric patients, however, are in considerable conflict with data collected on such supposedly normal populations as high school and college students. This second body of research has generally employed the Minnesota Multiphasic Personality Inventory (MMPI), a self-administered true-false psychometric instrument designed to measure an array of psychiatric symptoms. Standardized on patient populations, the MMPI collects information about relatively distinct patterns, each of which corresponds to the symptoms and problems of a clinical category of mental illness such as depression. These investigations have consistently obtained clear-cut results: prejudice is positively correlated with symptoms corresponding to hypochondriasis, depression, psychopathic deviations, schizophrenia, and hypomania and negatively correlated with defensiveness and hysteria (Altus and Tafejian 1953; Freedman, Webster, and Sanford 1956; Gough 1951; Jensen 1957).[6]

Additional studies of normal subjects using other methods have revealed similar, if not as striking, trends. Courtney, Greer, and Masling (1952) found no significant differences in responses on the Rotter Incomplete Sentences Test between those scoring high and low on the famous measure of the prejudice-prone authoritarian personality, the F Scale. But Jones (1955) found in two samples of naval aviation cadets that the F Scale related positively to the Taylor Manifest Anxiety Test. Furthermore, Meer (1952, 1955) noted significant differences in the affective content of the dreams of high and low authoritarians. In his undergraduate sample he noted that high authoritarians had more aggression toward outgroup characters than toward ingroup characters and that low authoritarians revealed no significant differences in aggression between ingroup and outgroup characters. In addition, only high authoritarians had more friendly acts with ingroup than with outgroup characters in their dreams. Meer contended that his results support the notion that the prejudice-prone cannot tolerate emotional ambivalence.

How these trends among the prejudiced were shaped in early life is suggested in the intriguing findings of Harris, Gough, and Martin (1950). They found that the mothers of

6. Interestingly, the MMPI's scale to measure paranoid trends has often not distinguished between prejudiced and unprejudiced subjects—despite the strong theoretical rationale for why it should. One investigation (Freedman, Webster, and Sanford 1956), however, found that this was due to items in the paranoia scale of the MMPI that measured naïveté rather than those tapping persecution fears. Another study (Jensen 1957) found that, in spite of this artifact of measurement, extremely prejudiced individuals (the extreme 7%) do score significantly higher on the paranoid scale.

fourth-, fifth-, and sixth-grade pupils tended to differ in their views on child-training according to their children's prejudices against minorities. Thus, the mothers of bigoted children were far more likely to believe that "obedience is the most important thing a child can learn," "a child should never be permitted to set his will against that of his parents," and "a child should never keep a secret from his parents." They preferred "a quiet child to one who is noisy" and, in the case of temper tantrums, believed that the child should be taught "that two can play that game by getting angry yourself."

How these trends manifest themselves in later life is shown in table 8.1. These data are from the same Gary survey in which Jack Hess, the steelworker, was interviewed. Two interesting findings emerge from this table. First, in the right-hand column, we see how a racism scale relates to a measure of suspicion and fear of crime among a probability sample of 230 White male adults of Gary, Ind., in 1968. As expected, the two measures are positively associated, but not consistently so, over their full distributions. Thus, among the highly anti-Black respondents, 69 percent (fifty-six out of eighty-one) are also extremely fearful of crime; but among the relatively unprejudiced, only 40 percent (twenty-nine out of seventy-two) are low in concern over crime. The relationship tends, then, to be one way; that is, we can predict fear of crime for the extreme bigots but not for the tolerant respondents. This is a general finding in this realm of research, and we shall return to it when we state our conclusions in this chapter.

Second, table 8.1 reveals that *both* racism and fear of crime independently relate to the view of Mayor Richard Hatcher despite their being highly interrelated. At the extremes, low racist and less suspicious respondents are almost four times more likely to hold a favorable impression of their Black mayor than high racist and suspicious respondents (83 percent to 21 percent). To interpret this finding, note that the

TABLE 8.1.   Racism, fear, and White views
of Mayor Hatcher of Gary, Ind.

Racism[a]	Suspicion and Fear of Crime[b]	White Gary Voters Who Perceive Mayor Hatcher Favorably[c]	Number of Respondents
Low	Low	83%	29
	Medium	61	28
	High	53	15
Medium	Low	63	16
	Medium	56	27
	High	41	34
High	Low	63	8
	Medium	47	17
	High	21	56

SOURCE: Unpublished survey study of Gary, Ind., conducted in October of 1968 (Pettigrew 1968).

a. Measured by agreement with such statements as: "Whites have a right to keep Negroes out of their neighborhood," "Negroes shouldn't push themselves where they're not wanted," "I would object strongly if a family member brought a Negro friend home to dinner," and "I would mind a lot if a Negro family with the same income and education moved next door."

b. Measured by agreement with such statements as: "Buses are not safe these days without a policeman," "Safety on the streets is the most important issue facing America now," "The major cause of race riots is ... Communists, outsiders," and "The assassination of national leaders was carefully planned by a group, not the work of individuals."

c. Respondents were asked to select three adjectives that were most descriptive of Mayor Hatcher from a card of 12 adjectives, half of which were favorable (e.g., intelligent, honest) and half unfavorable (e.g., corrupt, prejudiced). Perception was rated favorable when 2 or 3 of the 3 adjectives selected were favorable.

items that comprise the suspicion and fear of crime scale are quite extreme, going beyond the reasonable limits of concern over Gary's realistic problems of crime. If we can accept this measure of suspicion, then, as a crude negative indicator of positive mental health, table 8.1 shows for this White male sampling that: (1) extreme racism is associated with suspicion and the absence of positive mental health and (2) racism and the absence of positive mental health combine to predict a strongly unfavorable reaction to a new and powerful Black leader on the local scene.

Two contradictions arise, then, between the results of these two types of research on the links between prejudice and mental illness. In the test studies of normal subjects, a clear pattern of psychological disturbance emerges for the prejudiced but does not emerge in the clinical studies of mental patients. Moreover, the one clear diagnosis which seems to characterize *unprejudiced* patients, depression, turns out to characterize *prejudiced* students.

Resolution of these disparities, Jahoda shows, requires the "not healthy" category in addition to "ill" and "healthy." She maintains that the psychiatric research indicates that severe mental illness is not associated with being more or less prejudiced, while the student research indicates that among normals the absence of positive mental health is associated with being more prejudiced. But bluntly, the highly prejudiced are probably not more prone to debilitating mental illness than others, but they do appear less often to possess positive mental health. Jahoda's conclusion receives support from such varied research as studies which indicate extraordinarily intense levels of intergroup prejudice among incarcerated criminals (Adorno et al. 1950) and which indicate that the presence of prejudice is an accurate inverse predictor of improvement through psychotherapy (Barron 1953; Dowling 1955; Haimowitz and Haimowitz 1950).

Additional research on members of the radical right also supports Jahoda's theories. Chesler and Schmuck (1969) reported after interviewing over sixty midwestern "superpatriots" that they "were not generally psychotic, irrational or severely disturbed; they were not suffering from excessive anomie and did not feel especially powerless." For the most part, they appeared to be "pleasant, considerate and law-abiding." Likewise Elms (1970) finds that with few exceptions the radical right believers he interviewed in

Dallas were not any "nuttier than anyone else." The political climate of their city strongly reinforced their beliefs. And, argues Elms, "radical rightism is a sort of quick-and-easy, mail-order-diploma way to gain political expertise, and its conspiracy theories supply the requisite titillations."

Jahoda's conclusion begs the further question as to just what is positive mental health. This is not the appropriate place to go into this matter in detail. However, we have already described Bradburn's (1970) operational approach of defining it in terms of a surplus of positive over negative affect. Following Jahoda (1958, 1961), therefore, a few tentative theoretical criteria can be listed and compared with the personality aspects of prejudice. She lists six categories of human functioning that have been suggested by various writers as useful, though admittedly value-laden, approaches to a concept of positive mental health: (1) the mentally healthy individual is self-aware, self-accepting, and enjoys a stable identity, (2) an individual's degree of development and actualization of his potential is indicative of mental health, (3) so, too, is an individual's integration of psychic functions, (4) an individual's autonomy, relative independence from social pressures, and ability to act independently under internal controls are also seen as revealing,[7] (5) the adequacy of an individual's perception of reality has also been suggested as a criterion, and (6) finally, positive mental health requires the ability to master one's environment at a reasonable level of competency.

How does such a definition of positive mental health fit with what is known of the personality features of extreme intergroup prejudice? Numerous investigations suggest that

7. Relevant to this criterion are the results of the intensive study by Myers and Roberts (1959) of 50 middle-class and lower-class ambulatory schizophrenics and their families. These researchers noted among the middle-class mothers, though not among lower-class mothers, a strong tendency toward demanding perfectionism and overconforming with extreme control of impulses.

deeply rooted prejudice is in fact relevant to all six of the criteria above. Antiintraception, the refusal to look within oneself, is the hallmark of the prejudiced personality as uncovered repeatedly in research (Adorno et al. 1950; Christie and Jahoda 1954; Christie and Cook 1958; Titus and Hollander 1957; Harding, Kutner, Proshansky, and Chein 1954; Harding, Proshansky, Kutner, and Chein 1969). Prejudice typically serves as a projection of the bigot's problem onto others, the very opposite of the first criterion of positive mental health. The second criterion of self-actualization is more difficult to apply, though it seems reasonable to infer that prejudice in general might well act to retard the full development of one's potential.

The integration and unity of psychic functions, the next criterion, is clearly blocked by the bigot's strong use of denial as a defense mechanism. A number of studies have demonstrated that those who harbor deep prejudice are more likely than others to conform to group pressure in a standard experimental situation (Block and Block 1952; Crutchfield 1955; Wells, Weinert, and Rubel 1956) and thus fail to meet Jahoda's fourth indicator of positive mental health. The extremely prejudiced individual has also been found to employ rigid stereotypes and dichotomized thinking more than others, and this tendency violates Jahoda's fifth indicator. Finally, the sixth criterion of environmental mastery introduces a more complicated picture. It can be argued that the bigot's environmental mastery is enhanced by prejudice when it bolsters his sense of worth and effectively organizes his world. But here again, it is not difficult to think of situations where these personality functions of prejudice would fail the bigot.

We can, then, accept Jahoda's basic conclusion: *the highly prejudiced may well not be more prone to severe mental illness than others, but they do appear less often to possess positive mental health.* Building on her conclusion, we can extend this analysis by recalling the two insights provided by

Jack Hess, the steelworker: prejudice is always embedded both in a social context of intergroup norms and expectations and in a personality context of other values and beliefs.

The Social and Personality Contexts of Prejudice

Attitudes of any sort serve three vital personality functions (Smith, Bruner, and White 1956). First, there is the *object appraisal* function, that is, attitudes aid in understanding "reality" as it is defined by the culture. As societies and cultures change, the social consensus as to what constitutes "reality" shifts and attitudes shift accordingly. This is one of the psychological processes underlying the individual adaptations to the sweeping social alterations of our times. Another and somewhat similar psychological process is involved in the second function of attitudes, that of *social adjustment*. Attitudes aid socially by contributing to the individual's identification with, or differentiation from, various "reference groups."[8] They can help him conform to what is expected of him.

Finally, attitudes can reduce anxiety by serving an expressive or *externalization* function, the prejudice function focused upon in our discussion to this point. This occurs when an individual senses an analogy between a perceived event and some unresolved inner problem; he then adopts an attitude toward the event which is a transformed version of his way of dealing with his inner difficulty. In short, he externalizes his personality problems by projecting them onto the world through particular attitudes. Thus if he has sexual problems, he may come to regard Blacks as dan-

---

8. "Reference group" is an important social psychological concept needed to relate the social and personality systems. A reference group supplies standards which an individual may use to guide his own behavior and with which he may compare his own position in life. Note that a reference group is not necessarily a membership group. See Hyman and Singer (1968), Merton (1968, chaps. 10, 11), and Pettigrew (1967).

gerously hypersexed. The most fashionable psychological explanations of prejudice — frustration-aggression, psychoanalytic, and authoritarianism theories — all deal chiefly with the externalization process. The last of these, authoritarianism, has received massive research emphasis and deserves our special attention.

Motivated by a need to understand the Nazi movement in Germany, a group of personality specialists at the University of California at Berkeley intensively studied the personality dynamics of anti-Semites in the United States during the 1940s. They found a syndrome of personality traits, labeled "authoritarianism," that consistently differentiated many highly anti-Semitic and ethnocentric individuals from others. We have already noted that central to the syndrome is antiintraception, the refusal to look inside of oneself and a general lack of insight into one's own behavior and feelings. Probably deriving from early childhood training, the authoritarian refuses to accept his own emotions and tries hard to deny them. For instance, as a child the authoritarian may have frequently been punished by a stern father and in turn felt intense hatred for him. Unable to express his feelings for fear of further punishment, the authoritarian found these aggressive emotions threatening and unacceptable, denied them, and instead began to project them onto others. If he felt hatred for his father, he saw hatred not in himself but in the dangerous outside world.

Consequently, the authoritarian typically conveys an idealized picture of his parents as absolutely perfect and loving. Generalizing this unrealistic view to other authorities, the authoritarian comes to view the world in good-bad, up-and-down power terms. He is generally outwardly submissive toward those he sees as authorities with power over him. Similarly, he is aggressive toward those he sees as being beneath him in status. This hierarchical view of authority has led to the label of "authoritarian personality." Prejudice becomes for individuals possessing this personality "a crutch" upon which to limp through life. Lacking insight into their inner feelings, they project their own unacceptable impulses on the minorities whom they regard as being beneath them.[9] Hartley (1946) demonstrated that such persons will often reject on a questionnaire groups which do not even exist.

The psychoanalytically inspired theory of the authoritarian personality is a valuable contribution to an understanding of race relations in America. But the almost exclusive attention given the externalization function of prejudice has caused a lack of attention to the equally important function of social adjustment. By no means do all White Americans who hold anti-Black opinions and participate in discriminatory actions exhibit the authoriatarian personality syndrome. For many, anti-Black views and behavior are not nearly so expressive as they are socially adaptive in a racist society. In sharp contrast to the deeply rooted bigotry of authoritarianism, the bigotry of "conformity" requires prejudice as a social entrance ticket. The conformity bigot wants to be liked and accepted by people important to him; and if these people are anti-Black, he reflects their attitudes.

Notice the two significant differences between the authoritarian and conformity varieties of intolerance. Those who are anti-Black for largely conformity reasons have antipathy only for those groups that it is fashionable to dislike; their prejudice does not spread to outgroups in general as does that of authoritarians. They follow the path of least social resistance, for they need to be liked rather than to hate. More important, conformity prejudice is not so deeply rooted in childhood socialization, but is only an attempt to "live down" to what associates expect. Thus as social expectations are altered,

9. Note that this description fits the authoritarian of the political Right. Authoritarians are also found on the political Left; with equal dogmatism, they reject all authorities and attempt a strangely condescending identification with minorities. The politics of the two authoritarian types may be polar opposites, but the personality style remains strikingly the same. The first statement on this point was provided by Shils (1954).

conforming bigots shed their bigotry with relative ease. They continue to conform, but there is change in customs and norms that guide their beliefs and actions. Obviously, conformity prejudice makes possible at the individual level the power of situational norms to determine racial attitudes and behavior at the social level (Pettigrew 1971*a,* chap. 6).

Hence, it becomes important to inquire about the distributions of authoritarian and conformity bigots across the United States. Do most White Americans *need,* in a deep authoritarian personality sense, anti-Black prejudice? Or do most White Americans who harbor anti-Black attitudes do so largely in order to follow racist dictates and expectations? The answers to these questions are of considerable importance for public policy and the future of American race relations as well as for our understanding of the links between racism and mental illness.

First, it must be realized that the two types of prejudice are ideal types. In practice, the two are seldom seen in pure form; more typically, anti-Black prejudice weaves together elements of both types. Yet it is still possible to ascertain roughly the prevalence of persons who are relatively authoritarian in their orientation against Blacks in contrast to those who are relatively more conforming.

After a close inspection of the relevant data in the 1950s, Allport (1954) estimated that roughly "four-fifths of the American population harbors enough antagonism toward minority groups to influence their daily conduct." This crude figure varies widely, of course, across groupings according to region, age, and social class, and it varies widely, too, according to the research question and method employed. Yet allport's estimate continues to receive support from divergent data sources. Furthermore, the unprejudiced one-fifth noted by Allport appears to be matched by a prejudiced one-fifth motivated largely by authoritarian personality needs. These are the citizens who place their racial beliefs so high in their value structure that they will follow them even when they conflict with their other values. They can be counted on to vote against any civil rights legislation, to favor political candidates who run on openly anti-Black platforms,[10] and to answer most survey questions on minority groups in general with bigoted responses.[11]

Roughly speaking, then, three-fifths of White Americans may well be conforming bigots. On racial issues that face considerable societal disapproval, such as the "bussing" of children to interracial schools, most of these citizens will join the authoritarians in forming a majority resistant to change. On racial issues that win wide societal approval, such as the 1964 Civil Rights Act after the assassination of President John F. Kennedy, most of these citizens will join the unprejudiced in forming a majority favorable to change. It is they, then, who are primarily responsible for the breath-

10. Thus at George Wallace's high point in national opinion surveys in his 1968 third-party candidacy for the presidency, he received support from 22% (25% of Whites) and secured almost 14% (16% of Whites) of the total vote (Pettigrew 1971*a*, chap. 10).

11. Thus 18% believed in December of 1963 that "White people should have the first chance at any kind of job"—the most extreme item in Sheatsley's (1966) prointegration scale. At the other extreme, only 27% disagreed that "Negroes shouldn't push themselves where they're not wanted." Similarly, the Harris national survey for *Newsweek* in 1966 found on its four most extreme anti-Negro items only "the authoritarian fifth" objecting "to using the same restrooms as Negroes" (22%), "to sitting next to a Negro in a movie" (21%), "to sitting next to a Negro on a bus" (16%), and "to sitting next to a Negro in a restaurant" (16%) (Brink and Harris 1967, p. 136). Finally, the "tolerant fifth" reveals itself sharply in four questions asked in a Gallup national survey of May 1968. When queries as to whether "White people or Negroes themselves" were more to blame for the present conditions of Negroes, only 23% of the Whites cited "White people" with 19% holding "no opinion." Similarly, only 17% of Whites (10% "no opinion") thought Negroes were being treated in their communities either "badly" or "not very well"; only 18% (14% "no opinion") thought businesses in their area discriminated against Negroes in hiring; and only 17% (31% "no opinion") thought labor unions in their area discriminated against Negroes in their membership practices (Erskine 1968–69).

taking swings in the national mood on racial change, swings from the high of 1964 to the low of 1972.

Crude as these ratios must necessarily be, they are accurate enough to put in order and render understandable a great mass of relevant data on race relations in recent years. Such an analysis suggests that persons who approximate the conformity-type bigot probably outnumber those who believe and act on racial questions with consistency, including both those who approximate authoritarian bigots and those who are not anti-Black. Even in the South, there is considerable evidence suggesting that conformity prejudice against Blacks is considerably more common than authoritarian prejudice (Pettigrew 1958, 1959, 1971a).

Two practical implications flow from this personality analysis. On the one hand, it suggests that White American racial opinion is more flexible than it might at first appear. If major sociocultural changes create optimal conditions for increased interracial contact, attitudes toward Blacks and racial change could continue to improve as they have since 1944 (Hyman and Sheatsley 1964; Pettigrew 1971a, chap. 8). Reform efforts for the needed structural changes should not be deterred by initial opposition of a majority of White Americans. On the other hand, it should give us pause that there is a strong possibility that the anti-Black sentiments of about one-fifth of White America reflect in varying measure deep externalizing functions. Twenty million adult citizens who approximate authoritarian bigots form a critical mass for societal conflict and make it likely the Wallace phenomenon of 1968 will be repeated throughout the 1970s.

Tentative Conclusions and Remedial Implications

We can draw together the various threads of our discussion and venture four tentative conclusions concerning the relationship between racism and the mental health of White

Americans. The following series of interlocking propositions
appears tenable:

1. *The highly prejudiced are not more prone to severe*
mental illness than the unprejudiced. There may well be,
however, differences between the two groups in symptoms,
with the prejudiced more prone to somatic complaints and
the unprejudiced more prone to depression. Moreover, the
relationship may in effect be one way but not two way. As
Jensen (1957, p. 303) has written: "It seems likely that the
relationship between mental ill health and authoritarianism
does not hold in both directions. In other words while it may
be possible to have any degree of mental illness without
showing authoritarian attitudes, it may not be possible to
manifest an extreme degree of authoritarianism without
being psychologically maladjusted." We have seen evidence
for Jensen's point in table 8.1. This trend leads to our second
proposition.

2. *The highly prejudiced less often possess positive men-*
tal health than others. Regardless of how positive mental
health is defined operationally and theoretically, the prejudiced as a group appear to possess less of it in "normal"
populations than do the relatively tolerant. This proposition,
then, assumes that mental health is more than just the absence of mental illness, that there is a middle state of "not
healthy" between those of "sick" and "well." This assumption is now firmly grounded in the results of research, including those of Bradburn (1970).

3. *At least two contrasting personality bases for prejudice*
must be distinguished—authoritarian and conformity, and
the impaired positive mental health implications of prej-
udice are most relevant for authoritarians. The research supporting the second conclusion, which states that highly prejudiced individuals are less healthy than others, measured
prejudice either with special MMPI scales of prejudice (e.g.,
Altus and Tafejian, 1953; Gough, 1951) or with the original F

Scale measure of authoritarianism employed by Adorno et al. (1950), (e.g., Freedman, Webster, and Sanford 1956; Jones 1955; and Meer 1952, 1955). In effect, then, conclusion no. 2 has been demonstrated only for the authoritarian type of prejudice, rather than the more situationally structured conformity type of prejudice. Thus, conclusion no. 3 is needed for further specification. Moreover, there is little reason to believe that these findings could be replicated on conforming bigots unless "positive mental health" were defined largely in terms of Jahoda's fourth criterion of autonomy and relative independence from social pressures.

4. *Crude approximations based on a vast array of national survey data suggest that one-fifth of White Americans are relatively unprejudiced against minorities, three-fifths are prejudiced for largely conformity reasons, and one-fifth are prejudiced for largely authoritarian, externalization reasons.* To the degree that these rough proportions are correct, the major mental health implications of White prejudice in the United States are narrowed to a minority of the population. Yet one-fifth of the White adult population of the nation constitutes over twenty million people. Not only does such a number represent a critical mass politically, but it also represents a sizable share of the nation's mental health problems.

Such an analysis casts serious doubt upon the appropriateness to this realm of the traditional case-by-case medical model for remedial action. In a society where racism, individual and institutional, is endemic, it is hardly surprising that prejudice appears to have little more significance for serious mental illness than symptom selection. Even the "not healthy" implications of prejudice seem concentrated among the minority of bigots with strongly authoritarian personalities.

More to the point is a structural model for remedial action, a model that places greatest importance as a target for change not on individual prejudice itself but on the racist institutional structures that shape and support the bigotry of individuals. Indeed, alterations of racist structures would offer aid to all three varieties of White Americans under discussion. For the tolerant fifth, nonracist institutions would act as vital supports for their position. For the authoritarian fifth, nonracist institutions would act at least to contain discriminatory behavior and at best to alter their racial opinions once their racial behavior had changed. But institutional change would have its greatest effects on the largest group of all—the conforming bigots—for nonracist norms would set a new reference and new expectations for conformers to live up to. There is every reason to believe that conformers can make this adjustment easily and without, as in the case of authoritarians, major personality change. The conformers go right on conforming, but what they are conforming to has shifted. Details on the social psychological mechanisms underlying this process are provided elsewhere by the writer (Pettigrew 1971a).

Recall Jack Hess, the outspoken steelworker in Gary, Ind., whose racial views opened this paper. How would this analysis of racism and mental health apply to him? Without more complete data on him, we can only speculate. But his ability to place values above his racism—that is, his caring more about closing the foul neighborhood dump than about his racial beliefs—strongly suggests that Hess is basically a conforming bigot. In fact, he obtained only a middle-range authoritarian score on the short form of the F Scale employed in his interview. His opposition to Richard Hatcher as mayor of Gary was undoubtedly shared by the vast majority of his White friends and acquaintances, for only about 15 percent of Gary's White voters cast their ballot for Mayor Hatcher in November of 1967. Consequently, his beliefs about Hatcher served a direct "social adjustment" function for Hess. Moreover, just as the present analysis would predict, Hess gave no indications whatsoever of mental illness. His pattern of answers to a variety of questions in the survey interview suggested that he possesses at least some of the ingredients of positive mental health. In Bradburn's (1970) terms Hess appeared to have a surplus of positive over negative feelings and, thus, a modicum of psychological well-being.

No simple theories of racism or prejudice can account for Hess. Yet we have seen that Hess and conforming bigots like him apparently outnumber the unprejudiced and the authoritarian bigots combined. Those proponents of remedies fashioned on older medical models of a doctor, a patient, and a couch or on ideological models of the profound "sickness" of all bigots will simply pass by Hess and overlook, perhaps, the most vital and vulnerable component of American racism today. Put bluntly, we do not need "to cure" bigots so much as we need to erode the bases of institutional racism which condition the bigot's attitudes and behavior.

REFERENCES

Ackerman, N. W., and Jahoda, M. 1950. *Anti-semitism and emotional disorder.* New York: Harper.

Adorno, T. W.; Frenkel-Brunswik, E.; Levinson, D. J.; and Sanford, R. N. 1950. *The authoritarian personality.* New York: Harper.

Allport, G. W. 1954. *The nature of prejudice.* Reading, Mass.: Addison-Wesley.

Altus, W. D., and Tafejian, E. 1953. MMPI correlates of the Californian E-F scale. *J. Soc. Psychol.* 38:145–49.

Barron, F. 1953. Some tests correlates to response to psychotherapy. *J. Consult. Psychol.* 17:235–41.

Block, J., and Block, J. 1952. An interpersonal experiment on reactions to authority. *Human Relations* 5:91–98.

Bradburn, N. 1970. *The structure of psychological well-being.* Chicago: Aldine.

Brink, W., and Harris, L. 1967. *Black and White: a study of U.S. racial attitudes today.* New York: Simon and Schuster.

Chesler, M., and Schmuck, R. 1969. Social psychological characteristics of super-patriots. In *The American right wing,* ed. J. Schoenberger. New York: Holt, Rinehart & Winston.

Christie, R., and Cook, P. 1958. A guide to published literature relating to the authoritarian personality through 1956. *J. Psychol.* 45:171–99.

Christie, R., and Jahoda, M., eds. 1954. *Studies in the scope and method of "the authoritarian personality."* New York: Free Press.

Courtney, P. D., Greer, F. L.; and Masling, J. M. 1952. *Leadership identification and acceptance.* Philadelphia: Institute for Research in Human Relations, Report no. 1.

Crutchfield, R. S. 1955. Conformity and character. *Amer. Psychol.* 10:191–98.

Dowling, B. 1955. Some personality factors involved in tolerance and intolerance. *J. Soc. Psychol.* 42:325–27.

Elms, A. C. 1970. Pathology and politics. *Psychology Today* 3:27–31, 58–59.

Erskine, H. 1968–69. The polls: recent opinion on racial problems. *Public Opinion Quarterly* 32:696–703.

Fein, R. 1966. An economic and social profile of the Negro American. In *The Negro American,* ed. T. Parsons and K. B. Clark. Boston: Houghton Mifflin.

Freedman, M.; Webster, H.; and Sanford, N. 1956. A study of authoritarianism and psychopathology. *J. Psychol.* 41:315–22.

Freeman, H. E., and Giovannoni, J. M. 1969. Social psychology of mental health. In *The handbook of social psychology,* ed. G. Lindzey and E. Aronson. 2d ed. Vol. 5. Reading, Mass.: Addison-Wesley.

Gough, H. G. 1951. Studies of social intolerance. *J. Soc. Psychol.* 33:237–69.

Haimowitz, M. L., and Haimowitz, N. R. 1950. Reducing ethnic prejudice through psychotherapy. *J. Soc. Psychol.* 31:231–41.

Harding, J.; Kutner,.; Proshansky, H.; and Chein, I. 1954. Prejudice and ethnic relations. In *The handbook of social psychology,* ed. G. Lindzey. Vol. 2. Reading, Mass.: Addison-Wesley.

Harding, J.; Proshansky, H.; Kutner, B.; and Chein, I. 1969. Prejudice and ethnic relations. In *The handbook of social psychology,* ed. G. Lindzey and E. Aronson. 2d ed. Vol. 5. Reading, Mass.: Addison-Wesley.

Harris, D. B.; Gough, H. G.; and Martin, W. E. 1950. Children's ethnic attitudes: II. Relationship to parental beliefs concerning child training. *Child Develop.* 21:169–81.

Hartley, E; N. 1946. *Problems in prejudice.* New York: Kings Crown Press.

Hyman, H. H., and Sheatsley, P. B. 1964. Attitudes toward desegregation. *Scientific American* 211:16–23.

Hyman, H. H., and Singer, E. 1968. *Readings in reference group theory and research.* New York: Free Press.

Jahoda, M.

    1958.   *Current concepts of positive mental health.* New York: Basic Books.

    1961.   Race relations and mental health. In *Race and science,* UNESCO. New York: Columbia University Press.

Jensen, A. R. 1957. Authoritarian attitudes and personality maladjustment. *J. Abnorm. Soc. Psychol.* 54:303–11.

Jones, M. B. 1955. Authoritarianism and intolerance of ambiguity. *J. Abnorm. Soc. Psychol.* 50:125–26.

Kerner Commission Report. *See* National Advisory Commission on Civil Disorders.

Meer, S. J.

    1952.   The relation between authoritarian attitudes and dreams. *Amer. Psychol.* 7:312 (abstract).

    1955.   Authoritarian attitudes and dreams. *J. Abnorm. Soc. Psychol.* 51:74–78.

Merton, R. K. 1968. *Social theory and social structure.* New York: Free Press.

Myers, J. K., and Roberts, B. H. 1959. *Family and class dynamics in mental illness.* New York: Wiley.

Myrdal G. 1944. *An American dilemma.* New York: Harper.

National Advisory Commission on Civil Disorders. 1967. *Report.* Vol. 1. Washington, D.C.: U.S. Government Printing Office.

Pettigrew, T. F.

    1958.   Personality and sociocultural factors in intergroup attitudes: a cross-cultural comparison. *J. Conflict Resolution.* 2:29–42.

    1959.   Regional differences in anti-Negro prejudice. *J. Abnorm. Soc. Psychol.* 59:28–36.

    1964.   *A profile of the Negro American.* New York: Van Nostrand.

    1967.   Social evaluation theory: convergences and applications. In *Nebraska symposium on motivation,* 1967, ed. D. Levine. Lincoln, Neb.: University of Nebraska Press.

    1968.   The voting behavior of White males in Gary. Unpublished manuscript, Dept. Social Relations, Harvard University.

    1971*a*.   *Racially separate or together?* New York: McGraw-Hill.

    1971*b*.   The role of Whites in the Black college of the future. *Daedalus* 100:813–32.

Poinsett, A. 1970. The "brain drain" at Negro colleges. *Ebony* 25:74–82.

Sheatsley, P. B. 1966. White attitudes toward the Negro. In *The Negro American,* ed. T. Parsons and K. B. Clark. Boston: Houghton Mifflin.

Shils, E. A. 1954. Authoritarianism: "right" and "left." In *Studies in the scope and method of "The authoritarian personality,"* ed. R. Christie and M. Jahoda. New York: Free Press.

Smith, M. B.; Bruner, J. S.; and White, R. W. 1956. *Opinion and personality.* New York: Wiley.

Stanton, W. 1960. *The leopard's spots: scientific attitudes toward race in America,* 1815–59. Chicago: University of Chicago Press.

Titus, H. E., and Hollander, E. P. 1957. The California F scale in psychological research: 1950–1955. *Psychol. Bull.* 54:47–64.

Wechsler, H.; Solomon, L.; and Kramer, B. M. 1970. *Social psychology and mental health.* New York: Holt, Rinehart & Winston.

Wells, W. D.; Weinert, G.; and Rubel, M. 1956. Conformity pressure and authoritarian personality. *J. Psychol.* 42:133–36.

CHAPTER 9

Self-Concept in White and Black Children

by Gloria Johnson Powell

A history is presented of investigations of the problems faced by Black youth in their development as individuals, followed by focus on preliminary findings of an ongoing study of the development self-concept in Black and White youth. A description is given of the tests and methods used and the possible implications of the scores of Black and White youth in a Northern and a Southern community.

In 1935 the American Youth Commission was established by the American Council on Education, and in 1938 a special advisory committee of that commission was called together to assist in organizing an investigation of distinctive problems Black youth face in their development as individuals. The central problem to be addressed was to determine what are the effects upon the personality development of Black youth because of their being members of a minority racial group. Several studies were conducted concurrently in different sections of the United States, and the reports of these studies are well known. Allison Davis and John Dollard (1964) went to the urban South, to New Orleans, and studied the life experiences of eight selected Black adolescents. E. Franklin Frazier (1940) went to Washington, D.C., and Louisville, Ky., and described the personal experiences of Black youth in those two communities. Charles S. Johnson (1967) went to eight rural counties in the deep South — in Mississippi, Alabama, Georgia, Tennessee, and North Carolina. The personality development of Black youth in a Northern city, the South Side of Chicago, was explored by Warner, Junker, and Adams (1969). These studies were made in the late 1930s during a time of sociopolitical changes and were originally published in 1940 and 1941. The findings of those scholars marked the beginning of the awareness concerning the psychological development and needs of Black children in this country. The awareness and research continued, and we note in 1950 the historical report of Kenneth Clark (1952) on the effects of prejudice and discrimination on children which was presented at the Mid-Century White House Conference on Children and Youth (Witmer and Kotinsky 1952) and cited in the famous footnote 11 of Chief Justice Earl Warren's pronouncement on school desegregation on May 17, 1954.

In June of 1969 the Joint Commission on Mental Health for Children (1970) responded to the mandate of the Congress of the United States to assess the mental health needs of children of the country. Very early in its study, the commission recognized that the mental health problems of minority group children were severe enough to warrant special consideration. The Committee on Children of Minority Groups was formed, and the summary of the commission's study identified racism as a major contributing factor to impaired self-image.

According to some studies, what an individual thinks and feels about himself is mediated through his perception of what others think and feel about him. Within a given culture and society an individual's self-perception is mediated via his status and role, which are acquired or assigned to him by the society. The studies of Frazier, Davis and Dollard, Johnson, and Warner et al. in the late 1930s seem to reiterate this theme — that is, that Whites acting in a culturally prescribed negative way adversely influence the development of the growing Black child. The dynamic formulation of the effects of racism on minority children as elucidated by the Committee on Children of Minority Groups in the 1970 report of the Joint Commission on Mental Health for Children would seem to be supported by the conceptualizations that cultures exist on psychological and behavioral levels and that learned cultural patterns are inherent in the formation of the ethnic personality.

However, the decades of the fifties and sixties have seen a resurgence of Black consciousness and Black identity. The new pride in Africa's achievements, the interest in the discovery of ancestral roots, the assertion that "black is beautiful," and the demands for Black power are cries for self-determination and self-definition. The new Black consciousness, with the impetus of the Civil Rights Movement and the Black Muslim ideologies, has helped the Black world confront itself and deal with the meaning of its Blackness, and has forced a confrontation between Whites and Blacks.

Study of self-concept has become a popular and important way of understanding human behavior, for the individual's concept of himself is related to his general personalty and his state of mental health. Inasmuch as the milieu to which a child is exposed influences this development, changes in that milieu should lead to changes in self-concept. Inasmuch as the social, political, and psychological milieus for Black people are changing, can we assume that these changes are affecting the development of self-concept for White and Black children? In addition, the amount and degree of self-concept change may be dependent not only on the degree of family stability and economic status but also on the amount, degree, and kind of social, cultural, and political change within a given community.

The major focus of this chapter will be on the preliminary findings of an ongoing study of self-concept development of Black and White youth in various parts of the country. We shall limit our presentation to a comparison of self-concept of Black and White youth in two of the six cities being studied,

GLENDALE COLLEGE LIBRARY

one Southern city and one Northern city. Hopefully, some of these data will begin to answer in part the question we have posed above.

Outline of Study

From Rogers' theory of the self has come the construct of the self-concept as a reasonable index of adjustment (Fitts 1965). Though Sears was involved in empirical studies including self-concept as early as 1941, self-concept studies did not appear in any great number in the literature until given the impetus of Raimey's development, in 1948, of a methodology for measuring changes in self-reference in the therapy interview (Raimey 1948). Since that time, however, research on self-concept as a generalized personality construct has stimulated the development of many different measuring instruments.

The students in our study were given the Tennessee Self-Concept Scale (TSCS), which is simple for the subjects, widely applicable, and multidimensional in its description of the self-concept (Fitts 1965). The standardization group from which the norms were developed was a broad sample of people from various parts of the country, ranging in age from twelve to sixty-eight, with equal numbers of both sexes and including both Negro and White subjects. The scale was devised on a phenomenological system, and the subject is asked to rate himself in terms of (1) what he is — identity, (2) how he feels about himself — self-satisfaction, and (3) what he does — behavior. Within these dimensions he also rates his physical self, his moral-ethical self, his personal self, his family self, and his social self. These self-descriptions coincide with Allport's seven aspects of selfhood which together comprise the self as felt and known, that is, sense of bodily self, sense of continuing self-identity, self-esteem and pride, the extension of the self, the self-image, the self as a rational coper, and the self as a favorable striver (Allport 1963).

In addition to the TSCS, the students were given the Powell-Fuller Socio-Familial Questionnaire which asked specific questions regarding family background (birthplace of parents, occupation and educational level of parents, the status of their family [broken, extended], size of family, etc.). Also included were statements to be completed regarding the aspirational levels and self-attitudes of the students. There were no questions regarding race or racial attitudes on the self-concept scale or the questionnaire. The students were told that the investigators were interested in how young people think and feel about themselves. At each school in the Northern city, the tests were administered by Black and White people because the schools were mixed. In the Southern city, Black and White interviewers appeared at the mixed schools, but at segregated schools the tests were administered by interviewers who were of the same race as the children.

The Black and White students in each city are compared according to four scores on the self-concept scale: (1) the total positive *(TP)* score, which reflects the overall level of self-esteem; (2) the self-criticism score *(SC)*, which is made up of mildly derogatory statements that most people admit as being true, high scores indicating a normal, healthy openness and low scores, defensiveness; (3) the variability scores *(V)*, which measures the degree of inconsistency from one area of self-perception to another; (4) the distribution score *(D)*, which measures the certainty about the way a person sees himself.

In each city junior high Black and White girls and boys from twelve to fifteen years of age were tested. The students tested attended schools which varied in racial composition. In the Southern city some of the students tested attended schools which were completely segregated (all-Black or all-White), some were partially desegregated (20 percent), some minimally desegregated (10 percent or less), and some predominantly Black (80 percent).

In the Northern city all the students tested were attending desegregated schools from 75 percent Black to less than 10 percent Black.

Results

Southern City

In the Southern city 614 students were tested: 261 males and 353 females, 317 white students and 297 Black students.

Total positive scores by sex and race. The Black students obtained a total positive mean score of 348, which falls into the fiftieth percentile range for the self-concept scale. The White students achieved a total positive mean of 332, which falls into the thirtieth percentile range. The difference in the total positive mean scores between the two groups is statistically significant with $p < 0.001$.

There is no significant difference between the total positive scores of the 133 White boys and the 183 White girls, nor is there any significant difference between the total positive scores of the 129 Black boys and 170 Black girls.

However, the Black boys $(TP = 351)$ scored significantly higher $(p < 0.001)$ than the White boys $(TP = 331)$, and the Black girls $(TP = 345)$ scored significantly higher $(p < 0.003)$ than the White girls $(TP = 333)$.

Self-criticism scores by sex and race. There is no significant difference between Black and White students on the SC score, both groups obtaining a mean of 34. There is no significant difference between Black boys and Black girls, between Black boys and White boys, or Black girls and White girls.

Variability scores by sex and race. There is no significant difference between the Black and White students on variability scores, the former achieving a mean of 54.2 and the latter a mean of 53.4. There is no significant difference between the Black and White girls. However, the Black boys

($V = 56$) differ from the Black girls ($V = 52$) with a significance at the 5 percent level, and the Black boys ($V = 56$) differ from the White boys ($V = 51.9$) with a significance at the 5 percent level.

Distribution score. The Black students have a mean D score of 129.7, the White students a mean D score of 124. The difference is significant at the 5 percent level. The Black boys ($D = 131.7$) scored higher than the White boys ($D = 124.4$), but the difference is not statistically significant. The Black girls do not differ significantly from the White girls; nor do the Black boys differ from the Black girls; nor do the White boys, from the White girls. A summary of the self-concept scores for Southern students is in Appendix 9.1

Questionnaire data. Of the Southern children 75 pecent of the Whites compared with 65 percent of the Blacks lived with both parents. About 40 percent of the White fathers compared with 55 percent of the Black fathers finished high school, and about twice as many Black fathers (23 percent) as White fathers (10 percent) are college graduates. Sixty-two percent of the Black mothers are high school graduates and 25 percent college graduates compared with 42 percent and 5 percent of the White mothers who are high school and col-lege graduates. More White fathers (54 percent) than Black fathers (43 percent) were employed in technical occupations, but more Black fathers (12 percent) compared with 6 percent of the White fathers were professionals. The Southern city is the location of several Black colleges. These institutions have had a favorable effect on the educational and occupational achievements of the Black parents of the students included in this study.

The aspirational levels of the students were expressed in part as follows: 52 percent of the Blacks wanted to attend college and 46 percent wanted a profession, compared with 39 percent and 25 percent respectively of the Whites who wanted a college education and a profession. In terms of attitudes toward self, 56 percent of the White students and 61

percent of the Black students indicated that they were satisfied with their self-image. Attitudes about themselves that
were classified as immature or inappropriate were given by
15 percent of the White students and 12 percent of the Black
students.

Northern City

The number of White students tested was 157, and the
number of Black students tested was 149.

Total positive scores. The Black students achieved a
lower *TP* mean score (321.9) than the White students (327.4),
but the difference is not significant.

The Black girls (*TP* = 317.1) and the White girls
(*TP* = 319.7) have similiar scores, with no significant
difference in *TP* means. The White boys achieved a *TP* mean
of 336.5 compared with that of Black boys of 328.5. The
difference is not significant, however.

Black boys (328.5) scored higher than Black girls (317.1),
although the difference is not significant. Likewise White
boys (*TP* = 336.5) scored higher than White girls (319.7); the
difference is significant at the 5 percent level.

Self-criticism scores. Not any of the *SC* scores differ
significantly for any of the groups of students (see Appendix
9.2). Black students (*SC* = 37.1) tended to score higher than
White students (*SC* = 36.7), although it is interesting to note
that the White boys (*SC* = 37.7) scored higher than the White
girls (*SC* = 35.8).

Variability scores. Black students (*V* = 52.8) made higher
scores than White students (*V* = 47.8), and the difference is
significant at the 1 percent level. Black girls (*V* = 51.0) scored
higher than White girls (*V* = 47.3) with a significance at the 5
percent level, and Black boys (*V* = 55.2) scored higher than
White boys (*V* = 48.3) with a significance at the 1 percent
level.

Distribution scores. Black students made higher scores

than White, but not significantly so. Black boys ($D = 132.6$) scored higher than the White boys ($D = 119.0$), with significance at the 5 percent level, and higher than Black girls (115.1), with a significance at the 5 percent level. (See Appendix 9.2.)

Questionnaire data. Of the students 40 percent failed to answer the questionnaire completely or consistently. In many instances they indicated that they thought the questions regarding family were "too personal." The socioeconomic data for the students tested in this Northern city are based largely on data provided by school personnel and data on the community where the schools are located. Our best estimates regarding family background indicate that at least 80 percent of the White students live with both parents and 65 percent of Black students live with both parents.

Fifty-seven percent of the mothers of the White students had completed high school and about 15 percent had completed college. Forty-one percent of the mothers of Black students had completed high school and 5 percent had completed college. The occupational status of parents was not reported for about 70 percent of the Black students. However, 60 percent of the Black students lived in a section of the city that had the highest rate of substandard housing; another 35 percent of the Black students lived in a lower-middle-class neighborhood, and about 5 percent of the Black students lived in a middle-class or upper-middle-class neighborhood. Among the White students 25 percent had parents who were professionals, while about 20 percent were laborers. The aspirational levels of Black students were uncertain and indefinite. About 40 percent of the White students indicated a desire to go to college or get a job. Among all students, the attitudes toward self were predominantly uncertain or inappropriate.

It was very clear that these students, both Black and White, felt threatened by the whole testing procedure and in many instances were hostile or uncooperative.

Discussion

During the ages from twelve to fifteen years, a period of rapid physical changes, the adolescent is especially sensitive to inner psychical pressures and outer environmental pressures. The adolescent's reactions to these pressures will have much to do with shaping his adult ego identity. The process of firm identification implies the need for clear cultural patterns of appropriate behavior. The mores, values, ideas, and aspirations that are available to the young person must come from the culture. If they are not clear to the family of the child, they will not be clear to the young person who must assimilate them. In order to find his identity, the young person must learn to read his culture as well as his family.

Self-awareness does not emerge in an all-or-none fashion. A child understands or realizes different aspects of himself with varying degrees of understanding at different points in time. The development of self involves the process of differentiation; that is to say, an individual makes the distinction between himself and other objects—animate and inanimate. It is important to remember (1) that these processes of self-discovery are actively continuous as long as the child is developing or discovering new potentialities and (2) that self-concept development is dependent on other variables whose absence or presence impede or enhance self-discovery. It is safe to say that a growing person's view of himself is shaped by everything that affects the entire scope of his development, from his genetic makeup to obvious social influences in the society in which he lives.

A significant phase in the process of differentiation and development of self begins when a child asserts himself, opposes others, and compares himself with his peers. Harry Stack Sullivan (1964, p. 68) emphasized that a young child's self-esteem comes into being through a process of expressed or reflected appraisal. That is to say, a child is appraised by significant others and in time begins to appraise himself.

Approval by others who are significant in his life plants the seeds of self-approval) In a child's life, the significant others vary according to his age. Very early in life the most significant person in a child's life is the primary mothering figure, and later on the significant people may be his peers or other adults. A part of self-differentiation occurs when a child is able to compare with his peers, at which time he also brings to form a more or less clear conception of his family's socioeconomic status or social class (Powell and Fuller in press).

(The cultural influences on a growing child can be described as being (1) what other people do to the child, (2) what other people consciously teach the child, and (3) the behavior of other people observed by the child. We need to ask ourselves, then, from the Black child's point of view: What does he see other people doing to him? What is he learning from other people? And what is he seeing in the behavior of other people? How do the experiences of a Black child compare with those of White children? Based on his experiences and his comparisons, how does a Black child evaluate and conceptualize himself as a self or person?)

From the data provided in previous paragraphs, it would seem that the development of self-concept is different for various groups of young adolescents. Most certainly there seem to be regional differences in development of self-concept as well as ethnic differences. These differences cannot be attributed entirely to degree of family stability or educational and occupational level of parents alone. Soares and Soares (1969) in their study of self-perceptions of culturally disadvantaged children found that disadvantaged children do not necessarily reflect negative self-perceptions or lower self-esteem than do advantaged children. Inasmuch as about 50 percent of the Black Northern students tested could be considered disadvantaged by socioeconomic standards and about 60 percent of the White Northern students tested could be considered advantaged, the total positive scores of the Northern sampling would support the Soares's study, for the Northern Black and White students scored about the same with no significant difference. However, it should be noted that the *TP* mean scores for the Northern Black group (*TP* = 321.9) and the White group (327.4) represent the twenty-fifth percentile range for the self-concept scale. This means both groups scored quite low in terms of self-esteem. However, the Black Northern students were more certain about their self-picture than their White classmates.

Southern Black students have significantly higher *TP* scores than Southern White students; Black Southern boys did significantly better than White Southern boys, and Black girls did better than White girls. While Northern Black students scored in the twenty-fifth percentile, the Southern Black students scored in the fiftieth percentile — a marked difference. It should be noted also that, although the majority of Northern Whites had parents with higher educational attainments and socioeconomic standing, the Southern White students scored in the thirtieth percentile — somewhat higher than the Northern Whites, who fell in the twenty-fifth percentile.

In order to begin to understand the difference in total positive self-concept scores between Southern and Northern Black students, it would be wise to look at the two cities in which the students lived. The Northern city has a population close to one-half million people with 6 percent of the population being Black. It is a university town which prides itself on racial liberalism (although unconfirmed reports are that the last recorded lynching of a Black man in the North occurred in this state). The Protestant ethic abounds; in fact in many respects it could be considered a Bible Belt because of the numerous conservative churches. The Black community is divided with the largest percentage living in a community that was previously predominantly Jewish and that now abounds with substandard housing. The other large percentage of the Black community is located in a smaller area in the opposite part of town. The last mayoral election resulted in the selection of a conservative, law-and-order, prevent-riots mayor who has been a source of embarrassment to the liberal White community, which has taken pride in the city's long history of political liberalism. About four or five years ago, there was a riot in the Black community that had previously been predominately Jewish. As a result of that riot, some poverty programs were initiated. At the present time the community is involved in the issue of pairing of schools for racial balance. There is a great deal of resistance to the plan for pairing, especially in the more conservative White sections of the city. Some Black political figures have emerged, but none of sufficient power to win an election.

The Southern city is also a university town located in a Bible Belt. It is a city that has several renowned Black institutions. The city's population is less than one-half million, with about 34 percent of the city's population being Black. As one of the major seats of Black higher education, it has a sizable group of Black professional and business people as well as a sizable Black student population. The Black college students have been very much involved in the Civil Rights Movement aided by a cadre of young Black ministers of Dr. Martin Luther King's Southern Christian Leadership Conference. It could be said that the Black community of the city has been in the foreground of the new Black Movement, as well as having historical roots in previous evolutions of Black people in the country. The city began to comply with the 1954 Supreme Court ruling on school desegregation, and schools were desegregated on a grade-a-year plan beginning in 1956; it complied with federal mandates to speed up the process.

It is obvious that the cultural milieu for the Southern Black adolescent in our study was very different from that for the Northern Black adolescent. A cohesive Black community with strong Black adult models could in part contribute to the high total positive self-concept scores seen among the Southern Black students.

Self-concept studies comparing Negroes and Whites carried out during the periods of 1943 to 1958 and 1959 to 1965 reported the differences to be marked, with self-concept being less adequate in Negroes (Dreger and Miller 1960, 1968). More recent studies of racial comparisons, utilizing a variety of self-concept measures, also support the earlier findings that Negroes have a more negative self-concept. But Baughman and Dahlstrom (1968) in their analysis of Southern rural Black and White eighth-grade students found that the Black students more frequently reported themselves as being popular with peers, being highly satisfied with the kind of person they were, and having a happier homelife than that of the average child. They concluded: "Clearly if the self-concepts of these Negro children have been unduly damaged, this fact is not reflected in their interview statements about themselves nor in the educational and vocational aspirations which they report for themselves and which they seem optimistic about realizing" (p. 462).

Morris Rosenberg and Roberta Simmons (personal communication September 1970) tested third- to twelfth-graders in Baltimore using a different self-concept scale and found that the Black students did better than White students and the Black students in high school tended to do better if they were in a segregated or predominantly Black school.

The low self-concept scores achieved by the Northern students would suggest that there are noxious elements in their milieu which do not not enhance self-concept development. Although the differences in self-concept scores are not statistically significant, the Black students nonetheless tended to score lower than the Whites. It has often been said that being a White person in a White society appears to mean very little to the development of self-concept but that being Black in a White society seems to be one of the most important factors in such a development. This seems to be so in a negative way for Black Northern students, but may have more positive effects for Black students in the South. In the South, because of the overt racism, one defines oneself at an earlier age and develops more substantial coping styles. Then, too, the winds of change are blowing harder in the South, with Black people assuming more control over their communities, especially in the Southern city in which we tested. In the Northern city, the racism is more covert, more difficult to fight, and thus the immortality of segregation is less easy to attack. The Black Community in our Northern city is too small to command any power base.

The issue of family instability and poverty cannot be overlooked. Even when socioeconomic status is held constant, the stresses imposed upon a Black family are qualitatively different from those in a White family in a number of ways. Thus it could be expected that the self that many Black children experience is a self that has many unmet dependency needs. Be that as it may, it would appear that Black children in a Southern city have a way of overcoming that Black children in a Northern city have not attained.

The low self-concept of White students, North and South, would seem to indicate a process of alienation, rootlessness, and maybe even guilt. Young White radical groups continue to identify the White adults as the oppressor. There are few White models, then, for White youth, and their search for some cultural communal selves goes on in the form of the hippie movement and the desire for communal living. It would seem that the sins of the fathers have been visited upon the children.

Summary

A group of 617 Black and White students, twelve to fifteen years of age, in a Southern city were given a socioeconomic questionnaire and the Tennessee Self-Concept Scale. A smaller group (306) of Black and White students, twelve to fifteen years of age, in a Northern city were given the same scale.

The most significant finding was that the Black students in the Southern city scored significantly higher on the total positive score ($p<$0.001), indicating more certainty about the self than the White students in the same city.

In the Northern city, the Black students did less well than the White students on the total positive score, but the difference is not statistically significant. The Northern Black students also achieved a higher variability score compared with the Whites, a difference which is significant at the 1 percent level. This indicates that the Northern Black students have greater inconsistency in their self-picture or that their self-concept is less integrated. In the Northern city boys scored higher than girls, with a significance at the 5 percent level for Whites. There is a tendency for Northern students to have a higher self-criticism score than Southern students, indicating a tendency to be more critical of themselves than are Southern students.

The variables for positive self-concept among the Southern Blacks have been considered elsewhere (Powell and Fuller 1970*a*; 1970*b*; in press). In comparing Southern Blacks with Northern Blacks, it would seem that, although both groups are subject to racism in our society, the capacity for the Southern Black students to overcome, as it were, is facilitated by a strong cohesive Black community which has some power base in terms not only of numbers but also of achievements.

The low scores of White students in both North and South would seem to be a general reflection of the alienation which White youth are experiencing and a general rejection of the White adult world.

APPENDIX 9.1

Southern Students

Comparison of Southern students' self-concept scores

Factor Tested	White ($n = 317$)	Black ($n = 297$)	Significance
Total positive	332	348	0.001
Self-criticism	34	34	N.S.
Variability	53.4	54.2	N.S.
Distribution	124	129.7	0.01

Comparison of Southern girls' self-concept scores

Factor Tested	White ($n = 183$)	Black ($n = 170$)	Significance
Total positive	333	345	0.003
Self-criticism	35.2	34	N.S.
Variability	54.5	52.7	N.S.
Distribution	123.6	128.1	N.S.

Comparison of Southern boys' self-concept scores

Factor Tested	White ($n = 136$)	Black ($n = 128$)	Significance
Total positive	331	350	0.001
Self-criticism	34.6	34.6	N.S.
Variability	51.9	56.1	0.01
Distribution	124.4	131.7	N.S.

Comparison of Southern Black students' self-concept scores

Factor Tested	Boys ($n = 128$)	Girls ($n = 170$)	Significance
Total positive	350	245	N.S.
Self-criticism	34.6	34	N.S.
Variability	56.1	52.7	0.01
Distribution	131.7	128.1	N.S.

Comparison of Southern White students' self-concept scores

Factor Tested	Boys ($n = 136$)	Girls ($n = 183$)	Significance
Total positive	331	333	N.S.
Self-criticism	34.6	35.2	N.S.
Variability	51.9	54.5	N.S.
Distribution	124.4	123.6	N.S.

APPENDIX 9.2

Northern Students

Comparison of Northern students' self-concept scores

Factor Tested	White ($n = 157$)	Black ($n = 149$)	Significance
Total Positive	327.4	321.9	N.S.
Self-criticism	36.7	37.1	N.S.
Variability	47.8	52.8	0.01
Distribution	118.6	122.5	N.S.

Comparison of Northern girls' self-concept scores

Factor Tested	White ($n = 85$)	Black ($n = 85$)	Significance
Total positive	319.7	317.1	N.S.
Self-criticism	35.8	37.1	N.S.
Variability	47.3	51.0	0.05
Distribution	118.3	115.1	N.S.

Comparison of Northern boys' self-concept scores

Factor Tested	White ($n = 72$)	Black ($n = 63$)	Significance
Total positive	336.5	328.5	N.S.
Self-criticism	37.7	37.0	N.S.
Variability	48.3	55.2	0.01
Distribution	119.0	132.6	0.05

Comparison of Northern Black students' self-concept scores

Factor Tested	Girls ($n = 86$)	Boys ($n = 63$)	Significance
Total positive	317.1	328.5	N.S.
Self-criticism	37.0	37.1	N.S.
Variability	51.0	55.2	N.S.
Distribution	115.1	132.6	0.05

Comparison of Northern White students' self-concept scores

Factor Tested	Girls ($n = 85$)	Boys ($n = 72$)	Significance
Total positive	319.7	336.5	0.05
Self-criticism	35.8	37.7	N.S.
Variability	47.3	48.3	N.S.
Distribution	118.3	119.0	N.S.

REFERENCES

Allport, Gordon W. 1963. *Pattern and growth in personality.* New York: Holt, Rinehart & Winston.

Baughman, E. E., and Dahlstrom, W. G. 1968. *Negro and White children: a psychological study in the rural South.* New York: Academic.

Clark, Kenneth. 1952. The effects of prejudice and discrimination on personality development. In *Personality in the making,* ed., Helen Witmer and Ruth Kotinsky. New York: Harper.

Davis, A., and Dollard, D. 1964. *Children of bondage: the personality development of Negro youth in the urban South.* New York: Harper. Originally published 1940 by the American Council on Education, Washington, D.C.

Dreger, R. M., and Miller, K. S.
1960. Comparative psychological studies of Negroes and Whites in the United States. *Psychol. Bull.* 57:361–402.
1968. Comparative psychological studies of Negroes and Whites in the United States: 1959–1965. *Psychol. Bull.* 70:1–58. Suppl.

Fitts, William. 1965. *Tennessee self-concept scale manual.* Nashville: Counselor Recordings and Tests. (Box 6184, Acklen Station, Nashville, Tenn. 37212.)

Frazier, E. F. 1940. *Negro youth at the crossways: their personality development in the middle states.* Washington, D.C.: American Council on Education.

Johnson, Charles S. 1967. *Growing up in the Black belt.* New York: Schocken Books. Originally published 1941 by the American Council on Education, Washington, D.C.

Joint Commission on Mental Health for Children, Inc. 1970. *Crisis in child mental health.* New York: Harper.

Powell, G. J., and Fuller, M.

    1970*a*.   School desegregation and self-concept. Paper presented at the annual meeting of the American Orthopsychiatric Association in San Francisco, March 1970.

    1970*b*.   The cultural effects of segregation and desegregation. Read at the First International Congress of the Founding Fellows of the Center for Human Development, July 27, 1970.

    In press.   The variables for positive self-concept among Southern Black adolescents. Presented to the National Medical Association Meeting, Atlanta, Ga., August 1970. *J. Nat. Med. Ass.*

Raimey, V. C. 1948. Self-reference in counseling interviews. *J. Consult. Psychol.* 12:153–63.

Rosenberg, Morris, and Simmons, Roberta. 1970. Personal communication, September 1970. See also Rosenberg, Morris, and Simmons, Roberta G. 1971. *Black and White self-esteem: the urban school child.* Washington, D.C.: American Sociological Association.

Soares, Anthony, and Soares, Louis. 1969. Self-conceptions of culturally disadvantaged children. *Am. Educ. Res. J.* 6:31–45.

Sullivan, Harry Stack. 1964. *The fusion of psychiatry and social science.* New York: Norton.

Warner, W. L.; Junker, B. H.; Adams, W. A. 1969. *Color and human nature: Negro personality development in a Northern city.* New York: Harper. Originally published 1941 by the American Council on Education, Washington, D.C.

Witmer, Helen, and Kotinsky, Ruth, eds. 1952. *Personality in the making.* Report of the Mid-Century White House Conference on Children and Youth, 1950. New York: Harper.

CHAPTER 10

Racism, Mental Health, and the Schools

by Reginald L. Jones

The desire of Black people for school reform as a mental health move is discussed in the light of various factors such as the history of education for Blacks, the effects of service for special children, teacher expectations for pupils, and racism in the curriculum.

Suggested paths for the future are considered with particular attention on reorganization and change in the schools and development of realization among teachers and parents of the need for change.

Nowhere is the effect of white supremacy more pervasive and more debilitating than in the American School. Whether it takes the form of textbooks which promulgate white supremacy by excluding the lives and accomplishments of blacks and other minorities, whether it takes the form of white teachers who have double standards of expectation, reward and punishment, or whether it takes the form of self-hating black teachers who despise black children — white racism has poisoned the American School. White supremacy has left many black teachers and white teachers paralyzed in its wake, and it has been most deadly when they are unaware of their sickness. (Smith 1969, p. 63)

The Black push for reforms in the schools is a mental health strategy. It is the Black American's assertion of worth and dignity. It represents a demand that the schools take account of the culture and heritage of Black Americans; that it remove vestiges of discrimination in the employment of Black teachers, counselors, and administrators; and that it

deal with racism in the school curriculum. It represents a
frank confrontation with institutional forces which dehumanize Blacks.

Now being accumulated is evidence which indicates that
Blacks making demands on the system for reform are psychologically healthier than those who passively accept racism
(Hilliard 1972). The psychological value of activism extends
even to violence, for as Fanon (1966, p. 73) notes: "Violence
is a cleansing force. It frees the native from his inferiority
complex and from his despair and inaction; it makes him
fearless and restores his self respect." Similarly, Clark (1965,
p. 88) has written: "In a very curious way the [Black]
delinquent's behavior is healthy; for, at least, it asserts that
he still has sufficient strength to rebel and has not yet given
in to defeat."

In general, concepts of mental health include the ability to
adapt to the environment, to perceive reality accurately, to
manage stress healthfully, to function independently, to
learn, and to experience a sense of well-being. Discrimination can thwart the development of children in these
important areas. It can reduce cognitive functioning, distort
perceptions of reality, and impair affective states and processes (Douglass 1967). To the extent that racism and discrimination exist in the schools, it is apparent that the schools
can affect the mental health of children.

Aside from racism in the schools, many other factors affect
the mental health and well-being of Black schoolchildren.
These variables have been treated elsewhere (e.g., Berman
1954; Bower 1966; Flanders 1965; Gordon 1966; Gray 1963;
Hill and Luckey 1969; Hunter 1957; Jackson and Getzels
1963; Jersild and Lazar 1962; Marburger 1966; Rabkin and
Suchoski 1967; Strom 1965; and Waetjen and Leeper 1966,
among many others) and hence will not be dealt with here.

The present chapter emphasizes racist practices within
educational settings which have been or can be shown on
logical grounds to affect the mental health of Black children

in the public schools (grades K–12). These factors include, but are not limited to: (1) the structure of the schools themselves, (2) the labeling and placement of Black children in special classes, (3) teacher expectations and the Black child, and (4) racism and the curriculum. Each of these topics is taken up in the present chapter. A final section presents a variety of strategies and viewpoints related to the elimination of racism in the schools.

Racism and the Structure of the Schools: An Overview

The evidence of racism in our schools has been documented so many times it seems incredible that we should pretend that it does not exist and have an effect. Consider the minuscule number of black administrators in white or integrated school systems. Consider, too, the large proportion of black administrators who have "black" jobs such as "Assistant Superintendent in Charge of Human Relations" or "Director of Federal Programs." Consider the ratio of black students to white students in any school system as compared to black-white ratio or other staff. Consider the racial make-up of school boards, teacher training institutions, publishers of educational materials or other school oriented business. Consider the tests, the curriculum materials—not those being developed on a crash basis, but those actually being used. And search to find how much of this new curriculum is being used in all-white schools where it is essential if we are not to raise a new generation as racist as its parents. (Jerrems 1970, p. 41)

This section presents an overview of racism in the schools. It begins with statements of demands for school reform now being made by Blacks.

Slavemasters learned early that the educated slave was the one most likely to be dissatisfied with his lot and to yearn for freedom. During the period of slavery, education of slaves took place only when some utilitarian purpose was served—that is, to the extent that it was necessary to carry out the business of the master. Slaves did, however, evolve a system of education of their own based on the apprenticeship system. This system began with the birth of the slave and became crucial when the slave went into the field or into the master's home. Mere survival dictated that the young slave learn his job at an early age. The pervasive thought during slavery, and now in various forms, was that Blacks were intellectually inferior and uneducable and were fit only for work in the fields under supervised conditions. Ostensibly such practices fitted the needs of the larger society for, as Brookover and Erickson (1969) assert. "So long as the society needed large proportions of people with relatively low levels of competence and our beliefs in equality of educational opportunity were not too strongly held, the maintenance of a differentiated school system [or none at all as was the case during this period] served the society adequately." A repressive system which denied basic human rights and dignity was thus justified.

The colonial period witnessed small but sustained interests in providing some education for Blacks, largely so that they could become Christianized. The fact cannot be escaped, however, that this education, such as it was, was offered in a manner which degraded the self of the Black child. He was not good enough to be educated with Whites, and questions about his educability and his intelligence remained.

Directions shifted during the period of the American Revolution when many, foreseeing the end of slavery, called for education to prepare Blacks for their anticipated freedom. There were promising developments during this period, including mixed schools. All of this disappeared, however, with the dawn of the nineteenth century. Some speculate that, since hope for freedom seemed remote, Blacks reacted in frustrated violence. In 1831, Nat Turner and his band murdered White Virginians while they slept. Turner had learned to read at an early age from his master and from the Sunday schools which taught Black children. His revolt caused great fear throughout the South and marked a milestone in the denial of education to Blacks. Southern legislatures immediately enacted laws to prohibit the instruction of Blacks in any way or by any one.

During the Civil War integrated schooling did occur in certain states and communities. By and large, however, race-mixing in the schools was constitutionally prohibited in spite of the fact that five Southern stated elected Blacks as state superintendent of education. In 1896 the U.S. Supreme Court decided in *Plessy* v. *Ferguson* that schools could be "separate but equal."

Segregated school systems in both the North and the South were developed following the Civil War. For the next half century, and to this day in many communities, expenditures for Black education either declined steadily or were far from equivalent to that of Whites. During the 1930s Black Americans began to attack segregated education and racism in the schools with small and essentially unremarkable results (Wilson 1968).

In 1954 the Brown decision gave explicit attention to the effects of segregated schools on the development and mental health of the Black child. The social science statement introduced as an appendix to the appellant's briefs summarized mental health arguments for desegregating the schools (Allport, et al. 1952, p. 168):

Segregation, prejudice and discrimination, and their social concomitants damage the personality of all children—the children of the majority group in a somewhat different way than the more obviously damaged children of the minority group....

As children learn the inferior status to which they are assigned—as they observe the fact that they are almost always segregated and kept apart from others who are treated with more respect by the society as a whole—they often react with feelings of inferiority and a sense of personal humiliation. Many of them become confused about their own personal worth. On the one hand, like all other human beings they require a sense of personal dignity; on the other hand, almost nowhere in the larger society do they find their own dignity as human beings respected by others. Under these conditions the minority group child is thrown into a conflict with regard to his feelings about himself and his group. He wonders whether his group and himself are worthy of no more respect than they receive. This conflict and confusion leads to self-hatred and rejection of his own group.

The pendulum has swung in two distinct directions following the *Brown* v. *Board of Education* decision. The first direction has been an all-out push for desegregation and integration of the schools, an activity which is still under way. There is also a swing in the opposite direction in a number of instances, particularly in urban communities. Here the emphasis is upon community control of the schools and upon confronting the variety of racist practices ingrained in the structure of the schools themselves:

Black children, preyed upon psychologically, destroyed spiritually, and confined physically, are victims of America's sickness bent upon devastating all hopes of innocent black boys and girls. . . . A new order is going to reign in the black community. Whites who remain in the ghetto schools are going to find it very hot. In fact, white principals must go. White glaziers must go. White imagery must go. (Jackson 1968, p. 10)

Many of the demands have been sparked by students who, taking cues from their elders, have sensed, and correctly so, that various institutionalized practices are responsible for the perpetuation of racism in the schools:

The Black Student Union of Berkeley High School in order to promote pride in being black, a knowledge of black heritage and culture, to rid ourselves of the results of centuries of racial oppression in America, and to make the school curriculum relevant to the needs of black people, do hereby make the following demands. . . .

Seven of the fourteen demands were the following (Rodeheaver 1970):

1. A Black Curriculum Coordinator Responsible to the Black Cur-

riculum Committee, Who Will Also Act as a Personnel Recruiter for Blacks.
2. The Offering of the Following Courses As A Part of the Black Curriculum:
   A. Black American Literature and Poetry
   B. History of African Art, Literature, Culture and Politics
   C. Black Journalism
   D. Black Socio-Economics
   E. Modern African Languages: 1. Swahili, 2. Igbo.
3. An Inservice Training Program in Black American History and Culture for All Teachers
4. Five Black Counselors and We Want Them in Two to Four Weeks
5. Tracking System of Berkeley High School Must Be Eliminated
6. All Racist Teachers and Administrators Must Be Removed From Our School
7. More Black Teachers and Administrators

The issues cited above, and others, have led to serious disturbances in the schools. More than six hundred and fifty racially motivated disturbances were reported in the nation's high schools in 1969–70. Many led to property damage, physical injuries, and even death (Hendrick and Jones 1972). There were also quieter rebellions which occurred in an atmosphere free of physical violence. Some students inconpicuously dropped out because the schools would not or could not give adequate attention to their cultural and unique needs.

Overall, many similarities exist among the grievances of Black students in diverse locations. They include: (1) ability grouping, which frequently places Blacks in the lowest tracks; (2) racist teachers and administrators, or those actually perceived to be so; (3) proportionately few minority teachers and administrators; (4) a curriculum which fails to give attention to the history and culture of minority groups; (5) a curriculum focus upon White middle-class values based on the Protestant ethic; and (6) the sheer isolation of Black students from the mainstream of school activities. Many of these concerns are taken up in the following sections.

The Delivery of Services to Special Children[1]

The racist in our schools ... does not say "nigger" or "boy"; his epithets are "culturally different" and "slow learner." (Jerrems 1970, p. 40)

There is widespread belief that the placement of disproportionately large numbers of minority children in various special education programs is yet another indication of racist practices in the schools. The concerns related to this theme have been expressed well by Johnson (1969, p. 244):

I am suggesting that the educational system has failed in its responsibilities to Black Americans.... Its Black clientele has been labelled delinquent and retarded, thus helping the general educational enterprise to avoid some of the responsibility for its failure to adapt to individuals and collective needs. Basically this labelling process imputes a lack of ability or a lack of values and behavior which are acceptable to the School....

The rule of thumb for Black children is: IQ below 75 = learning problem or stupidity; and IQ above 75 = behavior problem or crazy.

Dunn (1968) has estimated that 60 percent to 80 percent of the students enrolled in special classes for the mildly retarded are from low-status and non-middle-class backgrounds — including Blacks, Mexican Americans, American Indians, and Puerto Ricans. Actual data on the disproportionately large numbers of minority children in special education classes for the mildly retarded were summarized in a recent survey of California public school districts. This survey showed that Blacks and Mexican-American children in special classes for the retarded exceeded their actual proportion in the schools in a sizable number of districts. Allegations about the placement of minority children in special classes thus appear to have some basis in fact.

Stigma and the mildly retarded. The very fact of minor-

1. Research in this section was supported in part by a grant from the Urban Research Program, University of California.

ity status presents difficulties for the Black schoolchild, and placement in special classes for the mildly retarded adds to this burden. Indeed, research by Meyerowitz (1962) indicates the young child's self-concept drops following placement in a special class for the educable mentally retarded. At the high school level the self-concept of special class retardates was found to be lower than that of students in regular classes (Jones 1968). It is not possible to establish cause-and-effect relationships between special education placement and lowered self-concept because of methodological problems in the above studies. The presumptive evidence, however, is that this is the case. Placement in a class for the mentally retarded is not a badge of distinction for, as one high school student notes: "Some of my friends won't even talk to me because they think I'm too dumb and dilentary." Another indicates: "If you want a girlfriend, she won't like you cause you're in the special class. She'll think you're stupid and kinda weird. They think you're retarded. Girls mostly, some boys."

A small pilot study of the management of stigma by a group of twenty-three senior high school boys (mostly Black) enrolled in a special class for the educable retarded was revealing. When asked about their schoolwork, seventeen of the twenty-three lied. Most indicated that they were enrolled in regular, not special, courses. Only two respondents indicated that they were enrolled in special education courses. Most respondents expressed a dislike for the special class because they felt different and were made fun of. Not one of the twenty-three respondents indicated that special classes were the preferred educational arrangement; most saw regular or honors classes as most desirable. Almost half (eleven) of the respondents expressed the view that the special-class placement would have a negative effect on their prospects for securing employment. More than half the respondents could find nothing about their school experiences that gave satisfaction with their special-class placement (Jones 1970).

The sentiments of the students are supported by those reported by teachers. Of a sampling of senior high school teachers of the retarded $(N=94)$, 83 indicated awareness of the fact that their students were ashamed of being placed in a class for the retarded, as was true for 82 percent of a sampling of junior high school teachers $(N=129)$ and 51 percent of a sampling of elementary teachers $(N=94)$. Moreover 80 percent, 90 percent, and 81 percent respectively of the senior high, junior high, and elementary teachers were aware of names and derogatory labels attached to their pupils (Jones 1971).

Children's perceptions of themselves as culturally disadvantaged and culturally deprived. The labels "culturally deprived" and "culturally disadvantaged" are currently fashionable and are the primary terms used to describe Black, lower socioeconomic status and in some cases other minority children (particularly Mexican American, Puerto Rican, and American Indian). That these terms in many instances apply to Blacks was explicitly noted by Johnson (1969, p. 242): "When we speak of inner city, or ghetto or core area and when we use euphemisms such as educationally disadvantaged, culturally deprived, and poverty-ridden, we are really talking about Black people or Afro-Americans."

Black children are familiar with certain frankly racist terms—for example, *nigger.* But what of certain other terms—for example, culturally disadvantaged and culturally deprived—said to reflect at least negative characterization? A survey of one school district (Jones 1970) was undertaken in which children in grades 4, 6, 7, 8, 9, 10, and 12 were requested to give a variety of perceptions of themselves. They were asked, for example: Do you see yourself as middle class? Do you see yourself as culturally deprived? The results revealed that proportionately few students labeled themselves as culturally deprived or culturally disadvantaged regardless of the objective circumstances. Most respondents saw themselves as middle class.

A methodological question, appropriate particularly for

subjects in the elementary grades, concerns whether or not the respondents were familiar with the terms used in the study — e.g., culturally deprived, culturally disadvantaged. Virtually no fifth- and sixth-graders could give satisfactory definitions of the terms. High school students were, in a number of instances, quite sensitive to the terms although those in schools enrolling substantial numbers of Blacks tended to be more evasive in their responses than others. Certain evidence of a cognitive nature then suggests that elementary children may be unfamiliar with the terms culturally deprived and culturally disadvantaged while older children may show some familiarity with them.

It seemed reasonably clear that the younger respondents were unfamiliar with the terms culturally deprived and culturally disadvantaged. But what of affective response to these terms? Do children have feelings about these terms despite their inability to define them? It was suspected that while the students could not give formal definitions of the terms, a number of affective responses fitting the stereotype would be given. In grades 3 through 6 in a small midwestern community, forty-nine Black children responded to a number of questions relating to their perception of various labels — for example, if someone were to call you culturally deprived would that be good or bad? The subjects responded to some nineteen different socioeconomic and class descriptive terms. However, the results of only a few terms will be discussed here. Most remarkable was the clear tendency to see the terms culturally disadvantaged and culturally deprived as negative descriptions — so perceived by, respectively, 78 percent and 68 percent of the respondents. Such terms as middle class, rich, and gifted, on the other hand, were perceived positively by, respectively, 66 percent, 94 percent, and 74 percent of the respondents (Jones 1970). Evidence now available, then, suggests that the terms culturally deprived and culturally disadvantaged are rejected by most schoolchildren as descriptive of themselves.

It is one thing to know that children reject such labels. A

more important question relates to the consequences of acceptance or rejection of the label and school attitudes. Here the data are clear. One study of 1,706 schoolchildren in grades 4 and 6 revealed that children who labeled themselves culturally deprived or culturally disadvantaged scored reliably lower on an inventory of school morale than those who described themselves as middle class—regardless of the objective circumstances of the child's socioeconomic status (Jones 1970).

It is debatable as to how much the labeling of a child as culturally deprived or culturally disadvantaged reflects a racist practice. The same can be said for practices for assigning Black children to classes for the retarded and disturbed. It can be asserted only that, to the extent that such practices appear to operate differentially for Blacks as opposed to other groups and to the extent that such practices support and maintain the host of stereotypes related to the ability and personal functioning of Blacks, such practices are racist. There is evidence that this is the case.

Teacher Expectations and the Black Child

The reality is . . . that a teacher in the black ghetto who does not expect children to achieve up to the level of white children is just as racist and is doing more harm to black people than a field full of southern farmers in white sheets. (Jerrems 1970, p. 40)

Teachers exert a powerful influence on the schoolchild. What the teacher thinks about the child—or, of more importance, how the child perceives the teacher's perception—can be a powerful factor influencing the child's learning and school attitudes. Within the context of school anxiety, these relationships have been summarized by Sarason et al. (1960 p. 272):

In some classrooms failure or lack of progress by a child is responded to by the teacher in a way that increases the child's feeling of inadequacy. In other classrooms the child is responded to in a way that, while it recognizes the child's failure or rate of progress, does not make him feel that the teacher is rejecting or derogating him, i.e. the teacher likes and accepts him despite his inadequacy or failure. It is too frequently forgotten by parents (and also by teachers) how important a figure the teacher is in the life of a child. From the standpoint of the child, what he thinks is the teacher's attitude toward him is of great moment to him.

Teacher expectations about the performance of minority children can come to serve as a "self-fulfilling prophecy." Such a possibility was brought to attention in a dramatic way by the research of Rosenthal and Jacobson (1968). The methods and conclusions of this study are by now well known and hence can be summarized briefly. A group of elementary schoolchildren was pretested with a standard nonverbal test of intelligence, the test being represented to the teachers as one that would predict intellectual blooming or spurting. Approximately 20 percent of the children in grades 1 through 6 were randomly identified as potential spurters. These children and others not so identified were retested with the same nonverbal I.Q. test after one semester and after one and two academic years. The results were remarkable: students in the control group made some significant gains in I.Q. (19 percent gained twenty or more I.Q. points); 47 percent of the special children, however, gained 20 or more total I.Q. points. A number of additional findings related to the age of the subjects (children in the upper grades maintained their advantage upon follow-up), sex (boys "bloomed" more in verbal I.Q., girls more in reasoning I.Q.), and educational track (most change occurred for those in the middle track).

The Rosenthal studies have been faulted on many methodological grounds (Barber and Silver 1968*a*, 1968*b*; Thorndike 1968). Taken at face value, however, the findings were interpreted by many critics as supportive of their perceptions of racism in school personnel. Given the methodological shortcomings of the studies, such inferences are clearly inappropriate. But the matter does not rest there. The results of related investigations suggest that teachers *do* hold low expectations for certain classes of students and that such expectations *do* relate to the ways in which teachers interact with their pupils. Corwin and Schmit (1970) in a study of a random sample of over thirty-four hundred teachers in a large midwestern city found that up to 70 percent of the teachers in the lower SES (socioeconomic status) school expressed the belief that their pupils's motivation was low or above average. Only 17 percent of the teachers in the low SES schools ranked inadequate curriculum and instructional materials first or second as reasons for poor educational performance. A similar number ranked inadequate preparation in previous grades as important (i.e., ranked it as first or second). Most of the teachers, therefore, were more likely to see the causes of the child's poor performance in the child's family background. In general, very few teachers blamed the schools for the students' problems. Teachers in the low SES schools did, however, complain in greater numbers than was true for teachers in the outer city that the schools were not adequate for training of the children, that staff morale was poor, and that they were unimpressed with the efforts of the Board of Education in behalf of the children. Finally, the teachers judged that there was less opportunity to innovate and participate in decision-making in their schools.

Herriott and St. John (1966), based on interviews with a national sampling of teachers and pupils in urban public schools, reported that the lower the socioeconomic status (SES) of the schools the smaller the proportion of teachers who held favorable opinions about the motivation of their pupils. (It will not escape the reader that a large majority of low SES schools in urban areas contain substantial numbers of Black students.) Moreover, these same teachers were less likely to report that they had personal loyalty to the principal, that they desired to remain at their present school, or that they enjoyed their work. The finding concerning work satisfaction is particularly important since there is evidence which indicates that reported satisfaction in teaching is directly correlated with pupil school morale (Jones 1968). Pearson product moment correlations between eight indices of school morale and reported teacher satisfaction for thirty-four randomly selected teachers and their fourth-grade students in thirty-four urban classrooms revealed significant correlations between reported satisfaction with teaching and (1) attitudes toward other pupils ($p < 0.01$), (2) pupil-teacher relationships ($p < 0.05$), (3) general feelings about school ($p < 0.01$), and (4) general school morale ($p < 0.05$). Similar analyses were carried out in twenty-eight sixth-grade classrooms. However, no significant correlations were found between reported teacher satisfaction and any of the morale subscales. The results are clear: for young children teacher satisfaction is related to pupil satisfaction. Unfortunately, it is not possible to know which group influenced which. Perhaps perceived poor pupil attitudes led to lowered satisfaction in teaching; or the situation could have been reversed with pupils responding to perceived poor teacher attitudes. Regardless of the order of development of the attitudes, it seems reasonably clear that lowered satisfaction in work with young children is very closely tied to pupil satisfaction with school. Apparently, teacher satisfaction has the more powerful effect on pupil morale in the early grades.

Significant correlations were obtained between total years of teaching experience and pupil attitudes on seven of the eight morale subscales at grade 6 but not at grade 4. Taken together the findings on teacher satisfaction and teacher experience and their relationship to pupil morale have definite implications for teacher placement in schools serving large numbers of Black and low SES children. Clearly only those who express a desire for such work and, among those already employed, those who express satisfaction with their work should be placed in these schools. Also preference should be given to the more experienced teachers, at least in the upper grades. These suggestions run directly counter to current assignment practices in many school districts where in-experienced teachers are given the more difficult and undesi-rable assignments—teaching Black children. Thus, Becker (1952) found that new teachers in Chicago were assigned against their wishes to inner-city schools and transferred away as soon as they had sufficient seniority to move to the more desirable (White, middle-class) schools.

The mediation of expectancy effects. What happens to the minority child in the classroom? If expectancy effects are operative at all, how are they mediated? Several studies have now examined the mechanisms through which expectancy effects become translated into actual teacher behavior. The first was that of Beez (1968). This experiment showed the effects of teacher expectation on pupil performance. Subjects were sixty teachers and sixty pupils in a Head Start program. Teachers taught each child the meaning of a symbol. Half the teachers had been given the expectancy that, based on a psychological appraisal of the child, good learning would occur; the remaining half were led to expect poor learning. The results were remarkable. Of those alleged to have good intellectual prospects, 77 percent learned five or more sym-bols, whereas only 13 percent of those alleged to have poor prospects achieved at this level. Moreover, teachers who had been given favorable expectations about their pupils actually attempted to teach more symbols than those teachers who had been given unfavorable expectations about their pupils.

Expectations not only cover subjective forecasts of pupil ability and motivation but extend to school attitudes as well. Expectations regarding the school attitudes of a "culturally disadvantaged" child held by a group of college students were investigated in a social cognition experiment (Jones 1970). Subjects were 119 female undergraduate students who volunteered to participate in a psychology experiment as part of an introductory psychology course requirement. Approx-imately 75 percent of the participants were prospective teachers. Seventy-five of the subjects were placed in the experimental group and were given the following instructions:

SOCIAL COGNITION EXPERIMENT

This is a study to determine the way in which individuals make certain kinds of predictions about the responses of others.

Please fill out the enclosed inventory according to the instruction on the booklet. However instead of answering the questions as you normally would, answer as you think the person described below would respond.

A twelve year old culturally deprived boy in the 6th grade in an inner city school.

Remember, you are to answer as you feel this person would.

Please answer every question, even though you may sometimes find it difficult to make a decision.

A second group of forty-four respondents (the control group) received instructions identical to those above except that the boy in the vignette was not described as being from the inner city or culturally deprived. Then all the subjects completed the School Morale Inventory (Wrightsman 1968), an inventory designed to measure student feelings about school in a number of important areas, according to the directions given above. The inventory was scored in the conventional manner, and the subtest scores given under the set to stimulate the culturally deprived child were compared (using t tests) with those given under the set to simulate the nondeprived child. The results were unequivocal: the deprived child was predicted to have reliably lower morale on all subscales of the School Morale Inventory, such as: (1) morale about the school plant, (2) morale about instruction and instructional materials, (3) morale about administration, regulations, and staff, (4) morale about community support of school and parental involvement in school, (5) relations with other students, (6) morale about teacher-student relationships, (7) general feelings about attending school, and (8) total school morale.

The study was replicated with a group of experienced teachers and counselors who had completed a year of study in an institute devoted to preparing counselors for "culturally deprived" youth. The responses of these specialists were identical to those by the undergraduate students: the school attitudes held by the "culturally deprived" were predicted to be reliably lower than those held by the "nondeprived." For both counselors and undergraduate subjects the cognitions given for the deprived child were considerably more discrepant than those actually given by children who could be so labeled. No pretests of counselor cognitions were obtained. It is difficult therefore to know the extent to which any changes took place in counselor attitudes toward the deprived as a function of the year-long institute. It is entirely possible that counselor attitudes were even more negative than those found at the end of their training. Obviously, it is not now possible to obtain this information, It can be asserted only that following a full year of training devoted to the culturally deprived the counselors held very negative and very stereotyped views of this group. If the program for counselors referred to above is any good at all, it suggests that prospects are not at all bright for modifying negative attitudes toward the deprived through formal training (including considerable field work).

Racism and the Curriculum

The textbook world is still white, middle-class and antiseptically unreal. (Bennett 1967)

The Black American has been systematically excluded from the curriculum. A student can complete twelve years of schooling with virtually no knowledge of Black literature or scanty knowledge of the contributions of Blacks to this country. He learns little of Black culture. His history of Black Americans is distorted. And, if the student himself is Black, his view of Black Americans as undervalued people is reinforced.

The curriculum includes all materials formally and informally available for presenting the subject matter of a given area. Curriculum materials include bibliographies, teacher guides, formal syllabi, records and tapes, films and filmstrips, educational television, and textbooks. The present section devotes attention to Blacks as treated in textbooks since most of the formal aspects of the curriculum are presented through this medium. There is existing evidence, however, which indicates that all activities in the development of Black curriculum are depressed. In one survey of Black curriculum materials available in 1968–69, W. L. Smith (1970) found that, of the fifty states and the District of Columbia, only twenty-eight had some type of material available (limited only to bibliographies in some instances); nineteen states had no material available or plans for developing any in the near future; four states were developing materials or had established what type of material would be needed. In a number of districts the Black studies curriculum was used only in schools enrolling sizable numbers of Blacks. Such materials are, of course, needed in these schools. It is apparent that the need is just as great in schools enrolling predominantly White students and also non-Black minority groups.

Racism in textbooks. Concern with racism in textbooks is not new. E. A. Johnson (1911), a Black historian, called attention to the racial bias of White authors in the early 1900s, while White (1939) gave attention to racism in textbooks in the late 1930s. In 1949 a committee of the American Council on Education found that Blacks were referred to almost exclusively in history textbooks only. Content was usually limited to the time of slavery and to Reconstruction. Slaves were typically depicted as happy, contented, and well treated. Africa was treated as a continent of backward, strange people whose primitive culture was vastly different from our own.

For the most part Blacks in contemporary America were ignored, as were problems related to discrimination in housing, voting, jurisprudence, education, and public accommodations (Banks 1969). A 1961 investigation of the treatment of minorities in the most widely used junior and senior high school social studies textbooks (Marcus 1961) revealed that few changes had occurred since the 1949 report of the American Council on Education. The most obvious shortcoming in the newer textbooks was the absence of the current struggles and changing status of Blacks. Few textbooks mentioned the achievements of contemporary Blacks, and Blacks were portrayed either as simple childlike slaves or as uneducated bewildered freedmen.

Distortions of the history and contribution of Black Americans were found also in textbooks for elementary schoolchildren. In one study of a sampling of elementary social studies textbooks, Anderson (1966) revealed that: (1) the textbooks overlooked the facts that Blacks were forced to come to America, (2) the slave trade and slavery as an institution tended not to be discussed, (3) abolitionism as a protest movement was omitted, (4) the emancipation of the slaves was interpreted as a kudo for Lincoln, and (5) Blacks were typically not mentioned between Reconstruction and the 1954 Supreme Court decision.

In comparing these results with those at the secondary level, Sloan (1966, p. 7) wrote:

In that part of her survey dealing with the treatment of the Negro in elementary school texts, Miss Anderson shows a far worse and therefore more deplorable situation than in the secondary school texts. Elementary school students . . . are in their most formative years and the need for historical truth and perspective is at least as vital as it is in the upper grades. . . . The grade school history texts are insipid, inadequate and inaccurate.

Racism extends to children's trade books as well as to textbooks. In one study of more than five thousand trade books for children published between 1962 and 1964 (Larrick 1965) fewer than 10 percent were found to include one or more Blacks. In a similar study of racism in interracial books, Glancy (1969, pp. 1–116) analyzed some 326 works of children's interracial fiction published between 1951 and 1967. Her results revealed the presence of negative stereotypes (poor and not striving, black-skinned, living in rural areas) in more than half the books. In addition, the "main White character" was always predominant. Two of the author's hypotheses were not found to be substantiated: (1) that the negative stereotype would be found to decline in frequency over the years and (2) that increases in the hypothetical positive stereotype would occur. Thus Glancy found that while negative stereotype of the Black American has disappeared from the fictional literature, it has not been, for the most part, replaced by a positive stereotype.

Despite some positive steps toward respresenting racial reality (e.g., increasing representation of Blacks, multiethnic readers, etc.), too many textbooks remain White, middle class, and antiseptic. The history and culture of Black Americans remains distorted in many instances. And importantly: "Far worse is the fact that almost all Black children are subjected to the maiming world of being taught to prefer others and to despise themselves. . . . In sum, most textbooks make learning a bore and a psychic insult for black children" (Bennett 1967, p. 138).

The critical question for the mental health of Black children is, of course, whether there is evidence which indicates that textbooks and curriculum materials do affect children's racial self-attitudes. The data here are slim. Indeed, there is only one known study which examined the effects of learning Black history on the racial attitudes of Black children (D. W. Johnson 1966). The children studied African and Negro history in a Freedom School each Saturday morning. Using interviews, Johnson determined "changes in superego strength, in self confidence, in attitudes toward Negroes and toward civil rights." The results were interpreted as indicating that the study of Black history can positively affect the racial attitudes of Black children. While this study is interesting, a number of questions can be raised about it. Could the fact that the participants were volunteers have influenced the results? Could bias have entered into the interview procedure, which was the sole method for gathering evaluation data? Since no control group was used, can change in the respondents' attitudes be confidently attributed to the Freedom School? In spite of this study's obvious weaknesses, this is precisely the kind of work that needs to be done. It is not enough merely to plan programs for enhancing the self-concept and racial awareness of the Black student. If we are to build a sound base for general practice and educational reform, careful evaluation of all programs, textbooks, and curriculums must be undertaken.

Education and the Reduction of Racism: The Future

We can ask that Brotherhood Week be changed to Racial Confrontation Week. We must no longer dread the confrontation but push it, so that people can be transformed. The educational process must be shifted in school so that every class at every grade level will discuss feelings, starting with feelings about race. We must make this nation one vast encounter group, dedicated to immediate change—to radical transformation of the national character. All schools such as those where you work should devote an entire semester to discussing nothing but race. (Cobb 1969)

The main elements of racism in the schools should by now be clear. Teachers, administrators, and the school curriculum are all implicated. All serve to shape and form the Black child's image of himself and his place in society. For many Black children the image of self is negative, the image of race is negative, and the perception of control of the environment is negative. For many Black children prospects for the future are not bright. It should be clear also that the school as an institution and its agents have failed many Black children.

A number of changes must be made in the educational establishment if positive mental health in Black children is to be developed and maintained. What can be done? Given the magnitude of the problem, no claim can be made for exhaustiveness of recommendations for changes in the school. Only the more obvious needs can be highlighted.

First, teachers, administrators, and other school personnel must somehow gain insight into their own racial feelings and attitudes. In some instances this goal may be achieved through introspection and reflection. For most, however, a more radical program may be needed—participation in sensitivity training or even in psychotherapy. Racial prejudice is an integral part of the person's total psychological makeup (Adorno et al. 1950). It thus may be impossible to modify prejudicial attitudes short of a total restructuring of the individual. Such a program is, of course, outside of the scope of the schools—if indeed it could be accomplished at all, given the primitive nature of our knowledge and skills in counseling and psychotherapy (Luborsky et al. 1971). What seems most reasonable is a policy for screening teachers who show themselves to be unfit for work with lower SES Black children. Such teachers, both Black and White, may well be quite satisfactory in work with Whites, with the middle class, or with other minorities. However if, after a program of education, orientation, role-playing, encounter-group participation, and other procedures of sensitization, teachers show themselves unable to relate effectively to Black children, then there is no alternative, if the mental and emotional health of both teacher and child is to be preserved, but to arrange some other educational placements for them. Effective techniques for screening teachers remain to be developed, but it does not seem unreasonable, as a beginning, to look for teachers who are emotionally stable and well adjusted. Conventional techniques of psychological assessment may be all that are necessary.

Secondly, schools must modify their curriculum to include

more of the history and culture of Black peoples. In a similar vein, curricula for the preparation of teachers must be dealt with. Strategies for the preparation of teachers for Black children, however, do not enjoy unanimity. On the one hand, there are those who suggest a variety of special curricula and experiences for the future teachers of Blacks. On the other hand, there are those who eschew such an approach: "examination of at least one particular aspect of the current trend in teacher preparation gives rise to the feeling that, advertently or inadvertently, teacher training institutes, if not one of the leaders of racism and its perpetration, are in the top ten institutes in our society doing so" (Hall 1969, p. 407).

Moreover, Hall notes that the problem with teacher-education programs is their tendency to dichotomize the problem into the "perpetrator of the evil, the bad white man; and the victim, the poor black man." This concern extends then to the curriculum:

The courses offered are based on the "we and them" syndrome. How do we get to know them? How do we get to understand them? How do we help them? It even goes further in this worship of differentiation, this denial of acceptance of a peer. . . . The special program phenomena often prey on some of the least sound, missionary, zealot, guilt ridden, self punishing hang-ups that young people (as well as others) have in our society today. Through exclusively perceiving the problem in a black-versus-white situation, we set the stage for the most crucial force of human resources, the teachers of our children, to perpetuate the very problem we are trying to solve and to extend the very viewpoint we are trying to eliminate. (Hall 1969, p. 407)

Such problems could be eliminated in Hall's view if teacher-education institutions accepted Blacks as falling on a continuum of all people. Teachers need to be trained, therefore, in skills of individual analysis and in techniques of responding to children in both individual and group situations. Ideally, the teacher himself "must be the most comfortable, swinging, loose human being possible, with minimum hang-ups about guilt and saving others, and thus himself secure enough to teach all people and learn from all."

A third area concerns personnel and racially integrated schools. Aside from the need to have good teachers of whatever race and to increase the numbers of minority teachers and administrators now employed by school districts, there would appear to be some advantage in having Black youngsters taught and administered by Blacks to provide models for the Black children. It will not escape the reader that it would be equally beneficial for White children to have Black teachers. If racism is to be eliminated at all, it is imperative that White children, particularly in their formative years, receive accurate perceptions of the range of talents and abilities possessed by Blacks. Such suggestions might seem to run counter to some work suggesting the value of desegregated and integrated schools for educating Black children. However, this is not the case. There is impressive evidence which documents the effects of school desegregation, school social class, and attending a racially integrated school on the Black child's achievement behavior (Coleman et al. 1966; U.S. Commission on Civil Rights 1967). The results of the Coleman study, with appropriate controls for school social climate, revealed that Black children in classrooms where more than half the students are White scored higher on reading and mathematics achievement tests than did Black children in classrooms having a smaller percentage of Whites. Various viewpoints relating to the likelihood that White students serve as achievement models are offered as an explanation of the above phenomenon. The Coleman study also presented evidence which indicates that "white students who first attended integrated schools early in their school career are [most] likely to value their association with Negro students" (Coleman 1966, p. 307). And further: "Whites who attended desegregated schools expressed greater willingness to reside in an interracial neighborhood, to have their children attend desegregated schools, and to have Negro friends. They consistently were more favorable toward the elimination of discrimination in employment against Negroes" (Coleman 1966, p. 112).

Evidence on the value of the integrated school for facilitating the achievement of the Black student and on influencing verbal attitudes toward Blacks in some future activities are impressive. But what of the present? What of the Black student's adjustment, his self-concept resulting from constant exposure to racism in teachers, students, and administrators? (Such unfortunately is also true for the Black student in the Black school, although perhaps these forces operate at a less intense level.) What evidence exists concerning the effects of school integration on intergroup attitudes and intergroup behavior? And what programs exist in the schools for modifying such attitudes and behaviors? If we are going to talk about integration as an educational goal, then we must have answers to these questions lest we err in developing cognitively able Black children at the expense of their social and emotional development. It is suspected that the recommendations offered earlier in this section for increasing the number of Black teachers and administrators would help to offset a number of the problems outlined above.

It has been generally assumed that integration will in and of itself lead to more positive attitudes and behavior towards Blacks. A recent survey of the literature in this area (Carithers 1970) suggests, however, that this is not the case. Rather, there appears to be no general agreement about the efforts of interracial contact on attitude change and intergroup behavior. Some studies have found heightened tolerance; some, heightened resistance; and some, no change. There is general agreement, however, that interracial contact per se will not in and of itself bring about increased tolerance and acceptance. Similar conclusions have been reached in a survey of studies concerned with modification of intergroup attitudes in a wide array of settings (Harding et al. 1969). What is needed in research in this area is more precise questions which focus upon the social groupings and social processes. What, for example, is the nature of the school social life? Does it foster competition among groups? cooperation among groups? What are the group processes and intergroup relations under different conditions of school integration? What different conditions of school integration exist? in different communities? (Carithers 1970).

A fourth area of need is for the development of school curricula to combat White racism. One of the best programs was developed in Ohio (Smith 1970). Four teaching units which actually involved teachers and students in study and discussion over a period as long as a year were developed. The first unit, "The Individual and Tolerance," required the student to concentrate on regarding himself as part of humanity and involved him in such searching questions as Who Am I? and What are my beliefs? The second unit, "Prejudice, Justice, Poverty, and Religion," dealt with causes of misunderstandings and prejudices. The third unit, "White and Black Race Issues," encouraged the student to probe psychological and sociological factors related to the race problem. It examined the nature of White racism and had as a central hypothesis that, until its pervasive nature is admitted, problems of racism will remain. The fourth unit, "The Reality of the Teaching-Learning Experience," described the winter and spring teaching efforts, in narrative form, of teachers who had participated in a summer project related to the development of the curriculum. Evaluative data on the curriculum are available as are evaluative instruments for assessing program outcomes.

Finally, elimination of racism in the schools may not occur solely by instituting changes in personnel and curriculum practices. In a number of instances, it may be necessary to bring help from outside the school itself. All failing, it may be necessary to reorganize the schools. Chesler (1969a), in a speech delivered at an Annual Meeting of the Metropolitan Detroit Bureau of School Studies, Inc., presented a number of "Promising Directions for School Change" stemming from his experiences in consultation with a variety of school districts on problems of student dissent. Among the key suggestions and critical needs he identified are the participation of a third-party negotiator and the necessity of generating and testing new models of organizing schools "along lines that do a more effective job of discovering and processing grievances and injustices." In a companion piece, Chesler (1969*b*) has also included work on role-playing, a potentially very useful device in ventilating feelings and sensitizing various protagonists to the feelings and attitudes of others. Similarly, Berlin (1970), following an examination of social and psychological conditions leading to confrontation and rebellion, has described group role-playing and discussion sessions (and individual consultation) with school administrators and teachers, using a psychiatric team.

Most suggestions for correcting the school's ills concern initiating changes in existing school programs — for example, providing for greater involvement of students, providing human relations training, exercising greater care in the selection of teachers, etc. Many of these activities have proved useful in a number of instances. Formidable obstacles make understandable the reluctance of educators to propose radical restructuring of the schools. The greatest obstacle may be the failure of parent and teacher to perceive the need for change at all. One of the more interesting findings of a Harris (1969) poll of a sample of high school students (both Black and White, presumably) conducted in 1969 revealed that curriculum innovations were favored by an overwhelming majority. More field work outside the schools was favored by 76 percent of the students, and 65 percent wanted more chance to work directly with the community. More student say in the area of policy-making was favored by 58 percent of the students (as compared with 35 percent of the teachers and 20 percent of the parents). A majority (54 percent) saw student participation in policy-making as "very important," compared with 30 percent of the teachers and 25 percent of the parents. Practically two-thirds of the students thought they should have more to say about making rules and determining the content of the curriculum; in both cases their feelings were not shared by nearly so many teachers or parents.

The many obstacles to radical school innovations make programs such as that at Parkway in Philadelphia all the more remarkable (Resnik 1969). Here in a "school without walls," using urban Philadelphia as a laboratory and classroom, are being implemented many suggestions designed to lead students toward greater involvement and meaningful learning on the one hand and a decrease in alienation, confrontation, and other forms of dissent on the other. According to one report (*Time* 1970), no racial incidents have occurred at Parkway. It may well be, if the social disease of racism is to be eradicated, that many of our current institutions — including the schools — will have to be radically altered if not dismantled altogether. We may have no choice —

> For unless man puts an end to this damnable sin,
> Hate will put the world in a flame —
> What a shame.
>
> (Cobb 1969)

REFERENCES

Adorno, T. W., Frenkel-Brunswik, Else; Levinson, J. D.; and Sanford, R. N. 1950. *The authoritarian personality*. New York: Harper.

Allport, F. H., et al. 1952. The effects of segregation and the consequences of desegregation: a social science statement. In *Prejudice and your child*, ed. K. B. Clark. Boston: Beacon Press, *1963*, pp. 166–84.

Anderson, Astrid C. 1966. The treatment of racial and cultural diversity in elementary school social studies textbooks. Report of the Lincoln Filene Center for Citizenship and Public Affairs, Tufts University.

ASCD. 1970. A selected bibliography of instructional materials. Supplement to *ASCD News Exchange*. Dec.

Banks, J. A. 1969. The need for positive racial attitudes in the textbooks. In

Racial crisis in American education, ed. R. L. Green, pp. 167–85. Chicago: Follett Educational Corporation.

Barber, T. X., and Silver, M. J.
  1968a. Facts, fiction, and the experimenter bias effect. *Psychol. Bull. Monograph* 70:1–29 (no. 6, pt. 2).
  1968b. Pitfalls in data analysis and interpretation: a reply to Rosenthal. *Psychol. Bull. Monograph* 70:48–62.

Becker, H. 1952. The career of the Chicago public schoolteacher. *Am. J. Soc.* 57:470–77.

Beez, W. V. 1968. Influence of biased psychological reports on teacher behavior and pupil performance. *Proceedings,* 76th Annual Convention of the American Psychological Association, pp. 605–06.

Bennett, L., Jr. 1967. Reading, riting and racism. 1967. *Ebony* 22:130–32.

Berlin, I. M. 1970. From confrontation to collaboration. *Am. J. Orthopsychiat.* 40:473–80.

Berman, L. 1954. The mental health of the educator. *Mental Hygiene* 38:422–29.

Bower, E. M. 1966. The achievement of competency. In ASCD Yearbook *Learning and Mental Health in the School,* ed. W. B. Waetjen and R. R. Leeper. Washington, D.C.: Association for Supervision and Curriculum Development.

Brookover, W., and Erickson, E. 1969. *Sociological foundations of educability.* Boston: Allyn & Bacon, in press. In Racism in education: a barrier to quality education, chap. 7 in *Racial crisis in American education,* ed. R. L. Green. Chicago: Follett Educational Corporation.

Carithers, Martha W. 1970. School desegregation and racial cleavage, 1954–70: a review of the literature. *J. Soc. Issues* 26:25–47.

Chesler, Mark A.
  1969a. Promising directions for school change. In *Dissent and disruption in secondary schools, ERIC document.* Washington, D.C.: Department of Health, Education, and Welfare, Office of Education, July, pp. 4–7.
  1969b. Role-playing exercises that highlight student-school conflict in secondary schools. In *Dissent and disruption in secondary schools, ERIC document.* Washington, D.C.: Department of Health, Education, and Welfare, Office of Education, July, pp. 1–4.

Clark, K. B.
  1965. *Dark ghetto.* New York: Harper and Row.
  1969. Learning obstacles among children. In *Problems of school men in depressed urban centers,* ed. A. L. Roaden. Columbus, Ohio: College of Education, Ohio State University.

Cobb, P. 1969. The Black revolution and education. *Bull. Nat. Ass. Sec. Sch. Prin.* 53:3–18.

Coleman, J; S.; Campbell, E. Q.; Hobson, C. J.; McPartland, J.; Mood, A. M.; Weinfeld, F. D.; and York, R. L. 1966. *Equality of educational opportunity.* Washington, D.C.: U.S. Government Printing Office.

Corwin, R. G., and Schmit, Sister Marilyn. 1970. Teachers in inner-city schools: a survey of a large-city school system. *Educ. Urban Soc.* 2:131–55.

Douglass, J. H. 1967. Mental health aspects of the effects of discrimination upon children. *Young Children* 22:298–305.

Dunn, L. M. 1968. Special education for the mildly retarded—is much of it justifiable? *Exceptional Children* 35:5–22.

Fanon, F. 1966. *The wretched of the earth.* New York: Grove Press.

Flanders, N. A. 1965. *Teacher influence, pupil attitudes, and achievement.* Washington, D.C.: Department of Health, Education and Welfare, Office of Education.

Glancy, Barbara J. 1969. *Children's interracial fiction.* Chicago: American Federation of Teachers.

Goldstein, H. 1963. Issues in the education of the educable mentally retarded. *Mental Retardation* 1:10–12, 52–53.

Gordon, I. J. 1966. New conceptions of children's learning and development. In ASCD Yearbook, *Learning and mental health in the school,* ed. W. B. Waetjen and R. R. Leeper. Washington, D.C.: Association for Supervision and Curriculum Development.

Gray, S. W. 1963. *The psychologist in the schools.* New York: Holt, Rinehart & Winston.

Hall, J; C., Jr. 1989; The Black thing: a small point, maybe. In Teacher education: White racism and inner city schools, ed. A. Pearl. *J. Teacher Educ.* 20:406–10.

Hampton, C. 1970. Rationale, development, and organization (of Black studies program in Berkeley, California—N. B.). *Bull. Nat. Ass. Sec. Sch. Prin.* 54:84–93.

Harding, J.; Proshansky, H.; Kutner, B.; and Chein, I. 1969. Prejudice and ethnic relations. In *The handbook of social psychology,* ed. G. Lindzey and E. Aronson. Reading, Mass.: Addison-Wesley.

Harris, L. 1969. What people think about their high schools. *Life* 66:22–23.

Haubrich, V. F. 1969. Preparing teachers for disadvantaged youth. In *Racial crisis in American education,* ed. R. L. Green, pp. 126–46. Chicago: Follett Educational Corporation.

Hendrick, I. G., and Jones, R. L., eds. 1972. *Student dissent in the schools.* Boston: Houghton Mifflin.

Herriott, R., and St. John, Nancy H. 1966. *Social class and the urban school.* New York: Wiley.

Hill, G. E., and Luckey, Eleanore B. 1969. *Guidance for children in elementary schools.* New York: Appleton-Century-Crofts.

Hilliard, T. O., 1972. Black psychology: personality characteristics of Black student activists and nonactivists. In *Black psychology*, ed. R. L. Jones. New York: Harper and Row.

Hunter, E. C. 1957. Changes in teachers' attitudes toward children's behavior over the last thirty years. *Mental Hygiene* 41:3–11.

Jackson, Rev. J. L. 1968. *Chicago Defender*. March 8, p. 10.

Jackson, P. W., and Getzels, J. W. 1963. Psychological health and classroom functioning: a study of dissatisfaction with school among adolescents. In *Educating for mental health*, ed. J. M. Seidman. New York: Thomas Y. Crowell.

Jerrems, R. L. 1970. Racism: Vector of ghetto education. *Integrated Education: Race and Schools* 8:40–47.

Jersild, A. T., and Lazar, Eve A. 1962. *The meaning of psychotherapy in the teacher's life and work*. New York: Teachers College, Columbia University.

Johnson, D. W. 1966. Freedom school effectiveness: changes in attitudes of Negro children. *J. Appl. Behav. Sci.* 2:325, 328, 329.

Johnson, E. A. 1911. *A school history of the Negro race in America*. New York: Golfman Company.

Johnson, J. J. 1969. Special education and the inner city: a challenge for the future or another means of cooling the mark out? *J. Spec. Educ.* 3:241–51.

Jones, R. L.

    1968.   Student attitudes and motivation. In *A report to the Columbus Board of Education*, ed. Ohio State University Advisory Commission on Problems Facing the Columbus (Ohio) Public School. June, pp. 272–300, 313–32.

    1969*a*.   School morale in the metropolis: pupil race, teacher race, teacher satisfaction, and other correlates. Paper presented at the annual meeting of the American Educational Research Association, Los Angeles, February.

    1969*b*.   The school morale of educable mental retardates. Paper presented at the annual meeting of the American Association of Mental Deficiency, San Francisco, May.

    1970.   New labels in old bags: research on labelling Blacks culturally disadvantaged, culturally deprived, and mentally retarded. Paper presented at the annual convention of the Association of Black Psychologists, Miami Beach, September.

    1971.   Teacher management of stigma in classes for the educable mentally retarded. Paper presented at the annual meeting of the California Educational Research Association, April.

Jones, R. L., ed. 1972. *Black psychology*. New York: Harper.

Larrick, N. 1965. The all-White world of children's books. *Saturday Review* 48:63–65.

Litcher, J. H., and Johnson, D. W. 1969. Changes in attitudes toward Negroes of White elementary school students after use of multi-ethnic readers. *J. Educ. Psychol.* 60:148–52.

Luborsky, L.; Chandler, M.; Auerbach, A. H.; and Cohen, H. 1971. Factors influencing the outcome of psychotherapy: a review of quantitative research. *Psychol. Bull.* 75:145–85.

Mackler, B., and Giddings, M. G. 1967. Cultural deprivation: a study in mythology. In *Education and social crisis,* ed. E. T. Keach, R. Fulton, and W. E. Gardner. New York: Wiley.

MacMillan, D. L. 1971. Special education for the mildly retarded: servant or savant. *Focus on Exceptional Children* 2:1–11.

Marburger, C. L. 1966. School-community relations and maladjusted youth. In *Social deviance among youth,* National Society for the Study of Education. 65th Yearbook, part I. Chicago: University of Chicago Press.

Marcus, L. 1961. *The treatment of minorities in secondary school textbooks.* New York: Anti-Defamation League of B'nai B'rith.

Meyerowitz, J. H. 1962. Self-derogations in young retardates and special class placement. *Child development* 33:443–51.

Rabkin, L., and Suchoski, J. F., Jr. 1967. Teachers' views of mental illness: a study of attitudes and information. *J. Teach. Educ.* 18:36–41.

Resnik, Henry S. 1969. High school with no walls—it's happening in Philadelphia. *Think* 35:33–36.

Rodeheaver, J. N. 1970. Black studies program in Berkeley, California. *Bull. Nat. Ass. Sec. Sch. Prin.* 54:77–84.

Rosenthal, R., and Jacobson, Lenore. 1968. *Pygmalion in the classroom.* New York: Holt, Rinehart & Winston.

Sarason, S. B.; Davidson, K. S.; Lighthall, F. F.; Waite, R. R.; and Ruebusch, B. K. 1960. *Anxiety in elementary school children.* New York: Wiley.

Sloan, I. 1966. *The Negro in modern history textbooks.* Chicago: American Federation of Teachers.

Smith, D. H. 1969. The Black revolution and education. *Racial crisis in American education,* ed. R. L. Green, pp. 56–71. Chicago: Follett Educational Corporation.

Smith, W. L. 1970. Critique of developments at the secondary level. *J. Negro Educ.* 39:239–61.

Strom, R. D. 1965. School evaluation and mental health. In *Mental health and achievement,* ed. E. Paul Torrance and Robert D. Strom. New York: Wiley.

Thorndike, R. L. 1968. Review of Rosenthal, R. and Jacobson, L., *Pygmalion in the classroom. Am. Educ. Res. J.* 5:708–11.

Time Magazine. 1970. 95, March 23.

Trager, Helen G., and Yarrow, M. R. 1952. *They learn what they live.* New York: Harper.

U.S. Commission on Civil Rights. 1967. *Racial isolation in the public schools.* Vol. 1. Washington, D.C.: U.S. Government Printing Office.

Waetjen, W. B., and Leeper, R. R., eds. 1966. *Learning and mental health in the school.* ASCD Yearbook. Washington, D.C.: Association for Supervision and Curriculum Development, National Education Association.

White, W. 1939. *Anti-Negro propaganda in school textbooks.* New York: National Association for the Advancement of Colored People.

Wilson, P. E. 1968. Negro education in a changing and racist America. *Virginia J. Educ.* 62:19–21, 38.

Wrightsman, L.; Nelson, R. H.; and Tranto, Maria. 1968. The construction and validation of a scale to measure children's school morale. Paper, George Peabody College for Teachers.

CHAPTER 11

Definitions and Distributions of Mental Disorders in a Racist Society

by *Morton Kramer*
Beatrice M. Rosen
Ernest M. Willis

This chapter presents findings of community studies developed to determine the prevalence of mental disorders in the United States and also data on patterns of the way that psychiatric facilities are used by race in the United States. Shown also are the inadequacy of present statistics on mental disorders by race, and recommendations are made for the development of statistics that can serve as the basis of programs to eliminate the attitudes, practices, and conditions that adversely affect the physical and mental health of citizens of the United States.

The assigned title of this chapter presumes that reliable and valid annual morbidity statistics on the group of mental disorders—which, collectively, are referred to as mental illness—are available and that it is possible to describe their occurrence and distribution in a society characterized as racist. However, the underlying presumption is incorrect. Annual morbidity statistics on the prevalence and incidence of mental disorders as a group or of individual disorders within the group do not exist for the United States or, for that matter, for any other society of the world, whether it is characterized as racist or not racist. Thus it is impossible to provide a precise description of the frequency of occurrence of the mental disorders by age, sex, race, marital status, occupation, place of residence, and a variety of other social and economic variables as of a given point in time or over time for the United States as a whole, its various geographic regions, divisions, or separate states.

The major impediments to the development of morbidity statistics on the mental disorders are the continued absence of standardized case-finding techniques capable of uniform application from place to place and from time to time for detecting persons in the general population with these disorders, the lack of reliable differential diagnostic techniques for assigning each case to a specific category, and the dearth of methods for determining dates of onset and termination. As Frost (1941) stated in his well-known paper on epidemiology: "since description of the distribution of any disease in a population obviously requires that the disease must be recognized when it occurs, the development of epidemiology must follow and be limited by that of clinical diagnosis and of the rather complex machinery required for the systematic collection of morbidity and mortality statistics." Up to now, this problem of the unavailability of reliable and valid criteria has defied satisfactory solution. Once it is solved, the collection of morbidity statistics on the mental disorders becomes possible.

However, it will still be necessary to develop the appropriate machinery for applying the case-finding techniques to target populations and collecting and analyzing the morbidity, disability, mortality, and related types of data required to develop a descriptive epidemiology of the mental disorders. In the absence of more precise statistics on the prevalence and incidence of mental disorders, statistics on the utilization patterns of psychiatric facilities, particularly mental hospitals, have been used as a first approximation to a descriptive epidemiology of these disorders. To date the number of trained persons engaged in the collection and analysis of such data is quite insufficient in relation to the job that needs to be done at the federal, state, and local levels. The situation is still more acute when it comes to the availability of trained epidemiologists, social scientists, biostatisticians, and related personnel who are needed to carry out surveys at the community level. Thus, even when the case-finding methods required for development of an epidemiology of mental disorders become available, much will remain to be done to develop the appropriate organizational structures and necessary manpower for applying such techniques.

It is the purpose of this chapter to review: (a) findings of community studies that have attempted to determine the prevalence of mental disorders for White and non-White groups in the United States and (b) available data on patterns of utilization of psychiatric facilities by race in the United States derived from national and state statistical programs related to these activities. It is important for the reader to bear in mind that neither the community studies nor the facility data-collection systems were designed for the specific purpose of determining the extent to which differences in the prevalence of mental disorders and in the rates of use of psychiatric services between Whites and non-Whites were due to racist practices and how much to other factors. The community studies were designed primarily to determine the prevalence of mental disorders in the noninstitutional populations in the areas studied. The national and statewide statistical reporting systems were designed to collect data on the age, sex, racial, socioeconomic, diagnostic, and other characteristics of persons using mental hospitals and other psychiatric facilities. At most, the data derived from these sources provide indicators which may suggest the presence and/or effects of racist practices.

Racist practices undoubtedly are key factors—perhaps the most important ones—in producing mental disorders in Blacks and other underprivileged groups, in determining the place where members of these groups receive diagnosis and treatment for these disorders, and in determining the quality of such clinical services. Indeed, the way in which racism has affected life-style, value system, socioeconomic and health status, opportunities for education, work, housing, medical care and recreation of the victimized groups accounts wholly or at least in part for the differences reported in these pages. In some instances the role of racism will be obvious; in others, not so obvious. Where possible, the authors have highlighted those differences which might have resulted from these practices.

This chapter also demonstrates the woefully inadequate statistics now available on mental disorders by race and makes recommendations which, hopefully, will lead to more complete and systematic statistics for this variable. Such data are needed to plan programs to eliminate the attitudes, practices, and conditions of life that have affected so adversely the physical and mental health and social well-being of so many of our citizens and to evaluate our efforts to accomplish this goal.

Some Preliminaries

In the preceding section some terms requiring definition have been used. These are: mental disorders, racism, incidence, prevalence, and rates of utilization of psychiatric facilities. In the paragraphs that follow, these terms will be defined — operationally where possible — so that the reader may understand more clearly the content and limitations of available data derived from community surveys and studies of patterns of care in relation to racism.

Definitions of Mental Illness and Mental Disorders

For purposes of this chapter, mental illness is defined in terms of the disorders listed in the diagnostic and statistical manuals of the American Psychiatric Association (1968, 1952). These classifications have been used in national and state activities related to the collection of statistical data on the care of the mentally ill. In addition, data collected from community studies have, for the most part, been reported in diagnostic categories that can be related to these classifications.

The major categories included in the second edition (DSM-II) of this classification are:

    I.   Mental retardation
   II.   Organic brain syndromes
        A. Psychoses associated with organic brain syndromes
        B. Nonpsychotic organic brain syndromes
  III.   Psychoses not attributed to physical conditions listed previously
  IV.   Neuroses
   V.   Personality disorders and certain other nonpsychotic mental disorders
  VI.   Psychophysiologic disorders
 VII.   Special symptoms
VIII.   Transient situational disturbances
  IX.   Behavior disorders of childhood and adolescence

A major advantage of the nomenclature and classification of mental disorders in this revised manual is that it provides a system of diagnostic nomenclature that is compatible with the eighth revision of the International Classification of Diseases (ICD-8) prepared by the World Health Organization (1967). Thus, it provides a basis for the development of comparable national and international statistics on the mental disorders. It should be noted that one category has not been included with the above list of mental disorders. This is category X, conditions without manifest psychiatric disorder and nonspecific conditions, which includes the following:

  316.   Social maladjustments without manifest psychiatric disorders
        316.0 Marital maladjustment
        316.1 Social maladjustment

316.2 Occupational maladjustment
316.3 Dyssocial behavior
316.4 Other social maladjustment

Category X is reserved for recording conditions of individuals who are psychiatrically normal but who nevertheless have severe enough problems to warrant examination by a psychiatrist. These conditions may either become or precipitate a diagnosable mental disorder.

This tenth category of disorders requires careful attention and study in the development of morbidity statistics on the mental disorders by racial groups. Types of behavior that are considered to be psychiatrically abnormal by one racial or ethnic group are not always so considered by members of another group. Criteria which make it possible to determine when such behavior should be included as a mental disorder (e.g., personality disorder) and when not must be developed. There is considerable overlap between conditions diagnosed as *antisocial personality* (a mental disorder) and those diagnosed as *dyssocial behavior* (one of the conditions without manifest psychiatric disorder). The social consequences of misdiagnosis may be considerable. The former diagnosis may result in a patient's being admitted to a psychiatric service for treatment, the other in an individual's being sentenced to a correctional institution or training school for delinquents.

One other point: The set of conditions included under the category of mental retardation will not be dealt with in this chapter except as this condition appears in community surveys and in other surveys of patterns of care of persons with mental disorders. This is a complicated and controversial subject in its own right and should be discussed by persons more familiar with the problem than we are.

Definitions of Racism

A number of definitions of racism are in use. In the absence of a generally agreed-upon definition, the one in the third edition of *Webster's Unabridged Dictionary* (1961), which gives the etymology and defines the word, may be cited:

racism ... *n − s* [prob. fr. *racisme,* fr. *race* + isme = ism] 1. the assumption that psychocultural traits and capacities are determined by biological race and that races differ decisively from one another which is usu. coupled with a belief in the inherent superiority of a particular race and its right to domination over others   2a: a doctrine or political program based on the assumption of racism and designed to execute its principles   b: a political or social system founded on racism

Kerner, in his discussion on the *Report of the National Advisory Commission on Civil Disorders* (Kerner 1969, pp. 537–41), defines the term as follows:

But first, what *is* racism? A simple definition of a complex phenomenon, bred into America for 300 years, may be impossible. In my view, however, white racism is expressed in the belief that if you are white, you are superior—and if you are black, you are inferior. The unfair effects of this way of thinking on American customs, actions, and even laws have been widespread. . . .

Racial stereotypes, in fact, are part of white America's world. Whites grow up with them, and we need not feel guilty or resentful about admitting it. Racism has been so deeply rooted in our society that it will require new attitudes, new understanding, new will, and new tolerance from every American, black as well as white, if we are to overcome it. If not, America will continue its disastrous drift in two societies, separate and unequal, locked in internecine strife.[1]

The above comment stresses attitudes of Whites toward Blacks. However, the problem goes much further. Whites manifest racist attitudes toward the American Indians, Orientals, and other racial and cultural groups such as Puerto Ricans and Mexican-American groups. In addition, they ex-

1. From *The World Book Year Book.* © 1969 Field Enterprises Educational Corporation. Used by permission.

hibit "within-ingroup" attitudes and practices that result, for example, in Whites' discriminating aginst other Whites — non-Jews versus Jews, native born versus foreign born, affluent versus poor — in general, attitudes that result in some members of one group, be they White or other than White, discriminating against other members of the same ethnic or racial group.

Definitions of Basic Epidemiologic Indices

This chapter deals essentially with epidemiologic concepts and measures involved in studying the relationship of racism to mental disorders. Epidemiology has been given various definitions, but one definition that seems to be most appropriate to the purposes of this book is "a science concerned with the study of factors that influence the occurrence and distribution of disease, defect, disability or death in aggregations of individuals" (Clark 1953).

It seems that the expectation of the organizing editors of this volume was for this chapter to review data on the variations in the occurrence of mental disorders in the United States with respect to the role of a stressor — racism — in the etiology of specific mental disorders and on the patterns of care of members of various racial groups, both the "superior groups" and the "inferior dominated groups." At the most elementary level, this would require basic data on the incidence and prevalence of specific mental disorders by age, sex, and race. The base population data required for the denominators of such rates are available from the U.S. Census of Population by racial groups (viz., White, Negro, American Indian, Japanese, Chinese, Filipino, Hawaiian, Aleut [Eskimo]) and by color (viz., White, non-White). Such data are provided in detail at the decennial census, and estimates for Whites and other races are given at various intercensal points. However, as indicated earlier, the numerator data required to compute incidence and prevalence rates (terms to be defined below) are nonexistent.

There are two basic ratios of cases to population that the

epidemiologist uses in studies of disease, the incidence rate and the prevalence rate. Because of their fundamental nature it is important that the concepts embodied in these rates be clearly understood by persons undertaking epidemiologic investigations. Understanding of these concepts also facilitates interpretation and critical evaluation of the published literature in this field.

Incidence rate.   Incidence is defined as the annual number of "new" cases of a specific disorder occurring within a specified period of time (usually a year). "New" case must be defined carefully as, for example, the first or initial attack of a disease during an individual's lifetime. The incidence rate is computed by taking the ratio of the number of new cases (as defined) in the specified interval to the appropriate population exposed to risk. In commenting on the role of the incidence rate in studies of infectious disease, Doull et al. (1942) have stated: "In general terms and assuming no restrictions on exposure, incidence is dependent upon the balance which exists between resistance of the population and pathogenicity of the microorganism. This balance may be called the force of morbidity."

The analogy is apparent between this concept and others that have been proposed with respect to the incidence of mental disorders in the population. Incidence of mental disorder would seem to be dependent upon the balance which exists between resistance of the population and those forces and stresses — biologic, cultural, psychologic, social, economic, and political — that produce mental disorder.

In this volume we are concerned with the effect of racism as an etiologic factor per se, as well as a factor that has played an important role in creating conditions that can result in mental disorder. Data included in table 11.1 may be used to illustrate these concepts.

Non-Whites have higher infant mortality rates and fetal mortality ratios than have Whites. Thus in 1945 the non-White infant mortality rate (57 per 1,000 live births) was

(Continued on page 365)

	1945			
Mortality Data	White Males	White Females	Non-White Males	Non-White Females
All causes of death	1,070.4	752.2	1,446.2	1,193.1
Tuberculosis	41.8	21.0	127.9	87.9
Syphilis and its sequelae	10.3	3.1	57.6	22.4
Malignant neoplasms	120.7	121.1	92.1	116.6
Vascular lesions affecting CNS	82.7	78.6	126.6	147.0
Arteriosclerotic heart disease	–	–	–	–
Hypertensive disease	–	–	–	–
Chronic and unspec. nephritis and other renal sclerosis	58.4	45.5	121.1	109.4
Influenza and pneumonia, except of newborn	48.1	33.7	98.9	77.7
Ulcer of stomach and duodenum	10.5	1.9	9.9	$(3.2)^a$
Gastritis, duodenitis, enteritis colitis	7.2	5.9	$(13.8)^a$	12.2
Cirrhosis of liver	11.8	5.9	8.5	$(5.4)^a$
Senility – ill-defined conditions	19.7	14.2	73.1	56.4
Accident	105.5	42.8	105.7	35.8
Suicide	18.5	6.3	5.7	1.5
Homocide	5.1	1.3	52.7	10.6
Infant mortality rates per 1,000 live births				
Under 1 year	39.9	31.1	63.2	50.8
Under 28 days (neonatal mortality)	26.4	19.9	36.0	28.0
Under 1 day	12.4	9.5	14.1	11.3
Fetal mortality ratios				
20 weeks or more	22.6	20.1	46.3	37.6
Maternal mortality rates	–	172.1	–	454.8
Estimated expectation of life at birth (in years)	64.4	69.5	56.1	59.6

SOURCES: 1945, 1955 (U.S. Dept. of HEW 1968*b*); 1967 (U.S. Dept. of HEW 1969*b*).

a. Parentheses indicate age-adjusted rates based on age-specific rates of which more than half were for frequencies less than 20.

TABLE 11.1 — *Continued*

	1955			
Mortality Data	White Males	White Females	Non-White Males	Non-White Females
All causes of death	905.0	572.8	1,187.5	909.9
Tuberculosis	10.0	3.6	32.1	16.5
Syphilis and its sequelae	2.2	0.7	(13.4)[a]	(4.9)[a]
Malignant neoplasms	137.4	114.3	138.7	124.7
Vascular lesions affecting CNS	82.7	73.2	136.2	139.3
Arteriosclerotic heart disease	281.6	130.6	188.8	126.8
Hypertensive disease	34.7	34.9	109.7	110.8
Chronic and unspec. nephritis and other renal sclerosis	8.4	6.0	20.5	19.6
Influenza and pneumonia, except of newborn	22.3	14.9	50.8	33.9
Ulcer of stomach and duodenum	8.4	2.0	7.2	2.5
Gastritis, duodenitis, enteritis colitis	3.3	2.8	(7.2)[a]	6.5
Cirrhosis of liver	12.9	6.1	10.3	6.8
Senility — ill-defined conditions	11.2	6.8	42.6	33.8
Accident	77.3	33.8	100.9	40.7
Suicide	17.2	4.9	6.1	1.5
Homocide	3.5	1.3	42.6	10.3
Infant mortality rates per 1,000 live births				
Under 1 year	26.7	20.3	46.9	38.6
Under 28 days (neonatal mortality)	20.3	15.1	30.2	24.1
Under 1 day	10.5	8.1	15.3	12.4
Fetal mortality ratios 20 weeks or more	15.8	14.5	31.0	25.8
Maternal mortality rates	–	32.8	–	130.3
Estimated expectation of life at birth (in years)	67.4	73.7	61.4	66.1

Continued on page 364

TABLE 11.1 — *Continued*

Mortality Data	1967			
	White Males	White Females	Non-White Males	Non-White Females
All causes of death	900.9	518.1	1,243.3	820.7
Tuberculosis	3.6	1.1	15.4	5.5
Syphilis and its sequelae	1.3	0.4	3.6	1.7
Malignant neoplasms	150.3	107.9	186.6	126.6
Vascular lesions affecting CNS	71.5	59.9	124.4	114.1
Arteriosclerotic heart disease	307.0	136.1	247.0	152.8
Hypertensive disease	14.7	14.2	58.1	55.0
Chronic and unspec. nephritis and other renal sclerosis	4.3	2.6	13.2	10.7
Influenza and pneumonia, except of newborn	24.2	14.3	47.6	26.6
Ulcer of stomach and duodenum	6.0	2.1	6.5	2.3
Gastritis, duodenitis, enteritis colitis	2.8	2.7	4.3	3.5
Cirrhosis of liver	17.2	8.4	27.2	15.0
Senility — ill-defined conditions	9.9	5.0	43.8	27.6
Accident	77.8	28.2	114.7	35.9
Suicide	17.1	6.7	9.7	3.2
Homocide	5.9	2.0	62.7	14.0
Infant mortality rates per 1,000 live births				
Under 1 year	22.4	16.9	39.3	32.5
Under 28 days (neonatal mortality)	17.2	12.7	26.3	21.2
Under 1 day	9.9	7.5	15.6	12.7
Fetal mortality ratios				
20 weeks or more	13.5[b]		25.8[b]	
Maternal mortality rates	–	19.5	–	69.5
Estimated expectation of life at birth (in years)	67.8	75.1	61.1	68.2

b. Includes males and females.

about 1.5 times as high as the White rate (36), and the non-White fetal mortality ratio (42 fetal deaths per 1,000 live births) was twice that of the White (21). Although considerable reductions occurred in these figures between 1945 and 1967 for all racial groups, as of 1967 the non-White infant mortality rate and fetal mortality ratio were, respectively, still 1.5 and 2 times those of the Whites (infant mortality rates: 36 for non-Whites vs. 20 for Whites; fetal mortality ratio: 26 for the non-Whites vs. 13 for the Whites). Also, despite striking reductions in the maternal mortality rates for both non-Whites and Whites during the same period, as of 1967 the non-White rate (69.5 per 1,000 live births) was 3.5 times that for the White females (19.5).

As a result of their research findings on the relationships of complications of pregnancy and the birth process to neuropsychiatric disorders in children, Pasamanick and Knobloch (1961, p. 91) formulated the following hypothesis: "there exists a continuum of reproductive insult, at least partially socioeconomically determined, resulting in a continuum of reproductive casualty extending from death through varying degrees of neuropsychiatric disability." They state further:

We also submit that this evidence — which supports the findings of other studies — is strong enough to warrant the institution of preventive programs in the prenatal period and preferably even before conception. . . .
These programs should be geared to the elimination and modification of such results of poverty and deprivation as malnutrition, infection, and other forms of stress, prenatally in the mother and postnatally in the child. In addition, it seems apparent to us that psychosocial deprivation and faulty stimulation in childhood require fully as much attention, if not more, in preventive programs. Hopefully, such programs would be established on a controlled experimental basis so that the hypotheses offered could be tested definitely.

Thus, the persistently higher infant mortality rates, fetal

mortality ratios, and maternal mortality rates for non-Whites as compared with Whites are very likely to have as their sequelae higher rates of neuropsychiatric disorders among non-White children than among White children. Similarly the fact that higher proportions of Negroes and other races than Whites have incomes below the poverty level (33 percent vs. 10 percent, respectively, table 11.2) means that higher proportions of non-Whites than Whites are subject to those stresses which accompany poverty, for instance, malnutrition, infection, psychosocial deprivation, and faulty stimulation in childhood. Racism has played a significant role in creating these conditions and the environment in which they thrive.

Blacks and members of other minority groups are subjected not only to the types of stresses first described but also to psychological stress resulting from discriminatory practices that have blocked opportunities for housing, education, and employment, regardless of educational level. To quote the recent publication *Toward a Social Report* (U.S. Dept. HEW 1969*a*, p. 24):

Because most Americans can realize their highest ambitions through education, it is often assumed that Negroes can similarly overcome the handicaps of poverty and race. But this has not been so in the past. To be sure, even in minority groups, better educated individuals tend to occupy more desirable occupational positions than do the less educated. Yet the returns on an investment in education are much lower for Negroes than for the general population. Indeed, for a Negro, educational attainment may simply mean exposure to more severe and visible discrimination than is experienced by the dropout or the unschooled.

Thus, in addition to the handicap of being born in a family with few economic or other resources, the average Negro also appears to have less opportunity because of his race alone.

The frustrations resulting from such racist practices produce psychological stress which in turn may be a key factor in the causation of various types of mental disorders (e.g., depressive disorders, psychophysiologic disorders, psychoneuroses, personality disorders, alcoholism).

TABLE 11.2. Persons below poverty level: United States, 1969

Family Status and Race	Number (in Thousands)			Percentage of Total[c]		
	All Persons in Families & Unrelated Individuals	Persons in Families with Male Head & Male Unrelated Individuals[b]	Persons in Families with Female Head & Female Unrelated Individuals	All Persons in Families & Unrelated Individuals	Persons in Families with Male Head & Male Unrelated Individuals	Persons in Families with Female Head & Female Unrelated Individuals
Total	25,389	15,025	10,364	12.8%	8.8%	38.9%
In families	20,695	13,705	6,990	11.3	8.3	38.7
Head	5,047	3,292	1,755	10.0	7.3	32.3
Family members < 18[a]	10,739	6,330	4,409	15.3	10.2	55.2
Other family members	4,909	4,083	826	7.8	7.0	17.8
Unrelated individuals 14 +	4,694	1,320	3,374	34.0	25.4	39.2
White	17,395	10,995	6,400	10.0	7.1	32.3
In families	13,546	9,995	3,551	8.4	6.7	29.1
Head	3,616	2,595	1,021	8.0	6.3	25.2
Family members < 18[a]	6,373	4,298	2,075	10.7	7.8	44.4
Other family members	3,557	3,102	455	6.3	5.8	13.1
Unrelated individuals 14 +	3,849	1,000	2,849	32.2	23.3	37.1
Negro and other races	7,994	4,030	3,964	33.5	23.6	58.4
In families	7,149	3,710	3,439	32.4	22.9	58.7
Head	1,431	697	734	28.2	18.9	52.9
Family members < 18[a]	4,366	2,032	2,334	41.6	28.3	70.4
Other family members	1,352	981	371	20.9	18.5	32.1
Unrelated individuals 14 +	845	320	525	45.7	34.8	56.7

SOURCE: U.S. Bureau of Census 1969, table 1.
a. Other than head or wife.
b. Includes head of husband-wife and other male-head families.
c. Percentage of persons in corresponding group in total population of the U.S.

Prevalence rate. Prevalence is the number of cases of disease present in a population as of a specified interval of time. The characteristics of the individuals who are to be counted must be defined carefully as, for example, all cases of individuals who have "active" disease during the interval of the study. The prevalence rate is computed by taking the ratio of the number of cases in the specified interval of time to the number of people in the appropriate population group for which the rate is being determined. There are several variations of the prevalence rate that have been used in surveys of mental disorders:

1. *The point-prevalence rate:* This is the ratio of the number of specified cases of a disorder alive as of a single day (e.g., the survey date) to the number of people in the appropriate population group as of the same date. This rate is a function of the incidence rate and the duration of the disorder.

2. *Period- or interval-prevalence rate:* This is the ratio of the number of cases of the disease present in a population during a specified interval to the population exposed to risk. In its simplest form, it is a combination of the point-prevalence rate at the start of the interval (e.g., beginning of the year) plus the incidence rate during the interval. In its more complicated form, the numerator of the ratio includes not only "new cases" but "reactivated old cases," that is, cases which were not included in the initial point-prevalence rate because they were inactive on the day of the survey but became active during the study interval. Thus the interval-prevalence rate may also be a function of the "reactivation" or "relapse rate" for a given condition.

3. *Lifetime-prevalence rate:* This is the ratio of the number of persons with a history of the disorder who are alive as of the survey date to the population exposed to risk. It is a function of the incidence rate and the survivorship rate of all persons who develop the disorder.

As can be seen, prevalence is a complex index. Interpretation of differences in this rate within and between groups on a cross-sectional or trend basis requires knowledge not only of factors that can affect incidence but of those factors that account for variations in the duration of the disorder following onset. This means we need knowledge of such things as the "cure," "relapse," and "mortality" rates.

As stated by Doull et al. (1942): "Prevalence is more complex than incidence. It is the resultant of the force of morbidity and those factors which determine whether the interval between onset and termination shall be long or short, whether a disease shall be acute or chronic."

To summarize, incidence measures the rate at which new cases are added to the population of sick persons; and, in conjunction with the decrement rate, that is, the rate at which the disease is "arrested" or "cured," or at which affected individuals are removed from the population by death, it determines the size and composition of the sick population, that is, the prevalence of the disease. Since the prevalence rate is a function of the annual incidence rate and duration of the disease, differences in prevalence of a mental disorder between Blacks and Whites are dependent on the relative differences between both the incidence rates and the duration of the disease following its onset (Kramer 1957). For example, it is possible to have equal incidence for a given disorder in Whites and Blacks but lower prevalence rates in Blacks because of their higher fatality rate. Or it is possible for Whites to have the higher incidence but a lower prevalence because of a more rapid "cure" rate for Whites as compared with that of the Blacks. It is essential to keep in mind that racist practices can affect not only the factors that produce mental disorders (the force of morbidity) and consequently the rate at which new cases occur but also those which affect the duration of illness and disability. The latter include the types and quality of care that individuals receive and the characteristics of the facility in which they receive it.

In turn, these factors are related to whether a patient is rehabilitated and recovers or whether he develops a more severe disability or dies.

Reporting of Data by Race

There has been no consistency in the way in which studies have been reported by race. Some report data for Negroes only; others report data for non-Whites, which includes Negroes and other races. Although Negroes constitute the largest proportion of the non-White group, their rates may be higher, lower, or equal to that for the other races. In the tables and text for this chapter, an attempt is made to use the categories as reported in the original sources, that is, Negro, non-White, Black, etc.

Underreporting of the Census of Population

Another limitation of the data that will be reported, particularly for the United States as a whole and for separate states, results from underenumeration of the population in the decennial census. These population data are used as denominators for rates presented for the United States and for separate states. Estimates of underenumeration in the 1960 census are shown in table 11.3. These estimates indicate considerably

TABLE 11.3.   Estimated net undercount in United States census, 1960

Age	Total	White Male	White Female	Non-White Male	Non-White Female
Total	2.3%	1.1%	1.7%	10.3%	7.1%
Under 5	2.6	2.1	1.4	7.9	6.4
5–14	2.1	2.3	1.3	4.9	3.8
15–24	4.0	3.3	2.3	13.9	9.5
25–44	2.6	2.2	0.7	16.0	6.2
45–64	2.3	0.2	1.8	13.0	12.8
65 and over	0.9	8.1[a]	4.5	7.9[a]	2.6

SOURCE: Taeuber and Hansen 1963.
a. Overcount.

larger undercounts for non-Whites than for Whites. As a consequence, the computed rates for non-Whites might appear somewhat higher than they actually are. Some of the rates are based on population estimates for intercensual years, which may be affected by such factors as in- and out-migration of an area. However, the differences reported between White and non-White rates are so extensive that the under-enumeration would have to be considerable in order to be the sole reason for them.

The reader should be aware not only of the denominator problems resulting from underenumeration of the population, but also of numerator problems that can result from incompleteness and errors in case reporting by race. Satisfactory measures of the latter type of error do not exist. Other numerator problems occur because of discriminatory practices which may result in Blacks' being sentenced to a correctional institution whereas Whites, with the same problem, may be sent to a mental hospital or some other type of health or social service facility.

Community Surveys of Mental Disorders

Prevalence Surveys of the Noninstitutional Population

A considerable number of community surveys have been carried out in different parts of the world to determine the prevalence and, in a few instances, the incidence of mental disorders in the noninstitutional population. These studies have been reviewed critically by many students of the epidemiology of mental disorders, including Lin and Standley (1962), Shepherd and Cooper (1964), and Dohrenwend and Dohrenwend (1969). The rates reported in these studies do not lend themselves to precise comparisons because of differences in the underlying purposes of each survey. Thus they require different definitions of a case of mental disorder, case-finding techniques, diagnostic categories, and data-analysis methods. The studies done in the United States,

TABLE 11.4.   Prevalence rates of mental illness for Whites

Location	Investigators	Date	Age Group
Nassau County, N.Y.	Rosanoff (1917)	1916	–
Baltimore	Cohen, et al. (1939)	1933	15+
Baltimore	Lemkau et al. (1942)	1936	All ages
Williamson County, rural Tenn.	Roth & Luton (1943)	1938–40	All ages
Boston	Hyde & Chisholm (1944)	1941–42	18–44
United States	Rowntree et al. (1945)	1942–43	18–37
Baltimore	Pasamanick et al. (1959)	1952	All ages

a. Methods of case-finding: (1) hospital records; (2) outpatient clinic and/or other agency records; (3) private psychiatrist and/or physician records; (4) population survey through informants; (5) population survey through household interviews; (6) verification through review by a psychiatrist of all or a sample of suspected cases and/or actual examination of members of target population by a psychiatrist and/or other M.D.

b. Type of prevalence measure: *Lifetime:* the number of active and inactive cases discovered through the specified case-finding methods alive as of the survey date per 1,000 population. *Point-prevalence:* The number of

several of which are summarized in table 11.4, emphasize that mental disorders afflict sizable proportions of our population both among members of minority groups and among majority groups, Blacks as well as Whites.

These surveys differ in their designs, particularly in definitions of a case, in the criteria for assigning cases to specific categories of mental disorders, in the classifications of mental disorders, in the age groups of the population studies, and in the types of prevalence indices computed. It is therefore impossible to determine whether differences in prevalence of mental disorders exist between Whites and others and, if they do, the levels of the differences. Dohrenwend and Dohrenwend (1969) recently reviewed a number of prevalence studies carried out in the United States between 1916 and 1952 in which findings were presented specifically for and Negroes in selected surveys in the United States

Size of Population	Case-Finding Methods[a]	Prevalence Measure[b]	Morbidity Rate		Ratio of Negro to White
			White	Negro	
–	1,2,4,5	–	1.8%	7.0%	3.9
56,044	1,2	Interval	2.2	2.8	1.3
57,002	1,2	Interval	1.9[c]	1.2[c]	0.6
24,804	1,2,3,4,6	Lifetime	7.8	4.2	0.5
60,000	6	Rejection Rate	11.1	37.2	3.4
–	6	Rejection Rate	7.1	5.0	0.7
809	5,6	Point	11.2	4.6	0.4

active cases discovered through the specified case-finding methods as of the survey date per 1,000 population. *Period or interval:* The number of active cases discovered through the specified case-finding methods that were active on the books of the specified agencies at some time during the study interval per 1,000 population. *Rejection rate:* Percentage of selectees examined during an indicated period who were rejected for psychiatric reasons.

c. Morbidity rate includes only persons with diagnoses of psychoses and adult and child neuroses.

Whites and Negroes (Rosanoff 1917; Cohen et al. 1939; Lemkau et al. 1942; Roth and Luton 1943; Hyde and Chisholm 1944; Rowntree et al. 1945; Pasamanick et al. 1959). From the reported findings they abstracted conditions referred to as psychological disorders, which include only the psychoses, neuroses, and personality disorders (table 11.4).

Two of these studies determined interval prevalence (Cohen et al. 1939; Lemkau et al. 1942); one study determined point prevalence (Pasamanick et al. 1959); and one determined lifetime prevalence (Roth and Luton 1943); and two reported selective-service rejection rates from World War II (Hyde and Chrisholm 1944; Rowntree 1945). There were no consistent differences between Whites and Negroes in the direction of the rates. In three studies, the Negro rates were the higher and, in four, the White rates were the higher.

However, it is important to understand differences in the prevalence measures used. As indicated in the earlier sections of this chapter, interval prevalence can be affected not only by differences in incidence and duration of disease but also by the length of the interval in which cases are counted. As Dorn (1951) has stated: "The length of the interval of observation must always be specified if a prevalence rate is to be correctly interpreted for we may speak of the number of persons who are sick at any time during a given day, week, month or other arbitrary interval."

The two studies that report rejection rates among selective-service registrants during World War II determined the percentage of selectees who were rejected for psychiatric reasons as a result of the selective-service examination (during the indicated periods). These rates do not provide an unbiased estimate of the rate of mental disorders in the male population aged eighteen through forty-four years. The standards for inductions were designed to afford the best means of procuring the needed number of men suitable for military service. However, to meet the manpower needs, which varied from time to time, there were changes both in the standards themselves and in their interpretation. There were also variations in the efficiency of screening for mental disorders at the induction stations. In addition, men examined through selective service were not representative of the total male population of their age groups. Losses to the examined group resulted from deferments for dependency, occupation, age, and voluntary enlistment as well as from the nonexamination of men who had certain obvious physical defects or who did not meet certain educational standards. Thus the prevalence rates from selective-service examination are not representative of the situation in the entire male population—either White or non-White—in the age group from eighteen through forty-four years.

The Effect of Racism on the Composition of
the Noninstitutional Population

The preceding surveys were carried out in noninstitutional populations. However, many factors can affect the composition of this population and the prevalence of the conditions being studied. These, in turn, can affect the level of the prevalence rate for these conditions. Pasamanick (1964) emphasized this point in explaining the lower prevalence rate for psychosis among Negroes as compared with Whites in the noninstitutional population of Baltimore (0.50 per 1,000 for Negroes and 5.20 for Whites). By including the number of persons in mental hospitals, he demonstrated that, though the rate for Whites remained higher than that for Negroes, the relative difference was considerably reduced (7.04 for Negroes and 9.46 per 1,000 for Whites). Thus the considerably lower non-White rate in the noninstitutional population was the result of a higher institutionalization rate for non-Whites.

Two factors deserve special attention because of their importance in the interpretation of differences in the level of prevalence rates between racial groups based on the noninstitutional population: (1) factors that result in the disproportionate representation of Whites or non-Whites in the various institutions which collectively form the institutional population of the United States and (2) factors that account for differential mortality between Whites and non-Whites.

Differential patterns of institutionalization. As shown in table 11.5 and in figure 11.1, data from the 1960 census of population demonstrate that the proportion of the non-White population who were inmates of institutions (1,490 per 100,000 non-White population) was considerably higher than the corresponding proportion for the White population (996 per 100,000 White population). Non-White rates were higher in nine types of institutional population, about equal for two, and lower in two. (Data on the inmates of institutions were not yet available from the census of population for 1970 as of the date of the writing of this manuscript.) Figure 11.1 indicates differences in utilization patterns by age group.

The factors that account for these differences are many and complex. Basically we are dealing with an "incidence" and "prevalence" type of problem. Annually some members of a population group (defined by such variables as age, sex, color, and socioeconomic status) develop and manifest a condi-

TABLE 11.5.   Persons who are inmates

Institution	Number		
	Total	White	Non-White
Correctional			
Prisons and reformatories	226,344	139,765	86,579
Local jails and workhouses	119,671	74,047	45,624
Mental hospitals and residential			
treatment centers	630,046	544,613	85,433
Tuberculosis hospitals	65,009	46,288	18,721
Chronic disease hospitals	42,476	36,117	6,359
Homes for aged and dependent	469,717	450,369	19,078
Homes and schools for			
mentally handicapped	174,727	161,271	13,456
Homes and schools for			
physically handicapped	24,291	21,404	2,887
Homes for dependent and			
neglected children	73,306	64,807	8,499
Homes for unwed mothers	3,497	3,029	468
Training schools for			
juvenile delinquents	45,695	31,294	14,401
Detention homes	10,821	7,342	3,479
Diagnostic and reception			
centers	1,367	995	372
Total	1,886,967	1,581,611	305,356

SOURCE: U.S. Bureau of Census 1963.

tion or behave in a way that results in their admission to a certain type of institution (incidence). Sometimes the admission is the result of a legal procedure whereby the individual may be sentenced to prison or committed to a mental institution.

Of those admitted, sentenced, or committed, as the case may be, some stay for short periods, others for longer periods (duration). The number in the institution on any day (prevalence) is a function of the number admitted and the duration

of institutions: United States, 1960

| Percentage Distribution | | | Rates per 100,000 population | | | Ratio Non-White to White |
Total	White	Non-White	Total	White	Non-White	
12.0%	8.8%	28.4%	126.2	88.0	422.5	4.8
6.3	4.7	14.9	66.7	46.6	222.7	4.8
33.4	34.4	28.1	351.3	342.9	416.9	1.2
3.4	2.9	6.1	36.3	29.1	91.4	3.1
2.2	2.3	2.1	23.7	22.7	31.0	1.4
24.9	28.5	6.2	261.9	283.7	93.1	0.3
9.3	10.2	4.4	97.4	101.5	65.7	0.6
1.3	1.3	0.9	13.5	13.5	14.1	1.0
3.9	4.1	2.8	40.9	40.8	41.5	1.0
0.2	0.2	0.2	2.0	1.9	2.3	1.2
2.4	2.0	4.7	25.5	19.7	70.3	3.6
0.6	0.5	1.1	6.0	4.6	17.0	3.7
0.1	0.1	0.1	0.8	0.6	1.8	3.0
100.0	100.0	100.0	1,052.3	995.8	1,490.2	1.5

FIGURE 11.1 Percentage distribution of persons who are inmates of institutions: United States, 1960 (U.S. Bureau of Census 1963)

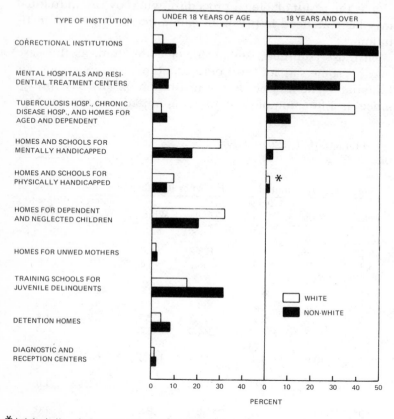

* Includes also Homes for Dependent and Neglected Children, Homes for Unwed Mothers, Training Schools for Delinquents, Detention Homes, Diagnostic and Reception Centers.

of stay. Explanations of differences in admission rates, duration of stay, and numbers of inmates as of a specific date require answers to such questions as the following:

1. What causes the problem(s) that result(s) in having a member of a defined group become a candidate for a medical, social, or correctional institution?

2. What factors account for the proportions of such persons being admitted (sentenced) to a certain type of institution?

3. What factors account for long or short stays in the institution?

4. To what extent do racist attitudes and practices on the part of personnel of the caretaker and law enforcement agencies and of the specific type of institution account for discriminatory practices in institutional placement, treatment, rehabilitation, disciplinary actions, parole, or discharge?

5. How do all of the above factors vary within and among the states of the nation?

The data reported in the census of inmates of institutions represent the end result of the interaction of all of the factors stated in or implied by the above questions plus others that we have not mentioned. The important point is that racist practices affect the composition and characteristics of the noninstitutional population by removing persons with various types of behavioral problems, diseases, disabling conditions, and social and economic characteristics from the non-institutional to the institutional setting at disproportionate rates. The removal rates (i.e., rates of institutionalization) and the durations of stay are not equal among the different age-sex-racial-socioeconomic classes of the population or among the various states.

Differential patterns of mortality.   Differential mortality between racial groups must also be taken into account in comparisons of prevalence since, as indicated, the level of such rates within and between groups can be markedly affected by the differences in survivorship of persons with a given condition. The differences in mortality patterns between racial groups at the time of the Baltimore studies in 1936 (Lemkau et al. 1942) and the Williamson County, Tennessee, study in 1938–40 (Roth and Luton 1943) were quite marked. These differences are illustrated in table 11.1, which presents the trends in mortality rates in the United States for

Whites and non-Whites by sex for the years 1945, 1955, and 1967 for selected causes. Although there has been marked improvement in the mortality of racial groups other than White during this interval, such rates were considerably in excess of the Whites during 1945 and earlier years. Rates for non-Whites were lower than the corresponding rates for Whites for only a few causes.

The impact of these mortality rates on differential survivorship of Whites and others even as late as 1967 is strikingly illustrated by a comparison by sex and race of the number of persons surviving to ages twenty, forty, sixty-five, and seventy-five out of 100,000 born alive. Such data are available from the life tables for 1967 (U.S. Dept. HEW 1969*b*) and are shown in table 11.6.

TABLE 11.6.   Survivorship from life tables for 1967

Age	Males		Females	
	Whites	Non-Whites	Whites	Non-Whites
At birth	100,000	100,000	100,000	100,000
20 years	96,298	93,982	97,486	95,485
40 years	92,583	85,013	95,662	90,529
65 years	65,990	50,180	81,486	64,255
75 years	39,716	25,605	62,403	41,069

SOURCE: U.S. Dept. of HEW 1969*b*.

In comparing prevalence rates of two racial or socioeconomic groups, it is important, therefore, to keep in mind that differential mortality among the persons who have a given disease or disabling condition determines the number of such persons who survive to a given date and would be counted in a prevalence survey. Thus, although the incidence of a given condition in two different population groups may be identical, prevalence can differ because of the intergroup differences in mortality following onset of the disease.

Incidence Surveys

Determining incidence of mental disorders is much more difficult than determining prevalence. Such investigations are plagued by all of the problems of case-finding and differential diagnosis already mentioned plus an additional one – determining the date of onset of the disease. Ideally, prospective studies of defined population groups are needed to establish incidence figures, but such studies are expensive and time consuming. They require periodic examination of members of the study population, with standard methods of systematic and uniform clinical examinations and of collection and evaluation of data on the person's life history, family relationships, marital adjustment, occupational history, participation in community activities, and related areas, if we are to gather the facts needed to determine the date of onset with reasonable accuracy. Thus, to establish this date, the psychiatrist faces the difficult task of evaluating data made available to him by the patient, members of his family, and other significant persons in the patient's life. Consequently, data on "true" incidence are not available except in very unusual situations (Hagnell 1966). A commonly used method for determining incidence of mental disorders is to determine the proportion of a population that has first contact with any one of a defined set of psychiatric facilities in a community during a defined time period. Since this procedure introduces another set of variables which may also be influenced by racist practices, namely those which determine admission to psychiatric facilities, this index – first admission to a psychiatric facility – will be dealt with in the following section concerning patterns of use of these facilities.

Patterns of Use of Psychiatric Facilities

The preceding sections have emphasized the sparse data available on the prevalence of mental disorders in the United

States, not only for minority but also for majority groups. This section presents data on patterns of use of psychiatric facilities. Although the situation is somewhat better for such data than for those on prevalence and incidence, it still leaves much to be desired. Unfortunately, national time series on patterns of use of psychiatric facilities by race are not available. The gaps in these statistics during the last two decades can be attributed for the most part to strong opposition on the part of key groups—governmental, professional, and lay organizations, as well as individual citizens—to the collection of social data by race. It was believed that the statistics derived from such data would be used in detrimental ways. As a result, we do not have the data needed currently to plan and monitor programs designed to eliminate problems due to racist practices and to evaluate the program effectiveness.

The data in this section are derived from the *Report on Inmates of Institutions* of the 1960 census of population, special studies conducted by the Departments of Mental Hygiene in several states, from psychiatric case registers, and from nationwide sample surveys conducted in 1969 by the National Institute of Mental Health when data collection was initiated on use of psychiatric services by race. The data from the census of population and nationwide surveys provide an overview of facility utilization by Whites and non-Whites. The data from smaller geographic areas (e.g., states, cities, counties) provide some insight into differential use of public and private facilities in such specified areas and can serve to illustrate the variation in utilization patterns in the areas they represent. However, they cannot be generalized for the country as a whole.

Although utilization data have limited uses for epidemiologic purposes, they are useful for defining high-risk population groups with respect to use of psychiatric services and for providing a firm starting point for planning and evaluating programs related to control and reduction of disability from mental disorders. Facts derived from such data can be used to demonstrate the volume of mental health services available, the extent to which such services are used, and the characteristics of persons using them. Such information can underline the need for additional knowledge to assess the effectiveness of programs for the care, treatment, and rehabilitation of persons with mental disorders.

It is not possible to estimate the extent to which racism by itself accounts for differences between the races in patterns of use of services. As already stated, racism has created many of the conditions that have produced factors that are related to mental disorder. It must be remembered, however, that for a long time the resources for the care of the mentally ill regardless of race, color, and socioeconomic status were quite limited and for many years the state mental hospital was the primary and, in many instances, the only resource for care and treatment. Similar situations have existed in other countries, and it is striking that the shape of the curve describing first-admission patterns by age and sex is essentially the same in the United States, Canada, and several other countries of the world. This fact is demonstrated in figures 11.2 and 11.3, which present the relative age/sex specific first-admission rates to mental hospitals in these countries (Kramer 1969).

These relative rates were obtained by determining the ratio of the actual rate in each age group to the total age-adjusted rate (specific for sex) for the country in question during the early 1960s. Although there is considerable variation in the actual numerical value of the total age-adjusted rate for each sex group (e.g., for males from 53 per 100,000 in Norway to 197 per 100,000 in Czechoslovakia and for females from 64 per 100,000 in Norway to 171 per 100,000 in Canada), the shapes of the curve for males and females in every country are strikingly similar when adjusted for the level of the rate.

Just as the curve patterns were so similar for the latter groups, so the relative first-admission rates in 1922 for Whites

(Continued on page 386)

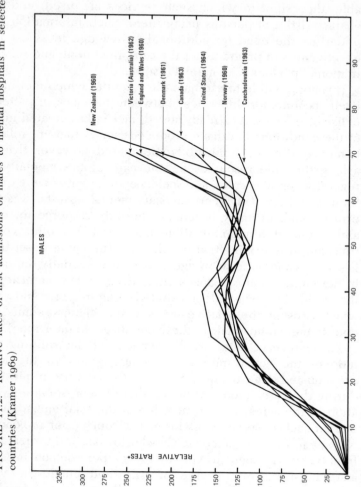

FIGURE 11.2. Relative rates of first admissions of males to mental hospitals in selected countries (Kramer 1969)

countries (Kramer 1969)

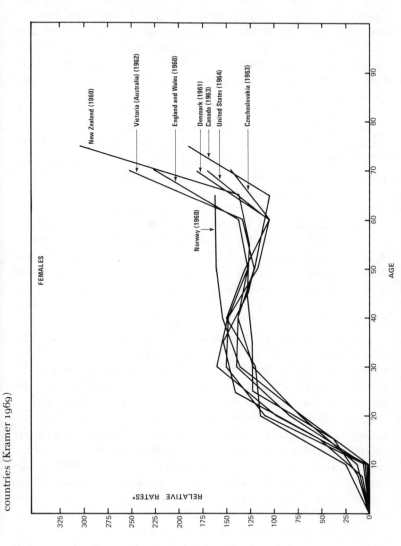

*RELATIVE RATE EQUALS AGE-SPECIFIC RATE AS A PERCENT OF AGE-ADJUSTED RATE.

and Blacks in the United States, computed in the same way, showed a similar pattern of use of psychiatric facilities—as have the rates for Whites and Blacks in New York State over many years (U.S. Dept. of Commerce 1926; Malzberg 1940, 1959). Thus racist practices may alter the magnitude of the rates, but may have only minimal effect on the pattern of the disease, by age.

Even if racist practices were eliminated completely, however, it cannot be assumed that all differences between the races in patterns of use of psychiatric facilities would be eliminated. Biological and genetic differences exist between groups and the diseases and disabling states caused by or associated with organic and physical factors are further modified by value systems and many other factors that characterize the life-styles of members of different cultural groups. Such variables as age, sex, marital status, education, occupation, income, access to facilities, living arrangements, attitudes toward mental illness, and acceptance of psychiatric treatment would still have to be taken into account.

First-Admission Rates

As a measure of incidence. Until quite recently, the first-admission rate to a mental hospital system has been defined as the annual number of patients admitted for the first time to these hospitals per 100,000 population exposed to risk of hospitalization. These rates have been used in studies attempting to measure incidence of mental disorders as well as to identify subgroups of the population which are affected by major problems of disability associated with mental disorders. Several of the classical studies in the epidemiology of mental disorders have used this rate as an index of the incidence of mental disorders (Jaco 1960; Malzberg 1959; Kramer 1957). These studies and many others were carried out for the most part during the 1930s, 1940s, and early 1950s, a period when public and private mental hospitals were the primary and, in some instances, the only facilities available for the treatment of the mentally ill. Since then, many changes have taken place in the care and treatment of the mentally ill so that the mental hospital is now only one of the possible sources of psychiatric treatment. The weaknesses of the first-admission rate to a mental hospital as a measure of incidence are now generally recognized so that variations in these rates from time to time and place to place within and between areas cannot be accepted confidently as reflections of changing incidence of the disorder.

With the increase in the number and types of psychiatric facilities now available at the community levels, the index of first admission to a mental hospital has been expanded to include first admission to a universe of psychiatric services (e.g., public and private mental hospitals, Veterans Administration hospitals, outpatient clinics, psychiatric services in a general hospital, private psychiatrists). This concept contains several underlying notions. Although it is impossible to establish with certainty the date of onset of a mental disorder (e.g., schizophrenia), it is possible to establish accurately the date of first contact with a facility (Dunham 1965). Also, the larger the network of facilities, the greater is the probability of a patient's coming into contact with a psychiatric service, particularly when the patient has a serious illness. The major problems involved in the use of these concepts are the variations in the number and types of psychiatric services available to the residents of an area, the extent to which all cases of a disorder will be admitted to a psychiatric service, and the time lag between the actual date of onset and the date of first contact.

Table 11.7 presents incidence rates of psychoses (functional and organic) computed from studies which have used definitions of new cases that include more than patients admitted to a state mental hospital. The cases included are first admissions with a diagnosis of psychosis to a universe of psychiatric facilities consisting of state hospitals, plus one or

(Continued on page 390)

TABLE 11.7. Incidence rates for psychosis and schizophrenia reported in selected surveys in the United States

	Texas	New York	Ohio	Maryland	Maryland	Louisiana
Investigator	Jaco (1960)	Malzberg (1959)	Locke et al. (1965a)	Warthen et al. (1967)	Pollack et al. (1964)	Pollack et al. (1964)
Date	1951–52	1949–51	1958–61	1961–64	1960	1960
Age group	All ages[a]	All ages[b]	15–64[a]	All ages[a]	All ages[a]	All ages[a]
Size of population						
White	5,699,089	13,872,095	3,470,770[a]	2,688,610[e]	2,573,814	2,211,715
Non-White	984,660	918,191[c]	428,097	551,323[e]	526,873	1,045,307
Population year	1950 census	1950 census	1960 census	7/1/62	1960 census	1960 census
Definition of incidence	A	A	B	C	B	B
Disorders						
All psychoses						
White	79	109.6	—	—	—	—
Non-White	54	213.7	—	—	—	—
Functional psychoses:						
Schizophrenic reactions						
White						
Male	32	33.0	45.7	57	36.4	38.5
Female	43	33.4	109.2	70	40.7	39.2
Non-White						
Male	30	110.8	62.4	120	73.7	33.5
Female	32	92.9	141.2	110	76.7	47.6

Other functional psychoses					
White					
Male	15	11.9	—	—	13.5	10.9
Female	26	23.5	—	—	14.3	19.4
Non-White						
Male	3	3.9	—	—	3.8	2.8
Female	3	9.2	—	—	15.9	11.5
Organic psychoses						
White	21	58.6	—	—	—	—
Non-White	20	105.9	—	—	—	—
Schizophrenic reactions:						
Ratio of non-Whites to Whites						
Male	0.94	3.36	1.37	2.11	2.02	0.87
Female	0.74	2.78	1.29	1.57	1.88	1.21

a. Age-adjusted rate.
b. Crude rate.
c. Black rather than Non-White.
d. Metropolitan-area residence.
e. Estimated.

A. Average annual number of first admissions to public and private mental hospitals.
B. Average annual number of first admissions to public and private mental hospitals, general hospitals with psychiatric facilities, outpatient psychiatric clinics, Veterans Administration hospitals.
C. Average annual number of new cases reported to psychiatric register during three years of operation (public and private mental hospitals, psychiatric services in general hospitals, outpatient clinics, Veterans Administration hospitals).

more of the following: Veterans Administration neuropsychiatric hospital, private mental hospital, psychiatric service in a general hospital, outpatient clinic, or private psychiatrist. The data were not reported in sufficient detail in each study so that a rate could be determined for all psychoses. However, each study did report a separate rate for schizophrenia. Among males the rates for schizophrenia were higher for non-Whites in four of the six studies and somewhat lower for non-Whites in two. Among females, the rates were higher for non-Whites in five of the six studies and lower in only one. Data on other functional psychoses were reported in four studies. In each of these studies the White rate for males was consistently higher than the corresponding non-White rate, and for females the White rate was higher in three.

Several of these studies examined first-admission rates for other variables such as age and sex for all diagnoses combined and for specific diagnostic groups. For example, the Malzberg studies for New York State mental hospitals by age, race, and sex for about 1930, 1940, and 1950 indicate that Negro admission rates for all diagnostic groups for each period were generally twice as high as those for Whites (figures 11.4 and 11.5: Malzberg 1940, 1959). Similarly, total age-adjusted first-admission rates to all psychiatric facilities in Maryland in 1960 were higher for non-Whites than for Whites while, in contrast, rates for Louisiana were higher for Whites (Maryland: White males, 321.7; non-White males, 407.1; White females, 254.7; non-White females, 306.5; Louisiana: White males, 303.9; non-White males, 175.0; White females, 262.6; non-White females, 172.6 [Pollack et al. 1964]).

Locke et al. examined first-admission rates to a universe of psychiatric services in Ohio for schizophrenia, alcoholism, mental diseases of the senium and psychoneurosis (tables 11.8 and 11.9: Locke and Duvall 1965a; 1964a; 1965b; Duvall et al. 1966). Rates were higher for non-Whites than for Whites for each disorder except psychoneurosis.

FIGURE 11.4. Average annual rates of first admission of males to all hospitals for mental disease in New York State, by specified years (rates per 100,000 population) (Malzberg 1959, 1940)

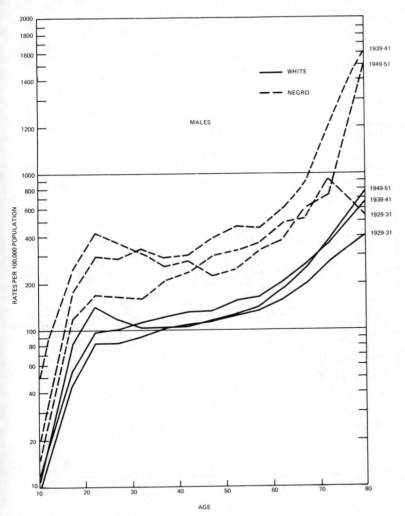

FIGURE 11.5. Average annual rates of first admission of females to all hospitals for mental disease in New York State, by specified years (rates per 100,000 population) (Malzberg 1959, 1940)

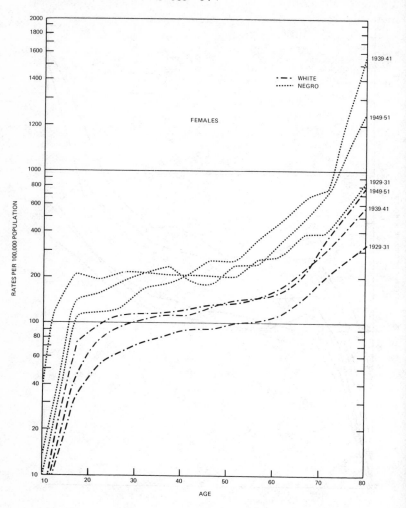

The interpretation of the differences reported in all these studies is not at all clear since we are dealing with differences not only in incidence of mental disorders but also in local practices, laws, and racial prejudices in the states where these studies were conducted (Texas, New York, Ohio, Maryland, and Louisiana). Such factors have marked effects not only on the life-style and value systems of Blacks, their health status, living arrangements, working conditions, and education, but also on their pathways to psychiatric care. Factors such as these can account for possible differences in both the incidence of mental disorders and the differential use of psychiatric facilities and other institutions by various racial groups. In addition, we are dealing with another variable that up to now has not been mentioned, namely, the consistency with which psychiatrists apply uniform criteria in determining presence or absence of mental disorders among Whites, Blacks, and members of other minority groups and in arriving at a diagnosis of schizophrenia, affective disorder, organic psychosis, neuroses, or personality disorder in persons of different racial origin.

Racist attitudes and practices can influence all of the factors mentioned above – life-style, value system, health status, use of psychiatric facilities, use of institutions other than mental hospitals, differential use of diagnostic criteria, and diagnostic labels. Thus, the data summarized in table 11.7 provide relatively little insight into the differential incidence of psychosis in Whites versus other racial groups. Furthermore, the problem of determining incidence is far more complicated when it comes to disorders other than the psychoses, that is, psychoneuroses, personality disorders, and psychophysiologic disorders. As indicated earlier, it would seem a priori that deprived and disadvantaged groups would experience higher incidence of mental disorders than other groups because of their greater exposure to the many biolog-

(Continued on page 396)

TABLE 11.8. Average annual admission rates to psychiatric facilities, residents from eleven metropolitan counties in Ohio, 1958–61 (rates per 100,000 population)

Diagnosis, Sex, and Color		Total	State Mental Hospitals	General Hospitals with Psychiatric Facilities	Private Mental and VA Hospitals	Outpatient Psychiatric Clinics
Schizophrenia						
Males:	White	45.7	28.2	6.4	3.5	7.7
	Non-White	109.2	80.9	10.5	1.4[a]	16.4
Females:	White	62.4	33.7	11.2	7.1	10.4
	Non-White	141.2	94.3	19.5	0.1[a]	27.3
Alcoholism						
Males:	White	40.6	24.2	—	12.1	4.3
	Non-White	82.9	61.6	—	12.3	9.0
Females:	White	9.6	5.2	—	3.6	0.8
	Non-White	34.5	23.0	—	7.4	4.1[a]
Mental disease of senium[b]						
Males:	White	60.0	45.6	7.2	5.9	1.2[a]
	Non-White	126.6	110.3	12.8[a]	—	3.1[a]
Females:	White	49.1	34.3	7.1	6.4	1.2
	Non-White	104.7	82.5	13.9[a]	—	8.4[a]
Psychoneurosis						
Males:	White	54.9	8.5	27.6	6.1	12.7
	Non-White	29.4	8.8	8.3	0.1[a]	12.2
Females:	White	106.6	13.3	59.0	14.1	20.2
	Non-White	80.7	17.8	23.9	0.5[a]	38.5

SOURCE: Locke and Duvall 1964a, 1965a, 1965b; Duvall, Locke, and Kramer 1966.
a. Fewer than 10 admissions a year.

TABLE 11.9. Ratio of non-White to White average annual admission rates to psychiatric facilities, residents from eleven metropolitan counties in Ohio, 1958–61

Diagnosis and Sex	Total	State Mental Hospitals	General Hospitals with Psychiatric Facilities	Private Mental and VA Hospitals	Outpatient Psychiatric Clinics
Schizophrenia					
Males	2.4	2.9	1.6	[a]	2.1
Females	2.3	2.8	1.7	[a]	2.6
Alcoholism					
Males	2.0	2.5	—	1.0	2.1
Females	3.6	3.7	—	1.9	[a]
Mental diseases of senium[b]					
Males	2.1	2.4	[a]	[a]	[a]
Females	2.1	2.4	[a]	[a]	[a]
Psychoneurosis					
Males	0.5	1.0	0.3	[a]	1.0
Females	0.8	1.3	0.4	[a]	1.9

SOURCE: Locke and Duvall, 1964a, 1964b, 1965a, 1965b; Duvall, Locke, and Kramer 1966.
a. Fewer than 10 admissions a year among non-Whites.
b. Rates for population 45 years of age and over. Age adjustment based on Ohio population 45 years and over.

ical, psychological, socioeconomic, and similar factors that can cause impairment of brain-tissue function, anxiety, and deeply ingrained patterns of maladaptive behavior. However, the measurement problems involved in determining incidence have yet to be solved satisfactorily. As a result, statistics are not available that provide a precise statement of the order of magnitude of differences in incidence of mental disorders within and among members of different groups in our society.

As a means of identifying high-risk groups.   Despite their limitations for determining incidence, first-admission rates to mental health facilities, specific for such variables as age, sex, color, marital status, etc., are useful for planning programs for the control of mental disorders. Indeed, such data are frequently the only systematic data available in a state for such purposes. They identify population groups in which high rates of disability exist and indicate groups which should be singled out for special attention in the planning of community mental health services. They also suggest important variables to be considered in the search for causes and effects of mental diseases per se and of hospitalization. Indeed, studies to illuminate the reasons for differential patterns of first admission that exist in various communities would provide very useful information (Clausen 1955).

1. Household and family composition.   Studies by Pollack et al. (1964, 1968; Pollack, 1968) in Louisiana and Maryland in 1960–61 investigated the relationship between family structure and the probability of admission to a psychiatric facility. First-admission rates for four variables — relationship of patient to head of family, size of family, type of family, and race — were determined (figures 11.6, 11.7, 11.8, 11.9, and 11.10). The White, non-White highlights of the findings are:

a. Overall, the rates for heads of female-head families were generally about 50 percent higher than those for heads

FIGURE 11.6. Age-adjusted first-admission rates for family heads, by family size, type of family, race, and residence: Maryland, 1960–61 (Pollack et al. 1968)

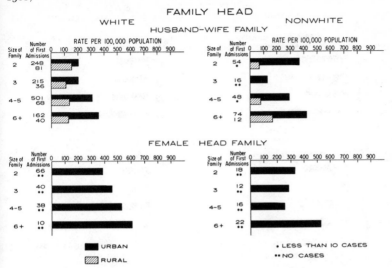

FIGURE 11.7. Age-adjusted first-admission rates for family heads, by family size, type of family, race, and residence: Louisiana, 1960–61 (Pollack et al. 1968)

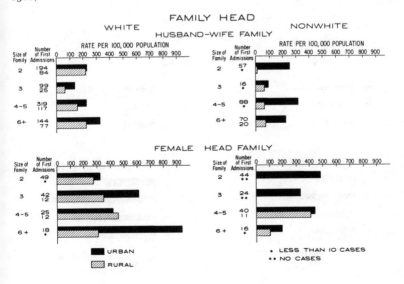

FIGURE 11.8.   Age-adjusted first-admission rates for wives of family heads, by family size, race, and residence: Maryland and Louisiana, 1960–61 (Pollack et al. 1968)

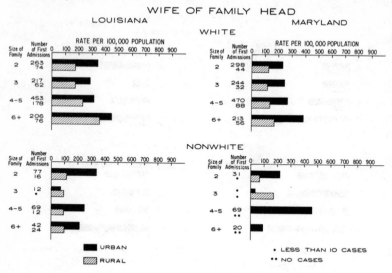

FIGURE 11.9.   Age-adjusted first-admission rates for children of family heads, by family size, type of family, race, and residence: Maryland, 1960–61 (Pollack et al. 1968)

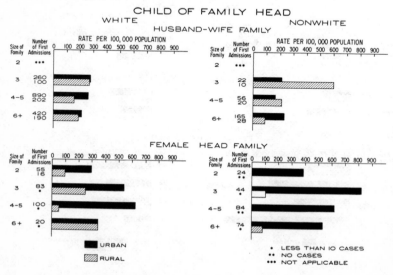

of husband-wife families, regardless of size of family.[2] The finding occurred for Whites for each family size in each state. For non-Whites, though this was true overall, some inconsistencies have been noted by family size.

b. The lowest rates for heads of husband-wife families were generally in families of three members. This is consistent for Whites and non-Whites.

c. Rates of first admissions to all psychiatric facilities were about twice as high among children living in broken families as for those living with both parents.

d. Rates for non-White children in husband-wife families in Maryland and female-head families in Louisiana were

FIGURE 11.10. Age-adjusted first-admission rates for children of family heads, by family size, type of family, race, and residence: Louisiana, 1960–61 (Pollack et al. 1968)

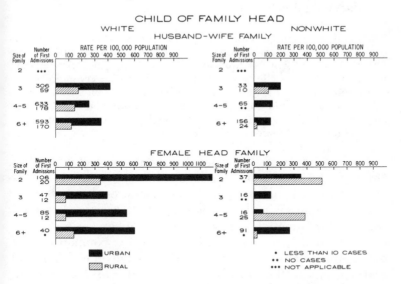

2. The overall finding that admission rates of intact families to psychiatric facilities are lower than those of broken families has been corroborated in a study by Ferber (1966).

higher for rural residents than for urban residents in families of sizes two through five.

If one can generalize beyond Maryland and Louisiana, it is possible to anticipate the task of providing adequate services for groups most likely to need them in the United States. For example, table 11.10 shows that there were almost six million broken families in the United States as of March 1969. Of these, about three-quarters were White; the remainder were of other racial groups. The proportion of husband-wife families among the Whites (89 percent) was considerably higher than among non-Whites (69 percent).

A study in a recent newspaper (Hamilton 1971) has highlighted the fact that the percentage of Black families headed by females increased from 22 percent in 1960 to 29 percent in 1969. Hamilton comments on how different interpretations are placed on this finding:

The familiar sociological analysts: A significant indication of continuing social deterioration and family instability. The view of the Urban League: The assumption of instability in "matriarchal" households ignores the extended-family adaptation common in the black community—the strong kinship bonds between aunts, uncles and grandparents and the family's children. Some black sociologists go further: they argue that in fact, roughly 70 percent of these families actually do have a father present.

The existence of strong kinship bonds among a family's children and their aunts, uncles, and grandparents is a phenomenon that is not unique to the Blacks. Such bonds exist between children and relatives in other groups. It would seem that information is lacking on several key issues: (a) the extent to which such kinship relationships compensate for the continued absence of strong bonds between children and both parents in the growth, development, physical, mental, and social well-being of children who are members of broken families; and (b) data on the number and proportion of families in different racial groups according to a distribution of

TABLE 11.10. Distribution of families: United States, March 1969

Type of Family and Marital Status of Head	Number (in Thousands)			Percentage		
	Total	White	Negro and Other Races	Total	White	Negro and Other Races
Total families	50,510	45,437	5,073	100.0%	100.0%	100.0%
Husband-wife	43,842	40,355	3,487	86.8	88.8	68.7
Other male head	1,229	1,028	201	2.4	2.3	4.0
Single	413	365	48	0.8	0.8	0.9
Widowed	447	365	82	0.9	0.8	1.6
Other[a]	368	298	70	0.7	0.7	1.4
Female head	5,439	4,053	1,386	10.8	8.9	27.3
Single	582	398	184	1.2	0.9	3.6
Widowed	2,364	1,927	437	4.7	4.2	8.6
Divorced	1,109	925	184	2.2	2.0	3.6
Separated	985	487	498	2.0	1.1	9.8
Married spouse absent	400	316	84	0.8	0.7	1.7
Broken families[b]	5,673	4,318	1,355	11.2	9.5	26.8

SOURCE: U.S. Bureau of Census 1970a.
a. Divorced, separated, married spouse absent.
b. Sum of other male-head families and female-head families in which heads are widowed, divorced, separated, and married spouse absent.

GLENDALE COLLEGE LIBRARY

strengths of kinship bonds and the effects of these bonds—positive and negative—on children in the crucial areas listed in (a). Acquiring the data to answer these questions requires a clear statement of the problems to be solved, operational definitions of the concepts involved, such as kinship bonds and their strengths, and the effects to be measured. Clearly an intensive research effort is needed to acquire the data needed to test the relevant hypotheses.

While the effects of the relative strengths and weaknesses of kinship bonds on members of the broken family are being debated, we should not lose sight of the fact that members of families with a female head regardless of race constitute a high-risk group with respect to health, social, and economic problems and need for human services if for no other reason than they contain sizable proportions of persons below the poverty level.

As of 1969, there were 18.3 million persons living in families with a female head (U.S. Dept. of Commerce 1970b). Of that number, 12.5 million were White and slightly fewer than 6 million were Negro and other races. Of the persons in White families, 29 percent (3.6 million) had incomes below the poverty level. Of those in the non-White families, 58 percent (3.3 million) were so situated. Female-head families—White, Negro, and other races—also contained high proportions of children under eighteen years of age. Thus, in the White poverty families there were 2.1 million children under eighteen, accounting for 58 percent of all members of such families, and in the poverty families of Negro and other races there were 2.3 million children under eighteen, or 67 percent of all the members of these families.

It is also important to remember that there are high proportions of persons below the poverty level in families with male heads. The numbers of Negroes and other races and of Whites living in families headed by males are, respectively, 16.6 million and 150.4 million. Of the persons in the non-White families 20 percent lived below the poverty level, while only a third of the corresponding percent (6 percent) of the White population had such low incomes. As indicated earlier, members of poor families, regardless of their composition and race, constitute high-risk groups with respect to physical and mental disorders.

2. Marital status. The relationship of marital status to rates of admission to psychiatric facilities — particularly mental hospitals — has been well documented (Rosen et al. 1964; Kramer 1966). In general, married patients have the lowest admission rates to mental hospitals and other services, and the not married (never married, separated, divorced, widowed) have considerably higher rates. This phenomenon occurs among non-Whites as well as among Whites in the limited number of studies that have investigated admission rates by race and age, sex and marital status (Pollack et al. 1968).

3. Level of education. The data reported by Locke and Duvall (1964*a* and 1965*b*) in their Ohio studies illustrate the differences found between Whites and non-Whites in admission rates to psychiatric facilities specific for level of education. Tables 11.11 and 11.12 show the associations between years of school completed and admission rates for alcoholism and diseases of the senium. In all cases the non-White rates were higher than those for the Whites. In addition, White rates were progressively higher as the amount of education decreased. However, this relationship was not so clear-cut among the non-Whites.

4. Migration. Table 11.13 and figure 11.11 show differences between admissions born in Ohio versus the corresponding group born in other states. With a few exceptions, non-White rates were higher than White rates. It should be noted also that overall rates were higher for persons born in other states than for native-born Ohioans regardless of race (Locke and Duvall, 1964*b*).

5. Residence. Studies cited in this chapter which have been based on Ohio and Monroe County populations report higher rates of use of psychiatric facilities by residents of

TABLE 11.11.   Average annual first-admission rates for alcoholism
per 100,000 population age 25–64 from eleven
metropolitan counties to state mental
hospitals: Ohio, 1958–61

Years of School Completed	Male		Female	
	White	Non-White	White	Non-White
Elementary (0–8)	37.5	60.2	7.0	18.8
High School	23.5	66.2	4.9	21.9
College (1 or more years)	10.0	16.8	3.5	21.1

SOURCE: Locke and Duvall 1964a.
NOTE: The counties are Cuyahoga, Franklin, Greene, Hamilton, Lake, Lucas, Mahoning, Miami, Montgomery, Summit, and Trumbull.

metropolitan than by residents of nonmetropolitan areas. They also report that admission rates for non-Whites are higher than for Whites in both areas. Other studies have shown that admission rates are generally higher in urban than rural areas (figure 11.12, Pollack et al. 1964; *see also* Locke and Duvall 1965a; Gorwitz et al. 1970). An examination of admission rates categorized by central city, suburban, and rural counties in the state of Maryland also reveals that rates were generally higher for non-Whites than for

TABLE 11.12.   Average annual first-admission rates for mental diseases
of the senium per 100,000 population 45 years and over
from eleven metropolitan counties to public
mental hospitals: Ohio, 1958–61

Years of School Completed	Male		Female	
	White	Non-White	White	Non-White
Elementary or none	56.9	82.2	49.6	65.8
High School	15.1	26.9[a]	16.1	24.4[a]
College	13.1	20.8[a]	8.0[a]	32.1[a]

SOURCE: Locke and Duvall 1965b.
a. Fewer than ten admissions per year.

TABLE 11.13. Age-adjusted average first-admission rates per 100,000 population to Ohio public mental hospitals, by place of birth, 1958-61

| | Male | | | | Female | | | |
| | White | | Non-White | | White | | Non-White | |
Diagnosis	Ohio	Other States	Ohio	Other States	Ohio	Other States	Ohio	Other States
All diagnoses[a]	113.2	143.1	249.2	254.7	82.6	105.9	163.0	208.4
Alcoholism[b]	27.0	39.9	64.8	61.6	4.0	7.6	21.3[e]	23.7
Mental diseases of senium[c]	51.1	61.6	93.3	113.0	32.7	41.6	37.0[e]	93.1
Schizophrenia[d]	26.0	29.9	72.8	81.9	29.4	36.5	80.2	93.0
Psychoneuroses[d]	10.6	12.4	16.0	8.1	16.6	20.0	22.6	19.9
Personality disorders[d]	21.4	24.5	51.3	27.0	7.4	9.0	11.1	9.2
All other diagnoses[a]	30.7	39.6	63.9	80.1	26.0	33.3	45.7	61.5

SOURCE: Locke and Duvall 1964b; see also Kramer et al. 1971.
a. Rates based on admissions and population 10 years of age and older.
b. Rates based on admissions and population 25-64 years of age.
c. Rates based on admissions and population 45 years of age and older.
d. Rates based on admissions and population 15-64 years of age.
e. Fewer than 10 admissions per year.

FIGURE 11.11.   Average annual first-admission rates in Ohio public mental hospitals for native-born males and females, by place of birth, all diagnoses, 1958–61 (Locke and Duvall 1964*b*)

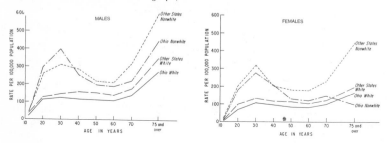

Whites for each area and for each sex-color group (table 11.14). However, the relative differences between non-White and White rates for both males and females residing in Baltimore (4 percent to 5 percent) and for females in the metropolitan counties (about 9 percent) were much lower than the corresponding differences between males living in metropolitan counties (30 percent) and males and females in the rural counties (36 percent for males and 19 percent for females).

Resident-Patient Ratios—Definitions and Limitations

Another index that has been used in studies of the mental disorders, particularly those relating to patients in mental hospitals, is the resident-patient rate. The resident-patient rate for a specific facility type is the ratio of the number of patients resident in the facility as of a given date to the population of the catchment area served by the facility. This rate bears the same relationship to an admission rate as the point-prevalence rate for a disease bears to its incidence rate; that is, prevalence of a specific disease is a function of its incidence and duration (i.e., interval between onset, recovery, or death) while the number of resident patients with a specific mental disorder is a function of the number of admissions and their durations of stay following admission.

The limitations of first-admission rates in reflecting in-

FIGURE 11.12.   Age-adjusted first-admission rates to outpatient psychiatric clinics facilities: Louisiana and Maryland, 1960–61 (U.S. total population as of April 1, 1960, used as a standard) (Pollack et al. 1964)

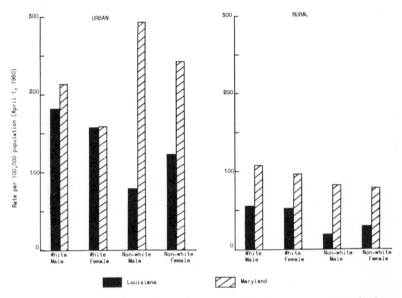

cidence were discussed in the preceding section. Similarly, the resident-patient rate has distinct limitations as a measure of the prevalence of mental disorders. These rates are a function of the rates of first admission, readmission, release, and death operating in mental hospitals. The level of resident-patient rate is, therefore, determined by the same factors that affect the admission rate plus the characteristics of the communities from which these patients are drawn and to which they return, the presence or absence of other facilities for the care and treatment of the mentally ill, the official and unofficial policies of the hospital which affect the admission or release of patients, the staffing patterns and treatment programs, the degree of improvement expected by the hospital staff of the patients before their return to the community, and the attitudes of the patients' families and communities

TABLE 11.14. Persons admitted to Maryland psychiatric facilities, July 1, 1965 to June 30, 1966 (rates per 100,000 population)

Residence	White Males	Non-White Males	Ratio: Non-White to White Males	White Females	Non-White Females	Ratio: Non-White to White Females
Total from state	688.4	1107.9	1.61	543.7	735.4	1.35
Baltimore	1264.2	1318.9	1.04	791.4	834.7	1.05
Metropolitan counties	539.6	700.9	1.30	476.3	517.2	1.09
Rural counties	632.5	862.9	1.36	514.0	609.2	1.19

SOURCE: U.S. Dept. of HEW 1966.

toward the mentally ill and the mental hospital (Belknap 1956; Brown, Monck et al. 1962; Dunham and Weinberg 1960; Greenblatt et al. 1955; Rawnsley et al. 1952). Here, again, socioeconomic conditions and discriminatory practices can influence all of these factors and thus affect the level of the resident-patient rates for Whites as compared with those for non-Whites.

Resident-patient rates for mental hospitals and residential treatment centers by race are available for the total United States from the 1960 census (table 11.15). Rates for all facilities were higher for non-Whites than for Whites for each age group with the largest differences occurring in the twenty-five- to thirty-four-year age group. In terms of specific facility types, however, rates were higher for non-White residents in public mental hospitals (federal, state, county, and city) than those for Whites. In sharp contrast, the rates for Whites in private hospitals were considerably higher than for non-Whites. Socioeconomic and other restrictive and discriminatory conditions were largely responsible for the greater use of public facilities by non-Whites and private facilities by Whites. Civil Rights and Medicare legislation should have had some effect on this differential use during the last decade (U.S. Congress 1964 and 1965). However, it is not possible at this writing to determine current patterns of use because comparable 1970 census data are not yet available.

One of the striking phenomena of the past sixteen years has been the sharp decline in the size of the resident population of the state mental hospitals of the nation (U.S. Dept. of HEW, 1970*b*). In the period 1955 through 1968, the population has declined steadily from about 559,000 to 399,000, a decrease of about 29 percent (table 11.16). Data are not available to chart the trend by race. However, trend data are available from the state of Maryland for the years 1961 through 1967 (table 11.17). Rates for non-Whites were considerably higher than for Whites at the beginning of the

(Continued on page 414)

TABLE 11.15. Patients in mental hospitals and residential treatment centers: United States, 1960

Color and Age	All Facilities	Federal Hospitals	State, County, City Hospitals	Private Hospitals & Residential Treatment Centers
Rates per 100,000 Population				
Whites				
All ages	342.9	33.3	295.6	14.1
Under 15	12.8	0.0	9.1	3.7
15–24	108.5	5.1	91.4	12.0
25–34	245.6	38.9	196.7	10.0
35–44	396.2	69.8	316.3	10.1
45–54	578.3	45.7	519.5	13.2
55–64	776.1	65.5	691.8	18.9
65–74	950.8	95.1	824.7	31.0
75 +	1,303.3	26.1	1,172.1	105.1
Non-Whites				
All ages	416.9	51.3	359.8	5.8
Under 15	17.0	0.2	14.1	2.7
15–24	196.2	13.0	176.1	7.1
25–34	546.4	91.7	449.1	5.7
35–44	723.1	123.8	593.0	6.4
45–54	842.2	80.5	756.1	5.7
55–64	1,042.9	102.4	932.5	8.1
65–74	1,026.5	147.6	867.0	11.9
75 +	1,334.2	66.1	1,236.2	31.9
Ratio of Non-Whites to Whites				
All ages	1.22	1.54	1.22	.41
Under 15	1.33	NA	1.55	.73
15–24	1.81	2.55	1.93	.59
25–34	2.22	2.36	2.28	.57
35–44	1.83	1.77	1.87	.63
45–54	1.46	1.76	1.46	.43
55–64	1.34	1.56	1.35	.43
65–74	1.08	1.55	1.05	.38
75 +	1.02	2.53	1.05	.30

SOURCE: U.S. Bureau of Census 1963.
NA = not applicable.

TABLE 11.16. Resident patients in state and county mental hospitals: United States

Age	All Mental Disorders		Schizophrenia		Diseases of the Senium		Other Mental Disorders	
	1955	1968	1955	1968	1955	1968	1955	1968
				Number				
All ages	558,922	399,152	267,995	194,922	73,772	49,158	217,155	155,072
Under 15	2,301	6,365	374	1,774	—	—	1,927	4,591
15–24	17,276	25,315	8,156	10,887	—	—	9,120	14,428
25–34	57,634	36,546	36,819	21,531	—	—	20,815	15,015
35–44	96,304	52,623	63,269	31,314	—	—	33,035	21,309
45–54	117,500	71,166	65,895	41,815	—	—	51,605	20,351
55–64	109,622	86,997	50,302	46,689	8,672	4,924	50,648	35,384
65 +	158,285	120,140	43,180	40,912	65,100	44,234	50,005	34,994
65–74	92,223	66,177	31,396	27,450	24,842	15,067	35,985	23,660
75 +	66,062	53,963	11,784	13,462	40,258	29,167	14,020	11,334
			Rates per 100,000 Population					
All ages	344.4	202.0	165.1	98.7	45.5	24.9	133.8	78.4
Under 15	4.7	10.7	0.8	3.0	—	—	3.9	7.7
15–24	86.1	79.9	40.7	34.3	—	—	45.4	45.6
25–34	246.0	157.8	157.1	92.9	—	—	88.9	64.9
35–44	427.2	226.4	280.6	134.7	—	—	146.6	91.7
45–54	622.8	312.2	349.3	183.5	—	—	273.5	128.7
55–64	753.7	486.7	345.8	261.2	59.6	27.5	348.3	198.0
65 +	1,125.1	627.9	306.9	213.9	462.7	231.2	355.4	182.9
65–74	979.4	561.5	333.4	232.9	263.8	127.8	382.2	200.7
75 +	1,419.8	734.9	253.3	183.3	865.2	397.2	301.3	154.4

SOURCE: U.S. Dept. of HEW, 1970b.

TABLE 11.17. Trends in patient statistics, Maryland psychiatric hospitals

Color and Year	Patients Under Care During Year	Average No. of Resident Patients	Admissions				Discharges	Deaths
			Total	First	Readmissions			
			Rates per 100,000 Population					
White								
1961	479.0	247.1	148.3	87.7	60.6	122.2	25.8
1962	500.1	238.6	175.1	98.9	76.2	149.0	27.6
1963	521.2	229.1	201.7	113.7	88.0	168.6	30.1
1964	498.9	210.4	198.1	110.5	87.6	181.2	26.4
1965	497.9	208.8	209.7	116.0	93.6	174.8	27.5
1966	517.7	198.8	230.3	118.7	111.7	208.4	27.7
1967	537.3	194.3	258.4	109.5	148.9	243.1	22.4
Non-White								
1961	787.7	363.6	256.9	140.4	116.5	260.8	27.4
1962	730.9	343.5	276.9	155.3	121.6	215.5	34.0
1963	816.1	356.2	332.7	201.3	131.4	286.4	30.9
1964	866.9	333.4	371.5	214.1	157.4	339.1	24.8
1965	906.3	336.3	412.8	242.9	169.9	325.3	31.6
1966	984.0	349.5	452.5	260.7	191.8	401.1	32.2
1967	1,071.3	342.6	528.0	267.9	260.1	497.4	29.1

Percentage Change, 1961-67

Whites	+12.2	−21.4	+74.2	+24.9	+145.7	+98.9	26.8[a]
Non-Whites	+36.0	−5.8	+105.5	+90.8	+123.3	+90.7	30.0[a]

Ratio: Non-White to White

1961	1.64	1.47	1.73	1.60	1.92	2.13	1.06
1962	1.46	1.44	1.58	1.57	1.60	1.45	1.23
1963	1.57	1.55	1.65	1.77	1.49	1.70	1.03
1964	1.74	1.61	1.88	1.94	1.80	1.87	.94
1965	1.82	1.61	1.97	2.09	1.82	1.86	1.15
1966	1.90	1.76	1.96	2.20	1.72	1.92	1.16
1967	1.99	1.76	2.04	2.45	1.75	2.05	1.30

SOURCE: Maryland Department of Mental Hygiene 1961–67.
a. Average, 1961–67.

period (1961). Although rates declined from 1961 through 1967 for both racial groups, they declined at a faster rate for Whites. As a result, the ratio of non-Whites to Whites under care during the period increased from 1.64 to 1.99.

Outpatient Psychiatric Clinics and State and County Mental Hospitals

This section describes total-admission rates to psychiatric outpatient clinics and state and county mental hospitals for the United States as a whole in 1969. These data, collected in sample surveys conducted by the National Institute of Mental Health, provide relatively current estimates of use of these facilities by age, sex, race, and diagnosis. These data include both first admissions and persons who may have had episodes of psychiatric care during an earlier time period.

AGE, SEX, COLOR

Outpatient clinics. Among clinic admissions, the age-adjusted admission rate for non-Whites was 30 percent higher than for Whites—564 per 100,000 population for non-Whites and 428 for Whites (table 11.18; figure 11.13). For males, the rate for non-Whites exceeded that for Whites by 40 percent (590 compared with 419) and for females, by 23 percent (537 compared with 435). Whites utilizing outpatient services were younger on the average than were non-Whites in terms of the median age at admission. Rates for Whites exceeded those for non-Whites for ages under twenty-five years while the reverse was true for groups twenty-five years and over. A similar pattern occurred in a 1961 study of clinic terminations (figure 11.14, Rosen et al. 1964).

Admission rates to clinics also varied by sex. Rates were higher for White females than for males except among children under eighteen years of age and among the elderly (sixty-five years and over). Among non-Whites, overall rates were higher for males than for females due to significantly higher rates for boys than girls and for men thirty-five to forty-four years of age than for women in this age group.

State and county mental hospitals. As in clinics, admission rates to state and county mental hospitals were considerably higher for the non-Whites than for the Whites—379

FIGURE 11.13. Admission rates to outpatient psychiatric services: United States, 1969 (rates per 100,000 population) (Taube 1970)

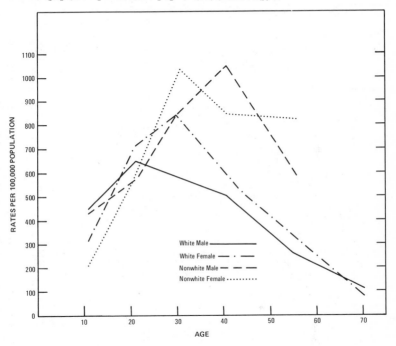

FIGURE 11.14. Clinic termination rate, 1961 (data for 579 of 682 clinics in 25 states) (Rosen et al. 1964)

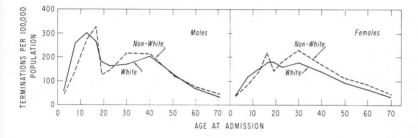

TABLE 11.18. Admissions to outpatient psychiatric clinics: United States, 1969 (rates per 100,000 population)

Sex and Color	All ages	Age-adjusted rates	Age					
			Under 18	18–24	25–34	35–44	45–64	65+
Both Sexes								
Total	441.1	441.1	370.2	671.9	746.4	594.8	338.9	106.1
Male	438.8	435.8	441.6	639.6	607.8	561.9	294.8	129.8
Female	443.7	443.3	296.2	698.9	874.8	625.4	379.3	88.5
White								
Total	426.6	428.4	378.9	687.0	718.9	549.8	298.9	99.2
Male	419.2	418.9	442.6	649.6	577.5	502.9	263.9	114.1
Female	433.5	434.8	312.6	718.1	851.3	594.2	331.0	88.2
Non-White								
Total	544.0	563.7	322.2	572.0	950.3	945.1	715.5	186.0
Male	575.2	590.2	436.0	572.8	844.0	1,058.1	592.5	a
Female	515.5	536.7	207.7	571.3	1,040.7	852.7	823.3	a
Ratio: Non-White to White								
Total	1.28	1.32	.85	.83	1.32	1.72	2.39	1.88
Males	1.40	1.41	.99	.88	1.46	2.10	2.25	a
Females	1.19	1.23	.66	.80	1.22	1.44	2.49	a

SOURCE: Taube 1970.
a. Five or fewer sample cases, estimates not shown because below acceptable limits of reliability.

per 100,000 for non-Whites and 234 per 100,000 for Whites
(table 11.19; figure 11.15). This was the case in almost every
age-sex-color group. For both Whites and non-Whites, the
male rates were higher than the female. In terms of age,
White persons admitted to state and county mental hospitals
were older than non-Whites. Except for a higher rate for
non-White girls under eighteen years of age, rates for males

FIGURE 11.15. Admission rates to state and county mental hospitals:
United States, 1969 (rates per 100,000 population) (Taube 1971)

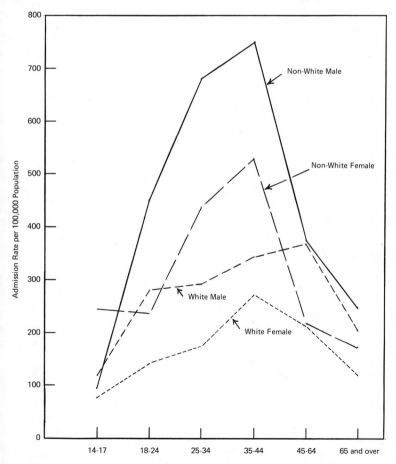

TABLE 11.19. Admissions to state and county mental hospitals: United States, 1969 (rates per 100,000 population)

Sex and Color	All Ages 14 & Over	Age-adjusted Rates	Age						
			14–17	18–24	25–34	35–44	45–64	65 +
Both Sexes								
Total	249.7	249.7	107.3	224.0	270.0	345.2	291.1	163.5
White	233.9	233.5	97.1	207.3	232.2	308.6	290.9	159.6
Non-White	379.1	373.1	170.9	336.7	553.2	632.0	293.1	208.4
Males								
Total	310.5	310.0	114.3	304.0	335.6	389.6	371.7	213.1
White	293.4	292.5	117.2	282.7	292.2	346.8	371.1	209.6
Non-White	452.8	452.3	95.7	449.5	680.4	753.1	377.5	251.0
Females								
Total	194.5	195.4	100.0	154.3	207.0	303.0	217.1	126.6
White	179.5	179.9	76.2	141.7	174.0	271.7	216.9	122.7
Non-White	314.5	305.6	245.6	239.5	442.4	531.3	218.8	174.0
Ratio:								
Non-Whites to Whites								
Total	1.62	1.60	1.76	1.62	2.38	2.05	1.01	1.31
Males	1.54	1.55	.82	1.59	2.33	2.17	1.02	1.20
Females	1.75	1.70	3.22	1.69	2.54	1.96	1.01	1.42

SOURCE: Taube 1971.

were considerably higher than for females for each age-color group.

Trend data on admissions to state and county mental hospitals by race are not available on a nationwide basis. From the limited data available, however, it appears that no consistent pattern of change exists in terms of differences between Whites and non-Whites for specified small geographic areas. For example, in Maryland State and county mental hospitals, the non-White admission rate in 1967 was 105 percent higher than in 1961 while the corresponding percent change in the White rate was 74 (table 11.17). In contrast, larger increases in admission rates to Tennessee public hospitals were noted for the Whites than for the non-Whites between 1960 and 1970 — 102 percent for Whites and 73 percent for non-Whites (Tennessee, State of, 1971).

DIAGNOSIS

Outpatient clinics. The diagnostic distribution of patients admitted to outpatient psychiatric clinics differed considerably by race (table 11.20). Among non-White males schizophrenia accounted for about 18 percent of the admissions, alcoholism disorders for an additional 15 percent, personality disorders (other than drug and alcohol addiction) for 9 percent. Among White males, schizophrenia accounted for about 14 percent of the admissions and alcoholism only 7 percent. Other disorders of importance for White males were neuroses (13 percent) and personality disorders (12 percent).

The differences in schizophrenic admissions were particularly marked among females. This mental disorder accounted for 30 percent of the admissions among the non-Whites but for only 17 percent among the Whites. Approximately one-fourth of the White and non-White females were admitted for neurosis.

In terms of age, rates for non-Whites were higher than were the corresponding rates for Whites for almost all age groups with alcoholism, schizophrenia, and drug addiction, while rates for Whites were generally higher than those for

TABLE 11.20. Admissions to outpatient psychiatric services: United States, 1969

| | Percentage Distribution | | | | Age-Adjusted Rates per 100,000 Population | | | |
| | Males | | Females | | Males | | Females | |
Diagnosis	White	Non-White	White	Non-White	White	Non-White	White	Non-White
All Disorders	100.0%	100.0%	100.0%	100.0%	418.9	590.2	434.8	536.5
Alcoholic disorders[a]	6.6	15.4	1.5	b	27.6	90.9	6.5	b
Schizophrenia	13.7	17.9	17.2	30.0	57.4	105.6	74.8	161.0
Neuroses	13.2	6.5	25.1	21.2	55.3	38.4	109.1	113.7
Personality disorders	11.9	9.1	10.8	5.9	49.8	53.7	47.0	31.7
Drug dependence	1.4	5.2	0.7	b	5.9	30.7	3.0	b
Other disorders	53.2	45.9	44.7	37.9	222.9	270.9	194.4	203.3

SOURCE: Taube 1970.
a. Includes alcoholism and organic brain syndromes associated with alcoholism.
b. Five or fewer sample cases, estimates not shown because below acceptable limits of reliability.

non-Whites with personality disorders, excluding drug and alcohol addiction (figure 11.16). Rates by sex for Whites with neuroses were higher than those for non-Whites among

FIGURE 11.16.   Admission rates to outpatient psychiatric clinics: United States, 1969 (rates per 100,000 population) (Taube 1970)

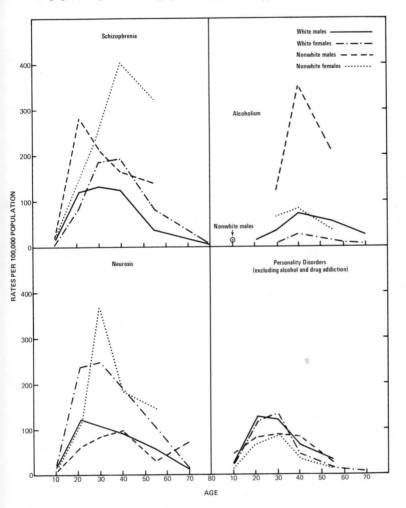

younger patients but were generally the same or lower among the middle-aged and older patients.

Comparison of the 1969 data with those from a similar study of clinics in 1961 highlights the overall increase in the use of clinics as well as the changes in utilization patterns by age, sex, and disorder. From figure 11.17 it appears that one

FIGURE 11.17. Percentage distribution of terminations from outpatient psychiatric clinics: United States, 1969 and 1961 (Taube 1970, Rosen et al. 1964)

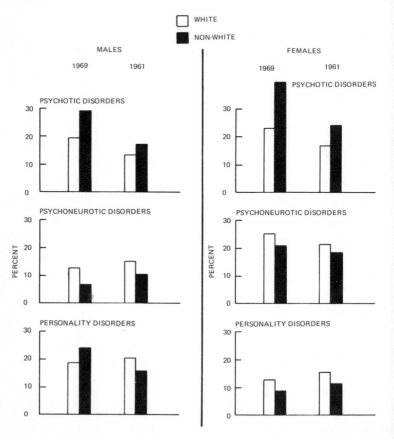

of the major factors contributing to the growth in the non-White rates was the increased proportion of non-White males and females diagnosed as schizophrenics and non-White males diagnosed with personality disorder.

State and county mental hospitals. Table 11.21 shows the percentage distribution of persons admitted to state and county mental hospitals by sex, color, and diagnosis. For White males, alcoholism comprised 39 percent of the admission diagnosis, and schizophrenia an additional 19 percent. In contrast, schizophrenia was predominant among non-White male admissions (36 percent) while alcoholism was the next largest category (30 percent). For women, schizophrenia was the most important admission diagnosis. A third of the White women and more than half of the non-White were assigned this diagnosis. Figure 11.18 shows the rates by age, sex, race, and diagnosis for the major disorder groups.

Recent trend data for the total number of persons admitted to state mental hospitals in Maryland (from 1961 through 1967) and in New York state (from 1960 through 1969) show no marked changes in the proportions of persons admitted for any major disorders with the exception of the diseases of the senium (Maryland Dept. Mental Hygiene 1961–67; New York, State of). For each sex-color group diagnosed with this disorder (except non-White women in Maryland), a gradual decline has been noted since the beginning of the decade.

SPECIFIC DISORDERS

Schizophrenic reactions. The serious nature of schizophrenia as a major public health problem has been described in other studies (Dunham 1965; Yolles and Kramer 1969). Our findings likewise indicate that patients with schizophrenic reactions comprise a major proportion of admissions to mental hospitals and outpatient psychiatric facilities, particularly among non-White patients. The nationwide data for schizophrenic reactions are shown in figures 11.16, 11.18, and 11.19. In both facility types (clinics and public mental hospitals), rates were generally higher for women than for

TABLE 11.21. Admissions to state and county mental hospitals: United States, 1969

| | Percentage Distribution | | | | Age-Adjusted Rates per 100,000 Population | | | |
| | Males | | Females | | Males | | Females | |
Diagnosis	White	Non-White	White	Non-White	White	Non-White	White	Non-White
All Disorders	100.0%	100.0%	100.0%	100.0%	292.5	452.3	179.9	305.6
Alcoholism	38.8	29.5	10.1	2.9	113.5	133.4	18.2	8.9
Organic brain syndromes	10.8	8.5	11.5	11.1	31.6	38.4	20.7	33.9
Schizophrenia	18.7	35.6	33.2	51.5	55.7	161.0	59.7	157.4
Neuroses	4.9	1.8	15.2	8.8	14.3	8.1	27.3	26.9
Personality disorders	9.5	10.5	4.2	3.9	27.8	47.5	7.6	11.9
Drug addiction	3.2	3.6	2.6	–	9.4	16.3	4.7	–
Other disorders	17.3	14.1	25.8	21.8	50.6	63.8	46.4	66.6

SOURCE: Taube 1971.

men and for non-Whites compared with Whites. In outpatient psychiatric clinics, rates by sex were consistently higher for non-Whites than for Whites for each age group. Rates for White and non-White males reached their maximum at eighteen to twenty-four years and for females of both racial

FIGURE 11.18.   Admission rates to state and county mental hospitals: United States, 1969 (rates per 100,000 population) (Taube 1971)

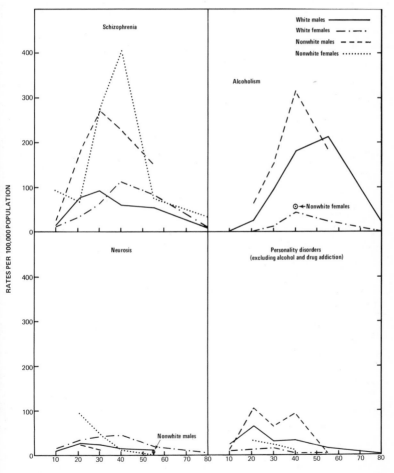

AGE

groups at thirty-five to forty-four years. For all age groups thirty-five years and over, rates for non-White females were at least twice as high as those for Whites.

FIGURE 11.19.   Schizophrenic admissions to outpatient psychiatric clinics and state and county mental hospitals: United States, 1969 (rates per 100,000 population) (Taube 1970, 1971)

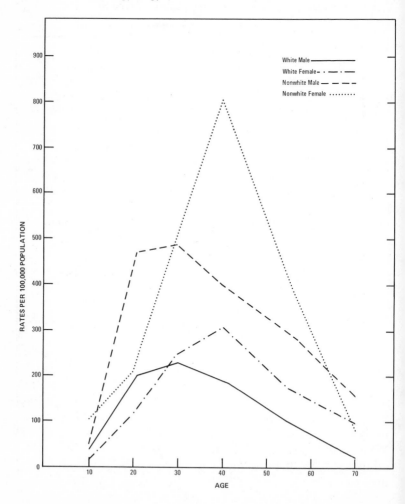

In state and county mental hospitals, rates for males were highest at twenty-five to thirty-five years of age and for females at thirty-five to forty-four years. As was the case in clinics, rates for non-Whites were higher than for Whites and at least three times as high during ages twenty-five to forty-four years. A similar pattern of relative magnitude, that is, non-White rates were about twice as high as those for Whites, is shown in a 1963 study of admissions to state and county mental hospitals by age, color, and diagnosis for Monroe County, N.Y., and Maryland (figure 11.20; Bahn et al. 1966).

Figure 11.19 illustrates the impact of schizophrenia on mental health facilities in the nation. Rates for non-White females exceeded 800 per 100,000 population in the age group from thirty-five to forty-four years. In other words, almost one out of every one hundred non-White women between thirty-five and forty-four years of age was admitted to either a public mental hospital or an outpatient psychiatric clinic with a diagnosis of schizophrenia in 1969.

Two studies concerned with the pathways of care for schizophrenics investigated the facilities at which schizophrenics received treatment. The facility of first contact, according to the study by Warthen et al. (1967), was generally an inpatient facility and, for non-Whites, primarily a state mental hospital. In their Ohio studies, Locke and Duvall (1965*a*) observed that relatively high proportions of Whites (41 percent of the males, 22 percent of the females) went to private or general hospitals while few non-Whites (4 or 5 percent) went to such facilities.

Alcoholism.   Alcoholism, like schizophrenia, is also one of our nation's major mental health problems. As stated before, alcoholism has been responsible for almost 40 percent of White male and 30 percent of non-White male admissions to state and county mental hospitals, according to the 1969 nationwide survey. In outpatient clinics, 7 percent of the White males and 15 percent of the non-White males were admitted with this disorder. In contrast, relatively few women were admitted for psychiatric care because of this disease.

FIGURE 11.20. Comparative psychiatric register admission rates to state and county mental hospitals: Maryland and Monroe County, N.Y., July 1, 1962, through June 30, 1963 (Bahn et al. 1966)

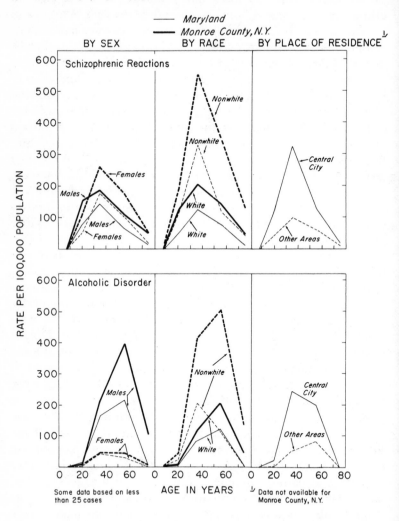

Rates reached their maximum between thirty-five and forty-four years of age for most sex-color groups in both inpatient and outpatient facilities. The one exception was for White males admitted to clinics; here the rates were highest between forty-five and sixty-four years. Rates were almost two times higher for non-White males than for White males in state and county mental hospitals but almost five times higher in outpatient clinics.

Diseases of the senium.   While schizophrenia and alcoholism accounted for the majority of admissions to mental hospitals among young and middle-aged adults, diseases of the senium accounted for the majority of admissions to state and county mental hospitals among the elderly.

Although the 1969 nationwide survey does not provide admission rates specific for diseases of the senium for patients sixty-five years and over, it does show rates for organic brain syndromes of which the diseases of the senium (senile dementia and psychosis with cerebral arteriosclerosis) comprise the largest part (U.S. Dept. of HEW 1968*a*). In the 1969 hospital survey, rates for organic brain syndrome among non-Whites sixty-five years and over were twice as high as those for Whites (153 per 100,000 population for White males, 237 for non-White males, 86 for White females, and 136 for non-White females).

Although rates were higher for non-Whites than for Whites, the percentage of patients admitted with diseases of the senium in each racial group may have been considerably lower for non-Whites. As an example, in 1967 in New York State, 27 percent of the White males first admitted to public mental hospitals were diagnosed with diseases of the senium compared with 8 percent of the non-White males (New York, State of). Similarly, 39 percent of the White females but 17 percent of the non-White were admitted with diseases of the senium. This pattern had been observed as early as 1930 in New York. Possibly due to efforts to place elderly senile patients in nonpsychiatric extended-care facilities, these proportions generally have decreased in the last few years. A similar admission pattern existed in Maryland in the early 1960s, but by 1967 the proportion of Whites and non-Whites admitted with senile brain diseases was about the same—4 percent of both the White and non-White males and 10 percent of the females (Maryland Dept. of Mental Hygiene 1961–67).

Nevertheless current data points to the greater use of public mental hospitals for the care of the aged non-White mentally ill. This situation cannot be attributed only to economic conditions or to greater incidence of mental disorder but in large part to racial discrimination that still persists with respect to care of the aged in nonpsychiatric resources. For example, in 1958, only four of some six hundred homes for the aged in Ohio accepted Negroes (Locke and Duvall 1965b). Resident-patient rates for homes for the aged and dependent further support this finding. According to the 1960 census, rates for Whites sixty-five years and over living in such homes were three times higher than those for non-Whites—2,463 per 100,000 population for Whites, 881 for non-Whites (U.S. Dept. of Commerce 1963). According to the 1968 Social Security Survey of the Demographic and Economic Characteristics of the Aged, the ratio of three to one still existed in 1968. While relatively more Whites lived alone or in institutions than did non-Whites, relatively more non-Whites lived with relatives or nonrelatives than did Whites (Murray 1971). The 1970 census data when available will provide more details relating to these living arrangements. Hopefully, Medicare and Civil Rights legislation have reduced markedly the many discriminating practices which may have contributed to these differences.

Drug abuse.   The role of racism in the etiology of drug dependence and its treatment is a complex subject in its own right and will not be dealt with in this chapter. Only brief mention will be made of some aspects of the problem as related to race. It has already been shown that for drug dependence the admission rates to mental hospitals and to outpatient clinics were considerably higher in 1969 for non-White than for White males (tables 11.20 and 11.21).

A study conducted in Maryland and related to the occurrence of drug abuse among patients who were under care in about 150 psychiatric facilities in the state of Maryland during 1967 provides additional information on this problem (Rosen and Goldberg 1972). During that year, about twenty-eight thousand persons were discharged from the Maryland facilities. Of this number, 1,055 (approximately 4 percent) had a history of drug abuse. Of these, only 458 were admitted with a primary diagnosis of drug addiction or intoxication. The remainder were admitted with a primary diagnosis of another disorder with drug abuse as an important associated problem. To obtain some notion of the relative racial distribution of drug abusers among these discharges in relation to their corresponding distribution in the population of the state of Maryland, an index was constructed consisting of the number of discharges per 100,000 population of the state of Maryland, specific for race. This index was also determined specific for age and sex as shown in table 11.22. There was little difference between the total age-adjusted index for White males and White females (23.2 and 23.9 per 100,000 respectively), while that for non-White females was only slightly lower (20.2). However, the index for non-White males (81.9) was three to four times as high as those in the other race-sex groups. Maximum levels occurred at eighteen to twenty-four years of age for each sex group except White women, for whom the maximum occurred at twenty-five to thirty-four years of age. The index attained its highest level among non-White males in age groups eighteen to twenty-four and twenty-five to thirty-four, with rates of 307.5 and 304.2 per 100,000 respectively.

The index was particularly high for non-Whites in public mental hospitals and for non-White men in outpatient clinics.

TABLE 11.22. Drug abusers discharged from psychiatric facilities: Maryland, January 1, 1967, through December 31, 1967

Sex and Color	All Ages		Age						
			Under 18	18–24	25–34	35–44	45–64	65 +
			Numbers						
All patients	1,055		81	326	312	178	139	19
White males	366		32	142	89	50	48	5
White females	369		29	64	99	83	81	13
Non-White males	257		15	91	106	38	6	1
Non-White females	63		5	29	18	7	4	–
			Rates per 100,000 Population						
All patients	28.6[a]	26.4[b]	6.3	92.4	68.2	35.0	19.3	7.0
White males	24.1[a]	23.2[b]	5.7	96.6	46.7	23.6	15.5	5.0
White females	23.8[a]	23.9[b]	5.9	44.5	51.1	38.4	26.0	9.4
Non-White males	83.2[a]	81.9[b]	10.9	307.5	304.2	95.8	11.6	6.6
Non-White females	19.9[a]	20.2[b]	3.6	89.5	46.5	17.0	8.1	–

SOURCE: Rosen and Goldberg 1972.
a. Crude rate.
b. Age-adjusted to 1967 U.S. population.

As has been the pattern for other diseases, relatively few non-White persons were admitted to private mental hospitals, general hospitals, and day-care facilities.

Narcotics were the drug type most frequently used by both White and non-White males and non-White females while depressants were the most frequent type reported among White women. Narcotic abuse was most commonly treated in public facilities, while depressant abuse was treated in general hospitals and in private mental hospitals.

PSYCHIATRIC CASE REGISTER[3] AND OTHER SMALL-AREA STUDIES

The nationwide surveys have as yet not collected data by race from private mental and general hospitals. Psychiatric case register and other small-area studies are useful in filling in this gap by describing utilization patterns among Whites and non-Whites for all types of psychiatric facilities (Maryland Dept. of Mental Hygiene and NIMH 1967). Table 11.23 shows utilization patterns in 1963 (all admissions) for three register areas, and page 390 gives first-admission rates in 1960 for two states where reporting was complete and unduplicated (one state, Maryland, subsequently became a register area).

As is evident from these tables, considerable variation exists both in the magnitude of the rates among areas and in the relationship between rates for Whites and non-Whites in each area. For example, age-adjusted admission rates for Monroe County in 1963 (ranging from 718 per 100,000 population for White females to 1,359 for non-White males) were at least 50 percent higher than those in Maryland for the same year: (485 to 772 per 100,000 for the same sex-color groups). In terms of the relationship between Whites and

---

3. A psychiatric case register is a data bank of information about individuals who have received service in any of a defined group of psychiatric facilities in a specified area (e.g., a state, county, etc.). Data on each psychiatric episode of these individuals are linked longitudinally to form cumulative records of their psychiatric careers.

TABLE 11.23.   Persons admitted to psychiatric facilities in register areas, 1963 (rates per 100,000 population)

Sex and Color	Maryland	Monroe County[a]	Hawaii[b]
	Rates per 100,000 Population		
Males			
White	577.8	854.8	397.0
Non-White	771.7	1358.9	369.3
Females			
White	485.4	718.4	409.6
Non-White	600.6	971.1	310.6
	Ratio: Non-White to White		
Males	1.34	1.59	0.93
Females	1.24	1.35	0.76

SOURCE: Bahn et al. 1966.
a. Does not include institutions for the mentally retarded.
b. Does not include private mental hospitals, general hospitals, and Veterans Administration hospitals.

non-Whites, Maryland and Monroe County had higher rates for non-Whites than for Whites for both sexes while in Hawaii the reverse was true. Similarly, in the 1960 data for Maryland and Louisiana, rates were higher for non-Whites than for Whites in Maryland but lower in Louisiana. It might be emphasized again that the differences between these admission rates probably do not reflect incidence of mental disorder as much as availability of mental health resources, referral patterns, social attitudes toward identification and treatment of mental disorders, and other socioeconomic and familial factors.

Table 11.24 shows the utilization patterns by Whites and non-Whites in different types of psychiatric facilities. The table emphasizes again that few non-Whites are admitted to private mental hospitals. It is interesting to note also that the differential use of inpatient services by males and females (that is, the larger proportion of women compared with men in private mental or general hospitals) is generally consistent for both Whites and non-Whites.

Nationwide data are not available on the differential utilization of private psychiatrists by race. However, such ⸢data are available in Monroe County and demonstrate a higher rate of admissions to private psychiatric practice among both White males and females as compared with the non-Whites (Bahn et al. 1966). The comparison shown in table 11.25 of outpatient psychiatric clinic rates with private psychiatrist rates indicates the differences in use of these services, by race. Even though rates are lower for non-Whites than for Whites, they probably represent a considerably greater non-White utilization of private psychiatrists than occurs in most areas. A nationwide sample survey held at about the same time indicated that less than 1 percent of the private psychiatric patients were not White (Bahn et al. 1965).

Discussion

This chapter reviews available data on the prevalence and incidence of mental disorders and patterns of use of psychiatric facilities with special reference to the role of racism in producing whatever differences may exist between White, Black, and other non-White groups in these indices. These data are of only very limited value for such purposes.

The community studies shown in table 11.4 provide various measures of prevalence which demonstrate that sizable proportions of Whites and non-Whites were affected by mental disorders. They do not provide data which describe the current situation in the United States. They describe the situation in Nassau County, New York, in 1916; in Baltimore in 1933, 1936, and 1952; and in Williamson County, Tennessee, a predominantly rural area, from 1938 through 1940. The two reports, based on selective service examinations carried out in Boston in 1941–42 and the United States dur-

(Continued on page 438)

TABLE 11.24. Persons admitted to psychiatric facilities in specified areas

Year, Area, Color, and Sex	All Facilities	Public Mental Hospitals	Private Mental Hospitals	General Hospitals	VA Hospitals	Institutions for Retarded	Outpatient Psychiatric Facilities
1967 Maryland							
White males	100.0%	35.9%	5.2%	6.3%	1.4%	1.0%	49.3%
White females	100.0	22.4	10.3	12.8	–	0.9	52.0
Non-White males	100.0	50.1	0.4	1.1	0.4	1.7	45.9
Non-White females	100.0	33.7	0.5	3.2	–	1.5	60.6
1963 Hawaii[a]							
White males	100.0	32.3	NA	NA	NA	1.4	66.3
White females	100.0	34.4	NA	NA	NA	1.6	63.9
Non-White males	100.0	27.7	NA	NA	NA	4.8	67.5
Non-White females	100.0	29.5	NA	NA	NA	5.0	65.5
1963 Monroe County, N.Y.[b]							
White males	100.0	40.4		6.7[a]		NA	52.9
White females	100.0	37.9		13.3[a]		NA	48.7
Non-White males	100.0	64.6		3.8[a]		NA	31.6
Non-White females	100.0	60.1		7.5[a]		NA	42.4

1960 Louisiana[d]						
White males	100.0	32.5	3.0	15.3	9.4	NA	39.8
White females	100.0	27.6	7.8	22.9	–	NA	41.6
Non-White males	100.0	34.8	–	20.7	9.3	NA	35.1
Non-White females	100.0	27.4	–	18.5	–	NA	54.1
1960 Maryland[d]						
White males	100.0	30.0	7.0	4.8	4.4	NA	53.8
White females	100.0	27.5	13.8	9.9	–	NA	55.4
Non-White males	100.0	40.3	–	0.7	3.6	NA	55.4
Non-White females	100.0	34.3	–	0.8	–	NA	65.0

SOURCES: 1960 (Pollack et al. 1964); 1963 (Bahn et al. 1966); 1967 (Maryland Dept. of Mental Hygiene 1961–67).
a. Private facilities not included in register.
b. Institutions for the retarded not included in register.
c. First admissions.
d. Includes private mental hospitals, general hospitals, and Veterans Administration hospitals.
NA indicates not applicable; a dash (–) indicates no cases.

TABLE 11.25. Admission rates per 100,000 population: Monroe County, N.Y., 1963

Color and Sex	Private Outpatient Psychiatric Practice	Outpatient Psychiatric Clinics	Ratio: Admissions Clinic to Private Practice
White males	156.2	452.3	2.9
White females	197.7	350.2	1.8
Non-White males	135.1	429.4	3.2
Non-White females	142.2	412.1	2.9

SOURCE: Bahn et al. 1966.

ing 1942 and 1943, apply only to males in the limited age range of eighteen to forty-four years of age and, for the many reasons discussed earlier, present a very biased picture of prevalence of mental disorders among both White and non-White males of this age range.

Prevalence rates by themselves can be misleading in assessing the role of racism and other factors in the causation of mental disorders in either Whites or Blacks. To illustrate: of the five community surveys three reported that the prevalence for Blacks was lower than that for Whites and two reported the reverse. Although it may seem paradoxical, racism can act in ways which under certain conditions can result in lower point-prevalence rates for Blacks as compared with Whites. To understand how this can happen, it is essential to remember that prevalence is a function of incidence of a disease and its duration. It is possible that the incidence for a given disorder in Whites and Blacks is equal but, because the disorder may be of shorter duration in Blacks—as, for example, resulting from a higher fatality rate—the prevalence for Blacks would be lower than for Whites. Thus, discriminatory practices that result in higher fatality rates for Blacks can account for the lower prevalence rate. On the other hand, Blacks may experience lower incidence of a disorder than Whites, but the disorder could be of much shorter duration in Whites because of their easier access to more effective treatment methods. Thus, despite higher incidence, the prevalence for Whites could be lower than that for Blacks because of discriminatory practices that prevent equal access to the more effective treatment methods.

Such incidence measures as are now available are based on rates of first admissions to state mental hospitals and other types of psychiatric facilities. These rates in turn are dependent not only on the factors that influence the incidence, duration, and prevalence of these disorders but also on socioeconomic, social class, attitudinal, and many other societal factors that determine who will receive psychiatric care, where, and when.

Clearly, then, investigations of the role of racism in the distribution of mental disorders require data on the incidence and duration of specific disorders and the way racist practices affect these indices. But this is no simple matter. Investigations of incidence of mental disorders are difficult to carry out not only because of the problems of case-finding and differential diagnosis but also because of difficulties in establishing date of onset. Isolating the factor or factors that caused the mental disorders is also a difficult and frequently impossible task since many etiologic agents may be involved. These range all the way from genetic factors, complications of pregnancy and delivery, organic diseases, trauma, infection, and drug and poison intoxication, to patterns of family relationships and stresses resulting from conditions of life and life-styles of persons in the various social classes. There are a host of similarly difficult problems to overcome to obtain appropriate measures of factors that determine duration of disease.

This chapter emphasizes several other points, demonstrating ways in which racism can produce problems that affect the components of morbidity rates. To illustrate, surveys of the noninstitutional population may yield a spuriously low estimate of the frequency of occurrence of a mental disorder in an area because discriminatory practices may have resulted in the admission of a disproportionate number of Blacks as compared with Whites to an institution (e.g., a prison, mental hospital, training school for juvenile delinquents). Such practices can bias both the denominators of the rates (i.e., the population exposed to risk) and the numerators (i.e., the number of persons with the characteristic under study in the population exposed to risk). Racist attitudes may also affect the consistency with which clinicians apply diagnostic criteria in determining either presence or absence of mental disorders in members of minority groups and in assigning a diagnosis of a specific mental disorder to a given individual. All such factors can bias comparisons of rates among different racial groups within and between areas as well as over time.

All of this emphasizes the need for an intensive research effort to acquire facts needed to assess the extent of mental disorders among Blacks and other minority groups, to test hypotheses concerning the role of genetic and social factors in the etiology of mental disorders (Kohn 1968) and the manner in which racism affects the incidence of such disorders and their duration, and to establish base lines against which to measure changes both in the extent to which racist attitudes and practices exist in different populations and in their effects on the persons toward whom these attitudes are directed.

The major stumbling blocks in such research continue to be the unresolved technical problems in the development for the mental disorders of case-finding and differential-diagnostic techniques which can be applied uniformly and reliably to various population groups. Without such techniques, systematic morbidity data on the mental disorders cannot be collected for either Whites, Blacks, or other racial groups. Although there has been much progress in research on this problem in the past ten years, still more is needed to solve the key issues involved (Gruenberg and Huxley 1961; Dohrenwend 1970). Indeed, it would be most desirable for members of minority groups to get the training needed to participate in such research and help to solve such problems.

When it comes to data on the patterns of use of psychiatric facilities, the situation is somewhat better and the solution is somewhat easier, but much still remains to be done to provide essential facts on a current basis. As was the case with the community studies, most of the available data are historical in nature and the more extensive tabulations come from a limited number of states (e.g., Maryland, New York, Ohio, and Louisiana). The lack of data on the patterns of use of psychiatric services can be attributed for the most part to the strong opposition on the part of key groups—governmental, professional, and lay organizations—as well as individual citizens to the collection of social data by race. It was the belief of such groups that the statistics derived from such data would be used in detrimental ways. But, as evidenced by the publication of *Racism and Mental Health*, this situation is changing. It is realized that the effective planning of services to all groups, be they White or Black, rich or poor, requires appropriate information. This problem is now being remedied at the federal level where sample surveys are being carried out periodically to determine the patterns of use of psychiatric facilities by race for the United States as a whole. Most state departments of mental health collect data on patient movement by race, but very few publish tabulations of these data in their annual reports (NIMH 1970). Publication of such data would add considerably to our knowledge of racial differences in patterns of use of mental hospitals, clinics, and community mental health centers.

The data on patterns of use of psychiatric facilities reported in this chapter demonstrate the generally higher admission rates for non-Whites as compared with Whites to mental hospitals and to outpatient services over a broad range of demographic variables—age, sex, marital status, income, occupation, education, migratory status, residence, etc. Such data, however, merely provide indicators of possible effects of racist practices. Studies are needed at the local, clinical, and community levels to investigate the extent to which such practices account for differences in admission rates to public mental hospitals as compared with outpatient services and community mental health centers, as well as for differences in quality of care, length of stay, and outcome.

There is urgent need not only to alleviate problems contributing to mental illness among minorities, but also to develop mental health programs which will provide more effective services to people in need. Projected population trends between 1970 and 1985 emphasize our concerns in this regard. Tables 11.26 and 11.27 demonstrate the expected changes in age, sex, and race of the population by 1985. Between 1970 and 1985 the total non-White population is expected to increase from 25.1 millions to about 32.3 millions, or by almost 29 percent. The White population is expected to increase from 179.8 millions to about 209.4 millions, or 16.5 percent. Thus, by 1985 the non-Whites will constitute 13 percent of the population. The increases in some of the age groups, particularly among the non-Whites, are extraordinary. The relative increases for the non-Whites range from 11 percent in the under eighteen-year age group to 86 percent of the age group of twenty-five to thirty-four years. These increases are considerably in excess of those for Whites. Such changes have important implications for the delivery of mental health services. To illustrate, tables 11.28, 11.29, 11.30, and 11.31 show what the expected number of admissions to both mental hospitals and outpatient services would be, assuming the rates determined in the national survey of 1969 would apply. As a result of the shifts in the age structure of the non-White population, the expected number of admissions to mental hospitals for non-Whites would increase from 64,000 to almost 93,000 (45 percent) and

(Continued on page 449)

TABLE 11.26. Estimated population in thousands: United States

Age	1970			1985		
	Total	White	Non-White	Total	White	Non-White
Total	204,923	179,794	25,129	241,731	209,427	32,304
Under 18	70,656	59,882	10,774	73,307	61,363	11,944
18–24	24,589	21,432	3,157	28,423	23,975	4,448
25–34	25,315	22,310	3,005	40,699	35,109	5,590
35–44	22,961	20,339	2,622	31,384	27,657	3,727
45–64	41,817	37,800	4,017	42,941	38,398	4,543
65+	19,585	18,031	1,554	24,977	22,925	2,052

SOURCE: U.S. Bureau of Census 1968.

TABLE 11.27. Estimated change in population: United States

Age	Change in Numbers of Persons (in Thousands) 1970-85			Percentage Change in Number of Persons 1970-85		
	Total	White	Non-White	Total	White	Non-White
Total	36,808	29,633	7,175	18.0%	16.5%	28.6%
Under 18	2,651	1,481	1,170	3.8	2.5	10.9
18-24	3,834	2,543	1,291	15.6	11.9	40.9
25-34	15,384	12,799	2,585	60.8	57.4	86.0
35-44	8,423	7,318	1,105	36.7	36.0	42.1
45-64	1,124	598	526	2.7	1.6	13.1
65+	5,392	4,894	498	27.5	27.1	32.0

SOURCE: U.S. Bureau of Census 1968.

TABLE 11.28. Estimated admissions to state and county mental hospitals: United States

Age	1970			1985		
	Total	White	Non-White	Total	White	Non-White
Total	379,891	316,000	63,891	476,226	383,577	92,649
Under 18	23,317	18,264	5,053	24,318	18,716	5,602
18–24	55,059	44,429	10,630	64,676	49,700	14,976
25–34	68,428	51,804	16,624	112,447	81,523	30,924
35–44	79,337	62,766	16,571	108,905	85,350	23,555
45–64	121,734	109,960	11,774	125,016	111,700	13,316
65+	32,016	28,777	3,239	40,864	36,588	4,276

SOURCE: NIMH 1970.
NOTE: Number is estimated on basis that admission rates per 100,000 population to state and county mental hospitals by age and color observed in 1969 would prevail in 1970 and 1985 (Taube 1971).

TABLE 11.29. Change in estimated admissions to state and county mental hospitals: United States

Age	Change in Number of Admissions 1970–85			Percentage Change in Admissions 1970–85		
	Total	White	Non-White	Total	White	Non-White
Total	96,335	67,577	28,758	25.4%	21.4%	45.0%
Under 18	1,001	452	549	4.3	2.5	10.9
18–24	9,617	5,271	4,346	17.5	11.9	40.9
25–34	44,019	29,719	14,300	64.3	57.4	86.0
35–44	29,568	22,584	6,984	37.3	36.0	42.1
45–64	3,282	1,740	1,542	2.7	1.6	13.1
65 +	8,848	7,811	1,037	27.6	27.1	32.0

SOURCE: NIMH 1970.
NOTE: Change is estimated on basis that admission rates per 100,000 population to state and county mental hospitals by age and color observed in 1969 would prevail in 1970 and 1985 (Taube 1971).

TABLE 11.30. Estimated admissions to outpatient psychiatric services: United States

Age	1970			1985		
	Total	White	Non-White	Total	White	Non-White
Total	914,955	777,213	137,742	1,127,778	939,183	188,595
Under 18	261,607	226,893	34,714	270,988	232,504	38,484
18–24	165,296	147,238	18,058	190,151	164,708	25,443
25–34	188,944	160,387	28,557	305,521	252,399	53,122
35–44	136,605	111,824	24,781	187,282	152,058	35,224
45–64	141,726	112,984	28,742	147,277	114,772	32,505
65 +	20,777	17,887	2,890	26,559	22,742	3,817

SOURCE: NIMH 1970.
NOTE: Number is estimated on basis that admission rates per 100,000 population to outpatient psychiatric services by age and color observed in 1969 would prevail in 1970 and 1985 (Taube 1970).

TABLE 11.31.   Change in estimated admissions to outpatient psychiatric services: United States

Age	Change in Number of Admissions 1970–85			Percentage Change in Admissions 1970–85		
	Total	White	Non-White	Total	White	Non-White
Total	213,223	161,970	50,853	23.3%	20.8%	36.9%
Under 18	9,381	5,611	3,770	3.6	2.5	10.9
18–24	24,855	17,470	7,385	15.0	11.9	40.9
25–34	116,577	92,012	24,565	61.7	57.4	86.0
35–44	50,677	40,234	10,443	37.1	36.0	42.1
45–64	5,551	1,788	3,763	3.9	1.6	13.1
65 +	5,782	4,855	927	27.8	27.1	32.0

SOURCE: NIMH 1970.
NOTE: Change is estimated on basis that admission rates per 100,000 population to outpatient psychiatric services by age and color observed in 1969 would prevail in 1970 and 1985 (Taube 1970).

in outpatient clinics from almost 138,000 to almost 189,000 (37 percent). In all the individual age groups, the percentage increase in the number of admissions would be exactly the same as the increase in population shown in table 11.27; that is, the expected relative increases in uses of these facilities would be as high as 86 percent in the age group of twenty-five to thirty-four years, a particularly high-risk group for schizophrenia and other major mental health problems.

Certainly such changes which result simply from population increases have important implications for developing plans to meet the increased needs for mental health services and for staff. Striking as the above facts may be, additional data on patterns of use of psychiatric facilities by race are still needed. Time series are not available by race to describe the trends in the resident patient population of the state mental hospitals. The decrease in total resident population during the fifteen-year period from 1955 to 1968 has been very striking, as shown in table 11.16. What is not known is whether the rates of decrease are the same, higher, or lower for Blacks as compared with Whites. More insightful computations of the future size of the state mental hospital population could be made if the trends in resident patients could be extrapolated specific for Whites and non-Whites and then applied to the expected population in 1985.

Considerably more data are needed to determine the extent to which the community mental health center program is attaining its goals in providing comprehensive mental health services to all the persons in our country regardless of age, sex, creed, national origin, or ability to pay. The details of this program, first authorized by Congress in 1963, are readily available — Public Law 88-164, 1963; Amendments to Public Law 89-105, 1965; Public Law 90-31, 1966; Public Law 90-574, 1968; Public Law 91-11, 1970 (U.S. Dept. of HEW 1970a). To provide a background for demonstrating some of the implications of this program in relation to needs for data, by race, on population, distribution of mental disorders, and patterns of psychiatric care and their effectiveness, we will summarize in the following paragraphs only the major elements of the program.

A community mental health center provides a comprehensive, coordinated program of mental health services located in one or more facilities in the community. Whether the services are offered at one location or more, they comprise a unified program permitting continuity of patient care. The centers' programs vary widely, each reflecting its community's special resources and needs. The purpose of each center is to provide a varied range of accessible and coordinated services to help prevent mental illness and to treat the mentally ill. Through a center's program a patient can find in his own community the type of care he needs. An essential feature of a center's program is to provide patients with "continuity of care" through a system of coordinated services which enables a patient to move easily from one type of service to another as his needs dictate so that the treatment he is receiving at any time is appropriate to the course of his illness. To help assure continuity of care, a central record-keeping system makes the patient's records readily available to authorized personnel of various services of the center.

To qualify for federal funds, a center must provide at least five essential services:

1. *Inpatient care,* which offers treatment to patients who need twenty-four-hour hospitalization.

2. *Outpatient care,* which offers patients individual, group, or family therapy while permitting them to live at home and go about their daily activities.

3. *Partial hospitalization,* which offers either day care for patients able to return home evenings or night care for patients who are able to work but are in need of further care and who are usually without suitable home arrangements. It may include both day and night care and/or weekend care.

4. *Emergency care,* which offers emergency psychiatric

services at any hour around the clock in one of the three units mentioned above.

5. *Consultation and education,* which is made available by the center's staff to community agencies and professional personnel.

In addition to the five basic essential services, a center may offer the following for a full comprehensive program: (6) diagnostic services, (7) rehabilitation services, (8) precare and aftercare, (9) training, (10) research and evaluation, and (11) special services offered to particular groups such as children, the elderly, citizens, alcoholics, or the retarded. Special services may also help to solve community problems such as drug abuse, suicide, or juvenile delinquency.

These services are to be provided on a catchment-area basis; that is, each center serves a defined population group of not fewer than 75,000 or more than 200,000 persons. For example, in an urban area a center may serve an inner-city neighborhood of up to 200,000. In a rural area smaller localities or counties in one or adjacent states may join together to form a center and share its facilities.

A select number of the program elements listed above can be translated into terms relevant to needs for statistical data to determine whether objectives — stated or implied — in the community mental health center program are being attained. This can be done by asking such simple questions as:

1. What is the population distribution of the catchment area by age, sex, race, and various socioeconomic and demographic factors?

2. How many White, Black, and other non-White persons have been admitted per year to the community mental health centers serving a specified catchment area by age, sex, income level, occupation, etc.?

3. What are the corresponding rates of admission for each group?

4. What is the distribution of persons according to the type of care received (inpatient care, outpatient care, partial hospitalization, emergency care)?

Answers to question 1 require base population data for a catchment area by age, sex, race, etc. The NIMH will be making such data available to each catchment area as determined by the 1970 census of population (Redick and Goldsmith 1971). Counts to answer questions 2 and 3 should be readily available from the center's records.

However, collecting the data to answer the question of differential rates of admission to public and private mental hospitals, outpatient clinics, and psychiatric services in general hospitals that are specific for residents of the catchment area being served requires a different approach, for example, periodic surveys of registers (Maryland Department of Mental Hygiene and NIMH 1967).

The answers to the above questions would also provide a starting point for various studies investigating the extent to which racist practices account for the differential patterns of utilization. For example, the NIMH survey of admissions to state mental hospitals in 1969 revealed that the rate of admissions for non-Whites was 60 percent higher than the rate for Whites (Taube 1971). Many factors, including racism, could account for this. An important question to answer is whether community programs designed to prevent admissions to state mental hospitals and to keep the mentally ill in the community are as effective for Blacks as for Whites.

More complicated kinds of survey designs are needed to answer other questions related to various objectives of the community mental health center program. For example, another goal is to maintain mentally ill persons in the community close to their own environment so as to protect their links with family and community. To quote from the president's message relevant to mental illness and mental retardation (U.S. Congress. House 1963):

It will be possible within a decade or two to reduce the number of patients now under custodial care by 50 percent or more. Many more mentally ill can be helped to remain in their own homes without hardship to themselves or their families. Those who are hospitalized can be helped to return to their own communities. All but a small proportion can be restored to useful life. We can spare them and their families much of the misery which mental illness now entails. We can save public funds and we can conserve our manpower resources.

Inherent in this statement is an objective that might be stated as follows: "Care for persons with mental health problems shall be provided close to their homes without hardship to these persons, their families, and other members of the community."

Developing the operational definitions and tools to determine the extent to which this can be accomplished is difficult. However, several important prototype studies of the burden of mental illness on the family have been done in England and could be adapted to conditions in the United States (Grad and Sainsbury 1963, 1966; Brown et al. 1962, 1966; Sainsbury and Grad 1966). Indeed, determining the burden that mentally ill persons constitute for members of minority group families as well as for the members of the families of the not-so-deprived groups of our nation would seem to be a study of a high order priority. Such studies would also provide further insight into the problem raised earlier concerning the relative strengths and weaknesses of various patterns of family organization and kinship bonds within White and Black families in relation to the community care of the mentally ill.

Suffice it to say, considerable basic and applied research is needed to provide the armamentaria required to prevent and control mental disorders. Hopefully, it will be possible to eliminate — or at least to minimize insofar as may be humanly possible — the role of racism in the chain of events that can not only cause these disorders but also obstruct and sometimes prevent delivery of effective methods for prevention and treatment of mental disorders in an environment most conducive to the achievement of maximum benefits. Epidemiology and biostatistics have important roles in providing the knowledge required to the achievement of these goals.

REFERENCES

American Psychiatric Association.
  1952.   *Diagnostic and statistical manual — mental disorders.* Washington, D.C.: American Psychiatric Association.
  1968.   *Diagnostic and statistical manual of mental disorders.* 2nd ed. (DSM-II). Washington, D.C.: American Psychiatric Association.
Bahn, Anita K.; Conwell, Margaret; Hurley, Peter. 1965. Survey of private psychiatric practice. *Arch. Gen. Psychiat.* 12:295–302.
Bahn, A. K.; Gardner, E. A.; Alltop, L.; Knatterud, G. L.; Solomon, M. 1966. Admission and prevalence rates for psychiatric facilities in four register areas. *Am. J. Pub. Health* 56:2033–51.
Belknap, Ivan. 1956. *Human problems of a state mental hospital.* New York: McGraw-Hill.
Brown, G. W.; Bone, Margaret; Dalison, Bridget; Wing, J. K. 1966. Schizophrenia and social care. Maudley Monographs, no. 17. London: Oxford University Press, p. 232.
Brown, G. W.; Monck, E. M.; Carstairs, G. M.; Wing, J. K. 1962. Influence of family life on the course of schizophrenic illness. *Brit. J. Prevent. Soc. Med.* 16: 55–68.
Clark, E. Gurney. 1953. An epidemiologic approach to preventive medicine. In *Preventive medicine,* ed. H. R. Leavell and E. Gurney Clark. New York: McGraw-Hill.
Clausen, John A., and Yarrow, Marian Radke. 1955. Paths to the mental hospital. *J. Soc. Issues* 11 (4):25–32.
Cohen, B. M.; Fairbank, R.; and Greene, E. 1939. Statistical contributions from the Eastern Health District of Baltimore, 111. Personality disorder in the Eastern Health District in 1933. *Human Biol.* 11:112–29.
Dohrenwend, Bruce P. 1970. Psychiatric disorder in general populations: problem of the untreated 'case.' *Am. J. Pub. Health* 60(6): 1052–64.
Dohrenwend, Bruce P., and Dohrenwend, Barbara S. 1969. *Social status and psychological disorder.* New York: Wiley.

Dorn, Harold. 1951. Methods of measuring incidence and prevalence of disease. *Am. J. Pub. Health* 41:271–78.

Doull, J. A.; Guinto, R. S.; et al. 1942. The incidence of leprosy in Cordova and Talisay, Cebu, P. I. *Internat. J. Leprosy*, Vol. 10.

Dunham, H. W. 1965. *Community and schizophrenia—an epidemiologic analysis.* Lafayette Clinic Monographs in Psychiatry, no. 10 Detroit, Mich.; Wayne State University Press.

Dunham, H. W., and Weinberg, S. K. 1960. *The culture of the state mental hospital.* Detroit, Mich.; Wayne State University Press.

Duvall, Henrietta J.; Locke, Ben Z.; and Kramer, Morton. 1966. Psychoneuroses among first admissions to psychiatric facilities in Ohio: 1958–1961. *Community Mental Health J.* 2(3):227–34.

Ferber, Andrew, et al. 1966. Current family structure: psychiatric emergencies and patient fate. Paper presented at 122nd meeting of the American Psychiatric Association, Atlantic City, N.J., May 13, 1966.

Frost, W. H. 1941. *Epidemiology.* Nelson Looseleaf System. Public Health Preventive Medicine. Vol. 2, chap. 7, pp. 163–90. New York: Thos. Nelson, 1927. Reprinted in Maxcy, K. F., ed. *Papers of Wade Hampton Frost: a contribution to epidemiologic method.* Commonwealth Fund, pp. 493–542.

Gorwitz, Kurt; Bahn, Anita K.; Warthen, Frances Jean; and Cooper, Myles. 1970. Some epidemiological data on alcoholism in Maryland. *Quart. J. Stud. Alcohol.* 31(2):423–43.

Grad, Jacqueline, and Sainsbury, Peter.

    1963.   Mental illness and the family. *Lancet*, March 9, pp. 544–47.

    1966.   Evaluating the community psychiatric service in Chichester: results. In *Evaluating the effectiveness of community mental health services*, ed. Ernest M. Gruenberg. New York: Milbank Memorial Fund.

Greenblatt, M. et al. 1955. *From custodial to therapeutic patient care in mental hospitals.* New York: Russell Sage Foundation.

Gruenberg, Ernest M., and Huxley, Matthew, eds. 1961. *Causes of mental disorders; a review of epidemiological knowledge.* New York: Milbank Memorial Fund.

Hagnell, Olle. 1966. *A prospective study of the incidence of mental disorder.* Stockholm, Sweden: Svenska Bokforlaget, Bonmers.

Hamilton, Charles V. 1971. The Black family in the United States—just how stable is it? *International Herald Tribune*, August 2, 1971, p. 7.

Hyde, R. W., and Chisholm, R. M. 1944. The relation of mental disorders to race and nationality *New Eng. J. Med.* 123:612–18.

Jaco, E. G. 1960. *The social epidemiology of mental disorders: a psychiatric survey of Texas.* New York: Russell Sage Foundation.

Kerner, Otto. 1969. The challenge of racism. In the 1969 *World Book Year Book*. Chicago, Ill.: Field Enterprises Educational Corporation.

Kohn, Melvin L. 1968. Social class and schizophrenia, a critical review. In *The transmission of schizophrenia*, ed. D. Rosenthal and S. S. Kety. Oxford, Eng.: Pergamon, pp. 155–73.

Kramer, Morton.

    1957. A discussion of the concepts of incidence and prevalence as related to epidemiologic studies of mental disorders. *Am. J. Pub. Health* 47:826–40.

    1966. *Some implications of trends in the usage of psychiatric facilities for community mental health programs and related research.* Public Health Service publication no. 1434. Washington, D.C.: U.S. Government Printing Office.

    1969. *Applications of mental health statistics.* Geneva, Switzerland: World Health Organization.

Kramer, Morton; Pollock, Earl S.; Redick, Richard W.; and Locke, Ben Z. 1971. *Mental disorders and suicide.* Vital and Health Statistics Monographs, American Public Health Association. Cambridge, Mass.: Harvard University Press.

Lemkau, P.; Tietze, C.; and Cooper, M. 1942. Mental hygiene problems in an urban district. *Mental Hygiene* 26:100–19.

Lin, Tsung-Yi, and Standley, C. C. 1962. *The scope of epidemiology in psychiatry.* World Health Organization. Public Health Papers, no. 16.

Locke, Ben Z., and Duvall, Henrietta J.

    1964*a*. Alcoholism among first admissions to Ohio public mental hospitals. *Quart J. Studies Alcohol* 25(3) 521–34.

    1964*b*. Migration and mental illness. *Eugenics Quart.* 11(4):216–21.

    1965*a*. Patterns of schizophrenic admissions to Ohio public mental hospitals. *Mental Hygiene* 49(2):220–29.

    1965*b*. First admissions to Ohio mental hospitals for mental diseases of the senium, 1958–61. *Pub. Health Report* 80(9):799–89.

Malzberg, Benjamin.

    1940. *Social and biological aspects of mental disease.* Utica, N.Y.: State Hospitals Press.

    1959. Mental disease among Negroes, an analysis of first admissions in New York state, 1949–51. *Mental Hygiene* 43:422–59.

Maryland Department of Mental Hygiene. 1961–67. Annual statistical reports for the fiscal years ending June 30.

Maryland Department of Mental Hygiene and National Institute of Mental Health. 1967. Maryland psychiatric case register: description of history, current status and future uses (Dec.).

Murray, Janet. 1971. Living arrangements of people aged 65 and older: findings from the 1968 survey of the aged. *Soc. Security Bull.* (Sept.), pp. 3–14.

National Institute of Mental Health. 1970. *A guide to data on patients in mental health facilities: state statistical publications, 1967 and 1968.* Washington, D.C.: NIMH Biometry Branch (Jan.).

New York, State of. Department of Mental Hygiene. Unpublished data.

Pasamanick, Benjamin. 1964. Myths regarding prevalence of mental disease in the American Negro. *J. Nat. Med. Ass.* 56 (1)6–17.

Pasamanick, Benjamin, and Knoblock, Hilda. 1961. Epidemiologic studies on the complications of pregnancy and birth process. In *Prevention of mental disorders in children,* ed. Gerald Caplan. New York: Basic Books, pp. 74–94.

Pasamanick, Benjamin; Roberts, D. W.; Lemkau, P. W.; and Krueger, D. B. 1959. A survey of mental disease in an urban population: prevalence by race and income. In *Epidemiology of mental disorder,* ed. B. Pasamanick, pp. 183–91. Washington, D.C.: American Association for the Advancement of Science.

Pollack, Earl S. 1968. Monitoring a comprehensive mental health program. In *Comprehensive mental health: the challenge of evaluation,* ed. Leight M. Roberts, Norman S. Greenfield, and Milton H. Miller, pp. 137–67. Madison, Wis.: University of Wisconsin Press.

Pollack, Earl S.; Redick, Richard W.; Norman, Vivian B.; Wurster, Cecil R.; and Gorwitz, Kurt. 1964. Socioeconomic and family characteristics of patients admitted to psychiatric services. *Am. J. Pub. Health* 54: (3):506–18.

Pollack, Earl S.; Redick, Richard W.; Taube, Carl A. 1968. The application of census socioeconomic and familial data to the study of morbidity from mental disorders. *Am. J. Pub. Health* 58(1):83–89.

Rawnsley, K.; Loudon, J. B.; Miles, H. L. 1962. Attitudes of relatives to patients in mental hospitals. *Brit. J. Prevent. Soc. Med.* 16:1–15.

Redick, Richard W., and Goldsmith, Harold F. 1971. *1970 census data used to indicate areas with different potentials for mental health and related problems.* Methodology Reports, Mental Health Statistics, Series C, Public Health Service publication no. (HSM) 72-9051. October. U.S. Department of Health.

Rosanoff, A. J. 1917. Survey of mental disorders in Nassau County, New York. *Psychiat. Bull.* 2:109–31.

Rosen, Beatrice M.; Bahn, Anita K.; Kramer, Morton. 1964. Demographic and diagnostic characteristics of psychiatric clinic outpatients in the USA, 1961. *Am. J. Orthopsychiat.* 34 (3):455–68.

Rosen, Beatrice M.; and Goldberg, Irving D. 1972. Drug abuse reported for patients seen in psychiatric facilities in Maryland, National Institute of Mental Health, Biometry Branch. (To be submitted for publication).

Roth, W. F., and Luton, F. B. 1943. The mental hygiene program in Tennessee. *Am. J. Psychiat.* 99:662–75.

Rowntree, Leonard G.; McGill, Kenneth H.; Hellman, Louis P. 1945. Mental and personality disorders in selective service registrants. *J. Am. Med. Ass.* 128:1084–87.

Sainsbury, Peter, and Grad, Jacqueline. 1966. Evaluating the community psychiatric service in Chichester: aims and methods of research. In *Evaluating the effectiveness of community mental health services*, ed. Ernest M. Gruenberg. New York: Milbank Memorial Fund.

Shepherd, Michael, and Cooper, Brian. 1964. Epidemiology and mental disorder: a review. *J. Neurol. Neurosurg. Psychiat.* 27:277–90.

Taeuber, C., and Hansen, M. H. 1963. A preliminary evaluation of the 1960 censuses of population and housing. U.S. Department of Commerce, Bureau of the Census (Sept.). Unpublished.

Taube, Carl A.

1970.   Differential utilization of outpatient psychiatric services by Whites and non-Whites, 1969. *Statistical Note 36*. National Clearinghouse for Mental Health Information, Survey and Reports Section (Dec.).

1971.   Admission rates by age, sex, and color, state and county mental hospitals, 1969. *Statistical Note 42*. National Clearinghouse for Mental Health Information, Survey and Reports Section (Feb.).

Tennessee, State of. 1971. Department of Mental Health. Unpublished data.

U.S. Congress. House.

1963.   Message from the president of the United States relative to mental illness and mental retardation. 88th Cong., 1st sess., February 5. Doc. no. 58.

1964.   Civil Rights Act of 1964. 88th Cong. July 2. H.R. 7152, Public law 88-352.

1965.   Social Security Act amendments of 1965, title XVIII. 89th Cong. July 30. H.R. 6675, Public law 89-97.

U.S. Department of Commerce. Bureau of the Census.

1926.   *Patients in hospitals for mental disease, 1923.* Washington, D.C.: U.S. Government Printing Office.

1963.   *Subject reports.* U.S. Census of Population, 1960: Inmates of institutions, final report (PC) (2)-8A. Tables 4–11. Washington, D.C.: U.S. Government Printing Office.

1968.   *Current population reports.* Series P-25, no. 388: Summary of demographic projections. Washington, D.C.: U.S. Government Printing Office.

1969.   *Current population reports.* Series P-60, no. 68; Poverty in the United States: 1959 to 1968. December. Table 1. Washington, D.C.: U.S. Government Printing Office.

1970a.   *Current population reports.* Series P-20, no. 200: Household and family characteristics, March 1969. May 8. Tables 1, 13. Washington, D.C.: U.S. Government Printing Office.

1970*b.*   *Current population reports.* Series P-60, no. 76: 24 million Americans—poverty in the United States, 1969. Washington, D.C.: U.S. Government Printing Office.

U.S. Department of Health, Education, and Welfare.

1966.   Maryland psychiatric case register statistical series, annual tables for year ended June 30, 1966. Vol. 5. Published in association with NIMH and Maryland State Department of Mental Hygiene.

1968*a.*   National Institute of Mental Health reference tables on patients in mental health facilities, age, sex, and diagnosis, United States.

1968*b.*   *Vital statistics rates in the United States, 1940–1960.* By Robert D. Grove and Alice M. Hetzel. Public Health Service publication no. 1677. Washington, D.C.: U.S. Government Printing Office.

1969*a.*   *Toward a social report.* Washington, D.C.: U.S. Government Printing Office.

1969*b.*   *Vital statistics of the United States, 1967.* Vol. II: *Mortality,* part A. Washington, D.C.: U.S. Government Printing Office.

1969*c.*   *Vital statistics of the United States, 1967.* Vol. II, sec. 5: *Life tables.* Washington, D.C.: U.S. Government Printing Office.

1970*a.*   *The comprehensive community mental health center, grants for construction and staffing.* Public Health Service publication no. 2136. Washington, D.C.: U.S. Government Printing Office.

1970*b.*   Trends in resident patients, state and county mental hospitals, 1950–1968. National Institute of Mental Health. Unpublished tables.

Warthen, Frances Jean; Klee, Gerald D.; Bahn, Anita K.; and Gorwitz, Kurt. 1967. Diagnosed schizophrenia in Maryland. In *Psychiatric epidemiology and mental health planning,* ed. Russell R. Monroe, Gerald D. Klee, and Eugene B. Brody, pp. 149–70. Psychiatric Research Report 22, American Psychiatric Association.

World Health Organization. 1967. *Manual of the international statistical classification of diseases: injuries and causes of death.* 8th rev., vol. I (ICD-8). Geneva, Switzerland.

Yolles, S. F., and Kramer, M. 1969. Vital statistics. In *The schizophrenic syndrome,* ed. L. Bellack and L. Loeb. New York: Grune & Stratton.

PART IV

Action Context

CHAPTER 12

Positive Mental Health in the Black Community: The Black Liberation Movement

by Preston Wilcox

This statement addresses itself to a definition of the concept of positive mental health from the Black perspective. It identifies the essential components of the Black Liberation Movement and some of the self-liberation activities in which Black communities are now involved. Finally, it addresses itself to the mental health implications of these new activities.

> To be a slave. To know, despite the suffering and
> deprivation, that you were human, more human than
> he who said you were not human. To know joy,
> laughter, sorrow, and tears and yet be considered only
> the equal of a table.
>
> To be a slave was to be a human being under conditions
> in which that humanity was denied. They were not
> slaves. They were people. Their condition was slavery.
> (Julius Lester, *To Be A Slave*)

To write this chapter is a challenge, largely because it provides the author with an opportunity to put on paper his own ideas about the subject. Having been trained in social work and having been employed in settlement houses, he soon learned that positive mental health really has meant the ability to conceal the fact that one was a white racist—whether his face were white or Black—without giving up the benefits of racism. One's mental health was in question if he questioned the white racist policies or attempted to uncover them. Blacks who chose to be themselves, then, found themselves in conflict with social work theories and practices and with the policies of settlement houses.

The late Martin Luther King, Jr., and Malcolm X were continually having their sanities questioned while they lived — by Blacks and whites alike. Both have been far more honored in death than they were while they lived. They were able to survive, then, by developing their own definition of themselves. They are living still because they decided to do so.

This analysis leads one to question the definitions that are used by the participating authors and the reader. Or is there a single definition?

- *Is white racism the same as white togetherness* — the suppression of white interethnic institutionalized conflict in order to contain Black people?
- *Is white racism white anti-Blackness* — the institutionalized white self-concept being based on *not* being Black?
- *Is there anything such as Black racism?* Is it antiwhiteness expressed by Blacks? Is it anti-Blackness expressed by Blacks? Is it pro-Blackness expressed *by* Blacks, *with* Blacks, *for* Blacks?
- Are Blacks the *majority* within the Black community or are such communities a "predominantly minority" group?
- *Are Blacks an American minority or a world majority?*
- How much will the theme of *control over definitions* permeate the concepts of mental health in America?
- Should efforts to improve mental health be designed to enable whites to be "kinder" to Blacks or to confront themselves and their own white racism?
- In considering mental health, should comments be addressed to a Black or to a white audience?

This chapter is addressed to the Black community. It is an attempt to put in one place a compilation of the

self-generated efforts by Blacks to manage their own liberation: to guard their own mental health. It focuses its attention on those efforts by Blacks to develop internal motion
within the Black community among Blacks themselves. To
that degree, this statement is—in itself—a mental health instrument: a mirror reflecting the exercise of a long-held and
increasingly actualized desire to have their own self-
determination.

It draws heavily upon the resources of the Action Library
located at Afram Associates, Inc., and the experiences of the
author in enabling Black communities to develop the desire,
skills, and talents to manage their own destinies.

A full exploration of this subject would require a book. The
limitations inherent in an article prevent any more than a
mere history of the original sources of information and such
topics. An unusually well-stocked Appendix, included as a
support of the basic content, begins on page 483. It is suggested that readers thumb through the Appendix now in
order to get a sense of from where the author is coming.

In this chapter, the *B* in Black is capitalized because the
word Black here does not refer to color. It refers to culture.
Using the same line of reasoning, the author in referring to
white uses a small *w* because he is referring to a color, not a
culture. In using the words Italian, Irish, Jewish, etc., he
would capitalize the first letter because in his mind he would
be referring to a culture not a color. He has no objection,
however, to other authors, including those in this book, using
a capital *W* in white.

Positive Black Mental Health Defined

This concept can be understood from the Black perspective only if one includes a full recognition of the following realities:

1. White institutional racism is a basic condition of this
society.

2. Such a condition renders large numbers of whites incapable of being able to perceive Blacks as humans and to respond to them on a human level.

The concept of positive mental health for Black people can be defined only by Black people for Black people.

The connotation of *positive versus bad* mental health should not be a part of the nomenclature of the Black community for several reasons:

1. The problems of the Black community were largely imposed on it by the oppressive exploitation of the white community. The health of the white community — in political, economic, educational, and psychological terms — is based on the systematic production of white-generated and defined pathology within the Black community (Wilcox 1970d, p. 42).

2. The problems of the Black community cannot be solved by the white community. The latter has a vested interest in the continued pathology of the Black community.

3. To accept white definitions of the Black condition is to rehabilitate Blacks to a state of "psychological whiteness" — anti-Blackness and antiselfness — rather than to restore them to a self-defined state in political, physical, and cultural terms (Action Stimulator #51, 1971).

If the above assumptions are correct, then, white humanists will (1) not separate professionalism from humanism, (2) work to confront white racism within the white community, and (3) deal with their need to make any decisions about the lives of Black people.

Black humanists will (1) refuse to respond to decisions made by non-Blacks that effect the internal relationships within the Black community, (2) acquire the skills, resources, and desire to control the institutions serving the Black community, and (3) enable the consumers themselves to control their own restoration programs such as drug treatment, alcoholism, etc.

The mental health states of Blacks are largely a reaction to or an adaptation to the conditions of white institutional racism. Indicators of healthy states of Black mental health are as follows:

1. Conscious awareness that this society is hostile to one's existence — that it is organized to destroy Black people as Blacks: that they live in a society where it is illegal to be Black and to be human. Black men earn "acceptance" when they deny their Blackness or feign whiteness.

2. A constant state of dynamic tension. Perpetual conflict becomes a static condition. Most mainstream crises do not have to be crushed — they will peter out if not escalated by oppressive or resistive tactics. "Conscious living" and resisting are the normal states of tension for Black people (Wilcox 1971*b*, p. 54).

3. Ability to deal with superordinates. The most consummate skill of Black people is to exercise power from a presumed position of powerlessness.

4. Lack of a desire to oppress or to be oppressed and a will to sustain one's existence on his own terms; refusing to be abused or to abuse.

5. A need to be involved in shaping and/or controlling one's own destiny; being suspicious of bewilderers and gatekeepers, that is, those who have a need to believe that they can save you or have a need to adjust your expectations.

6. Steady involvement in self-confrontation — engaging one's "I" institution *first* before confronting other institutions, that is, killing one's old inner self first.

7. Being steeped in an identity of one's own culture — history and values — at a gut level.

8. A basic knowledge of the society's destructive characteristics: racism, capitalism, classism, sexism, materialism, and the like.

9. An ability to perceive the humanity of oppressed people and to enable them to utilize it in their own liber-

ation; ability to perceive the relationship between the exploiters and those they exploit.

10. Desire to think, feel, and act in a single motion; not to fragment oneself into emotion, intelligence, and action.

Such a conception of mental health as it relates to Black people forces Black therapists and/or other professionals to examine their roles as *members* of the Black community *first*. A second question would relate to their *psychological identity* with and their *accountability* to the Black community. A third aspect would relate to involving the consumer—along with the professional—in attempting to change the conditions which contributed to his problems in the first place. They become partners in subverting the system, rather than retaining the traditional patient-worker relationship.

The implication for these conceptions as they relate to white professionals is that they will recognize that the only interface they can enjoy with the Blacks is one which is based on their confrontation of the white racism within the white community. They will recognize that, when they aid in the rehabilitation of Blacks into a sick society, they are only postponing the revolution. They are not helping to remove the need for it.

The Thrust of the Black Liberation Movement

In years gone by, American social institutions have approached Blacks as being "inferior white people." They were not perceived as being human beings in their own right. The humanitarian goal of white people was to make Black people "equal to white people." Those Blacks who subscribed to such a policy had to perceive themselves as being outcasts—off-whites if you will—rather than human beings in their own right. They had to become civil rights advocates, striving for equal treatment, school integration, and such.

Authentic Black men recognize that to be "equal" to

whites is to agree to participate in one's own oppression and to agree to oppress others. Recall that the original Uncle Toms are white men, not Black men. White youth who sought to think for themselves were forced into being hippies, Weathermen, beatniks—and were shot down on university campuses. The thrust for Black men, then, is to become equal to the occasion. Table 12.1 presents this point with greater clarity.

TABLE 12.1.   Comparison of characteristics of civil rights orientation with characteristics of Black nationalism orientation

Civil Rights Characteristic	Black Nationalism Characteristic
1. Search for new and kinder masters	1. No need for masters
2. Assimilation	2. Reenculturation and restoration
3. White approval	3. Black sanctions
4. One-by-one improvements	4. En masse improvements
5. Reaction to white goals	5. Enactment of group's own goals
6. Confront The Man	6. Confront oneself
7. Individualism	7. Collectivism
8. "Whites on the mind"	8. "Blacks on the mind"
9. Appeal to white conscience	9. Appeal to Black consciousness
10. Evaluate the ghetto	10. Elevate the Black community
11. Aimed toward the talented one-tenth	11. Aimed toward the Black masses

SOURCE: Wilcox 1971*a*, p. 47.

The Black Liberation Movement, then, is a movement to engage Black people in managing their own restoration to an original state of humanity. In the process they must redefine themselves on their own terms: the goal of Black people should not be one of producing more humane prisons, but of removing the need for prisons (Writings 1971, pp. 8–9; Aswadu 1971). That is, Black people can understand that prisons are not necessary in a healthy society; and thus, if they don't imitate the white society that uses prisons, the Black community can change society so that prisons will not be needed. In the same way, within the Black community there is a search to find a way to prevent the sale of dope within the Black community and to reach the international sources of dope so as to eliminate them. Within the white society there is a search for more effective drug cures without necessarily dealing with basic causes.

The thrust of the Black Liberation Movement can be catalogued as follows:

1. To control those institutions which serve the needs of Black people within the Black community and to subvert and/or mute the negative impact of all oppressive institutions

2. To identify and exercise those decisions which can be made about Black people only by Black people

3. To decide on how much it will not take from white people and to steadily push the level of tolerance to higher levels of conscious resistance

4. To humanize the existence of Black people even within a white racist society

5. To heighten the consciousness of Black people:
   • About their undying love for one another in order to increase the possibility that they can prevent themselves from being divided and conquered
   • To understand that they (Pan-Africanists) are a world majority with a common human destiny
   • To understand that every act is a political act, even the one of producing this chapter
   • That all Black people are ultimately accountable to each other

6. To ensure that these concerns pervade every act and every fabric of their lives

This thrust represents a conscious nation-building endeavor by Blacks, a recognition that Blacks exist as a physical and psychological nation in this society – colonized and controlled by whites. To understand fully the thrust to Black nationalism, one has only to examine the failure of this country itself to deal with the process of building a human nation:

1. The country's involvement in war
2. The existence of starving people in a land of plenty
3. The high incidence of mental sickness
4. The need for prisons and all other "controls"
5. The separation and distrust among all parts of society so that, for instance, the institutions of public safety and protection (police) are distrusted by the public and, even more amazing, the police fear the public.

Such a conception of the Black community as a nation is only perceivable by Black people who are an integral part of the Black community themselves. Insiders within the Black community can easily subscribe to such definitions. Outsiders – Black and white – will refute this thrust because of their inability to comprehend it.

Self-liberating Activities Present
Within the Black Community

An increasing number of Black communities are currently engaged in efforts to redefine themselves by:

1. Determining who speaks for the Black community through:
   - The utilization of Black caucuses
   - The nomination of their own candidates for public office, as occurred in NewArk, N.J., and in New York State: Kenneth A. Gibson was nominated for mayor by a Black and Puerto Rican convention, and Basil Patterson was nominated to run for lieutenant governor of New York State by the Black Elected Democrats (Chalmers and Cormick 1971, p. 63).
   - The proliferation of Black urban coalitions to replace

interracial councils at the local level: Afram Associates, Inc., is currently compiling a roster of such coalitions for thirty-four cities which have the largest Black
populations — ranging from Milwaukee with 62,458 to
New York with 1,087,931 (see Action Stimulator #53,
in Appendix).
- The increase in the number and quality of national
Black organizations and caucuses: Afram is currently
compiling such a directory under the direction of
Charles L. Saunders. As of this writing 247 such or-
ganizations have been identified.
- The role of the Black caucus within the Department
of Health, Education, and Welfare, called DRUM (see
Appendix, page 000).
- The development of the Congressional Black Caucus
(Congressional Black Caucus 1971).
- The establishment of linkages with African govern-
ments (Congress of African People, 110 Arlington
Street, Boston, Mass. 02116).

2. Moving to control the schools, police precincts, hospitals, health centers, and publicly financed programs that
serve their communities (Mamis and Wilcox 1968).

3. Defining and controlling the research activities which
take place within their communities (Community Research
Review Committee 1971).

4. Developing their own fund-raising mechanisms, for example:

United Black Appeal	United Black Fund
416 Warren St.	715 G. St., N.W.
Roxbury, Mass. 02119	Washington, D.C. 20001

Black Women's Community Development
Foundation
1028 Connecticut Ave., N.W., Suite 510
Washington, D.C. 20036

5. Developing new organizational models for establishing

coalitions among a variety of groups within the Black community around partisan political issues. The United Front in Cairo, Ill., is a case in point. Its counterpart at the national level at this time is the Congress of African People (see *United Front News*, P.O. Box 544, Cairo, Ill. 62914, $7 per year).

6. Developing comprehensive organizational strategies that include a variety of concerns under one umbrella. The Muslims provide a national model which combines economic, religious, educational, and sociopsychological concerns under a single umbrella. The Committee for a Unified New-Ark has produced a Black nationalist constituency whose concerns include politics, education, art and culture, physical fitness, and nation-building under a single sponsorship (Nation of Islam, 5335 S. Greenwood Ave., Chicago, Ill. 60615; Committee for a Unified NewArk, 502 High St., NewArk, N.J. 07102).

This shift toward the conscious development of Black-oriented Black-controlled organizations has built within it:

1. Opportunities for Blacks to learn how to accept direction and leadership from other Blacks

2. Opportunities for Blacks to learn how to work with each other

3. Opportunities to learn how to prevent one's group from being "divided and conquered"

4. Opportunities to humanize the institutions that Blacks control or influence:
   - To end brutality against Black prisoners by white police
   - To end violence among prisoners against each other (Humanizer #16, in Appendix)
   - To end corporal punishment, school suspensions, and expulsions in community-controlled schools (Action Stimulators #18 and #13, in Appendix)

- To introduce Black culture, history, and values into the curriculum (Wilcox 1970*a*)
- To define the role of outsiders within the Black communities (Technology or Tricknology 1970; Hall 1969; Haskins 1970; Wilcox, ed. 1970*a*)
- To develop consumer-controlled programs (Lewis 1969; Wilcox 1966, 1968, 1970*e*)
- To develop new criteria for the evaluation of the consumers' own programs and to manage these evaluations themselves (Thomas, White, and Wilcox 1971)
- To redefine the structure and relationship of the programs so as to reduce the possibilities of oppression and conflict (Lewis 1969)

What comes through when Black communities get involved in such activities is that such communities learn:

1. That Blacks would never treat each other the way The Man has treated them.

2. That Blacks are less concerned about panaceas than they are in preventing even *one* more person from falling into the cracks.

3. That prisons have nothing to do with rehabilitation; courts, little to do with justice; the antipoverty program, little to do with helping consumers to overcome poverty, etc. (Burns 1970).

4. That people tend to make decisions in their own interest no matter about whose life the decision is made.

5. That there is a set of nonnegotiable decisions that fall within the purview of Black people. These decisions should not be made by anyone else.

6. That the exercise of Black Power in most instances is not an infringement upon white power. It is merely a return to Blacks of the power which was rightfully theirs but which has been historically exercised by white people.

Mental Health Implications

The mental health implications of the Black Liberation Movement are clear. As the opportunities are increased for Black people to become whom they want to become and as Black people begin to assume control over the definitions of their own problems and goals, then new organizational forms will begin to unfold.

New Professional Roles

Efforts are already underway to redefine the role and concept of the Black professional. Two examples are worthy of mention: (a) the Code of Ethics of the Atlanta Chapter of the National Association of Black Social Workers (Thought Stimulator #83, in Appendix) and (b) the *Declaration of Black Teachers* (Thought Stimulator #82, in Appendix).

A recent statement by the Atlanta University School of Social Work traces its historic commitment to Blackness from the school's beginnings in 1920 and asserts that the school is no longer ashamed of Blackness (Atlanta University 1971). Atlanta, along with the Howard University School of Social Work, makes two schools which are beginning to produce a new breed of Black social workers.

The increasing withdrawal of Black teachers from the National Education Association and the American Federation of Teachers portends a new relationship between Black teachers and students. Such teachers will refuse to strike for teachers' benefits only; they will view themselves as part of the Black community and will join with parents and students in holding school systems accountable to parents and students as well as teachers. The recent school strike in NewArk, N.J.—the longest strike to date in the history of teacher unions—is a case in point (Thomas, White, and Wilcox 1971; Means 1970; Wilcox, ed. 1970*b*; Satterwhite, Amoureaux, Johnson, and Payne 1970; Vann 1970; Wright 1970).

Black professionals who perceive themselves as being accountable to the Black communities—and not to the institutions which employ them—will acquire the skills and insights to advocate along with their clients in order to make such institutions more responsive. They will not blame the client. Rather, they will begin to see that many delivery systems are organized to perpetuate the problems they were set up to alleviate (Ryan 1971). They will begin to blame the system, to deal with basic causes, and to perceive the politics inherent in the presenting problems. Importantly, they will learn that they cannot really assist a client who is unwilling to assist himself. Also they will learn to comprehend the politics behind the problems of their clients.

Such an approach by professionals will tend to *multiply* the number of local persons who are equipped to help others to understand the political nature of their problems. A second contribution of this approach is that the professional develops a vested interest in enhancing the strength of the clients rather than in emphasizing their weaknesses.

Consumer Control Over the Treatment Process

As professionals become involved within the Black communities, they will soon become aware of the possibility that some of the victims—pimps, prostitutes, drug addicts, excons, and alcoholics—have a greater ability to treat each other than have nonvictims. Importantly, the victims themselves soon come to realize that they must acquire the skills and insights to manage their own devictimization. The victims define their own problem by acknowledging that they have one. They literally learn how to help themselves by empathizing and working with each other. Malcolm X describes such a process himself (Humanizer #5, in Appendix). The following is a personal diary of an anonymous addict who went through a process of detoxification. It is an example in microcosm of Malcolm's thesis:

First Day. I found out it isn't what you know but who you know. Meaning, I was put into the hospital so fast that it made my head spin; thanks to Miss Kornegay [Alice Kornegay, Director, The Service Association, 156 E. 127th St.. Harlem, N.Y. 10035; (212) 534-3367. Don't phone; send a check!]

Second Day. I had not yet began to have drugs get out of my system. But because of personal reasons, I was put in my place but good.

Third Day. Was one of the most important, for I was put in my place by a patient. I found that my actions offended a lot of people, and was causing bad situations through being loud.

Fourth Day. I learned to respect others through respecting myself. We had a man-to-man discussion that night.

Fifth Day. This was the day of days; for once I was cut off medication and cut up at a therapy meeting. I cried but learned.

Sixth Day. We had church; after services I was left with two very strange feelings. I learned that I could make it in society with a Godly vice, like the one I had that was extremely devilish.

Seventh Day. This day completes the cycle. Now I have much more to live for, because in my stay it give more to work on, and for, and the mental constitution to work with. Now I feel good, look good, and sincerely hope I can make it. My deep and sincere thanks to all workers and counselors, working as hard as they can to save one; *me.*

A group to which the above addict belonged developed the following criteria for evaluating the success of its self-treatment program. What is obvious from a reading of the criteria is that the problem of drug addiction was perceived as a political problem — not just as a psychological one.

1. Increase in number and frequency of arrests of non-addict pushers by locally based police

2. Number of locally based police fined, suspended, or fired for collusion with drug pushers

3. Number of drug pushers run out of community by local residents

4. Decline in burglaries and muggings locally by drug addicts

5. Increase in programs involving the leadership of addicts and their legitimate advocates

6. Control of narcotic treatment programs by consumers, not professionals

7. Use of public funds (Medicaid, Medicare, etc.) by addict population

8. Employment of addicts in other fields locally — education, health, etc.

9. Control over job placement or job opportunities by addicts or their advocates

10. Increased public appropriations based on political pressure and competence of the exaddicts with concomitant development of new tax sources, etc.

The process of consumer control signals a redefinition of the problem and a redefinition of the person who has the problem. It invests that person not only in his own cure but in the process of curing others. It predisposes one to distrust "do-gooders" — most of whom have a vested interest in creating dependence within others. It predisposes one to seek the basic causes — within himself *and* within the system — for his problems. It predisposes one not to have a need to contribute to the production of more victims in the way in which the system produces its own victims.

The economic and medical consequences of consumer control are considerable. Fewer professionals are required; funds are utilized to meet program expenses — not necessarily for personnel services — but for subsistence purposes only. A focus is placed on self-treatment and consumer involvement in that process. Methadone as a treatment modality is viewed as a "medical fix" in many Black communities: a crutch for doctors, not a cure for addicts.

Finally, consumer control over the treatment process ensures control over definition of the problem. The problem of drug addiction within the Black community can be fully understood only if seen as a *political problem* despite the psychological predisposition of those who fall victim to addiction. The implications are as follows:

1. The sale of drugs is deliberately concentrated within the Black community.

2. The primary economic benefactors from the sale of drugs reside in communities which frequently discriminate against Black residents.

3. The police within the Black community are a part of the problem: the drug problem requires their collusion to exist and persist.

4. The "consensus for Black genocide" sanctions the sale of drugs to Blacks. A character in Mario Puzo's *The Godfather* (1969) is quoted as saying: "In the city I would try to keep the traffic in the dark people, the colored. They are the best customers, the least troublesome, and they are animals anyway. They have no respect for their wives or their families, or for themselves. Let them lose their souls with drugs."

The drug problem, then, cannot be dealt with by producing more therapists. Neither can it be dealt with by self-treatment programs alone. It will require a combination of (a) control and management by Blacks of the treatment facilities, (b) control over the police, and (c) control over the schools.

New Social Values

The problems of Black people have been derived largely from their oversubscription to a set of values which have been talked about but, in action, systematically rejected by white America: democracy, the melting pot, integration, equality, and cooperation. When analyzed these values have different meanings to Black and white Americans (table 12.2).

Blacks with key leadership, like Brother Ron Maulana Karenga and Imamu Amiri Baraka, have begun to articulate a new set of values. These values, when internalized and actualized by the Black community will render obsolete nega-

TABLE 12.2. Concepts frequently talked about in the United States with their different meanings for whites and Blacks

| Concept | Meaning for | |
	Whites	Blacks
Democracy	For whites only	Hypocrisy
Melting pot	Anglo-Saxon Protestantism	Instant whiteness, self-rejection
Integration	"There are no Black people"	Domination by others
Equality	Equal to whites	Equal to the occasion
Cooperation	Cooptation, selection of suitable associates	Mutual sharing

tive self-definitions of Blacks by Blacks. Such definitions emanating from outside of the Black community will be ignored. Of course, this process will require a double murder: (a) killing within oneself the need to comply with definitions from outside of oneself and (b) killing within oneself the need to define others. The students within NewArk's African Free School (33 Sterling St.) have put it this way: "Before we can love all people, / We must first love ourselves." "Disruptive," troublemaking children when viewed from the perspective of such a value system may, in fact, be politically disruptive, but they are not by any means psychologically disruptive.

New Social Institutions

The drive by Black therapists to be included in leadership positions within mainstream mental institutions is a basic contradiction (Douglas 1965). Residents of poor communities who have had tenure in prisons, residential treatment centers, jails, hospitals, and the like tend to agree that two things happen to a patient in a mental institution: (a) he is tamed, as was "Hard Rock" as described by Etheridge Knight (1970) and (b) he ages; that is, he gets older.

Such institutions are usually established to perpetuate

themselves, not to work themselves, of necessity, out of a job. They are established to become permanent, not to learn, of necessity, how to be of service. Their primary function is not treatment. Their main functions are related to employment needs, training needs, etc. Patients are important only as diagnostic studies, seldom as people. In fact, few therapists — Black or white — are free enough to respond to patients as people (as potential members of their own families).

Most such institutions are organized to perpetuate racism, not to confront it; to sustain mental illness, not to cure it; to attract mental patients, rather than to enable them to treat themselves; to promote scientific colonialism, rather than scientific humanism.

A Black who succeeds in being promoted *up the organization* has to acquire consummate skill to avoid exercising the Peter Principle (Laurence and Hull 1967). Such Blacks are in danger of being trapped by the system: they will be called upon to cure Blacks *faster* than white therapists, to admit them at a *slower* rate, but *not to deal with basic causes*. The need for new structures and relationships within such institutions is clear (Wilcox 1970g). Such institutions must *destroy the barriers between*

- Consumers and participants
- Institution and community
- Therapists and patients
- The decision maker and the targets of those decisions.

They must

- Build problem-solving processes and mechanisms that ensure law and justice, not just law and order
- Involve the patients and the staff as equal partners in the problem-solving process

Such institutions must

- Become part of a social movement and not focus on its institutional aspects

• Become political instruments, not psychological dumping grounds

• Must involve all their participants in a search for the truth, not an avoidance of it

My message has been that people have a right to suffer mental health problems; that for Black people many of these problems emanate from the condition of white institutional racism; that many of these problems will disappear the moment that Blacks begin to define themselves; that the treatment of Blacks must be officially assigned to Blacks or the consumers themselves; that no one has a right to exploit the illness of another person; that the current definitions of mental illness are more of the same-o, same-o—white institutional racism poorly concealed.

Right on!
Power to the correct people.

APPENDIX 12.1

The following Thought Stimulators, Action Stimulators, and Humanizers are produced by

Afram Associates Incorporated
68-72 East 131st St.
Harlem, New York 10037
Phone (212) 690-7010

Thought Stimulator #5

*Straight Talk Between Blacks and Whites?
Is It Possible?*

Those who know, don't tell, those who tell, don't know — Bobby Seale paraphrasing Malcolm X in *Jet*, January 15, 1970, p. 30.

Oppressed people have two sets of feelings: one for home consumption and one for export — Richard Wright in *White Man, Listen*, p. 21.

... draw on the insights, the knowledge, the experience that we [Black colleges] have in educating Black students — Vivian Henderson in the *New York Times*, October 10, 1969, p. 10.

From adolescence to death there is something very personal about being Negro in America. It is like having a *second ego* which is as much the conscious subject of all experiences as the natural self — Saunders Redding in *On Being Negro in America*, p. 3.

One ever feels his two-ness — an American, a Negro; two souls, two thoughts, two unreconciled strivings; two warring ideals in one dark body, whose dogged strength alone keeps it from being torn asunder — W. E. B. Dubois in *The Souls of Black Folk*, pp. 16–17.

These five Blacks seem to agree that there is a medium of communication which is Black and which operates to define "others," as outsiders. It's knowledge, it's feeling, it's psychological, it's political, it's experimental, it's conscience, and *it exists*.

This reminds this observer of a Black woman whom he met in Mississippi who was describing her cagy dealings with a white "tooth doctor" for whom she worked. He was always questioning her about what was going on in the Black community. She stated that she would *speak once*, and *think twice* about (a) why he was asking, and (b) what she should tell him!

What is your assessment of this situation?

Thought Stimulator #6

Differential Ethnic Group Reactions to Dual Caucus Experiences

A. DIFFERENTIAL RESPONSES TO CAUCUS EXPERIENCES: BLACKS VS. WHITES

BLACKS	WHITES
1. Feelings of togetherness and cohesiveness.	1. Feelings of rejection.
2. Class and color differences are subordinated in interest group cohesiveness.	2. Class and ethnic differences are heightened.
3. Task orientation.	3. Emotion laden.
4. Sense of belonging develops.	4. Divisiveness develops.

B. DIFFERENTIAL RESPONSES: MIXED GROUP ACTION VS. MULTI-RACIAL ACTION[1]

	1. *Mixed Group Action*	2. *Multi-racial Action*
BLACKS	Divided by white togetherness	Togetherness based on prior preparation

1. Multi-racial action is differentiated from mixed group action in that in the latter instances the Blacks and whites met together to discuss the subject issues. In the former instances, the Blacks met alone as did the whites, *before* they came together for multi-racial action.

| WHITES | Cohesiveness of whites | Divided through reaction to Black rejection of subservient roles |

SUMMARY AND ANALYSIS

These data were collected by observing participant behavior in several Problem-Solving Encounters. They are based on observations and experiences reported by the participants after having participated in caucuses, mixed and multi-racial groups. The data are based on reactions to initial participation in such experiences. They do not purport to make statements about participant behavior over a long period of time. In each instance, the subject under discussion was of a Black-white nature.

One can posit from the above findings that:

1. Black togetherness develops as a reaction to the sanction to meet alone. Black togetherness develops as a consequence of a *deliberately planned effort*.
2. Whites are *automatically* organized against Black togetherness. White togetherness is automatic as long as it is anti-Black. Without Blacks to reject, white in-group divisiveness comes to the surface.
3. The divide and conquer strategy emanating from white anti-Blackness turns Blacks against each other regardless of social class and complexions.

One can conclude from this transitory paradigm that:

a. White group acceptance of Blacks requires that the Blacks who are accepted reject other Blacks.
b. Black group acceptance of Blacks is experienced as a new phenomenon by many; acceptance of whites by this group requires that the white confront racism.

These data have implications for such issues as community control of schools, police precincts, etc. There is a suggestion that such efforts have counterracist, power-developing, skills-building opportunities embedded within them. It is apparent from my observations that the feelings of rejection experienced by the whites emanate from a *loss of control* over the Black agenda.

Thought Stimulator #40

Sex and Race: The White Man's View

A. THE WHITE MAN'S RANK ORDER OF DISCRIMINATION[1]

Rank I   *Intermarriage* (bars against intermarriage and sexual intercourse involving white women)

Rank II   *Social Equality* (specifically concerned with behavior in personal relations)

Rank III *Use of Public Facilities* (use of public facilities such as schools, churches, and means of conveyance)

Rank IV   *Political Disenfranchisement*

Rank V   *Discrimination by Public Servants* (in law courts, by the police, and by other public servants)

Rank VI   *Economic Exploitation* (securing land, credit, jobs, or other means of earning a living; discriminations in public relief and other social welfare activities)

Next in importance to the fact of the white man's rank of discriminations is the fact that *the Negro's own rank order is just about parallel but inverse to that of the white man.*[2]

B. THE "SPLIT IMAGE" THEORY

It seems possible that the image of the white woman is partly conserved against sexual thought and allusions, where-

1. Adapted from Gunnar Myrdal, *An American Dilemma: The Negro in a White Nation* (New York: McGraw-Hill, paperback edition, 1944), pp. 60–61. See also Emory S. Bogardus, "Race, Friendliness and Social Distance," *Journal of Applied Sociology* (1927), pp. 272–87.

2. Myrdal, *American Dilemma*, p. 61.

as the Negro woman tends to draw the full burden of the unsublimated sexual feeling. . . .

. . . In this case it would appear that the white men are defending their women not only from the sexual thoughts and attention of Negroes, but also from their own, and what they denied to themselves in fantasy they will hardly permit Negroes in fact.[3]

The interrelationships between "sexism" (myth of white male supremacy) and racism (myth of white supremacy) are highly correlated. The literature on the Women's Liberation Movement is a case in point.

3. John Dollard, *Caste and Class in a Southern Town* (Garden City, N.Y.: Doubleday and Co., Inc., 1937, 1949), pp. 137–38.

Thought Stimulator #43

Who Am I?

The President of Michigan State University was quoted at the time of his assumption of his current position as follows:

I'm a man first, an American second, and a black man third.[1]

Have you asked yourself *that* question?

WHO AM I?[2]

    a. I am a person.
    b. I am an American.
    c. I am a Black Nationalist.
    d. I am a member of the Third World.
    e. I am a Black person.

1. *New York Times*, October 18, 1969, p. 16.
2. Preston Wilcox, *A Black Experience Test: A Self-Examination* (New York: Afram Associates, Inc., March 31, 1970). 5 pp. (mimeo), 50¢.

f. I am a person who is Black.
g. I am a Black man.
h. I am a Black woman;
i. I am a woman who is Black.
j. I am a man who is Black.

Please rank in order of IMPORTANCE.

Rank Order	Letter
1	
2	
3	
4	
5	
6	
7	
8	
9	
10	

Please feel free to duplicate and pass on to others. Afram Associates will appreciate receiving copies of *your* findings (68–72 East 131st St., Harlem, N.Y. 10037).

Prepared by Afram Associates, Inc., under contract to SEDFRE, 164 Madison Ave., New York, N.Y. 10016.

Thought Stimulator #44

White Tricknology: Example #1

A Black activist in Harlem was recently quoted as saying that he was not worried about white technology. He stated that Harlemites were concerned about "white tricknology." Tricknology is herewith defined as the accumulation of experience and repertoire of language, style, intellectual and emotional guilt games played by whites to justify their continued delusions of supremacy. Tricknology is a term utilized by liberated peoples to decode the technology of oppressors.

One of the reasons that white America's essential uptightness is becoming public knowledge is that the Blacks, Puerto Ricans, Chicanos, poor whites, Indians, and the disenchanted white middle-class youth have developed a consummate skill in deciphering the language of oppression.

The example herein deals with an effort by a group of Indians — the Onondaga Tribe — to have the New York State Department of Education return 26 wampum belts which the state has stored in the State Museum and Science Service Building. The belts, valued at $300,000.00, were presented to the state in 1898 by Chief Baptist Thomas. A bill has been introduced to have the belts stored in a museum on the Onondaga Reservation.

A story was carried in the Syracuse *Herald-Journal* on April 17, 1970 (p. 27) describing an exchange in the State Assembly Chambers between an assistant state commissioner of the state museum and a third party as follows:

Commissioner: Why should they have the wampum belts? They can't even read them.
Third Party: How do you know they can't read them if you can't read them yourself?

Please note how the white tricknologist attempted to use technology (the ability to read Indian signs) as a basis for denying the return of the belts without *first* testing out his assumptions and *secondly* having the requisite skills to evaluate whether or not the Indians could read them.

And even if the Indians cannot read them, it is an irrelevant issue and, in fact, an attempt to divert attention from the main issue: the return of the wampum belts.

Prepared by Afram Associates, Inc., in contract to SEDFRE, 164 Madison Ave., New York, N.Y. 10016

Thought Stimulator #44

White Tricknology Example #2

In a continuing effort to decode white tricknology, the Action Library of AAI presents the following statement for analysis and interpretation. South Africa's Prime Minister John Vorster was quoted in the *New York Times* on April 18, 1970 (p.9) as follows:

But we are building a nation for whites only. We have a right to our own identity just as blacks and other non-whites have a right to theirs. Black people are entitled to political rights, but only over their own people — not my people.

Even as Vorster made this claim he was in control of the political rights of 13 million Black Africans, 1,850,000 mixed-blood coloreds, and half million Asians. While it sounds as though he is protecting the right of Blacks to their own identity, his real message was that his own white identity was intricately tied to the continued control over Blacks by whites.

What he fails to understand is that whites will actually have no rights as long as they have a *need* to control Black people. They will not have the right to sleep at night without having a gun at their sides.

Prepared by Afram Associates, Inc., under contract to SEDFRE, 164 Madison Ave., New York, N.Y.

Thought Stimulator #50

Fourteen Points of Blackness[1]

"Our diversity defines our unity."

1. Black control of the total educational process within the Black community

1. Prepared for consideration at a planning meeting (A One-Day Black

2. Black community control of the police
3. Black community ownership of all land and control of all business and economic institutions in the Black communities
4. Establishment of a National Black University
5. Formation of a Black Political Party, *the Liberation Party*
6. Formation of a National Black Media Committee (*Black Organized to Oversee the Media* — BOOM)
7. Endorsement of the historical legitimacy of all Black rebellions — past, present and future — and the right of all Black self-defense activities
8. Formation of a National Black Consumer Action Committee to expose white fraudulent practices and initiate selective buying campaigns
9. Construction of a Black Theology and National Black Church
10. Support of the Republic of New Africa and *any other Black nation-state alternatives*
11. Demand the implementation of Black Reparations
12. Establishment of a National United Black Fund
13. Support of *only* those Black politicians, educators, businessmen and civic leaders who are controlled by and responsive to the Black community
14. Formation of a *Global Alliance of African Peoples* in Africa, the Caribbean, Latin-America, and the United States

Chuck Stone, Chairman
National Conference on Black Power
April 18, 1970

Strategy Session) held at the Douglas Memorial Methodist Church, 11th and H Sts., N.E., Washington, D.C., on Saturday, May 16, 1970.

Thought Stimulator #51

Gradual Black Genocide[1]

It goes on daily — gradual Black genocide as follows:

- Life expectancy for Blacks in the U.S. is 63.6 years while for white Americans it is 70.19.
- Out of every 100 babies who die in infancy, 75 percent are Black babies.
- In 1968, 42 percent of Blacks 20 and 21 years of age had not completed high school while 18 percent of whites had not completed high school.
- Eighteen million dwelling units in the city (N.Y.) are lead-paint dwellings. Approximately 30,000 New York City children between the ages of 12 months and 6 years have absorbed an excessive amount of lead poisoning.
- In 1968, the income of Black families was only 60 percent of the median income of whites.

1. "We Charge Genocide" in *Harlem News*, March 1970, pp. 11. (c/o ARCH, 221 W. 116 St., Harlem, New York 10026.) See also William L. Patterson, ed., *We Charge Genocide—The Crime of Government Against the Negro People: A Petition to the United Nations* (New York: Civil Rights Congress, 1951).

Thought Stimulator #54

Indicators of Feelings of Inferiority

The consequence of residency in a white-controlled society has conditioned far too many people to receive and absorb white-generated messages that suggest that Black people are inferior to white people. It's a *myth* which white people have a need to turn into a reality largely because white institutional racism failed to turn all Black people into lambs. If Black people were inferior to white people, white people would not have had to develop a "tricknology" to convince Black people of this myth.

In order to help the Brothers and Sisters look at their own feelings of inferiority, the following indicators are listed:

1. *Anti-whiteness* — may be a sign that one cannot accept himself as being Black and perceive the beauty of Blackness
2. Belief that "white is right"
3. Fear of white people: unable to say what one feels to white people; scratching when one doesn't itch; lowering one's voice when whites enter the room; being ashamed of Black, etc., *only* in the presence of whites
4. "Chasing" white women because they are white
5. Being jealous of white women who date Black men
6. Inability to instinctively understand what motivates the Black Panthers without necessarily condoning their behavior
7. Inability to instinctively blame the system for the problems of the Black community without helping Brothers and Sisters to *learn* how to help them
8. Condescending attitudes toward Blacks as Blacks
9. Being Blacker than thou with other Blacks and whiter and brighter in presence of whites
10. Speaking to whites as a "Black expert" without the sanctions of the Black community
11. Starting a movement to get a job in the homes of helping Black people
12. Behaving white in a Black caucus
13. Competing with rather than cooperating with a Brother
14. Not having a need to stand with Black Sisters in time of need
15. Not investing bread in Black enterprises
16. Not being able to understand why the Toms behave as they do

17. Rationalizing the behavior of whites and kicking Toms in the ass
18. Playing games with Black people and dealing above board with white people
19. Expecting Black leaders to be supermen
20. Hustling off the Brothers
21. Not banking in Black-owned banks
22. Rapping without doing: no follow-through
23. Feelings of being overlooked

Can you list some more indicators? Please send them to us at the Action Library, Afram Associates, Inc., 68–72 East 131st St., Harlem, New York 10037.

Thought Stimulator #59

The Power to Oppress: Behavioral Characteristics

Power has been defined as the ability to get others to behave the way those in power want others to behave. It is most frequently perceived as the ability to get people to *line up:* to respond to orders and to think the way those in power want others to think. Seldom is power utilized to enable those who bestow power by compliance to the orders from above to develop a need *not* to want to line up, to *not* have to have orders before acting and to learn to think for oneself.

One way to examine this question is to outline the behavioral characteristics of those who view power as a tool of oppression and not as a tool of liberation.

1. They are fearful of *establishing precedents,* i.e., a favorable decision is exercised as a *tactic* and not a philosophy.
2. They are fearful that a *specific* decision will become *generalized,* even if appropriate.

3. They are fearful that people will act *without* their approval.
4. They are fearful that their subordinates will *bypass* their authority.
5. They are fearful that subordinates will not *show deference*.
6. They are fearful that subordinates will inadequately represent them or their organizations they head before others.
7. They are fearful of *sharing information* fully with their subordinates.
8. They are fearful that subordinates will plan joint actions to question the use of their powers so they *divide in order to conquer*.
9. They tend to want to have *the last word*.
10. They tend to listen to one subordinate's complaint against another without bringing the two subordinates together.

List your own additions to this. How do subordinates learn how to deal with such persons, that is, help persons to give up their need to oppress?

Thought Stimulator #68

From the Rhetoric of Repression to the Language of Liberation

RHETORIC OF REPRESSION
(This............really means ....this)

1. Model Cities	Model Colonies
2. Urban Renewal	Negro Removal
3. Human Relations	Colonial Relations
4. Integration	Nonexistence for Blacks

5. Nonwhite	Nonexistence for Blacks
6. Open Society	Series of Closed Doors
7. Brother	Brother-in-Laws
8. Brotherly Love	Big Brother— Little Brother
9. American Dream	American Nightmare
10. Race, Creed, or Color	White Only
11. Patriotism	Service in Vietnam

LANGUAGE OF LIBERATION

(This..........really means ....this)

1. Model Cities	Black Community Control
2. Urban Renewal	Cooperative Housing Development
3. Human Relations	Counterracist Relations
4. Integration	Multi-racial
5. Nonwhite	Black; non-Black
6. Open Society	Human Society
7. Brother	Soul Brother
8. Brotherly Love	My Brother's Brother, not my Brother's Keeper (man-to-man)
9. American Dream	The Struggle to Resist Oppression—Night and Day
10. Race, Creed, or Color	Content of One's Person Despite Race, Creed, or Color
11. Patriotism	Right to Dissent

NOW LIST YOUR OWN!

1. _____ _____ _____
2. _____ _____ _____
3. _____ _____ _____
4. _____ _____ _____
5. _____ _____ _____

Prepared by AFRAM ASSOCIATES, INC. under contract to SEDFRE, 164 Madison Avenue, New York, N.Y., 10016

Thought Stimulator #78

A Monument to the Past, Present, and Future of Casualties of the African Revolution

I. THE PAN-AFRICAN UNITY PRAYER

Our father who art in African Unity. Hollowed by the name. Thy Glory and Power come. Thy will be respected Overseas as it *Must* be in Africa. Give us now our daily dose of resistance to betray thee to thy enemies. And help us forgive only those who sincerely repent their inhuman wrongs against us. And lead us not into the temptation of accepting everyone who simply says he is for our course. For by their fruits, the sons and daughters of Africa shall know them; through One Hope, One Destiny, One Africa, Amen.

II. THE PAN-AFRICAN BEATITUDES FOR REVOLUTION

1. Blessed are the masses: for theirs is the future Glory of Africa.
2. Blessed are they that mourn for the welfare of the masses: for they shall be comforted.
3. Blessed are those who side with, live with, work for, and fight for the masses: for they shall inherit Africa.
4. Blessed are they who hunger, thirst, and die for the African Revolution: for they shall become Africa's martyrs.
5. Blessed are the conscientiously committed to Africa: for African Unity shall reward their conscience.
6. Blessed are the totally committed to the African Revolution: for they shall bring about Africa's Glory.
7. Blessed are they that will leave their houses, countries, material well-being to campaign for, work for, and fight for African Unity: they shall be called the Children of Africa.

8. Blessed are they that are ridiculed for believing in the "idea" of Pan-Africanism: for theirs is the Glory of Africa.

9. Blessed are you when enemies shall revile you, and persecute you, and shall say all manner of evil against you, for your Pan-Africanist Convictions.

   Rejoice, and be exceedingly glad: for great is your reward in a Union Government for Africa: for so they persecuted the Originators of Pan-Africanism before you.[1]

Okiya Omtata Okoiti

1. Reprinted by permission of *The Pan-African Voice*, vol. 1 (February 1968). (Center for Black Education, 1435 Fairmont Pl., N.W., Washington, D.C. 20009.)

Thought Stimulator #80

Liberation Alphabet[1]

A   Accountability of Administrators and Teachers!

B   Beauty in and of Blackness!

C   *Community control* of information and Learning for Black Self-Reliance!

D   Disciplined teacher participation in new Black teacher groups!

E   English the second language of Black people!

F   Federal monies controlled, supervised, and administered by Black people!

G   Grading standards revised!

H   History — told like it WAS!

I   Integration — not a panacea!

J   Judgments using a yardstick of *needs!*

K   Kindergarten is where it begins!

1. Foresight, February, 1969, inside back cover. (P.O. Box 494, Detroit, Mich. 48204).

L   Literature by and about Black people!
M   Middle-class (powerless) values OUT!
N   New materials – new approaches – new Black ideas!
O   Objectives relevant to Black determined aspirations!
P   Parent participation in planning, supervision, and in the total school activities!
Q   Quit *rapping!*
R   Racism not the issue – *control* of racism the issue!
S   Social promotion *out!*
T   Teach Black history and culture in all schools!
U   Understanding and implementing Black goals!
V   Veto-ing "establishment" goals!
W   Wider use of materials by Black writers!
X   X-ray treatment of all school procedures!
Y   Youth participation in the total school, including curriculum planning!
Z   Zero in on the issues!

Adapted from recommendations of Workshops of the Black Ministers – Teachers Conference, Detroit, Mich., April 1698.

Thought Stimulator #82

Declaration of Black Teachers[1]

We maintain that the present system of education is not organized for the benefit of Black youth.

We have collectively dedicated ourselves to the following *commandments* which we recommend to all Black teachers:

1. We shall know no other loyalty than to the children we teach.
2. We shall create no false images of loyalty for them.

1. *Foresight,* February 1969, p. 4. (P.O. Box 494, Detroit, Mich. 48204.)

3. We shall not defend our own inadequacies by blaming our children.
4. We shall labor six days and nights devoting our talents and energies to our responsibilities to the children we teach.
5. We shall honor the mothers and fathers of our children.
6. We shall not kill the minds and bodies of our children with underestimations of their worth and the worth of Black people.
7. We shall not adulterate our instruction but shall enrich it with the aim of developing Black youth who will be of service to the Black community.
8. We shall not steal their time and energies in busy work or in activities designed to promote middle-class values and goals.
9. We shall not bear witness against our children or against our fellow Black teachers but shall do our best to lift them from the hell of ignorance, confusion, and despair in which a racist society has placed them.
10. We shall not covet that status in society which will serve to isolate us from our goals and those of the Black community.

We earnestly seek the cooperation and assistance of those who work with Black youth in the formulation and immediate implementation of a program to achieve these goals.

Adopted at the Black Ministers — Teachers Conference, April 27, 1968, Detroit, Mich.

Thought Stimulator #83

*Code of Ethics of the Atlanta Chapter of the
National Association of Black Social Workers*

In America today, no person of African ancestry, save the

selfish or irrational, can claim to be neutral to the events taking place in our society. Therefore, this is a statement of ideals and guiding principles based on functionalism and not professionalism.

If a sense of community awareness is a precondition to humanitarian acts, then, we as social workers must look to our own skills and commitments and translate them into concrete benefits of the African community. We will serve mankind best by serving our own African people first. When we address our expertise to the quality of life of African people in America, the appropriate roles for us must be guided by African consciousness and advocacy in addressing the security and needs of the African community.

As a Black social worker I commit myself to the interests of my Black brethren and *subscribe* to the following statements:

1. I regard as my primary obligation the welfare of the Black community, the Black family, and that which includes action for improving social conditions.
2. I give preference to this mission over my personal interests.
3. I adopt the concept of a Black extended family and embrace *all* Black people as my brothers and sisters, making no distinction between their destiny and my own.
4. I hold myself responsible for the quality and extent of service I perform and the quality and extent of service performed by the agency or organization in which I am employed, as it relates to the Black community.
5. I accept the responsibility to protect the Black community against unethical and hypocritical practice by any individuals or organizations engaged in social welfare activities.
6. I stand ready to supplement my paid or professional advocacy with voluntary service in the Black public interest.
7. I will consciously use my skills, and my whole being, as an instrument for social change, with particular attention

GLENDALE COLLEGE LIBRARY

directed to the establishment of Black social institutions such as schools, hospitals, and voluntary agencies.

The above statement of conduct and commitment is based on a Code of Ethics that was developed by the New York Chapter of NABSW.

In our Code of Ethics, *African* and *Black* are used to denote the same phenomena — Africans. Black people in this country are an African people. For a rationale of this position see Humanizer No. 1 (originally circulated by the Action Library, Afram Associates, Inc., 68–72 East 131st St., Harlem, New York 10037, [212] 690-7010).

Action Stimulator #6

The Community Takes a Stand!

DECLARATION OF INDEPENDENCE:

Dayton Model Cities Planning Council
Education Committee
Joint Community School Council (September 13, 1969)

On August 14, 1969, the Dayton Board of Education signed an agreement with the Model Cities Planning Council that stated:

The Board and the Council will determine the qualifications for the selection of the Project Director. . . .

Recognizing the importance of close liaison between this position and the Education Committee in the appointment or termination of the Project Director, recommendations of the Planning Council will be sought and considered. Termination of the employment of the Project Director' shall be consummated only upon the concurrence of the Board and the Council.

In issuing his directive of September 9, 1969, relieving Arthur Thomas from administrative responsibilities in any school and directing him to "refrain from entering any school or grounds other than his office at Louise Troy," Dr. Wayne Carle acted outside the limitations of his authority. Dr. Carle usurped the prerogatives of both Model Cities Planning Council and the Dayton Board of Education. Dr. Carle is clearly out of order.

The Model Cities Planning Council's Education Committee and the Joint Community School instruct Arthur E. Thomas, the Project Director of the Model Cities Education Component, to continue to report to work and to carry out his regular duties.

Mr. Arthur E. Thomas is instructed that if he is called to report to the Superintendent of Schools or any of his subordinates, he is to report this information to the Chairman of the Education Committee of the Model Cities Planning Council for further instructions.

Since our major concern is the education of our children, the Education Committee and the Joint Community School Council wish to announce that schools will be open on Monday, September 15, 1969, and operating fully under the Model Cities Education Component.

We demand that the Superintendent of Schools and the Board of Education and the law enforcement agencies of the city of Dayton fulfill their responsibilities in insuring the safety of all Model Cities children attending schools inside and outside the target area.

For clarification and further information, call the Model Cities Planning Council, 224–7422, 1100 W. Fifth St.—our center of communication.

CommUNITY School Chairmen

Mrs. Juanita Johnson, Dunbar
Mr. Horace Kelly, Edison

Mrs. Sudie Allen, Grace A. Greene
Mr. Peter Hill, Irving
Miss Barbara Dennis, Louise Troy
Mrs. Lillian Walker, MacFarlane
Mr. Augustus Beal, Miami Chapel
Mr. Robert Allen, Roosevelt
Mrs. Ida Page, Acting Chr. Weaver
Mr. Levoyd Thomas, Whittier
Mr. George Self, St. James

Prepared after 5 hours of discussion at a joint meeting, Saturday, September 13, 1969, Dunbar High School.

Action Stimulator #13

Objective Achievements and Community Control

The School-Community Control Movement has been under attack as a mere move to substitute parent power for professional power, rather than as a move to increase the possibility that minority and poor youth will be responded to as they really are: *educable human beings.* Until recently, little has been written about the objective educational changes which have resulted. The table below is based on an article by Dr. Mario Fantini, Ford Foundation.

"Pre-experiment" refers to the period when the schools were totally integrated into the central school system. "Since inception" relates to the period since the subject schools first began to restructure their relationships with the central school system.

| | Pre-experiment | | Since Inception | |
	MC[1]	OH-B[2]	MC[1]	OH-B[2]
Suspensions		628		less than 30
Vandalism	?	2 per week	70% decrease	2 per year
Attendance		70–75%		90%
Daily teacher absence		15%		2%
Teacher turnover		20–25%		3%
Reading			Gain: 2 years in row	98% average gains, 1½ years

Source: Mario D. Fantini, "Participation, Decentralization, Community Control and Quality Education," *Teachers College Record*, vol. 71, no. 1 (September 1969), pp. 106–07.

1. Morgan Community School, 1773 California St., Washington, D.C.
2. Ocean Hill–Brownsville Demonstration School District, 249 Hopkinson Ave., Brooklyn, N.Y. 11233.

Action Stimulator #17

A "Community-Educator" Speaks!

By Preston Wilcox

The I.S. 201 Complex has proved to be a fruitful experiment in education. In fact, it is on the basis of the success of decentralized authority as practiced within the demonstration districts that the recent decentralization law was drafted. Yet, the Interim Board has chosen to overlook the Arthur A. Schomburg community and overlook the educational value of the demonstration districts in favor of personal and political considerations. Therefore, contrary to what we see being done in this plan, let us consider only educational factors in relation to demonstration districts:

The Arthur A. Schomburg I.S. 201 Complex has initiated several programs which are to be found nowhere else in the city (but then, isn't that the nature of an experimental project?). They include the Gattegno "Schools of the Future" method — for teaching math and reading to both students and their parents; the "Tri-University staff development program"; the use of innovative multi-media techniques for both student instruction and teacher training. Equally as important are the intangibles — the air of confidence that parents, students, and teachers project as they work together and as our students approach their studies. Black and Puerto Rican parents feel free to help teachers and students and they take part in all that goes on in our schools.

We in our community are living examples of the saying: "excellence in education can be achieved only when a community values education as a precious goal and has the power and resources to manage its own schools."[1]

1. David X. Spencer, *Statement at Interim Board of Education Public Hearing* (New York: I.S. 201 Complex, December 4, 1969), p. 1.

Action Stimulator #18

Progress at Ocean Hill-Brownsville

1. INCREASE AND PRODUCTIVE USE OF PARAPROFESSIONALS

Ocean Hill-Brownsville, like other city school districts, is allotted 75 paraprofessionals. The district has reallocated other funds to increase that to 325. Instead of pencil sharpening, the paraprofessionals are used for teaching and testing.[1]

2. TEACHER ACCOUNTABILITY

Each teacher has four paraprofessionals and the team covers two classes of about 25 children each. They also enable

1. Rhody A. McCoy, "Ocean Hill Struggles for Identity," *New York Times*, January 12, 1970, p. C-69.

use of an assessment program to permit student grouping by achievement, not by chronological age. While providing an objective report card, they also insure teacher accountability.[2]

3. DECREASE IN VANDALISM, HIGHER DAILY ATTENDANCE, LOWER STAFF TURNOVER,

Other facts are equally important. Vandalism, for example, has practically stopped. Daily attendance is up, staff turnover dropped from 50 percent to 8 percent.[3]

2. Ibid.
3. Ibid.

Action Stimulator #27

Black Community Development Technique, #1

HOW TO HELP PEOPLE COMPREHEND THE NATURE OF THEIR OWN POWER

1. Compile information about the total rents paid on a given block to help the residents become aware of their *collective economic power!*
2. Attempt to get them to agree to withhold all of their rents for a 15-day period without explaining to the landlord *why* they are doing it. Watch how up tight he gets!
3. Refuse to permit the landlord, utilities and telephone companies, etc., to send workmen into your building unless they are members of minority groups.
4. Take slum landlords into court to justify *why* they are continuing to collect rents for indecent, deteriorated housing!
5. Have every tenant in the building and the landlord contribute one dollar per month per apartment toward a

cooperative economic fund—not to be touched for any purpose for a year. Use the money as a down payment on the building and, then, pay off the balance and maintenance, etc., through the monthly rentals (now called mortgage payments).

6. Set up a schedule to have a parent *sit* in every elementary school classroom everyday to ensure that your children are respected. *Classroom Parent Groups* can chip in to pay a senior citizen or an unemployable person to sit in each classroom to make sure that their children are taught and respected. It can also be done on a school-aide basis with several parents moving from class-to-class. *No one has a right to destroy your children.*

7. Have the local police precinct captain report to all community groups on the number of arrests made each month for:
   a. *Pushing* dope, not using it
   b. *Acceptance* of bribes *by* the police
   c. *Brutality* by the police against local citizens
   d. Etc.

8. Request reports from public agencies—welfare, education, hospitals, health, youth board, police, housing authority, sanitation, etc.—as to the *number* of local residents who are employed in *decision-making* and *staff* positions.

9. Encourage everyone you know to deposit one dollar per week in the local minority-group-owned bank, at least one per week *by mail.*

10. Ask all salesmen, insurancemen, local businesses, and the like where they have their money deposited *before* making a purchase. Find out why they are *not* depositing their funds in minority-group banks, if this is the case.

11. THINK THE WAY YOU WANT TO THINK, BUT ACT TOGETHER!

Action Stimulator #32

A Twenty-Point Program for
Real School-Community Control

The struggle to control the schools in their own community began in the poorest section of Harlem in September 1966. It began with a mere request for the privilege to participate in the selection of the principal. The resistance of the N.Y.C. Board of Education and its school staff has served to escalate the struggle. Minority-group communities across the country are now demanding a voice in the education of their children. Importantly, the concept of education as a professional employment system has been modified and humanized as a consequence of the learnings that have accrued from that struggle. The following statement, developed by parent/community leaders at Harlem's I.S. 201 Complex, represents a new level of understanding by the people themselves. It was such an impressive document that we have decided to give it wide circulation. It follows[1]:

1. District boundaries defined by the communities themselves — organized on the basis of one district for each intermediate or junior high school complex.
2. School board election procedures developed by the school communities and held by the communities. This includes determining number of members, qualifications, and voter eligibility.
3. Full employment of community residents; all available positions to be filled by residents *first*.
4. Accountability of all administrative and teaching staff. Teachers must believe in our children's ability to learn; teachers must respect the children and the community.

---

1. Reprinted by permission of *Position Paper: The Future of the Arthur A. Schomburg, I.S. 201 Complex Demonstration Project*, April 1970, pp. 3–5. (103 E. 125th St., Harlem, New York 10035.)

5. Full utilization of school buildings. Facilities must be available to the communities for afternoon, night, and weekend use.
6. Availability of adult education programs for all, including both academic and job-training courses.
7. Abolition of all testing until tests can be developed which are relevant and geared to the requirements of individual communities.
8. Control of all school construction and maintenance funds.
9. Free breakfast and lunch programs for all children. No more soup and bread-and-butter sandwiches. Nutritious and appealing meals, including soul food, rice and beans, and Chinese food, will be served.
10. Establishment of educational programs which teach modern-day awareness of the real world. This includes Puerto Rican, Black, and Chinese culture and history, problems of unemployment, poor housing, malnutrition, police brutality, racism, and other forms of oppression.[2]
11. An end to all suspensions, dismissals, and other abuses against children until fair procedures can be devised to deal with each individual case.
12. Development of programs to deal with drug addiction.
13. Establishment of student participation in the decision-making process, both at junior high and high school levels.
14. Immediate repair of all deteriorated school buildings and start of new construction to reduce overcrowding; renovation of city-owned, but abandoned, structures to be considered for this purpose.
15. Immediate changes in the teacher and supervisory licensing and certification procedures so as to eliminate

2. The subject school-community does not serve Indians, Chicanos, and Orientals, but this statement should be viewed to include their interests as well as those of poor whites.

practices which have been used to exclude minority group persons from teaching and supervisory positions; abolition of the Board of Education, which exists only in New York City.

16. Development of bilingual classes and programs at all levels.

17. Establishment of medical and health services for all children; mandatory assignment of at least one full-time doctor and one full-time nurse to each school.

18. Establishment of equitable grievance procedures to protect the rights of parents, children, and students.

19. Free access to their children's records for all parents, as is their legal right, with nothing to be put in children's records unless approved by parents.[3]

20. Abolishment of the tracking system which was declared unconstitutional and discriminates against Black, Puerto Rican, and poor.

3. See *Guidelines for the Maintenance and Discussion of Pupils' Records* (New York: Russell Sage Foundation, 1970). 42 pp.

Action Stimulator #48

The 7 Principles of Blackness

1. UMOJA (UNITY)   To strive for and maintain unity in the family, community, nation, and race.

2. KUJICHAGULIA (SELF-DETERMINATION)   To define ourselves, and speak for ourselves, instead of being defined and spoken for by others.

3. UJIMA (COLLECTIVE WORK AND RESPONSIBILITY)   To build and maintain our community together and to make our brothers' and sisters' problems our problems and to solve them together.

4. UJAMAA (cooperative economics)   To build and maintain

our own stores, shops, and other businesses and to profit together from them.

5. NIA (PURPOSE) To make as our collective vocation the building and developing of our community in order to restore our people to their traditional greatness.

6. KUUMBA (CREATIVITY) To do always as much as we can, in the way we can in order to leave our community more beautiful and beneficial than when we inherited it.

7. IMANI (FAITH) To believe with all our hearts in our parents, our teachers, our leaders, our people, and the righteousness and victory of our struggle.

Action Stimulator #53

The Black Nation in White America

U.S. CITIES RANKED BY BLACK POPULATION[1]

1	New York	1,087,931
2	Chicago	818,647
3	Philadelphia	529,240
4	Detroit	482,223
5	Washington	411,737
6	Los Angeles	334,916
7	Baltimore	325,589
8	Cleveland	250,818
9	New Orleans	233,514
10	Houston	215,037
11	St. Louis	214,377
12	Atlanta	186,464
13	Memphis	184,320
14	Newark	138,035

1. Imamu Amiri Baraka (LeRoi Jones), "The Pan-African Party and the Black Nation," *The Black Scholar*, vol. 2, no. 7 (March 1971), p. 29. (Numbers in left-hand column mine.)

15	Birmingham	135,113
16	Dallas	129,242
17	Cincinnati	108,754
18	Pittsburgh	100,692
19	Indianapolis	98,049
20	Richmond	91,972
21	Oakland	83,618
22	Kansas City, Mo.	83,146
23	Jacksonville	82,525
24	Norfolk	78,806
25	Columbus	77,140
26	San Francisco	74,383
27	Buffalo	70,904
28	Louisville	70,075
29	Gary	69,123
30	Mobile	65,619
31	Miami	65,213
32	Nashville	64,570
33	Boston	63,165
34	Milwaukee	62,458

(All these figures are white-low.)

Humanizer #5

The Cure of Addiction — to Anything

The addict was first brought to admit to himself that he was an addict —

Secondly: he was taught *why* he used narcotics
Third: he was shown that there was a *way* to stop addiction
Fourth: the addict's shattered self-image, and ego, were built up until the addict realized that he had *within* the self-power to end his addiction
Fifth: the addict voluntarily underwent a cold turkey break with drugs
Sixth: finally cured, now an ex-addict completes the cycle by

"fishing" up other addicts whom he knows, and supervising their salvaging.[1]

This communal education and liberation process, as outlined by Malcolm X, requires that the addict be helped to accept his true condition, to understand *why* this is the case, be shown a *way*, get involved in building (restoring) his own self-image, invest *himself* in his own cure, proceed to try to help others to experience what he has experienced. Seemingly the key to this deprogramming process beyond what is spelled out is that it converts the helpless into helpers themselves. It modifies the relationship between the helper and the helpless as it takes place.

A second thread in this process is described by Malcolm X elsewhere. Malcolm X suggested that one had to first change his philosophy, then change his thought processes, change his attitudes and finally his behavior.[2]

The human-ology outlined herein has potential uses in helping to overcome a variety of addictions other than those derived from narcotics.

1. Alex Haley, ed., *The Autobiography of Malcolm X* (New York: Grove Press, Inc., 1965), pp. 262–63.

2. *Message to the Grass Roots from Malcolm X* (Detroit: Afro-American Broadcasting and Recording Co., 1965), recording, side I. (Suite 503, Tobin Building, 1308 Broadway, Detroit, Mich.) See also Preston Wilcox, "So You Want to Be Black," *Black Caucus*, vol. 1, no. 1 (Fall 1968), pp. 32–36.

Humanizer #14

Black Human Nature!

The late W. E. B. Dubois made these observations in 1935:

Hundreds and thousands of slaves were evidently leaving their masters' homes and plantations. They did not wreak vengeance on unprotected women. They found an easier more effective and more decent way to freedom. Men go wild and fight for freedom with bestial ferocity when they must—where there is no other way; but human nature does not deliberately choose blood—at least not black human nature.[1]

In describing a slave uprising planned by Brother Gabriel Prosser in August 1800, Lindenmeyer writes:

All slaveowning whites were to be killed, but poor and elderly women, sympathetic French and peaceful Quakers were to be spared.[2]

To deny the rare quality of humanity embedded in Black thought within a racist society is to deliberately avoid a search for the truth.

1. W. E. B. Dubois, *Black Reconstruction in America* (New York: The World Publishing Co., 1935), p. 66.
2. Otto Lindenmeyer, *Of Black America, Black History: Lost, Stolen, or Strayed* (New York: Avon Books, January 1970), p. 108.

Humanizer #16

Young Blacks Humanizing the Prison

In the months to come, the beneficial effect of the young blacks was to be proved: knifings and fist-fights among "brothers" decreased; the boxing program, once a main sports interest, went out of existence; interest in things "black" increased to such a degree that a history book, such as Lerone Bennett's *Before the Mayflower*, was worth ten cartons of cigarettes—prison currency; and even though the guards tried, gangs were formed to protect the more timid young blacks from some of the old convicts who wanted to make "girls out of them."[1]

1. "The Day the Young Black Came," in *Black Voices from Prison*, by Etheridge Knight (New York: Merit Books, Pathfinder Press, 1970), p. 165.

Contrast this action by young Blacks in prison with that described below:

You always had to be tough. That was the big thing, to be tough. Don't feel tough, but I couldn't let on. Even when the guys would take off (sodomize) somebody, it would turn my stomach sick, but I'd have to be one of the leaders or get marked chicken. What I'd do, I'd help to make the guy give in, then when it came my turn I'd say, "Ah, the hell with it," and I'd head for my cell. Night after night, I'd lay there masterbating—that was all there was for me.[2]

The young Blacks utilized violence or the threat of it to protect the humanity of others and their own. In the second case, the participant condoned violence against others by others in order to guard his need not to be violent against others. But, is he any less guilty than those who perpetuated violence against others? Are the young blacks saying something to us? As one prisoner put it,

There is no excuse for making sick people sicker and therefore more of a threat to society when they return to it.[3]

2. Harvey Swados, "The City's Island of the Damned," *New York Times Magazine*, April 26, 1970, p. 25.

3. William Healy, "Another Day Coming," in *Black Voices in Prison*, p. 52.

APPENDIX 12.2

To Whom It May Concern

FROM: Preston Wilcox, Educational Consultant

SUBJECT: A Social Study: *What Would You Do and How Would You Feel if You Woke up Tomorrow Morning as a Black Man or Woman?*

The above stated question is being circulated to leading and non-leading white Americans as a means to collect information on their perceptions of the question being raised. As a frequent author on the issue of Black-white encounters, I am interested in compiling this information into a book, if appropriate.

I am requesting a response hopefully limited to two pages, typed double-spaced. If selected, it will be used in its entirety — verbatim. If you do not want your statement identified please indicate accordingly. The final product will contain a listing of all persons to whom this memorandum was sent whether or not they replied.[1] Their statements will be identified only if they indicate that they want to be identified.

Any statement which is received may be used. AAI will assume that if the statement is received permission to publish it has been granted. In any case, however, permission to publish will be sought where there is a traceable name and address.

Your response and the insight revealed may be helpful in aiding white America to understand itself. Black Americans, too, will be interested.

February 3, 1970

1. AAI understands that the bases for not responding will be varied and valid. Failure to respond will not prejudice the senders of this memorandum. A reason for *not* responding forwarded to us by such recipients however would be helpful.

Political Action

Black Interests Come First[1]

BY PRESTON WILCOX

A new militant black middle class is developing in the United States. It is very different from the old black bourgeoisie. Rather than being ashamed of its color, the militant middle class sees beauty in blackness. Rather than putting extraordinary value on associating with whites, it tends to recognize the value of its own integrity.

It is this class that has the most to gain from the kind of disruptions that have been triggered throughout the country. It is a class that views its destiny as being tied directly to the destiny of the black poor. It is a class that is expanding, through defectors from the black bourgeoisie, returning veterans from the Vietnam war, the growing cadre of college graduates and the penetration of the black-power ethos into the social fabric of the ghettos.

More and more black people who were psychologically white are now addressing themselves to the question of who they are and what their responsibilities are in the racist society in which they live.

One aspect of the movement that is sweeping America is seen on the college campuses, where black students are revolting and looking for some kind of integrity in the educational process. In the past, the great majority of black people who were educated in this country turned out to be psychologically white — they then imposed the oppressor's definition on the black community. Take as an example the famous document about Harlem, *Youth in the Ghetto,* which was subtitled, *The Consequences of Powerlessness.* The subtitle reflects a white position; the problem of Harlem is that it is a black community. The black position would have been,

1. *New Generation,* Fall 1967.

The Consequences of Victimization, recognizing the racist nature of our society.

There is a growing ability in the black community to handle these black spokesmen who are psychologically white. And as this ability increases, the elected officials who happen to be black are beginning to make a shift. It's very interesting that the Negro politicians from around the country who recently assembled in Chicago took a stand not to take a stand about the uprisings this summer. This is progress. Five years ago they would have taken a white position.

Over the next couple of years the black communities, led by the new militants, will have to engage in non-partisan political action. Actions such as New York's I.S. 201 struggle are political action, and there have been ramifications from that all over the country. More of those kinds of activities are necessary to de-program the people who are black and who oversubscribe to white definitions.

Non-partisan political activity will be necessary to develop leadership that truly feels responsibility to black people, leadership that asks what something will do for black people before they ask what it will do for America, leadership that puts black people first. Black people and their concerns have been overlooked by America.

The basis for deciding on alliances should be: Will it help blacks? This criterion should be applied to each individual issue, for it really makes very little difference now whether the Democrats or the Republicans win. The Democrats may have passed more legislation, but they have not enforced it.

The kind of political action I see, therefore, is one that starts out non-partisan and moves to a partisan level at the point when a larger group of Americans sees its destiny as being tied to that of the black community.

This political action should begin at the local level within the black communities through a demand for black leadership of the institutions that serve or feast off such communities.

Psychologically black leadership is herewith defined as that which is responsible and responsive to the black community. Such leadership should be characterized by the transmission of skills, know-how, competence and opportunity to black people; most importantly, the desire to think for oneself. Such leadership must function as an *advocate* in behalf of black people and not as an "expectations adjuster" for the system.

The relationship between elected officials and such leadership should be based on the willingness of elected officials to promote the self-interests of the black community. The traditional pattern attempts to soften the impact of the colonialistic relationship between black communities and the broader city without effectively altering the colonialistic relationship itself.

The new strategy will require a deepening capacity of black communities to hold elected officials and social institutions accountable. The national welfare rights movement and the struggle in a number of cities over the control of ghetto schools are cases in point.

A further aim of this effort is to develop and cultivate *black thinking* leadership and competence, to increase the level of political awareness of the black community, and to *integrate* the power structure—politically and economically. This is not a separatist or segregated endeavor. It will include anyone who acknowledges that we live in a racist society that will remain stacked against the black people unless black people can bring about an effective redistribution of our nation's power and resources.

The question is not social integration, social separation or social segregation. None of these in themselves can advance the cause of black people. What is required is the integration of the self-interests of black people into the political processes of the nation. The ethos of black power offers this opportunity.

REFERENCES

Action Stimulator #51. 1971. Black restoration processes. New York: Afram Associates.

Aswadu, Ahmad Al. 1971. A Black view of prison. *Black Scholar* 2:28–31.

Atlanta University. Faculty and Students. 1971. Atlanta University School of Social Work projects: the Black experience in social work education. Atlanta, Ga.: Atlanta University School of Social Work. Mimeographed.

Baraka, Imamu Ameer. 1969. A Black value system. *Black Scholar* 1:54–60.

Barbour, Floyd B., ed. 1970. *The Black seventies.* Boston, Mass.: Porter Sargent.

Beck, Robert (Iceberg Slim). 1969. *Mama black widow.* Los Angeles, Calif.: Holloway House.

Black economic development: a bibliography. 1970. New York: Afram Associates. Mimeographed.

Burns, Haywood. 1970. Can a Black man get a fair trial in this country? *New York Times Magazine* (July 12), pp. 5, 38, 44–46.

Chalmers, W. Ellison, and Cormick, Gerald W., eds. 1971. *Racial conflict and negotiations: perspectives and first case studies.* Ann Arbor, Mich.: Institute of Labor and Industrial Relations, University of Michigan, Wayne State University, and the National Center for Dispute Settlement of the American Arbitration Association.

Community Research Review Committee. 1971. *Requirements for research involving the Black community.* Boston, Mass.: Boston Black United Front.

Congressional Black Caucus. 1971. *Statement to the president of the United States.* Washington, D.C.: U.S. House of Representatives, March 25.

Douglas, Joseph H. 1965. Racial integration in the psychiatric field. *J. Nat. Med. Ass.* 57:7.

Douglass, Frederick. 1968. *Narrative of the life of Frederick Douglass.* New York: New American Library.

Dubois, W. E. B. 1969. *The souls of Black folk.* New York: New American Library.

Ellis, William W. 1969. *White ethics and Black power: the emergence of the West Side organization.* Chicago: Aldine.

Hall, Robert. 1969. White teaching cannot motivate our children. New York: Afram Associates. Mimeographed.

Haskins, Kenneth W. 1970. *Community control comments: Some of the ways that those in power try to maintain their power and/or confuse the issue—or resistance to community control is. . . .* New York: Afram Associates.

Jones, LeRoi. 1963. *Blues people*. New York: William Morrow.

Knight, Etheridge. 1970. Hard Rock returns to prison from the hospital for the criminal insane. In *Black voices from prison*, pp. 122–23. New York: Pathfinder Press.

Laurance, Peter J., and Hull, Raymond. 1969. *The Peter principle*. New York: Morrow.

Lester, Julius. 1968. *To be a slave*. New York.

Lewis, Toye Brown. 1969. Black agency control: an action manual. New York: Afram Associates. Mimeographed.

Mamis, Nancy, and Wilcox, Preston. 1968. *Community control of police: a bibliography.* New York: Afram Associates.

Means, Fred E. 1970. Teachers unions: yes, poor children: no. New York: Afram Associates. Mimeographed.

New York Times. 1971. Peoples verdict in Bedford-Stuyvestant killing due tomorrow, p. 30. June 1.

Oosterwal, Gottfried, and Wallace, Elton. 1971. *A student missionary orientation course*. Washington, D.C.: Missionary Volunteers International, General Conference of Seventh Day Adventists.

Puzo, Mario. 1969. *The godfather*. New York: Putnam.

Ramsay, Annette M. 1970. *Understanding White racist thought: a bibliography*. New York: Afram Associates.

Ryan, Willam F. 1971. *Blaming the victim*. New York: Pantheon.

Satterwhite, Frank J.; Amoureaux, Hilda; Johnson, Jeffalyn; Payne, Toni. 1970. *Workshop in independent Black institutions*. Palo Alto, Calif.: College Entrance Examination Board.

Seven Hills Neighborhood House. 1970. Resolutions, demands and recommendations, techni-culture conference. Cincinnati, Ohio: Seven Hills Neighborhood House. Mimeographed.

Social casework. 1970. Vol. 51, no. 5, May. The entire edition deals with the Black perspective.

Technology or tricknology: White teachers in the Black community. 1970. *Social Policy*, November–December, pp. 67–68.

Thomas, Arthur E. 1971. *An evaluation of the Dayton experience: an experiment in community control*. Wilberforce, Ohio: Institute of Research and Development in Urban Areas, Central State University.

Thomas, Arthur E., and Burgin, Ruth W. 1971. *Community school council: philosophy and framework for urban educational change*. Wilberforce, Ohio: Institute for Research and Development in Urban Areas, Central State University.

Thomas, Joyce Ware; White, Gardenia; and Wilcox, Preston. 1971. *The African free school: toward a design for self-assessment*. New York: Afram Associates.

Vann, Albert. 1970. The agency shop. In *What Black educators are saying,* ed. Nathan Wright, Jr., pp. 234–35. New York: Hawthorn.

Weusi, Sultani Mtetezi. 1970. Community organization. New York: Afram Associates. Mimeographed.

Wilcox, Preston

1966.   Economic potential in a ghetto: credit unions and security deposits in East Harlem. New York: Afram Associates. Mimeographed.

1968.   The meaning of community control. New York: Afram Associates. Mimeographed.

1969*a*.   Bibliography: women and race. New York: Afram Associates. Mimeographed.

1969*b*.   The Black condition: a bibliography. New York: Afram Associates. Mimeographed.

1969*c*.   Self-liberation: some indicators. New York: Afram Associates. Mimeographed.

1969*d*.   The crisis over who shall control the schools: a bibliography. *Foresight* 1:3.

1970*a*.   Black studies as an academic discipline. *Negro Digest* 19:75–87.

1970*b*.   Humanness in a racist society. *Black Caucus* 3:50–59.

1970*c*.   Integration or separatism: K–12. *Integrated Education: Race and Schools* 3:23–33.

1970*d*.   Social policy and White racism. *Social Policy,* May–June, p. 42.

1970*e*.   *How to develop "operational unity" among Blacks: preface and bibliography.* New York: Afram Associates.

1970*f*.   Making social work relevant to Black people: a bibliography. New York: Afram Associates. Mimeographed.

1970*g*.   *On the way to school-community control: some observations.* New York: Afram Associates.

1971*a*.   To negotiate or not to negotiate: toward a definition of a Black position. In *Racial conflicts and negotiations,* ed. W. Ellison Chalmers and Gerald W. Cormick, p. 47. Ann Arbor, Mich.: Institute of Labor and Industrial Relations, University of Michigan and Wayne State University.

1971*b*.   Book review of *Black voices from prison* by Etheridge Knight. *Black Scholar* (April–May) 2:54.

Wilcox, Preston, ed.

1970*a*.   *White is.* New York: Grove Press.

1970*b*.   *Workshop on education and Black students, Congress of African People.* New York: Afram Associates.

Wilcox, Preston, and Harvrilesky, Catherine. 1969. A selected bibliography on White institutional racism. New York: Afram Associates. Mimeographed.

Wright, Nathan, Jr. 1970. Shankerism. In *What Black educators are saying,* pp. 79–81. New York: Hawthorn.

Wright, Nathan, Jr., ed. 1970. *What Black educators are saying.* New York: Hawthorn.

The writings of Black prisoners. 1971. *Black Scholar,* vol. 2, April–May.

Yette, Sam R. 1971. *The choice: the issue of Black survival in America.* New York: Putnam.

CHAPTER 13

The Formation of the
Black Psychiatrists of America

by Chester M. Pierce

In this history of the Black Psychiatrists of America, brief mention is made of the circumstances which made such an organization seem necessary and the reason for particular orientation to the development of the Black child. Relationships are given with the National Institute of Mental Health, the National Medical Association, and the American Psychiatric Association. Presented also are aspects of the work of the Black psychiatrists, including the newsletter, the establishment of the Solomon Fuller Institute, various Black caucuses, the film project, and the methods of government.

My assignment is to write a history. The tragedian Euripides used the word ιστορια when he said, "He is happy who has learned to *search into* the ceaseless and deathless causes of things, the whence they arose, the how and the why." When referring to his own work, Thucydides, the first scientific historiographer, wrote, κτεμα τε ες αιει, "And indeed it is a possession forever." So it is that I present this history of the Black Psychiatrists of America in the hope that many of the ceaseless, deathless causes of problems in Black-White relations in America will be illuminated so that we can work toward their elimination. And indeed such things should be obliterated forever. For there is no doubt that the motivation and necessity for the birth of the Black Psychiatrists of America were secondary to a few of the countless and incessant degradations that Blacks suffer in this "democracy."

The reader is alerted, therefore, that the fraction of truth to be presented may be strongly biased since it was forged in the crucible of hopelessness that all Blacks know, and it was shaped of the frustrated despair and bitter defeat that all Blacks have felt. Yet in accordance to my classical education, I will strive to present an honest and objective view. I will insist that many of the events to be unfolded were generated under this honest bias, so in that sense everything you read is absolute truth — from the vantage point of my fraction of truth.

Before recounting the significant events in this history, it is necessary to make a few preliminary observations about the Black Psychiatrists of America. It was born to be action oriented. As such, the organization, regrettably, has not been afforded the luxury of long-range contemplation. In a general way the key figures in the organization took the position that while our White counterparts could debate whether or not psychiatry should become more "involved," we the Blacks had no choice, given the conditions of our people, but to opt for action programs far beyond the walls of the consulting room and the clinic.

I think most of my colleagues would agree philosophically that our group had a special obligation to emphasize the mental health and emotional development of our children, the twenty-first-century adult. Therefore, it seemed important that underlying whatever thrust we made there had to be attention to the precious Black child.

Since, in fact, we are a segregated, urban people, most of our consideration had to be in some relationship to what was happening to the inner-city Black child. By the close of this decade well over 90 percent of Blacks will live in segregated housing. Almost all will be living in urban areas, and the chances of their housing being adjudged, on very generous grounds, to be substandard may reach the fifty-fifty level. So the prime concern of the Black Psychiatrists had to be on the withering effects of these demographic realities. When such unhappy circumstances are made additive to the ongoing ego erosion visited on Blacks by the unsavory influences of the mass education and mass media systems, one begins to grasp the gravamen of our problem.

It was in this vein that the founders of the Black Psychiatrists of America formulated ideas concerning the need for interdisciplinary action and definition of problems. For instance, in a world grown small by communication and transportation advances, how does one give the inner-city child sufficient hope that he will operate as a twenty-first-century cosmopolite?

In order to appreciate the forces that compelled the engagement that has been taking place between Blacks and Whites in American psychiatry, one should realize that to most Blacks there is no doubt that racism is a mental health illness. Prior to the publication of the Kerner Commission Report, several of us were able to confirm the commission's own theory which it elaborated independently that White racism was the major domestic issue of our times. The Blacks reasoned that racism was a delusion, built upon the false belief of ideas of superiority as a function of skin color. When no evidence can alter this belief, it is by definition delusional. In the United States in the overwhelming weight of its history and actions, Blacks have been both legally and informally victimized by this delusion. Since in effect the delusion affects virtually everyone in this land, it makes racism both a mental health and a public health problem. A public health illness such as racism, affecting masses of people, by definition cannot be treated on a one-to-one basis. Also it leaves chronic, sustained disabilities as sequelae, and it costs large sums of money to control or eliminate.

This was the type of thinking that many Black psychiatrists were doing as early as 1964. It was about that time that steps were taken to confront, in our opinion, one of the great purveyors of racism in this country, the National Institute of Mental Health (NIMH). It made no difference that the men in NIMH as well as in the Department of Health, Education and Welfare (HEW) might be, as individuals, as liberal as any White men in America. Our position was and remains that, if racism is a mental health problem of ubiquitous magnitude, then the arm of the federal government most responsible to stop its cancerous growth must be the National Institute of Mental Health. To our perception of reality, the NIMH was a sorry model to look toward for surcease from this problem since that organization itself was infected in its operation with the manifestations of racism.

With these few introductory words I will proceed to a presentation of a conspectus of our history leading up to the caucus by Blacks at the American Psychiatric Association meeting in May 1969 at Miami Beach, Fla. Then I will spend the bulk of this chapter on the basic efforts that resulted from this caucus. Finally, I will dwell on some of the present directions toward which our group would like to project American psychiatry. Like all histories the matters and people selected to be discussed are only a small, weighted sample of what one could elect to discuss. For the significant omissions, particularly those names of those friends who helped our cause (which we see as congruent to helping the best interest of both this nation and the world), I apologize.

History in Overview

Stage 1: The NIMH

Some years ago a Black whose name is lost amid the interstices of history visited Oklahoma City as a delegate from the Department of Health, Education and Welfare. On this occasion this high-ranking official was informed that Black psychiatrists were sorely distressed because NIMH, giving away perhaps $400 million per year, was essentially bereft of Black input. The opinion was expressed to this gentleman that much help in solving the beleaguered racial problems in this country, silently and effectively, could be provided merely by expanding Black input at the decision-making level about how NIMH spent its $400 million. The official agreed and promised to have HEW's chief physician contact several of us within two days. Needless to say, we are yet to hear from this chief physician. My own reading is that the Black man, as many of us know so well, did present our plight and our moderate proposal, but that the White authorities declined to act.

Yet all was not lost. Some positive things emerged from this brief contact with HEW. Dr. J. Alfred Cannon of Los Angeles agreed to bring this matter to the attention of Congressman Augustus Hawkins, a Black legislator, who has continued to befriend our cause. It was suggested to the congressman that all the Blacks in Congress should apprise themselves of how Blacks were circumvented at HEW. We like to think that such information helped the Black congressmen organize the thinking in their own caucus, which is still to reach its potential.

Similarly, the incident focused the attention of a growing number of Black psychiatrists on the importance of the NIMH in the lives of all Blacks. By that time we could say that what was essential was for us to find ways to affect the lives of all citizens in this land. This concept, perhaps the most critical in our organization, demanded certain social and political activity. It resulted, also, in causing Blacks to take a systematic inspection of those institutions whose influence touches every life in America. This idea became ingrained as a guiding principle and was coupled with the care that we took to be sure that we could gather sufficient data to speak as experts concerning such an institution's deficiencies.

Stage 2: The National Medical Association

Many Black psychiatrists regularly attended meetings held by the American Psychiatric Association and the section on neurology and psychiatry of the National Medical Association. Already in 1966 at the National Medical Association

(NMA) meeting in Chicago, Dr. Charles Wilkinson of Kansas City, Mo., was culling interest by a small group over the need for more rigorous organization of Black psychiatrists. The following year in St. Louis this interest was very lively, and Dr. Wilkinson took the leadership in calling together a group of participants to concern itself with growing racial misunderstanding. It was believed that Black psychiatrists might have some worthwhile contributions in this area.

At this point the NIMH did render assistance when it provided a small grant to Dr. Wilkinson for the purpose of holding several meetings with invited participants. Dr. Wilkinson, at the time a councilor at the NIMH, held the first meeting in Kansas City, Kans., on February 9 and 10, 1968. The initial organizational meeting went well, and two months later the same participants were joined by Dr. Cannon of Los Angeles and Dr. Alvin Poussaint of Boston. This meeting took place on April 5 and 6, 1968, in New York City.

Thus it happened that by chance many of Black America's senior psychiatrists were coming together into New York the night that the Reverend Martin Luther King was assassinated. Doubtlessly, this happenstance entered into the events that followed insofar as Black psychiatry was concerned. As we listened to radio reports and called to various sections of the country for on-the-spot reports in inner cities, our moderation weakened and our alarm hardened.

It was in this guise that we turned again to the NIMH as an institution which had to be more responsible than others both for what was happening and for what could be done to ameliorate things. Now I will elaborate, from our viewpoint, the sorry model that NIMH presented that very night when we anguished in our grief for a great moderate leader. At this point, let the reader be reminded that the informed opinions around the table that night represented as wide a range of psychiatric knowledge by Blacks that could be assembled in this country.

To our informed knowledge, the NIMH had never had a

Black resident in its inhouse program. To our informed knowledge, no Black had ever been "principle investigator" on a research grant from NIMH, that is, no Black had ever had primary check-writing responsibilities for research. To our knowledge, NIMH employed only two Black inhouse professionals, one of whom would be returning to academe in the not too distant future. To our knowledge, only *four* Blacks had ever been councilors, site visitors, review committee members, or consultants at NIMH when it disposed of its $400 million yearly. All four of us who had ever had such jobs were seated at the table. Let the reader be reminded that much of the site-visiting and reviewing is done by persons of far less academic rank than that held by numerous Blacks at prestigious universities. This chapter is not the place to recount the enormous advantages to an academic of having access to information garnered while serving NIMH.

At any rate, the New York meeting resulted in deciding that there were specific questions Black psychiatrists should research and that there was an important need for Black psychiatrists to communicate with as many other Black psychiatrists as possible (including residents in training). It was at the Kansas City and New York meetings that the idea of recognizing our own history was discussed. It was here that the name Solomon Fuller, a hero in Black psychiatry, was first mentioned as someone whose accomplishments we should memorialize.

In the following month the Black psychiatrists in the unnamed group were contacted by Dr. L. J. West, now chairman of the Department of Psychiatry at University of California, Los Angeles. Dr. West, then department chairman at the University of Oklahoma, was on the program committee of the American Psychiatric Association and was counted among our friends even at the confrontation of the APA trustees in 1969. He asked the group to present a session entitled "Black Power: An Identity Crisis." At this panel in May 1968 in Boston, Mass., Drs. Cannon, Comer, Pierce,

Pinderhughes, and Poussaint presented papers. Dr. Hyland Lewis, an eminent sociologist, joined the panel. Dr. Wilkinson was an officer of the panel as was another Black psychiatrist, Dr. Charles deLeon of Cleveland, Ohio. The panel was well attended, and among the things that happened were the first public attacks on the NIMH for sustaining racism. Of perhaps more historic importance was the penetrating paper on racial psychodynamics presented by Dr. Charles Pinderhughes of Boston, Black America's leading psychoanalytic theoretician. The momentum achieved by this group was stopped. Yet the ideas and spirit that were developed continued, and the group served as a vehicle for initiating meaningful contacts among Black psychiatrists.

Stage 3: The Gardner Letter

In late 1968 the Honorable John Gardner was luncheon guest at Harvard University. Mr. Gardner was then president of the Urban Coalition, but he was discussing his experiences when he had served as secretary of HEW. I gave him my views of HEW, placing emphasis on the responsibility of NIMH to the nation: since NIMH money provides training or support for institutions throughout the nation, all patients in the nation are influenced. In this way NIMH affects the lives of virtually everyone because everyone's doctor has been trained somewhere along the line by money given to a department of psychiatry or a hospital by NIMH. Mr. Gardner was thoughtful about these charges and suggested I put them in letter form. This was accomplished. Soon afterward a letter was received from Dr. Stanley Yolles, director of NIMH, asking for a delegation of Black psychiatrists to come discuss the matter brought up in the Gardner letter.

By means of a series of strategies and tactics by Blacks, it ended up that Dr. Yolles and his superior, Dr. Joseph English, arrived in Cambridge on April 12, 1969, to meet with a delegation of Black psychiatrists. This meeting took place at

Harvard University. Drs. Yolles and English answered questions about the organization of NIMH and, in fact, acted like the cordial friends we knew them to be from other contacts. Bureaucratic and political considerations may have kept them from acting more directly to help the Black cause. As individuals they were far, far more liberal than most Whites.

In frankness it has to be stated that the Harvard University meeting was of very limited value, chiefly due to the emotional overreaction of several Black psychiatrists, who declined to behave in a previously agreed-upon manner. Nevertheless, the meeting was profitable in that new allies were being included.

At the Harvard meeting there was a large contingent of Black psychiatrists from Washington, D.C., under the leadership of Dr. Charles Prudhomme, Black America's senior psychoanalyst. In addition, there were psychiatrists from as near as Boston and as far as Los Angeles. The importance of the Washington group cannot be overstated, however, since their local organization of fifty-five Black psychiatrists had the biggest concentration of Black psychiatrists in the land. This organization in the Washington and Baltimore area was called the Black Alliance of Psychiatrists.

It was after Drs. Yolles and English departed that the Blacks decided that we must proceed on plans to organize nationally and that we must articulate our wants to the White psychiatric establishment. Thus the mandate was given to organize at the May 1969 meeting in Miami, although organizational talk had been bruited about for some months. This information was circularized to Black psychiatrists all over the land.

Stage 4: The American Psychiatric Association Confrontation

On May 5, 1969, a number of Black psychiatrists at the Miami meeting began to discuss what we should articulate. That evening about one hundred Blacks at the American

Psychiatric Association (APA) meeting held an election making me the chairman and Dr. Cannon the vice-chairman. By May 6, the demands of the caucus had been elaborated. The framers of the demands and resolutions were Drs. James Comer of New Haven, Conn.; Hiawatha Harris of Los Angeles, Cannon, and Pierce. These demands were discussed and modified with all the Black psychiatrists present on Wednesday, May 7. The framers of the demands had selected as its working group the "Executive Committee," which was announced after the group approved the demands. It was the task of this Executive Committee to take the demands of the Black Psychiatrists to the Board of Trustees of the American Psychiatric Association.

The morning of Thursday, May 8, 1969, while the trustees breakfasted, the Blacks presented their demands. President Raymond Waggoner of the University of Michigan then continued the discussions in a small session of his Board of Trustees and our Executive Committee. On May 8 a news conference was called by the Black Psychiatrists of America. The incoming and outgoing APA presidents (Raymond Waggoner and Lawrence Kolb of Columbia University) were with the Executive Committee members and answered questions put to them by the press.

It was here perhaps that one of the fundamental problems of our organization developed. By a slim margin the Blacks had agreed on May 5 to remain within the boundaries of the APA. The Executive Committee operating on that wish *always* thought the time would come for separation and that we should belong to the APA and NMA, and yet have our own organization of the same people in order to give ourselves more flexibility and latitude. Having the press conference with two APA presidents may have delayed separation. Yet the establishment we first had to challenge was the most powerful professional organization in American psychiatry. The demands we articulated still are mostly unmet; however, some may view our progress as extremely salutary. The next section of this chapter is devoted to our basic and initial efforts in effecting change in American psychiatry.

The Basic Efforts

Where, then, could the Black Psychiatrists hope to work in order to effect change in the lives of all Americans both Black and White? While this question was being cogitated, the group got the vital assistance of the Maurice Falk Medical Fund of Pittsburgh. A generous grant allowed the group to work toward its goals. Fluid funds were necessary in order for key members of the organization to travel, to meet each other, and to communicate.

The APA

As a result of the caucus, ten demands were thrashed out. There was general endorsement of the demands, but at this writing, nearly two years later, there is still much to be desired. In *Item* 1 the demand for a task force of Black psychiatrists was granted. In essence the Executive Committee was given the status of a committee (therefore the Executive Committee had the use of travel monies and the chance to bring data to the attention of the president).

Item 2 called for a significant increase in Black members on APA committees, task forces, and positions of responsibility and decision-making. Since May 1969 the number of Blacks on national committees, commissions, task forces, and councils has increased by at least a factor of six. The group mobilized considerable political effort to place Dr. Charles Prudhomme on the ballot for the vice-presidency of the American Psychiatric Association. One group of Whites contested this name on the ballot (an almost unprecedented action in the history of elections of vice-presidents). Only the charity of Dr. Prudomme kept this incident from being inflamed since, at the very time it occurred, Black students at Howard, angry at not having seen a Black psychiatrist in their first two years of medical school, were looking for an issue to justify their strike. Many who signed the petition to place a White man on the ballot against Dr. Prudhomme were Whites teaching psychiatry, that is, interpersonal relations, to Blacks at Howard. Fortunately a combination of pressures and events caused the rival candidate to withdraw. Another part of item 2, however, called for the immediate appointment of five Blacks onto the APA Board of Trustees. This demand was turned down on the basis of being unconstitutional since trustees are elected by the general membership. The trustees did appoint Black "consultant-observers" to each of the APA councils as an alternative.

Item 3 urged the APA to be more rigorous in effecting desegregation of mental health facilities. As far as I know, no effort has been expended in this direction except to reiterate a resolution saying in effect that the APA endorses democracy. Legal pitfalls are alleged to be of concern if the APA becomes too active politically. Further, besides the fund loss in terms of the benefits resulting from being a nonprofit organization, there was a real concern about the sympathy of the total membership in regard to this issue.

For the same stated reasons the American Psychiatric Association has not taken, to my knowledge, a powerful position about recruiting more Black residents, faculty, and medical students, as demanded in *Item* 4. Yet there is much interest by significant individuals in the APA to move in this direction. The Manpower Commission, for instance, established during the tenure of President Dan Blain (1963), has done a great deal to show the problems that result from failure to utilize more Blacks. Moreover, as of this spring the Medical Education Committee has come out with a set of strong endorsements to the benefit of the Black cause, including the suggestion that, if training funds from the federal government are curtailed, Blacks should be given preference for what funds happen to be available. But the question remains, Where do the endorsements go and with what force?

It may be instructive to state that the set of liberal recommendations made by the APA Medical Education Committee was made while the author met with it in his capacity as representative from the Medical Education Council. These recommendations, therefore, were sent to the Board of Trustees via the approval of this Medical Education Council. This is an example of the value of having Blacks participate in the shaping of ideas and their dissemination.

Item 5 is difficult to evaluate. Since in fact many more Blacks are now known to the APA establishment, they are more likely to be considered in leadership and planning roles than formerly. However, this involvement has not yet reached an entirely satisfactory level, even when it comes to planning to involve Black people. As of spring 1971, plans were afoot, without Black input, concerning Africans who were to be trained by the United States. From its inception the Black Psychiatrists had emphasized the need to have Blacks be involved in planning for international programs, particularly when those programs involved Blacks.

In my opinion the item which may have had the most far-reaching impact has to do with our attempt to get the APA to use its influence in getting Black psychiatrists' ideas about the mental health of children before the Congress. This was not successful, nor in fact were our own efforts to mobilize Black child psychiatrists to take a leadership role in securing informed opinions about the recommendations to be made by the Joint Commission on Mental Health for Children from psychiatrists, teachers, nursery school workers, mothers, etc. In a separate book now being edited, the author is writing a couple of chapters dealing with the formation and function of the Committee on Minorities of the Joint Commission on Mental Health for Children. Suffice it to say at this time that Black psychiatrists must be held remiss in their failure to help make all Black America realize the enormity of the consequences of proposed legislation affecting children that would spend in the vicinity of $10 billion per year. Hence *Item* 6, an important concern, must continue to seize the attention of any Black interested in the emotional and mental welfare of Black citizens when the twenty-first century arrives.

The APA was encouraged to use its influence to help reduce the racism at NIMH. As far as I know this *Item, number 7,* also was never given actual energy by the APA. There have been very salutary changes at NIMH compared with the conditions there in 1964. Most of these developments have taken place since 1969, and the Black Psychiatrists of America take some credit for initiating the pressures which have rendered some change. Doubtlessly, a host of other political and social considerations were in operation. Yet two points can be made cautiously by the historian. On the one hand, the APA did not as an organization apply significant pressure at NIMH on behalf of the non-White minorities. On the other hand, we see again the operation of the lesson in Black-White relations in this country that states that any gain is made under the accompaniment of constant Black force and dissatisfaction. The Black Psychiatrists continued, despite pitiably puny resources, to press for more things from NIMH.

It is pleasant to report that *Item* 8, which demanded office space and staff at APA headquarters, resulted in the APA's agreeing (one year after the demand) to hire a Black psychiatrist, full time in a staff position. The original job description for this position was written initially by Drs. Pierce and Cannon from their seats on the APA Manpower Commission. However, it is easy progress, and such easy reports fail to reflect the nuances and battles required for the most simple objective. For instance, somehow this job position related to the most unpleasant struggle the new organization undertook. Shortly after we began, the APA decided to use public-grant funds to conduct a survey of the Office of Economic Opportunity programs. A White psychiatrist was hired for this task. Due to strenuous objections by our group, which took the view that a Black should have this title, the study was postponed.

In essence we had blocked a White from a job which past tradition would indicate would project this man into a role of Black expert. His opinions might weigh heavily on legislative spending or the institution of new programs. We had objections about this principle more than we did about the specific individual. We believed that Blacks should be made into Black experts and that Blacks might be better able to assess and evaluate predominantly Black programs. It is a regret to report that the whole project was put into abeyance presumably because of the intractable attitude of our group and our own failure to provide alternative solutions. But human events steer by serendipity. Thus this event in contesting the APA Board of Trustees and staff gave us vigor and confidence in our early weeks of life. And it led to the increasingly persistent demand for a full-time staff appointee.

As is the reaction of most American institutions, APA did not deal with the content of *Item* 9. Thinking Blacks in 1969 or 1970 would not expect a professional organization of about nineteen thousand to be vociferous and tough in denying memberships to those who discriminate in their practices against Blacks. The APA rebuttal was easy since it could be stated that an allegation of this sort against any member would be extremely difficult to prove.

Finally *Item* 10, which dealt with the relative lack of Black employees in the convention site, was not listened to with any urgency for change. In truth, however, I can report only that I do not know if more than usual sensitivity for this item was regarded in the selection of future meeting sites.

There are a couple of other places where our group tried to influence American psychiatry. We took a strong antiwar stance. So it was that, prior to the 1970 annual meeting in San Francisco, our group was on record to the president-elect of the APA (Dr. Robert Garber) that we believed the APA had to take more action to make known its abhorrence of war and the emotional damage caused by continuing our involvement in the Vietnam War.

Finally it was our hope that the APA might take a more

long-range view about mental health problems and decide that the time has come to act to insure requisite Black re-search skill. Our people and therefore the nation will be diminished if there are insufficient Blacks able to participate in scientific research. Too many pressures are pushing our youth toward "community" careers. This is well and good, but special protection must be rendered to select, nurture, and develop certain Black psychiatrists to become top-flight investigators.

The NIMH

Enough has been said about our efforts to effect change at NIMH. During our early years the negotiation for a minority center with NIMH was deemed to be our number one short-term goal. This delicate negotiation was in the capable hands of Dr. James Comer. The chief has now been appoint-ed, Dr. James Ralph, and the Center for Minority Group Mental Health Programs is in operation (see chapter 14). Naturally enough, from the beginning, we took the position that the director should be a Black psychiatrist. We initiated the plan to invite other minorities and other disciplines to negotiate with us at NIMH both because it was morally correct and politically necessary. Yet, not only because we began the proceedings but because we feel we are the ba-rometer minority (and the largest and perhaps the best edu-cated) in this country, we felt that we should have a more significant role in the formation and early functioning of any center. Let me anticipate some objections by saying that, in the course of my year as chairman, I wrote perhaps one thousand letters (each having carbon copy recipients) about our organization. Dozens of those reflect an unswerving be-lief in the necessity for minorities in the United States to collaborate (and many of the letters are to Spanish-speaking and Indian allies). Further, these minorities must band to-gether with others in the rest of the Third World. Black America's most crucial contribution has to be in leading such an organization due to the sheer numbers of educated Blacks available to lend meaningful collaboration; for example, if tomorrow this country had to provide the entire personnel for a first-class medical school or engineering school, Black America could export such schools (but of course nowhere near what it should be able to do as a part of the general population of the United States).

Other activity with NIMH has been an attempt to step up recruiting of Blacks on both an intramural and extramural basis. This project was delegated to Dr. Joseph R. Phillips of Nashville, Tenn. He kept on the project team with a tenacity. I can report that in the two years since we began systematic pressures more Blacks have been recruited at all levels by NIMH. We feel that our group helped bring about some of this change.

What I cannot report, because the information is unavailable, is how many Blacks have now sat on committees dealing with the disposal of funds.

American Board of Psychiatry and Neurology

Another institution in this country that the Black Psychiatrists looked at was the American Board of Psychiatry and Neurology. We reasoned that if the written and oral examinations were altered to include more material of relevance to minorities there would come about a shift in the training of physicians and psychiatrists.

In order to accomplish this goal we believed it was necessary to get a Black onto the Board of Directors of the American Board of Psychiatry and Neurology. The next vacancy to occur on this Board after the organization formed would be that held by the APA representative. Thus the APA could make recommendations to the Board for replacement.

Dr. Hugh Butts of New York City began making inquiries of the American Board. His aim was to find out how many Blacks had been examiners, how did Blacks fare on taking the exam, which Blacks sought certification. Underlying these questions was the assumption that, by teaching more about Blacks and non-Whites, the training of all psychiatrists could be augmented and made more valuable to the service of our times. Furthermore, in order for departments and hospitals to provide this sort of teaching, it meant that non-Whites had to be included in patient loads, and, more important, that a more perspicacious faculty supervision would be necessary. Thus there could be indirect yields in regards to the number of Black faculty and students.

By May 1970 the American Board of Psychiatry and Neurology had designated the author for the directorship to be made vacant in December 1970 by its outgoing president, Dr. Walter Barton. This was done after the recommendation by the APA. Dr. Jeanne Spurlock, chairman of the Department of Psychiatry at Meharry Medical College, declined the invitation to join the Board due to the pressures of her other responsibilities. I believe that, had she accepted, it would have been the first time a woman had been a director of the Board.

Newsletter

The budding organization of Black Psychiatrists of America was obliged to perform Hegelian syntheses concerning long-range versus short-range goals. As indicated, the chief short-range goal was accomplished under the sagacity and diplomacy of Dr. James Comer. The establishment of the center, as an immediate objective, should however have continuing long-term effects.

Early in our thinking it was deemed important to have a variety of communications to bring us together, to keep everyone informed of ongoing progress, to help disseminate job opportunities, to exchange experiences while learning who we were, where we were located, and what we did. The best way of accomplishing this would be by having an elaborate computerized registry which received and elaborated data to be sent to all Black psychiatrists. Dr. Lloyd Elam, now president of Meharry Medical College, and the author began planning such a registry in Toronto, Canada, in 1961. A more practical and immediate method would be to establish a newsletter. This was made the chief intermediate goal.

We are indebted to Dr. James Ralph not only for volunteering to put out the newsletter of the Black Psychiatrists of America, but also for recruiting the money necessary for the undertaking. The patron of our communication became the Shepherd Enoch Pratt Hospital, Baltimore, Md.

To his everlasting credit, Dr. Ralph managed to put out the first three editions of our newsletter. They were circulated free of charge to all our membership as well as to certain members of the medical and psychiatric power structure. The impact that these newsletters made on boosting our morale and making us aware of our potentialities cannot be exaggerated. We hoped too that the newsletter would become the medium through which we could increase our pride by keeping live the memories of our giants. Our first giant was indeed a genuine hero.

Solomon Fuller Institute

Professor Solomon Fuller trained all the first Black psychiatrists and many of the nation's top White psychiatrists. Living in Boston, he was a teacher and investigator of much distinction. In 1909 when Freud lectured at Clark University, Professor Fuller was on the same program, indicating the position he occupied in American medicine.

We will cherish Solomon Fuller's example and keep it before us by incorporating a nonprofit institute named for him. This institute will perform a variety of service, research, consultation, and teaching functions. Hopefully, it will be able to be a conduit through which can be funneled Black-oriented projects funded by government or private sources. The details of the institute have not been agreed upon, but it is hoped that all Black psychiatrists will have an allegiance to it and make it the hub around which a multitude of professional actions will take place. Currently, Dr. Robert Sharpley of Boston, Mass., is heading a team which is to give an opinion about where the institute should be located, what range of activities it should undertake, who should direct it, etc.

Dr. Sharpley was made treasurer of our organization on August 11, 1969, at a National Medical Association meeting in San Francisco. In May of 1970 in the same city, other formal organizational matters, such as the decision to make bylaws and to pay dues, were attended to. Already in that spring steps were taken to incorporate the Solomon Fuller Institute as one more evidence toward concerted unity.

Other Black Caucuses

The introduction of a concept of concerted unity demands a consideration of the obvious appropriateness of the Psychiatric Black Caucus to collaborate with other Black caucuses, particularly those in the mental health fields. As it turned out, in the first year our collaboration for the most part was only at the level of exchanging communication.

This was no small accomplishment, however, and when it is realized that our prime natural ally in the mental health field, the Black Caucus of Psychologists, was made aware of each move we made or intended to make, one can grasp the spin-off value. Not one of the one thousand letters sent from my office, for instance, was not seen first by Mrs. Ernestine Thomas, a consultant and liason administrator between the two caucus groups. Oftentimes Mrs. Thomas would be a formal recipient of a carbon copy. But at all times she was shown the correspondence. This chanced to be convenient because Mrs. Thomas was on the Harvard staff and quite literally was officed in the same module as myself.

Furthermore, we did make valiant and repeated efforts to meet our brothers. A particularly informative and gratifying exchange took place in San Francisco during our first year's operation. Drs. Cannon and Pierce met with members of others caucuses, including Dr. Charles Thomas, the national chairman of the Black Psychologists. A major limitation to our further collaboration was that all of us were in the throes of organizing ourselves. Doubtlessly, in coming years such collaborative efforts will be routine and effective, but in the early years the struggle to survive took precedence. From the viewpoint of the Black Psychiatrists, we had a more definite work plan than the other groups. Yet, just as in our negotiations for a center or for jobs at NIMH, our teams always insisted that other Black caucuses be included. In fact, we told them of our position so that they could delegate whom they wished to work with us.

In these dealings we discovered more and more about the importance of plans and the need for fluid funds. It was in this fabric that we saw one of our master designs. However, we have not been able to get any of the cloth.

Foundation Boards

Decision-making capacity at the level of money allocation again was the generating force leading us to try to find ways to get more Blacks on foundation boards. We had hoped to get Blacks placed in national situations where psychiatric knowledge would be useful when funds were dispensed. The sorts of boards we considered ranged from voluntary mental associations through medical foundations.

Recognizing the complexity of the task, we should be pleased with our record. In one instance, a member was placed on a board in which we and our psychologist colleagues had exerted what efforts we could. Whether or not these efforts were persuasive, we have no way of knowing.

However, in the second instance Dr. Alvin Poussaint, now associate dean of the Harvard Medical School, was placed on a mass media board after our group had interceded with a former board member, Mrs. Fran Morris of Oklahoma City. Mrs. Morris led a long arduous fight on behalf of our candidate. Great was our joy to have a Black on a mass media board (American Women in Radio and Television). To our way of thinking, this should be the direction of the future for Black psychiatrists. We had hoped to get Blacks placed on other boards, but we did not succeed. However, we had better results in our effort to get Blacks onto editorial boards.

Editorial Boards

We calculated that Black expertise in mental health should be of value in diluting the isolating effects of racism if Blacks were on the editorial boards of trade, lay, and professional journals. Again our zeal promoted desires to have Blacks as editorial consultants on trade publications in mass media. However, we would welcome the opportunity to place Black psychiatrists on the boards of a vast array of publications.

Naturally, we raised the question of putting Blacks on the learned journals in psychiatry. Before we could articulate this concern to the *American Journal of Orthopsychiatry*, its editor-in-chief, Dr. Leon Eisenberg of Boston, Mass., another long-time friend to our cause, requested Drs. Comer and Pierce to join his editorial board.

When the issue was brought to the APA concerning the desirability of having a Black on the editorial board of the *American Journal of Psychiatry*, we ran into a problem which confounded us from the start. Many of the positions in the APA require that the appointee be a Fellow in the organization. Unfortunately a disproportionately low percentage of people of color have been elevated to Fellowship. The reason for this dearth needs to be clarified and rectified. In general, it seems that Blacks do not participate in sufficient quality or quantity at the district branch levels of the APA. Further, since for most of us Fellowship confers no special privilege, we have been lackadaisical in its pursuit.

At any rate, following the search for Fellows who might be appropriately qualified to be on the *American Journal of Psychiatry* editorial board, the author was appointed. I am also on the Board of *Psychiatry Digest*. I am not sure whether there are Blacks on other editorial boards. What I am sure about is that there are too few Blacks on editorial boards. Of course, we must keep in sight that we must be training young Blacks who could someday become editors-in-chief.

Incidentally, local APA interest has seized more Black psychiatrists. The state of Missouri can be singled out since it has produced local state-level district branch presidents in Drs. Charles Wilkinson and John Anderson. Dr. Anderson is from St. Louis.

The Executive Committee gave much thought to how we could interest our youth in organized psychiatry. In the early 1960s when I attended an APA meeting as a state delegate, I was told that no other Black had ever voted in the assembly. The APA and older Black psychiatrists must find ways of extending our participation not only to get appointments to decision-making arenas such as editorial boards, but also to anticipate and participate in the direction of American psychiatry in such movements as community mental health.

From day one of our existence, we have stressed the need to have those just out of residency and those in residency take active leadership. The best example of such a leader is found in the person of Dr. Gail Burton Allen of New York City, the first secretary of our group. Dr. Allen was able to secure our greatest foundation support from the Grant Foundation. With these monies she initiated the Black Psychiatrists of America film project.

Black Psychiatrists of America Film Project

Probably the most important administrative task is choosing key people. In this regard my chairmanship was made easy by three critical selections: Drs. Comer, Ralph, and Allen, who worked with the most vital of our needs. Coupled with this task, in terms of the long-range goal, the understanding and manipulation of the mass media must also be the special province of Black psychiatrists.

The author was greatly influenced by the manner in which

Sesame Street was planned by the Children's Television Workshop. It was my privilege to participate in these planning sessions and to continue as a member of its National Advisory Board. The format of brainstorming with people from professions, from the creative arts, and from the community was very compelling.

Accordingly, Dr. Allen was persuaded to use such a format in seeking new ways to make films for Black children. Over the course of a year, the film project had such brainstorming sessions, enjoying the input of many dedicated individuals from all over our land — some famous, some obscure, but all willing and eager to find ways to help Black children. This project was helped immensely by the consultation and continued support of Mrs. Joan Ganz Cooney, the president of Children's Television Workshop and the originator of Sesame Street.

At this time the project has found a number of exciting production ideas. The project occupies space in the quarters of the Children's Television Workshop in New York City. We are seeking funds to complete our first film, an animation of a true incident that occurred in a ghetto kindergarten. We think we will be able to do new and impactful things for Black children.

Our project has built into it large components for evaluating and assessment, on the one hand, and for training and development, on the other hand. The basic philosophy of the films will be to increase the child's awareness of the microaggressions he suffers and teach him how to deal with them. This theory, now published (Pierce 1970c), was elaborated at an unusual laboratory: the football practice fields of Harvard, where I worked during the fall of 1969 as an assistant coach of the freshman team.

An ideal would be to reach a state in which every Black would be an expert demographer who knew antipropaganda techniques. We would expect such a person to have hope, and, in the sense that he would control his destiny, he would have a positive self-image and group image. He would be able to unify his community (the inner city) and cooperate to make it a vibrant, dynamic, cosmopolitan place, controlled by his group. To us, films seem to be one way to arrive at this state. Thus as more Blacks are trained and as more Blacks operate, say, cable TV stations, more Black psychiatrists should be learning about mass media techniques. We must be informed about cassettes and about geosynchronous satellites which can beam material all over the world. A trip to Europe is scheduled for several of us so that we can become informed about special film techniques.

Still another aspect of the Black Psychiatrists of America film project is a TV monitoring study. The funds for this come from the Markle Foundation, whose president, Dr. Lloyd Morrisett, is president of the Board of Trustees of the Children's Television Workshop. With this money we are developing more sophisticated techniques of observation and recording the nuances of White-Black behavior as witnessed over television.

Miscellaneous

There are items too numerous to mention that have occupied our organization in its early years. We are proud, for instance, that a couple of our grants were given to the Roxbury Action Program to administer. George Morrison, its director, aided us greatly, and we are happy that a Black community organization got the overhead of the grant. Similarly, we are obliged to Vernon Jordan of the United Negro College Fund who administered one grant gratuitously. This is another glad sign of cooperation among Black folk.

During the course of the year, some of us have testified or otherwise been involved in the Black Panther trials in New York and New Haven. We have discussed the need to involve ourselves in the problems of drug addiction. Answers are slow in coming, however.

Also the Black Psychiatrists of America initiated a project

through Columbia University in which we hope to bring Black doctors from Africa and Latin America to our cities. Our Black doctors will visit foreign countries too, in an effort to make Blacks see that we can be contributors rather than always being contributed to and, in addition, to build bonds of solidarity with our Black brothers everywhere. Accordingly, several of us plan to visit Africa in an effort to cement the details of this program, which we hope will gain wide-based support from all Black doctors. Incidentally, some of us are now corresponding members of the newly formed Association of Psychiatrists of Africa.

Propinquity has dictated that our eyes turn southward before we gaze to the east. It is our dream that in the not too remote future we will actualize projects with our brothers in Latin America. It was our honor and delight that Dr. Michael Beaubrun, chairman of the Department of psychiatry at the University of the West Indies, joined all our sessions in Miami. Another who has extended friendship to us from that time was Dr. Angel Gomez of Puerto Rico. The Executive Committee succeeded in bringing to the attention of White planners of Latin American conferences the special qualities of Dr. Jamie Smith e Incas, a Peruvian-born, American-educated Black psychiatrist on the faculty of the Ohio State University. Dr. Smith e Incas, who is fluent in Portuguese, Spanish, and Quechua and thoroughly versed in South American culture, should prove an asset to such conferences. Incidentally, much of our first year's effort was directed in bringing qualified individuals to the attention of interested parties.

Present Directions

Throughout this chapter present directions have been indicated as natural growth from projects already initiated. Thus in the APA we must do more to get our doctors elevated to Fellowship so that they can participate in the organization at its critical levels. Also, we need to increase our tie with federal, state, and local legislators and officials both Black and White. We must continue to search the literature for references on race by Black psychiatrists (Dr. Sharpley completed such a bibliography last year).

Dr. Charles Prudhomme has donated an oil painting of Solomon Fuller to the APA. There is a precedent of such donations from outgoing vice-presidents, but Dr. Prudhomme had decided to get the painting done for the benefit of the posterity before he was aware of such a tradition. Even more meaningful is the fact that Dr. Prudhomme and Dr. Montague Cobb, the venerated editor of the *Journal of the National Medical Association*, are undertaking a historical study of Solomon Fuller.

It is a pleasure to write that the Black Psychiatrists of America, after two years in existence, offered several special awards in the spring of 1971. The honorees were two Black psychiatrists and one Black general practioner. Drs. Charles Wilkinson and Charles Prudhomme were honored for their singular struggles to energize Black psychiatry. Dr. Robert Smith of Jackson, Miss., was rewarded for his incredible battles in the Civil Rights War.

Dr. Frances Bonner of Boston is deliberating over the role of psychoanalysis in the lives of Black psychiatrists and Black communities. The implications of this deliberation and what actions stem from it can have far-reaching effect. These are present directions that have been started, and I am sure they will continue.

Conclusion

Our organization is too organic, too fervent, to use a word such as "conclusion." I will end by stating what I hope have been and will continue to be intrinsic conditions for our existence. I hope we never lose sight of the fact that we must live in the future and as such our special strength must be utilized to help our children. I hope we develop a "conveyer belt" so that young leaders will be helped into significant and responsible positions. After they work in that position for an abbreviated time and they have surveyed the factors driving American medicine, they should step off the belt so that someone else can be given the view and so that we can spread our talents and broaden our expertise. I hope too that we never lose our desire to include youthful colleagues at all entry points of our proceedings.

Now there is a feeling of *déjà vu*. In the early 1960s, while others were toasting HEW, some were in thirst for something more, something like a powerful minority center at NIMH. A center is here, but its power is yet to come. Even so, many of my White colleagues are ready to quench thirst by a toast to the new center. But Blacks have a terrible dryness. Hence, they look about and realize that in the final analysis the only way that thirst can be slaked is by a massive and unprecedented commitment of effort and resources by White America. This is the only way that in two generations from now no person in this country will have to pause a millisecond a day in concern about skin color. This is the only way that the managers of American life can be seen on this globe as legitimate.

So once again one should look to the federal government to begin an inroad and to assume leadership. Perhaps the first step would be to establish a National Institute of Minority Affairs, funded with sufficient money and legislative teeth to allow it to complete its mission and eliminate itself by 2100. Such an institute would be charged with correcting the contagious and lethal mental health and public health illness, racism.

Our needs are great. Our time is short. We shall endure. We will prevail. To all who have read these words this far, I render the valediction of Black brothers on the streets, "Peace and Black blessings."

Note: The formation of the Black Psychiatrists of America involved a considerable amount of work that was carried out through letters and other documents. This material, which is written verification of the historical facts, is available for inspection from the files of Dr. Pierce and Dr. Gail Allen, the organization's first secretary. Inquiries should be made to Dr. Pierce.

REFERENCES

Pierce, C. M.

1959.   A psychiatric approach to present day racial problems. *J. Nat. Med. Assoc.* 51:207–10.

1968a.   Is bigotry the basis of the medical problems in the ghetto? In *Medicine in the ghettos,* ed. John C. Norman. New York: Appleton-Century-Crofts.

1968b.   Manpower: the need for Negro psychiatrists. *J. Nat. Med. Assoc.* 60 (1):30–33.

1968c.   Possible social science contributions to the clarification of the Negro self-image. *J. Nat. Med. Assoc.* 60 (2):100–03.

1968d.   Problems of the Negro adolescent in the next decade. In *Minority group adolescents in the U.S.,* ed. Eugene Brody, pp. 17–47. Baltimore, Md.: Williams and Wilkins.

1969a.   Our most crucial domestic issue. *Am. J. Psychiat.* 125:1583–84.

1969b.   Violence and counterviolence: the need for a children's domestic exchange. *Am. J. Orthopsychiat.* 39:553–68.

1970a.   Black psychiatry one year after Miami. *J. Nat. Med. Assoc.* 62 (62):471–73.

1970b.   Effect of television on equal educational opportunity. In *Hearings before the Select Committee on Equal Educational Opportunity of the U.S. Ninety-First Congress,* pp. 948a–928m. Washington, D.C.: U.S. Government Printing Office.

1970c.   Offensive mechanisms. In *The black seventies,* ed. Floyd Barbour, pp. 265–82. Boston, Mass.: Porter Sargent.

1970d.   Research and careers for Blacks. *Am. J. Psychiat.* 127:817–18.

1970e.   Xenophobes and cosmopolites? *Am. J. Orthopsychiat.* 40:560–61.

1971.   New modes of education: the pre-school years. Paper presented at the First General Assembly of the World Future Society, Washington, D.C., May 14.

Pierce, C. M., and West, L. J. 1968. Six years of sit-ins: psychodynamic causes and effects. *Int. J. Soc. Psychiat.* 12:29–34.

CHAPTER 14

Key Issues in Developing a National Minority Mental Health Program at NIMH

by Frank M. Ochberg
Bertram S. Brown

Given in this chapter is the administrators' perspective, reviewing the issues which were debated and clarified prior to the establishment of a federal center to deal with minority mental health concerns. Problems of conflicting ideologies, questions of priority, and concerns related to bureaucratic details which are explored here can be generalized to other programs currently being designed to meet minority group needs, in schools, in industry, in communities, and in government.

On November 19, 1970,. Secretary Elliot Richardson announced the establishment of the Center for Minority Group Mental Health Programs within the National Institute of Mental Health. He explained that the new center would serve as a focal point for all activities within the institute which bear directly on meeting the mental health needs of minority groups, including programs of research, training, services, and demonstration projects (see Appendix 14.1, "HEW Press Release, November 19, 1970"). Culminated in this announcement were two years of formal and informal negotiations between leaders of the Black Psychiatrists of America and the National Institute of Mental Health officials—years characterized by organization of Black psychiatrists (see chapter 13), forceful criticism by Black professionals of federal agencies for their failure to include more Blacks in decision-making roles and an acceleration of equal employment opportunity activities in federal government.

At the American Psychiatric Association meetings in May 1969, a caucus of Black psychiatrists led by Dr. Chester Pierce of Harvard University selected Dr. James Comer, associate dean of Yale Medical School, as their liaison representative to NIMH. One month later Dr. Comer, along with Dr. J. Alfred Cannon of the University of California School of Medicine and Dr. Joseph R. Phillips of Nashville, Tenn. represented the Black caucus in a meeting with the director and deputy director of the institute. There were two important results of this meeting. One was a commitment by the leadership of the NIMH to establish an identifiable organizational unit to foster the development of mental health programs for minority groups. The other was a plan for a special effort in the recruitment of minority personnel for NIMH. Staff work for this recruitment effort was delegated to the chief of personnel of NIMH and Dr. Phillips, who expanded the task force to an eight-man group comprised of NIMH staff and outside consultants. Separate strategies were designed to implement each of these objectives.

Several critical issues relating to the first objective, the establishment of a minority center, surfaced in this meeting and were elaborated over the ensuing year. A review of these key points is the subject of this chapter. It should be clearly understood that this review is based on the observations of two administrators who were actively involved in the discussions, decisions, and events described throughout this chapter. Therefore, this is not objective history. It is a presentation of issues and events which are still fresh and subject to lively debate.

A brief description of the National Institute of Mental Health will provide a context for understanding these issues.

The Institute

The institute provides national leadership for the improvement of mental health through the conduct and support of

programs for the discovery and demonstration of new knowledge; the training and development of specialized manpower; and the inauguration, demonstration, and support of services to promote and sustain mental health, prevent mental
illness, and treat and rehabilitate mentally ill persons. The
NIMH also serves as a principal focus for behavioral science
activities and for the study of cultural and social problems
related to mental health. It is part of the executive branch of
the federal government, located within the Health Services
and Mental Health Administration of the Department of
Health, Education, and Welfare. The annual budget (as of
this writing in mid-1971) of approximately $400 million is
divided roughly into four quarters of close to $100 million
each for support of research, training, community mental
health services, and special programs. The special programs
include narcotics addiction and drug abuse, alcoholism, suicide, crime and delinquency, child and family mental health,
aging, and metropolitan problems (see figure 14.1). As national concern and demand for federal programs in certain of
these specific areas have increased, budgets have expanded
and organizational changes have occurred. A striking example of this is the national program for alcoholism, which
grew from a center within a division of special programs to a
full division, to an institute within the National Institute of
Mental Health – all in the year 1970.

Although the scope and hopefully the impact of some of
these targeted programs have increased in recent years, the
total institute budget, after a period of vigorous growth in the
1950s and 1960s, has leveled off. Since costs continue to
escalate beyond federally budgeted resources, these recent
years have been marked by serious reductions in the support
of mental health research, training, and service programs.
Furthermore, the presidential policies of grant consolidation,
regionalization, and revenue-sharing challenge the ability of
centralized national programs to mount new initiatives.

In the context of these financial and administrative trends,

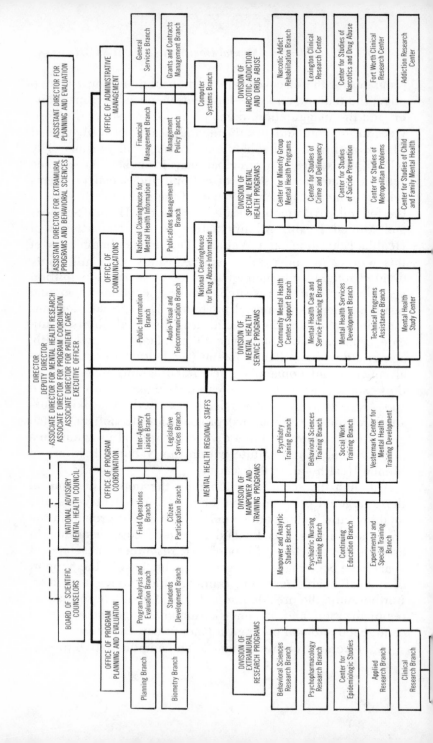

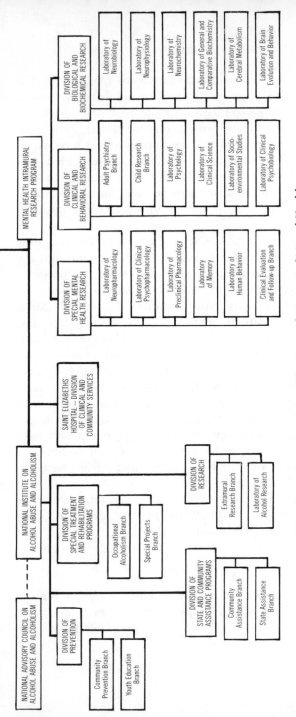

FIGURE 14.1. Organization of the National Institute of Mental Health

three new major programmatic thrusts were planned by the leadership of NIMH in mid-1970: (1) children's mental health programs, (2) programs relating to violence and social deviance, and (3) minority group mental health programs. Plans for implementing the first two areas relied heavily on collaboration with other governmental agencies. Plans for implementing the third area, minority group mental health programs, initially focused on internal reorganization, transferring funds from existing programs to support new projects in the new center.

In the early planning phase, it was assumed that this new center could provide leadership in the development and application of fresh knowledge from the view of the minority groups. It could lend support to professional and nonprofessional training of minority group members. It could stimulate, support, and evaluate mental health service programs for minority groups. It could collect and disseminate information about mental health problems and resources related to cultural, ethnic, and racial issues. And it could advocate priorities within the institute based on mental health needs of minority groups. These missions are consistent with the general goals of the institute, responsive to needs forcefully outlined by minority-group proponents, congruent with federal emphasis on targeted programs in areas of great need, but counter to the trend in government away from new national categorical programs.

This, briefly, is the stage on which was set a vigorous debate over the concept, functions, powers, and pitfalls of establishing a minority center at NIMH.

Key Issues

Definition of minority.   Although early impetus for the establishment of a special center came from Black psychiatrists who proposed a program on aspects of Black community health utilizing Black professionals, agreement was quickly reached between leaders of the Psychiatric Black Caucus and NIMH that the concerns of other minority groups should be represented. But which other minority groups? The other racial minorities in America are Indians and Asian Americans. The former already have a federal health program with a significant mental health component: the Indian Health Service. The Asian Americans have seldom presented themselves as needing or wanting special health service benefits. On the other hand, Mexican Americans, Puerto Ricans, Cubans, and other Spanish-speaking citizens form a significant subgroup in America, have suffered restricted economic opportunities, have in many cases identified themselves as a minority group with specific problems and needs, and have requested new federal service programs to meet these needs. The Department of Health, Education, and Welfare in its Equal Employment Opportunity Program defines all of these groups as minorities: Negroes, Spanish Americans, American Indians, and Orientals (see Appendix 14.2). At this moment, the same definition of minority pertains for the Minority Center.

Specifically excluded from consideration as minority group members are White ethnic minorities and White women. Certain White ethnic groups have claimed to be victims of systematic discrimination and degradation. Some have sought government grants and contracts for research and services pertaining to their particular condition. Women in the labor force are a minority and have recently been organizing special efforts to rectify institutional practices and individual attitudes which serve to limit their freedom and opportunity. The decision not to include issues relating to White ethnics and White women within the purview of the Minority Center was pragmatic: a new, visible, specialized center with a limited budget could not serve the needs of too many discrete and different groups; racism is currently perceived as a more

destructive force than prejudice based on sex or ethnicity,
and therefore the racial minorities and Spanish Americans
were seen as warranting this special targeted program.

Relationships among minority groups. Defining the target populations as Negro, Spanish-American, American Indian, and Asian-American raises the question of how these
four separate groups can best be served by a single administrative entity. Must all racial groups be represented? Should
one group have a clearly defined leadership role? Should
efforts be made to develop separate programs for each minority group, or should one consolidated program be administered by all minority groups? In preliminary discussions
among members of the Black Psychiatrists group and the
NIMH staff, it was the institute personnel who argued for
adequate representation from other minority groups. Black
leaders observed that their current concern was for Black
people, that, while sympathetic to the plight of other minority groups in America, they found that combining ranks
among minority groups often diluted rather than strengthened their efforts. However, the Blacks felt that if the federal
government were going to force the American racial minorities to combine on this particular project, as the "majority
minority" they should be in charge.

Some opposition to this idea was voiced by Span-
ish-Amererican representatives in several meetings. Although they would not argue for a leadership role themselves, they wanted to be sure that their interests would not
be superseded by those of another group. The issue of the
relative status of Indian and Asian interests has never fully
surfaced. There are several possible explanations for this: the
number of Americans in these categories is relatively small.
There were no representatives of Indian or Asian-American
groups at early negotiations on the design of the Minority
Center. Asian Americans have not characteristically allied
with other American racial minorities to demand targeted
federal programs, and Indians have used the existing chan-

nels of the Bureau of Indian Affairs and the Indian Health Service, rather than creating new alliances. There are so few Indian mental health professionals that the identification of one or two to represent the total population of Indians in America poses a significant problem. There are many Asian-American mental health professionals but few whose racial identification and concern are as great as are those of the Black or Spanish-American professionals.

Several programmatic options relate directly to this issue of minority group relationships and relative power. The center could be organized along ethnic lines, with separate sections for Black, Spanish-American, Asian-American and Indian problems. This was actually suggested at one conference, with strong support from several Spanish-American representatives. Each section could then have its own budget determined by a capitation formula. On the one hand, this would maximize racial focus and prevent domination of the program by one racial group. On the other hand, it would undercut an opportunity for "Third World" cooperation, would necessitate a quadruplication of bureaucratic procedures, and, with little new money available for the total program, would result in meaninglessly small budgets for each of the four subgroups.

The issue of a segregated center.   Although it was stated early in 1969 that the National Institute of Mental Health should have a separate program conceived by and for minority group persons, debate about such a segregated center continues. Is it legal? Is it moral? Is it practical and in the best interests of the minority constituents themselves?

Some have argued that the creation of a new program with explicit responsibility for minority concerns would relieve other divisions of the institute of their responsibility to respond to these same concerns. Since the budget, power, and scope of these other divisions, particularly the Divisions of Extramural Research Programs, Manpower and Training Programs, and Mental Health Service Programs far exceed that of any center, this effect could be devastating. The Minority Center might then be a token response to the demands of the vocal minority groups and would be held responsibile for meeting these demands in the future, yet it would be relatively powerless to do so. Furthermore, concentration of the minority staff in one segment of the institute would bleed other divisions of their minority personnel. Arguments to the contrary have, so far, been convincing. Directors of the powerful Divisions of Research, Training, and Services have themselves pointed out the dangers of slackening an institutewide effort at upgrading minority mental health programs in response to the development of a new center and have called for even greater efforts to recruit minority staff and to develop programs relating to needs of minority persons in their own divisions. It was suggested that the presence of a critical mass of minority staff, hired within this new center, could attract more minority employees for other sections of the institute.

The question of reverse discrimination was raised when Black studies programs in certain federally subsidized colleges limited their enrollment to Black students, thereby jeopardizing federal support on the basis of racial discrimination. However, there is no legal sanction against devoting a single federal program to the problems of one or more disadvantaged groups. As long as recruitment for staff is not strictly limited to any race and no candidates are excluded from consideration because of race, the Federal Equal Employment Code is honored. Therefore, a segregated center is legal, but the segregation must be de facto and not de jure.

Hiring preference by race is based on the perceived importance of the experience of being a minority group member. The concept that problems of minority groups are best understood and solved by members of those minority groups is open to debate and raises the next set of issues.

Maintenance of professional standards. Should existing

standards of quality be applied in the recruitment of minority staff and in the selection of grantees to receive awards for research, training, and mental health service programs? Although existing standards of quality are seldom defined objectively, a panel of "experts" can usually reach agreement with fair reliability on whether or not a candidate or a program measures up. Some have argued that these experts base their common judgment on "White education" and that White insight is blind to Black problems. This argument holds that the traditional methods of inquiry and of education upon which we rely in this country have failed to break the cycle of minority group degradation, powerlessness, and ignorance, and therefore this White educational system must itself be broken. In advocating a rejection of traditional White standards of research and training, there may be posed an alternative emphasis on minority services. The obvious question has not been answered: "How are non-White standards of excellence in research and training to be defined?"

There are some who argue that the whole issue of White versus non-White standards is a sham. Science knows no color distinction. Methods of observation and verification are common to all people, and the crucial point is that *all* people have an opportunity to learn these basic skills which can then be applied in the service of humanity. The current NIMH research policy is to maintain traditional scientific standards and methods, but to experiment with innovative approaches. How this will be translated into a specific program for the Minority Center remains to be seen.

Scope and focus. The three integral component functions of the NIMH are research, training, and service. As described previously, separate divisions administer grants and contracts in these three areas at an annual budget level of approximately $100 million each. An "operating center" within the NIMH is one which provides any combination of these functions in a specific area. The Center for Studies of Suicide Prevention, for example, provides research grants in suicidology and funds professional and paraprofessional trainees in this field. Other centers, such as the one for child and family mental health, coordinate grant programs of the major divisions but provide no direct grants of their own. This type is known as a coordinating rather than an operating center.

The issue of whether the Minority Center should be an operating center was debated. This would mean that the bulk of minority mental health grants could be administered by the center. Arguments in favor of this arrangement included precedents and available blueprints for managing such a structure. This was seen as the simplest, most straightforward administrative plan for a new program; The center could be located within the Division of Special Mental Health Programs, along with a full spectrum of other operating and coordinating centers. The chief responsibility for all institute minority programs could be in the hands of minority people. A comprehensive operating center would allow for the best overview of minority mental health problems in America, the development of the most exhaustive registry of mental health personnel, and the stimulation of the greatest amount of minority mental health grants in all problems areas.

Opposing arguments were stated: a comprehensive program staffed with relatively inexperienced people could lower standards for research and training. A comprehensive center, with a small operating budget, would at best have a token impact on nationwide problems and at worst a deleterious effect by reducing the effort of all other divisions and centers in the area of minority mental health. Therefore, it was argued, the scope should be limited to either training or research and the center placed within the appropriate training or research division.

There were interesting points raised regarding the choice of a research or a training focus. Favoring research was the fact that curricula for training programs and basic concepts for developing service programs rely on available knowledge in order to be effective. Because of the lack of useful, tested knowledge relating to the mental health of minority groups, a research approach should be primary. Also, since research grants tend to be awarded for a shorter length of time than are training grants, it would be easier to free money for new research grants within the institute. Research is the area of highest prestige of the institute and should be opened to meaningful minority participation through this mechanism.

On the other hand, those who argued for a focus on training saw the immediate need for minority studies to be that of training researchers rather than doing research. If the greatest shortage of minority skills is in research, they observed, the quality of research will be low until training is improved. Furthermore, new trainees could fill staff positions throughout the institute leading to an increased awareness and understanding of minority mental health concerns in research, training, and service programs.

The exact purview and focus of the Minority Center was deliberately left unsettled for future consideration by the center's chief and his staff. However, authority for the broadest possible scope was granted by the administrator of Health Services and Mental Health Administration and supported by the secretary of HEW.

Style and emphasis. A staff group within NIMH debated whether the programs funded by the Minority Center should be innovative or traditional and whether the mental health personnel trained should be professionals or nonprofessionals. A relatively small program can have a large national impact if energies are targeted on one area of need or if a bold and imaginative new approach is developed. Mental health manpower needs in general are great, but one area of particular concern currently is training the nonprofessional or paraprofessional care giver. The present supply of psychiatrists, psychologists, social workers, and psychiatric nurses is inadequate to meet the national demand for mental health services, and the future supply of these professionals will be far more overburdened. It has been demonstrated convincingly that many of the mental health services currently performed by these professionals can well be administered by persons with less specialized education than that of fully trained professionals. So, it was argued that in order to prepare for future manpower needs, the Minority Center should emphasize training this new breed of nonprofessional. However, if a policy of training minority nonprofessionals and Caucasian professionals were to prevail throughout NIMH, the gap in career status between the races would only be widened. Therefore a counterargument was to place high priority on training minority professionals to do mental health research or even to emphasize training teachers of researchers, since such a program would have great impact on generations to come.

Similarly, an emphasis on traditional mental health research, such as "the etiology of depression and schizophrenia in a minority population," was seen as important by some from both a scientific and a political point of view. Tested research designs exist. There are important data to be gathered and analyzed in these areas. The risk of wasting money is lower in conventional programs. Gains would accrue not only to the general public, who would receive relevant public health information, but to the minority administrators, who would master the operation of conventional research-grant programs and could then experiment with innovative designs.

The opposition argument stressed the importance of discarding traditional public health models, of focusing on racism as a cause of physical and mental illness, and, particularly, of examining the effects of White racism on Whites. This side saw the greatest yield coming from a deliberately controversial and innovative research approach.

Again, these issues were not resolved and were deliberately left unresolved, to be decided after the hiring of a chief for the new center.

Power. Power within the federal bureaucracy is derived

from a complex interaction of variables and is considered quite differently from different perspectives. One over-simplified formula is that power is a function of budget size and access to those with even greater power. Therefore, the crudest power issues regarding this center were, "How big a budget?" and "Where does it stand on the organizational chart?" There was, at one point in the discussions between representatives of minority professionals and members of NIMH staff, debate over total budget size. However, the center was planned to begin operations before a new congressional appropriation could be requested, received, and allocated. (This process routinely takes two years.) Therefore the budget for operations and original programs had to be drawn from a limited fund of money within NIMH that was not obligated elsewhere. A fraction of this "free money" was set aside for the center. In addition, grants were earmarked in other parts of the institute for transfer to the Minority Center. This created a balance of new and continuing administrative responsibilities.

The organizational issue was also debated. At first the minority representatives wanted a full division with separate centers for the various minority groups. Most centers are one echelon lower than this or equivalent to branches of divisions. The advantage to NIMH of launching a Minority Center at a divisional level was the symbolism, establishing this area as one of highest priority for the institute and gathering the support of those minority consultants who favored this plan. There were convincing opposing arguments. Sufficient funds were not available to staff a division adequately in its first year of operations. A branch could easily grow into a division after a brief period of development, if the program warranted this administrative growth. Examples already existed in the drug and alcohol programs. Therefore, the issues were settled in favor of a center within the Division for Special Mental Health Programs.

Recruitment of a chief. After these questions were defined, discussed, and decided or deliberately left undecided until a center chief was selected, the issue of paramount importance was the selection of a chief. In the best of all possible worlds, this chief would satisfy all concerned. He (or she) would represent all minorities, all professionals, and all nonprofessionals; be experienced in research, training, and administration of service programs; and be skilled in bureaucratic manipulation while remaining an advocate for the concerns of several outside groups. A selection procedure was developed, involving wide advertising and an initial selection panel composed of representatives of several racial groups and professional disciplines from within and without NIMH. The advertisement for a center chief read as follows:

Position available: Chief, Center for Minority Mental Health Programs, National Institute of Mental Health. Salary—GS-15, $22,885–$29,752, or higher dependent on qualifications . . . [there followed a description of the goals of the Center]. The Chief, CMMHP, conceives, plans, and directs the Center program in training and utilization of the minority group members for mental health services, the improvement of services to minority groups, and the development of increased knowledge relevant to minority group issues.

Qualifications: Must have substantial experience in the administration or conduct of research, training, or service programs relating to urban and minority groups. Must have doctorate or its equivalent experience in one or more of the social, behavioral, or biomedical sciences.

All qualified applicants for the position were Black, so the sensitive issue of choice among various racial groups did not arise. However, the professional discipline of the chief was of great interest to several constituent groups, most particularly the Black Psychiatrists of America and the Association of Black Psychologists. In addition, the National Association of Black Social Workers and the Black Caucus of the American Public Health Association were concerned. The issue became not only one of getting a person with the most appropriate professional training for the job but also of finding a person who could represent the interests and approaches of a particular constituent group. On April 28, 1971, Dr. James Ralph, a thirty-nine-year-old psychiatrist from Baltimore, Md., was selected as the Center's chief.

Conclusion

The issues described above illustrate some of the practical problems and options which face an administrator who would respond to the special needs of minority groups in America with special efforts in their behalf. These needs are abundantly clear in the field of mental health:

1. Nationwide admission rates to both inpatient and outpatient psychiatric facilities are higher for non-Whites than for Whites.

2. Non-Whites show minimal use of private psychiatric facilities.

3. Puerto Ricans in New York State constitute 9.1 percent of first admissions to state schools for the retarded, while their proportion of the state population is only 4 percent.

4. The 1960 census indicated that 48 percent of the institutionalized non-Whites lived in hospitals and homes for the physically and mentally handicapped while 80 percent of the institutionalized Whites lived in such facilities. In contrast, 49 percent of the non-Whites were in correctional institutions compared with only 16 percent of the Whites. These data suggest vast inequities in the handling of behavior problems of persons from different social and racial backgrounds.

5. Available data reveal a pattern of exclusion of Negroes from health and related professions: Negroes constitute about 2 percent of all physicians, 1.8 percent of psychiatrists, 2 percent of psychologists, 5.6 percent of nurses, and 10.9 percent of all social workers. A recent study revealed that, be-

tween 1920 and 1966, the ten most prestigious departments of psychology in the United States granted only 8 Ph.D.s to Negroes out of a total of 3,767 Ph.D.s. Six of these departments did not grant a single Ph.D. to a Negro. The departments included in this study supply most psychologist consultants to federal training and research programs.

6. In 1969 one-third of the non-White households lived below the poverty level compared with 10 percent of the White.

7. The average length of life for White males is sixty-eight years, White females seventy-five, non-White males sixty-one, and non-White females sixty-eight.

8. Infant mortality rates were almost twice as high for non-Whites as for Whites in 1967 (36 per 100,000 for non-Whites, 20 per 100,000 for Whites).

9. Mortality rates for non-White babies are 58 percent higher than among Whites for those under one month old and almost three times as high among those from one month to one year old. One-third of all Indian infants die between the first month and first year of life — largely from preventable diseases. An Indian child's average life expectancy is only forty-three years.

10. Non-White families in 1962 with incomes under $2,000 spent less than one-half as much per person on medical services as did White families with similar incomes. While this discrepancy declined in families with annual incomes of $10,000 or more, total non-White medical expenditures per person averaged only 74.3 percent of White expenditures.

It is our contention that institutional rearrangements in service to these minority groups is crucial. To be effective, these rearrangements must involve a realistic sharing of power and expertise. Issues such as scope and focus of programs, initial levels of budget and administrative authority, innovative and professional styles, and standards of excellence will be difficult to resolve in a way that satisfies the majority of those who seek the institutional rearrangement. These issues are not limited to a federal health program, but pertain to schools, industries, and all levels of government.

The future of the Center for Minority Group Mental Health Programs at NIMH is uncertain. Until more data are available, we cannot draw conclusions, for our experience in institutional rearrangement in the service of minority group needs is limited. But this much is clear: in the next edition of this book, the chapter on minority centers will more likely be written by the staff of the Center for Minority Group Mental Health Programs than by two White administrators.

APPENDIX 14.1

HEW Press Release, November 19, 1970

The establishment of a Center for Minority Group Mental Health Programs within the National Institute of Mental Health was announced today by Bertram S. Brown, M.D., NIMH Director, on behalf of Secretary of Health, Education, and Welfare Elliot L. Richardson.

The announcement was made by Dr. Brown in an address at the 1970 Annual Meeting of the National Association for Mental Health in Los Angeles, California.

Secretary Richardson said, "The new Center will serve as a focal point for all activities within NIMH which bear directly on meeting the mental health needs of minority groups, including programs of research, training, services, and demonstration projects. This new Center, which will have a staff recruited from minority groups, will provide additional channels of communication between NIMH and minority communities. These will aid the Institute in developing and conducting a comprehensive program to help meet the mental health needs of minority groups in the United States."

According to Dr. Brown, the Center will administer programs of grant support for research to develop increased knowledge of minority groups, their relationships to other groups, and the particular mental health concerns in their communities.

Dr. Brown commented, "In our research programs, we look forward to supporting skilled persons from minority groups who will conduct studies of the problems of their own communities."

The new Center will also support projects designed to prepare minority group members for professional and paraprofessional careers in the mental health field.

According to Dr. Brown, "The Institute is conducting an

extensive effort to recruit a Chief for the Center from among minority groups. The new Chief will undertake the job of selecting the Center's staff and formulating the specific directions of its programs."

The Center for Minority Group Mental Health Programs will be a part of NIMH's Division of Special Mental Health Programs.

APPENDIX 14.2

292-4-30 from DHEW Personnel Manual

Updating Automated Minority Group Statistics

292-4-00   *Purpose*

This Instruction supplements FPM Letter 290-2,[1] "Automated Procedures for Processing Minority Group Statistics." It states the responsibility for the collection and maintenance of minority group statistics within DHEW, following the initial identification and collection of data used in preparing the 1969 Minority Census Report as requested by the Civil Service Commission.

292-4-10   *Responsibility*

A. The Director of the Equal Employment Opportunity Staff-Office of the Assistant Secretary for Administration, has the prime responsibility for the establishment, update, and maintenance of the automated minority identification file, in-

1. Note that FPM Letter No. 290-2 is published in advance of incorporation in FPM ch. 713.

cluding the release of any reports derived therefrom. Requests for all reports based on the minority group statistics must have the written approval of the Director, Equal Employment Opportunity Staff–Office of the Assistant Secretary for Administration.

B. The personnel office servicing employees will be responsible for furnishing input data on new and separated employees for updating the statistical file.

292-4-20   *Procedure For Updating Statistical File*

A. To assure the statistical data file is current, the addition of new employees and deletions of separated employees must be processed into the automated system on a regular two week cycle.

1. *Coverage.* This procedure covers all the full-time employees except those in Hawaii and the commonwealth of Puerto Rico and foreign nationals outside the United States.

2. *Effective Date.* These procedures are effective with actions processed on and after December 1, 1969.

3. *The servicing personnel office* that inducts the employee when he enters on duty will make a minority group identification. The employee's social security number and minority identification code will be recorded on a memorandum form

used for submitting the data to the Director, Equal Employment Opportunity Staff. (See X292-4-1 for sample of memorandum format).

4. *The social security number and minority code* will also be entered on the memorandum form for separated employees. The minority code need not be shown on separated employees if it is not readily available. However, when the employee is moving to another operating agency within DHEW the SPO number of the gaining office must be entered in the right hand field on the form opposite the social security number.

5. *Due dates.* The additions and deletions for each pay period are to be listed and sent to the Director — Equal Employment Opportunity Staff, Office of the Assistant Secretary for Administration. Room 5412, 330 Independence Avenue, S. W. Washington, D.C. 20201 by close of business Tuesday following the end of each pay period.

292-4-30   *Minority Group Designation*

The minority status of employees through visual observation will be coded according to the following minority group designations of race and national origin:

Code Designation

1. Negro — Persons having visual characteristics of this group and who are so regarded in the establishment where they

work or in the community where they live.

2. Spanish American—This group includes persons of Latin-American, Mexican, Puerto Rican, or Spanish origin or ancestry.

3. American Indian—Persons who are regarded in the establishment or community as members of this group.

4. *Oriental*—Employees who are regarded in the establishment or community as members of this group, which includes persons of several national origins; e.g., Japanese, Chinese, Filipino, Korean, Polynesians, Indonesians, etc.

5. *Aleut Employment in Alaska*—Employees who are regarded as members of this group in the establishment or community.

6. *Eskimo Employment in Alaska*—Employees who are regarded as members of this group in the establishment or community.

7. *None of these*—Employees not otherwise included in the above designations.

NOTE: These designations are necessarily broad and therefore not anthropologically precise; however, they are adequate to meet program needs. In this connection, note further: Do not ask any employee what his ethnic identification is. Where in doubt, it will be better to base designation on an educated guess.

CHAPTER 15

Mental Health Action
for Human Rights

by Charles V. Willie
Bernard M. Kramer
Bertram S. Brown

What can be done about racism in mental health?

How can energies from the field of mental health be mobilized to overcome racism and its impacts?

How can we discover why people hate and discriminate?

How can we convince the vast public that White racism hurts not only Blacks but also Whites?

How can we move away from antihumanism to prohumanism as identified by John Ordway in chapter 4?

How can institutions and laws be cast to favor positive components in the majority psyche, where prejudices are of the conformity type described in chapter 8 by Thomas Pettigrew?

How can resources for mental health be focused to enhance positive strengths in minority communities?

How can mental health programs be strengthened to heal wounds and give counsel to those exposed to mental health risks of discrimination, bigotry, segregation, and the residues of slavery?

These are some of the items to place on the agenda for action. Many suggestions appear on the preceding pages, and others are easily read between the lines. The aim of this chapter is to bring into focus suggestions for action that might stimulate effective use of the human powers of reason, compassion, and necessity.

This book has wrestled with broad but crucial issues: How has mental health affected racism? How has racism affected mental health? Imbedded in these are questions of institutional arrangements as well as individual adaptations.

The contributing authors agree that all institutions in the United States are racist, including those in mental health. They agree also that institutional changes (as opposed to personality changes) are needed to root out and eliminate racism. We share Thomas Pettigrew's definition of institutional racism as "that complex of institutional arrangements that restrict the life choices of Black Americans in comparison to those of White Americans." In mental health, major manifestations of institutional racism are that members of racial minority groups have had limited opportunities to train and practice as mental health specialists and that facilities and services have often been unavailable, insufficient, or inadequate.

Stresses endured by racial minorities in the United States because of racism have been unrelenting. And they have been as severe as the greatest stresses experienced by Whites in this society—or more severe. Oppressed Blacks face double jeopardy—damned if they actively resist and damned if they passively accept. The result is much anguish, especially in interpersonal relations.

What has not been recognized by professionals and the public is the extraordinary way in which many Blacks and members of other racial minority groups have coped with adversity. How they have strengthened themselves to overcome the obstacles of racism is worthy of careful studies. Such investigations would make significant contributions to the accumulated body of knowledge and clinical practice in mental health. Well-documented life styles of effectively coping individuals and families could serve as models for dealing with danger and difficulty.

The present state of knowledge about racism and mental health is confusing. It is hard to sort out fact from fiction. Self-concept among Black children, for example, is said to be negative by some behavioral scientists, while others have found it to be positive and even stronger than the self-concept of Whites. Role relationships between Black men and women are varyingly described as cooperative or competitive. Some of our authors say that Black family life is disorganized while others believe that it has shown great strength and staying power as one of the most adaptive institutions in our society. Obviously more effective research is needed to clarify these and other issues in racism and mental health.

The absence of conceptual clarity and the presence of contradictions in the findings of different scholars reflect, in part, the underdeveloped status of this field. Moreover, the relationships between the races in this society are in a state of transition. Goals for community life and related strategies are in a fluid condition. Movements toward integration and separatism coexist. Consolidation of societal resources as a way of sharing risks and responsibilities could stifle the call for self-determination, decentralization, and local control. Subdominant people of power tend to be interested in local determination. Each concern is valid. Each, in fact, may be subjugated to its own opposite. A problem for the field of racism and mental health is to determine under what conditions different approaches may yield maximum opportunities for all.

The value placed by mental health specialists upon varying goals and strategies will affect their interpretations of individual and group behavior of racial minorities. Evidence is provided by several authors that mental health professionals are affected by the racism that permeates our social institutions. Such awareness may help reduce impediments to change erected by professionals as well as by the public. Foremost among the impediments most frequently encountered is a lack of awareness of racist tendencies in personal and organizational policies and procedures. One need not be a racist to contribute to and perpetuate institutional racism (see Thomas Pettigrew, chapter 8).

We turn now to some specific suggestions for action and research that might forward the mental health of minorities and the nation at large. One important task has to do with the fate of thousands upon thousands of Blacks and other minority members now incarcerated in mental hospitals and other institutions across the country. How many of these were illegally detained in the first instance? How many have continued in captivity beyond what may have once been legal conditions but this fact is no longer recognized? How many should be released? In how many instances can and should damages be retrieved? It is a massive job that cries to be done, that is, to canvass *all* people now in mental hospitals and other institutions beyond a given duration, to identify those detained illegally and unjustly, and to secure their release and just compensation for damages done. It needs no special clairvoyance to see that those so identified and released among Blacks and other minorities will far exceed their expected proportions in the population. A campaign to achieve this just and humane goal would be a most worthy undertaking.

Another important need, advanced by Chester Pierce in chapter 13, is that of nurturing the growth of research capacity in mental health among Blacks and other minority groups. The unacceptable alternative is to confine their role to that of service with research and teaching functions restricted to dominant White groups. Key positions of power and control over mental health resources will then continue to be denied to Blacks. And the charge that the institutions of mental health are racist in nature will continue to be justified. Additionally, research and teaching will not be available as models for emulation to future generations of Blacks who choose careers in mental health.

Academic departments in mental health occupy a very special position from which they can influence the spirit and style of future mental health practitioners. They can exercise leadership to improve mental health's role in racial matters, or they can play a passive role to support the status quo.

Departments of psychiatry, psychology, social work, and nursing, for example, educate thousands of individuals each year for professional work in the mental health arena. A small number of these students are Black colleagues of a much larger number of White students. For both Black and White students the questions of race and racism constitute a core issue to their performance as mental health professionals in a society where race is such a pivot in human relations. Yet most departments of psychiatry, for example, tend to adopt the position that they are "race free." They frequently argue that human motivation transcends race and that there can be no racial psychology as such.

The conclusion emerges from this line of argument that teaching programs in mental health need not present material on racism beyond what students learn through liberal education or current events. Even progressive students will say that they already know about racial differences in life expectancy, that they know that mental health services are inaccessible and unacceptable to Blacks. They want to *do* something about it, they will say, not hear more about it.

But, one asks, *do what?* In the light of what knowledge? Faculties in the mental health disciplines have an obligation to convey through courses and other teaching modes the facts and figures, concepts and ideas, issues and problems relating to racism as it affects and is affected by mental health. And students, both Black and White, have a reciprocal obligation to learn about these so that they may be armed with information to act in this nation's foremost mental health problem — racism. Courses such as the following would go a long way toward filling a serious vacuum in the education of mental health professionals:

Psychology of Racial Prejudice
History of Racism in Mental Health
Patterns of Segregation and Discrimination in Mental Health Services
Impact of Racism on Mental Health of Blacks and Whites

Positive Mental Health Implications of the Black Liberation Movement
Epidemiology of Mental Health and Illness among Minority and Majority Groups
Current Strategies for Reducing Institutional Racism and Individual Prejudice

There is a need to create machinery for a continuing surveillance of developments in the field of racism and mental health. One possibility is the publication of a periodical entitled, perhaps, *Abstracts in Racism and Mental Health* or *Annual Review of Racism and Mental Health.*

A need exists to explore the relation between health and mental health with respect to the issue of racism. Although this volume has concentrated on the relation between racism and mental health, it is nonetheless true that a significant portion of the mental health field is linked, for better or worse, with medicine and health at large. It is, therefore, important to consider how the structure of health care is affected by racist elements and how this, in turn, relates to the structure of the activities in mental health. The professional referral system, for example, plays an essential role in shaping the nation's teaching hospitals. This in turn affects mental health referrals in such ways as to restrict Black access to mental health segments of the general health-care system.

Another proposal for action would be to develop a roster of targets for institutional change to reduce institutional racism. Schools, churches, hospitals, prisons, armed services, recreational facilities, and social services all are arenas in which practice could be tipped to favor antiracist or nonracist outcomes. Potential consequences for improved mental health could be enormous.

But resistance to institutional change is frequently emboldened by widespread prejudice or individual racism in the White population. The need is great for a new appraisal of the roots of White prejudice. This would help identify leverage points for improving the climate of opinion within which efforts to reduce institutional racism could flourish. We submit that, contrary to antiresearch sentiments in the wind, the time is right for a resurgence of research into the basic causes of White racism in so many individuals. Our current knowledge in this sphere is dated, drawing on information obtained prior to the dramatic and deep-going change in the role of Blacks from passive objects to active protagonists. It is now necessary to embark on a new series of investigations aimed at understanding the nature and motivational base of White responses to the changed situation. Such understanding would make a critical difference in developing strategies for the struggles that lie ahead.

Of particular importance is the need to identify and analyze areas where Black and White interests coincide. Thomas Pettigrew has cogently argued that many prejudiced Whites will relinquish specific anti-Black dispositions when specific points of self-interest come into conflict with their racism. A roster of possible points of mutual interest to overcome institutional racism could be a valuable contribution. In the long run, for example, it may well be that the interest of White parents in their children's education will lead them into unexpected alliances with Black parents. It is our hope that publication of this volume will assist mental health workers in articulating other mutualities in the service of human rights.

Contributors
Index

Contributors

Bertram S. Brown
Director, National Institute of Mental Health, Rockville, Md.

James P. Comer
Associate Dean, Yale Medical School; Associate Professor of Psychiatry, Yale Child Study Center; New Haven, Conn.

Jacquelyne Johnson Jackson
Associate Professor of Medical Sociology, Center for the Study of Aging and Human Development, Duke University Medical Center, Durham, N.C.

Reginald L. Jones
Professor of Education, University of California at Riverside, Riverside, Calif.

Bernard M. Kramer
Professor and Chairman of the Department of Psychology, College II, University of Massachusetts — Boston, Boston, Mass.

Morton Kramer
Chief, Biometry Branch, Office of Program Planning and Evaluation, National Institute of Mental Health, Rockville, Md.

Thurgood Marshall
Associate Justice, United States Supreme Court, Washington, D.C.

David F. Musto
Assistant Professor of History and Psychiatry, Yale Child Study Center, Yale Medical School, New Haven, Conn.

Frank M. Ochberg
Director, National Institute of Mental Health, Western Regional Office, HEW Region IX, San Francisco, Calif.; pre-

viously Executive Assistant to the Director, National Institute of Mental Health, Rockville, Md.

John A. Ordway
Psychiatrist in private practice, Pine Ledge Road, Bangor, Maine

Thomas F. Pettigrew
Professor of Social Psychology, Harvard University, Cambridge, Mass.

Chester M. Pierce
Professor of Education and Psychiatry, Faculty of Medicine and Graduate School of Education, Harvard University, Cambridge, Mass.; Founding National Chairman, Black Psychiatrists of America

Charles A. Pinderhughes
Professor of Psychiatry, Boston University School of Medicine, Boston, Mass.; Lecturer in Psychiatry, Harvard Medical School, Boston, Mass.; Director, Department of Psychiatry Research, Boston Veterans Administration Hospital, Boston, Mass.

Gloria Johnson Powell
Assistant Professor of Child Psychiatry, University of Minnesota, Minneapolis, Minn.; Director of Mental Health Services, Community-University Health Care Center, Child and Youth Project 603, Minneapolis, Minn.

Charles Prudhomme
Psychiatrist in private practice, Washington, D.C.

Beatrice M. Rosen
Biometry Branch, Office of Program Planning and Evaluation, National Institute of Mental Health, Rockville, Md.

Jeanne Spurlock
Chairman, Department of Psychiatry, Meharry Medical College, Nashville, Tenn.

Claudewell S. Thomas
Director, Division of Mental Health Service Programs, National Institute of Mental Health, Rockville, Md.; Associate Professor of Psychiatry, Public Health, and Sociology, Yale University School of Medicine, New Haven, Conn.

Preston Wilcox
President, Afram Associates, 68–72 East 131st Street, Harlem, N.Y.

Charles V. Willie
Vice-President of Student Affairs and Professor of Sociology, Syracuse University, Syracuse, N.Y.

Ernest M. Willis
Biometry Branch, Office of Program Planning and Evaluation, National Institute of Mental Health, Rockville, Md.

Index

Titles in the Series

METHODOLOGY IN EVALUATING
THE QUALITY OF MEDICAL CARE
An Annotated Selected Bibliography, 1955–1968
Isidore Altman, Alice J. Anderson, and Kathleen Barker

MIGRANTS AND MALARIA IN AFRICA
R. Mansell Prothero

A PSYCHIATRIC RECORD MANUAL FOR THE HOSPITAL
Dorothy Smith Keller

RACISM AND MENTAL HEALTH
Charles V. Willie, Bernard M. Kramer, and Bertram S. Brown, Editors

2256